WE, OF OUR BOUNTY
A History of the Sheffield Church Burgesses

Graham Murray

David Wilson

Peter Holt

Peter Lee

Paul Ward

The Sheffield Church Burgesses 1997

George Tolley

Leslie Fletcher

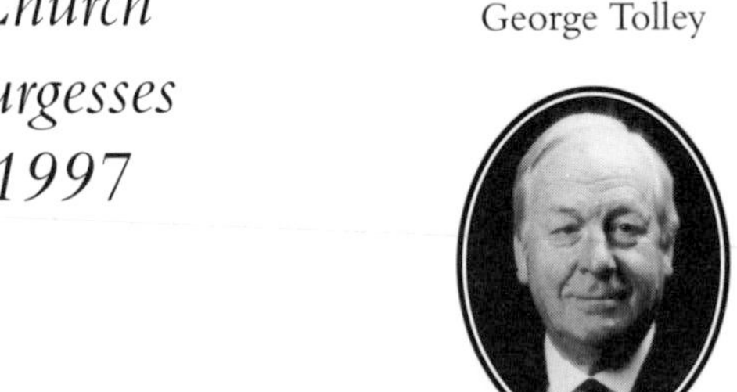

John Peters

Stewart Hamilton

Geoffrey Sims

Nicholas Hutton

Stephen Hunter

We, of our Bounty

A History of the Sheffield Church Burgesses

(The Twelve Capital Burgesses and Commonalty
of the Town and Parish of Sheffield in the County of York)

by

George Tolley

We of our bounty have willed and ordained appointed decreed and granted that the said Burgesses from henceforth may and shall be one Body corporate and politick for ever.

(From the Charter of Queen Mary Tudor, granted to the Sheffield Church Burgesses 8 June 1554)

The Memoir Club

First published in 1999 by
The Memoir Club
The Old School
New Road
Crook Town
Durham

British Library Cataloguing in
Publication Data.
A catalogue record for this book
is available from the
British Library.

ISBN: 1 84104 004 5

Typeset by George Wishart & Associates, Whitley Bay.
Printed by Bookcraft (Bath) Ltd.

Dedicated

to

Martin Lee

Law Clerk to the Sheffield Church Burgesses Trust
1968-1997

A trusted adviser and wise counsellor;
guardian of tradition and strategist of change

Contents

Illustrations

Foreword

By the Rt. Revd. David R. Lunn, Bishop of Sheffield 1980-1997

WHAT AN EXTRAORDINARY story this is; a living and unbroken link between the country village that was medieval Sheffield and the great city of today that is busy getting ready for the excitements of the new millennium.

The key word is TRUST: for nearly half a millennium the twelve Church Burgesses have held in trust those ancient lands that a generous (but long-forgotten) piety had given to be used for the well-being of the parishioners of Sheffield. We live in a cynical age, in which we very readily assume that power is invariably abused. No one can be trusted. All must be publicly 'accountable'. Yet this self-perpetuating oligarchy of the 'great and the good' (or, at least, moderately great and good) have exercised this trust for over four hundred years without reward, without theft, without scandal and with astonishing financial acumen. It is an amazing record, of which the Church Burgesses, and indeed Sheffield itself – for they have very nearly all been Sheffielders – should be proud.

But – as this splendid book shows – the Church Burgesses have had their critics. Basically the charge has been that they are the wrong people to be doing the job. Some of the less gripping pages of this book wrestle with the attempts of the 19th-century critics to rewrite the history of 16th century Sheffield. This (retired) Bishop of Sheffield rejoices that the Church Burgesses survived the onslaughts more or less unscathed. The defeats of the rapacious Londoners of the 16th century central government and of the power-hungry local councillors of the 19th century have made possible that vast range of practical good done for the Church and people of Sheffield today.

Thank you, Church Burgesses, for your faithful, careful hard work through the centuries. A trust very well kept.

Thank you, Church Burgesses, for all you are doing today for the parishes and people of the City of Sheffield.

And thank you, George Tolley, and the Burgesses of today, for opening up this history and letting us read this astonishing page in the history of our City.

Introduction

ANCIENT CHARITIES are commonly either moribund or quaint. Sheffield has two ancient charities which are neither. The Town Trust, claiming its origins in the 1297 Charter of Thomas de Furnival, for several centuries fulfilled many of the responsibilities now undertaken by local government, and remains an active and substantial supporter of many of the town's activities. The Church Burgesses Trust, established in 1554 by a Charter of Mary I, although charged with some responsibilities for the relief of the poor and the maintenance of highways and bridges, had, and still has, as its major responsibility, the support of the Established Church in the old parish of Sheffield, an area which now includes some 40 parishes. Since, until late Victorian times, ecclesiastical affairs were also the town's affairs, these responsibilities placed the Church Burgesses in a significant position of influence and authority. They appointed and employed assistant clergy and lay staff of the Parish Church; they maintained the building and paid for expenses of worship. And, alongside these ecclesiastical responsibilities, they provided charitable support for the poor and, from time to time, were active in educational developments in the town.

Rapid and far-reaching social change in the 19th and 20th centuries might have meant, as it did for so many ancient charities in other towns, a loss of purpose leading to desuetude or to a recasting of objectives. Whilst there has been some broadening of objectives for the Church Burgesses, their essential purposes remain as set out in their Tudor Charter. Their financial support, of the Cathedral and of clergy stipends in the four Sheffield Deaneries, is not a mere token of ancient custom, but is a significant part of current budgets. Their contributions also to the building of churches are, from time to time, substantial. And, in addition, their secular charitable activities, especially in education, continue to grow. Far from being an anachronistic survival, the Burgesses fulfil an active, continuing role.

Much of the history of Sheffield is bound up with its topography and its lack of local aristocracy. Its topography, its hills and valleys and fast flowing streams, led to small, discrete communities, each in its own enclave as it were, and gave the town an effective source of water power which encouraged and sustained industrial development. As to aristocracy, Gilbert, the 7th Earl of Shrewsbury, who died in 1616, was the last Lord of the Manor to reside in Sheffield. Shortly after his death, the cutlers, in 1624, sought protection through incorporation as the Company of Cutlers in Hallamshire. Thereafter, there was de facto tri-partite governance of Sheffield: the Cutlers' Company in industry and business, the Town Trust in maintenance of the town's services, and the Church Burgesses in ecclesiastical and related matters. This continued in its essentials until the town was incorporated in 1843. The independence, and insularity, of Sheffield people were allied with, and reflected in, the independent, and independently-minded, corporations who governed the town. All this was to change, of course, in the mid- and late-19th century, but the three bodies remain significant because they are embedded in the social fabric of the town. Neither the Town Trust, nor the Church Burgesses, have the visibility, the prominence or the cachet of the Cutlers' Company, as seen in the prestige of the Master Cutler. But there remains a respect and regard for both Trusts, even though very few Sheffield citizens have an understanding of the history of either body or of their current activities.

The very title, 'The Twelve Capital Burgesses and Commonalty of Sheffield', can only cause confusion, compounded by the commonly accepted description as 'The Church Burgesses'. For the Church Burgesses are not a 'church body'. True, from very early times, they described their meetings as 'Church meetings', with proceedings recorded in 'the Church Minutes'. Their estates and property they often referred to as 'Church lands', and their detailed involvement in the affairs of the Parish Church might, at times, have suggested that they were co-managers with the Vicar, and, in some respects, that was true. Yet, notwithstanding the responsibilities placed upon them in their Charter for maintaining the fabric of the parish church, for paying the stipends of its assistant clergy, and for meeting costs of divine worship, they support but do not manage, they influence but do not direct. The story of this self-perpetuating body, rarely, if ever, now in the limelight, is one of stewardship; the quality of which depends much more upon the firm discipline of tradition, upon the acceptance of a personal mandate of trust and responsibility, than upon public accountability, though modern charity law requires greater formality in this regard.

The responsibilities of Trustees of grant-making charities are essentially four-fold:

- to maintain and, if possible, to enhance, the capital of the Trust.
- to generate income for the purposes of the Trust.
- to disburse that income in accordance with the stated purposes of the Trust.

– to have regard to changing circumstances of the constituencies served by the Trust and to seek to respond to them.

Failure in any one of these responsibilities is a failure of stewardship, from which decline may commence, the decline which has either led to the demise of, or has made ineffective anachronisms of, so many charitable Trusts. But we are entitled to ask: 'What difference would it make if the Church Burgesses ceased to operate? And a further question: 'What place does such a charitable institution have in a complex world, where so much social action is dependent upon government funding and direction?' The questions are especially relevant at a time when the welfare state is visibly breaking up and when the voluntary sector is growing vigorously, not merely filling the gaps in necessary social provision, but serving as a major partner in the provision of social services funded by the government. For the Church of England in Sheffield, the answer to the first question is clear enough. Some means would have to be found of replacing, or re-assigning, the very substantial sums that go towards the Cathedral and to clergy stipends, and which provide significant support for church building and other activities. But with the Church Burgesses, as with so many other major charitable Trusts, other issues are more important than money. It is probably very rare that a major social or community initiative is totally dependent, for its inception or survival, upon a single, substantial charitable contribution from a grant-making Trust. True, there are many examples where a major grant appears to have been crucial in establishing some initiative or in giving new life to a faltering cause. But, had such support not been forthcoming from that particular source, other ways would almost certainly have been found of achieving the desired objective, albeit within a different time-scale or within a reduced level of provision. Grant-making charitable Trusts undoubtedly make things possible, but rarely is the action of a single Trust decisive in determining the success or failure of some major project. Grant-making Trusts do not allocate money in the knowledge or expectation, nor with the intention, that this thing shall happen and that shall not happen. This would both limit their value and give them wholly unwarrantable power. Their important roles, both subtle and pervasive, are to encourage, to affirm and to confirm. Their support encourages those who are recipients of grants and encourages others to give also. Their support affirms the value and the worth of the work that is being done and confirms the standing of the organisation responsible for the work. These roles apply to the Church Burgesses across the whole range of their responsibilities.

The history of the Church Burgesses could have been very different. Within the terms of their Charter, they could have followed a narrowly denominational path. In so doing, they would have become more and more constrained in their activities. The decisive time for the Burgesses came in the 1850s, when they were under public scrutiny and faced considerable public criticism. They might then have chosen a defensive route of retreating into an ecclesiastical enclave. They chose, rather, to broaden the base of their activities and placed themselves firmly within the context of a Sheffield that was changing rapidly. What this history shows is that decisive action in 1854, whereby the future of the Burgesses was secured as a multi-purpose Charitable Trust, was essentially one of continuity. The Church Burgesses had their origin in meeting the social and spiritual needs of the whole town of Sheffield. Four hundred and fifty years ago, the resources could hardly be said to match the tasks; nowadays it is an impossible task. Yet the needs are there to be met. This history might enable some judgements to be made on the effectiveness, or otherwise, of the Church Burgesses in deploying their resources to meet those needs. It might also be of value, as history often is, in helping to decide future directions of policy.

The burgesses are conscious of the weight of tradition inevitable in an ancient institution, but do not allow tradition to stand in the way of effective discharge of their responsibilities. Their prayer (used at all Trust meetings) acknowledges the strength of the past, but demonstrates a ready acceptance of the need to respond, with God's help, to current and future needs. That prayer (written by Canon Christopher Smith) runs:

> 'Almighty God, whose kindness and mercy provided for those who have gone before us, accept our thanksgiving for the historic trust given by Mary Tudor, Queen of this realm, to the Church Burgesses of Sheffield; Grant to us, who inherit these responsibilities, wisdom and dedication in carrying out our duties, so that all may be done to the glory of God and for the benefit of your Church and Kingdom; through Jesus Christ our Lord. Amen.'

Acknowledgements

PROFESSOR DAVID HEY encouraged me to undertake the writing of this history and has been most supportive in his help and advice. Mr. Martin Lee, Law Clerk to the Burgesses until very recently, has given freely of his time and expertise and, much more than that, has been an active participant in the whole project. His constructive and searching comments have improved the text and he took on much of the task of bringing it to publication. Mrs. Doreen Conley, Personal Assistant to the Law Clerk, was willing at all times to meet my requests for information and help. It is a matter of great regret that she died before seeing this History in print. Mr. Nicholas Robinson, Surveyor to the Church Burgesses, has been very kind in allowing me access to plans in his possession.

To my fellow Burgesses I am most grateful for all that I have learned from them over many years and to Mr. Graham Murray and Mr. David Wilson I owe especial gratitude for their comments and the information they have provided from their long personal experience of the Burgesses' activities and their unique family connections. The late Mr. Paul Ward read the final draft with meticulous care and thereby helped to remove ambiguities and errors.

Staff of the Sheffield City Archives and the Local Studies Library have been unfailingly helpful in meeting my many requests for documents.

To my wife, as ever, I owe a deep debt of gratitude for her encouragement, interest and constant help, without which this History would not have been completed.

CHAPTER 1

Origins

FOR NEARLY 450 YEARS, the Sheffield Church Burgesses have sought to fulfil the responsibilities laid upon them in their Charter of Incorporation granted to them by Queen Mary Tudor on 8 June 1554. Joseph Hunter, writing in 1819, was fulsome, yet measured, in his praise of their record of achievement.

> 'To the credit of the body, and to the honour of the individuals in whose hands this trust, so important to the best interests of the inhabitants of Sheffield, has been placed, let it be observed, that it has been uniformly administered with a due regard to the benefit of those for whom they were placed in trust. Unlike other small corporate bodies, at whose disposal church-preferment has been placed, here no private inclination, no personal or family interest, has intruded to divert them from paying an honourable and Christian-like regard to the interest of that part of the church of Christ for which they stand intrusted. They seem to have resisted the temptation before which many might have fallen of regarding trustee property in the light of private property, and of administering it not so much for the benefit of those from whom they are placed in trust as for their own.'[1]

Yet the origins of the Church Burgesses have attracted partisan controversy, not yet fully resolved. As recently as 1948, the then Law Clerk of the Sheffield Town Trustees fanned the flames of controversy yet once more when he claimed that the Church Burgesses 'came into being on faulty premises and perjured evidence and by means of a specious piece of special pleading.'[2] That partisan comment, it has to be said, was not intended in any way as a reflection upon the stewardship of the Burgesses down the centuries.

We cannot now recover the significance and the nuances of the ecclesiastical and doctrinal in-fighting of Tudor Sheffield. What is significant is that the body established by Charter nearly 450 years ago is now a substantial charity, having great responsibilities for maintaining the Cathedral Church; a body which contributes significantly to the stipends of Anglican clergy in Sheffield, and which has provided substantial sums for Church building in Sheffield during the past one hundred years. Furthermore, its contributions to secular charitable purposes are considerable, especially for education. But origins are important and, as we shall see, controversies that surround them have a habit of re-surfacing from time to time.

Because of past controversies it is necessary to relate and to assess the facts, so far as these are known.

The 1554 Charter

A copy of the Charter and its translation are shown on pp. 26–29. What does the document tell us?

1. That land and property specified in the Charter had 'for time out of mind' been in the possession of the Burgesses and Inhabitants of Sheffield, the income therefrom being used for specific purposes for the benefit of the town.

2. These purposes were:
   - the repair of the Parish Church;
   - the repair of bridges and common ways;
   - the relief of the poor and needy of the parish.

3. Prior to the thirtieth year of the reign of Henry VIII (1539), the inhabitants had, by voluntary contributions and by the proceeds of May Games, maintained three priests, to 'celebrate and administer' in the Parish Church.

4. By that year, such voluntary contributions could no longer be depended upon ('their Charity decreased, waxed cold and was utterly diminished and extinct'); no doubt because of uncertainty created by Henry's plundering of Church property.

5. Accordingly, the salaries of the three priests were met by contributions from the income deriving from 'the town's lands and property'. In addition to paying £16.10s.0d. for salaries, a further sum of 19.0s was found for maintaining an altar lamp and an anniversary mass.

6. In the first year of the reign of Edward VI (1547), under the Act for Dissolution of Chantries, the lands and properties providing the income for these 'superstitious' purposes was confiscated to the Crown, in sum £17.9s.4d. Nevertheless, despite the confiscation, the salaries of the three assistant priests continued to be paid by the Crown, annual 'pensions' being granted for life to the three men then serving in that capacity: Alexander Booth (£6.13s.4d); Richard Bewick (£5.0s.0d.); William Hall (£5.0s.0d.).

7. In response to a petition, Queen Mary revoked the confiscation, but did not merely restore the situation to what it had been before the Act of Edward VI. (And it is difficult to determine precisely what that situation was.)

8. The Charter:
   - establishes the Burgesses and Inhabitants of the town as a body corporate and politick by the name of the Twelve Capital Burgesses and Commonalty of Sheffield;
   - names the Twelve Capital Burgesses and grants them perpetual succession, stipulating only that any vacancies as they arise shall be filled by 'discreet, reputable and honest men' chosen by the Capital Burgesses;
   - grants to the Capital Burgesses and Commonalty lands and property specified in the Charter and the right to purchase and accept additional land and property;
   - specifies the uses to which the proceeds of the land and properties shall be put, namely:
     - payment of the stipends of the three priests assisting the Vicar of the Parish Church and of the costs of divine worship there. The Capital Burgesses were required to accept the continuing payment of the 'pensions' granted by Edward VI to the three former assistant priests;
     - whatever is left over and above these stipends and costs shall be used towards the repair of the Parish Church, for bridges and highways and for the relief of poor and needy inhabitants of the parish.

The Charter is admirably explicit in its directions and clear and unequivocal in its statements of the responsibilities to be exercised by the Twelve Capital Burgesses and Commonalty of Sheffield. Why, then has there been controversy? Essentially, controversy has been concerned with two issues:

a. whether the establishment of the new corporate body of Twelve Capital Burgesses represented an undermining and curtailing of the freedoms granted to the free tenants of Sheffield in the Grant of Thomas Furnival of 1297;
b. whether it was fair and just to appropriate town lands for the prime purpose of paying the stipends of the three assistant priests, bearing in mind that such payments had been made from 'town's' income only since 1539. This is not an issue that is essentially ecclesiastical, but concerns the justice of imposition, by the Crown, of what some might claim as arbitrary and unjustified priorities for the application of the resources of the Burgery.

The Furnival Grant of 1297 and developments thereafter

The Furnival Grant of 1297 (pp. 30-31) marked an historic advance in the status of freeholders in the township of Sheffield and, therefore, of the status of the town itself. In return for assured payments by the freeholders of a rent of £3.8s.9¼d, per annum, Thomas de Furnival, Lord of the Manor, demised the land and properties and granted important rights and privileges to the free tenants:

- freedom from feudal duties;
- a Court to be held in the town every three weeks, with right of trial by jury;
- freedom of movement, without payment of tolls, throughout Hallamshire;

It is important, also, to note what the Furnival Grant was not. It was not:

- a charter of incorporation of the Burgery of Sheffield;
- a deed of trust establishing a scheme of administration of the town's lands;
- an endowment.

As the Report of the Inquiry of the Charity Commissioners in 1897 puts it:

> '... popular belief long maintained and embodied even in legal documents that the property now administered by the Town Trustees was originally given to them upon charitable trust by the ... grant of Thomas, Lord Furnival. That this result, however, was not effected by the deed is plain from a perusal of it ... The sole objects of the deed, therefore, were to assess at a fixed sum the fee farm rents payable to the Lord of the Manor by the free tenants, or freeholders, for these holdings, to provide for the due holding of the Court Baron at the will of the vill or township of Sheffield and the administration of justice there, and to grant to the said freeholders freedom from toll throughout Hallamshire.'[3]

John Wheat at a later date, and when he was Law Clerk to the Church Burgesses, states: 'you have only to look at the Deed itself and consider what it really did – and all that it did – to see that it had nothing whatever to do with any Trust ... It has been assumed that the Grant is the root of title to all the old public Trust property in Sheffield, or at least to such of it as is administered by the Town Trustees. But this is not so.'[4]

However, in the years after the Furnival Grant, income from the freeholders' lands beyond that payable to the Lord of the Manor, together with the proceeds of other public bequests, must have been used for public purposes. An Indenture dated 12 May 1498 lays down the conditions under which William Hyne bequeathed in his will of 10 May 1498 three tenements and a 'smeethy house' in Water Lane upon trust that the four Church-maisters of Sheffield and their successors should receive rents and pay for certain obits, masses and other services in the Parish Church for the benefit of the said William Hyne, his wife Felice, their fathers and mothers and all Christian souls. If these duties are not performed, then the premises are to be held by 'the freeholders of Sheffield called the burgesses' and income expended in 'mending bridges, causeways, highways most defective and within one mile of Sheffield, and in other deeds of charity as they should think most meritorious for the health of the said William Hyne and the souls aforesaid.'[5]

By the time of Henry VIII, Sheffield was a town of 2000 inhabitants, pursuing its civic responsibilities with some seriousness, utilising money from a number of sources:

1. There was the income from the lands and properties of the free tenants of Sheffield, over and above that which had to be paid over to the Lord of the Manor under the Furnival Grant.

2. There was a variety of bequests, mostly for Church purposes, commonly for commemorative masses, for maintenance of the Parish Church, and, occasionally, for the poor.

3. There were voluntary contributions, through Church collections, for stipends of the three assistant priests operating from the Parish Church.[6]

4. There was income from the May Games ('and other Vain Plays and Interludes'), for support of the three assistant priests. 'A great number of people at divers times in the year, resorted unto the said town, to view and see the said Games, of whom much money was collected.'[7]

The Vicar and Churchwardens appeared to carry the prime responsibility for administering these moneys. This would not necessarily imply prior claim for Church purposes, or ecclesiastical control of the income, but would reflect the centrality, at that time, of the Parish Church and its officers in the affairs of the town.

Confiscation under Edward VI

With the great uncertainties created by the attacks of Henry VIII upon Church revenues and possessions (chiefly through the dissolution of the monasteries), people became less willing to contribute voluntarily as the long arm and grasping hand of the King reached ever deeper into Church revenues. We are told that round about 1538

> 'the said inhabitants and others, resorting to the said Church on Sundays and other holidays, withdrew their liberality and devotion as to any such purposes, and would give very little money, or none, for the maintenance of the said

priests; and about this time also, such May Games and other like fantastical pastimes did cease, for divers good considerations, as things not to be frequented among civil people . . . whereupon it was thought convenient by many of the said inhabitants, that part of the issues of the said premises in Sheffield should (as might be conveniently spared after other more necessary charges done) be given to the said three priests . . . but as it was not certain what the yearly charges of the repairs of the said Church, and the amendment of the highways and bridges would be, nor how much was necessary to be detained for the relief of the poor; it was not specially declared by the inhabitants what the three priests should have . . . the said inhabitants did . . . give to the three priests, to two of them severally £5.6s.8d. and to the third (because he did more service in the Church than the other two did) 10.0s more than his fellows, i.e. £5.16s.8d.'[8]

Herein lies the origin of the Church Burgesses Trust – the acceptance, or, at least, the institution, of the practice of contributing, from public monies, to the stipends of the three assistant priests at the Parish Church. It was the formalisation of this arrangement, under the Charter granted by Mary Tudor, which constituted the Trust, formalisation which would, presumably, not have been necessary had the ad hoc arrangements of Henry's time been allowed to continue. But the Act for the suppression of Chantries in the first year of King Edward VI's reign resulted in the confiscation to the Crown of the lands which provided the wherewithal for the maintenance of the three priests. The Act reflected the power of the Protestant juggernaut which, under the Lord Protector Somerset, got under way during Edward's brief reign. The object of the Act was to do away with superstitions and errors held to be associated with Catholic ways. In its preamble the Act states,

'that a great part of the superstitions and errors, in Christian religion, had been brought into the minds and estimations of men, by reason of their ignorance of their very true and perfect salvation, through the death of Jesus Christ; and by devising and phantasysing vain opinions of purgatory and masses satisfactory, to be done for them which be departed; the which doctrine and vain opinion, by nothing more was maintained and upholden than by the abuse of trentals, chantries and other provisions made for the continuance of the said blindness and ignorance.'[9]

The Act stipulated that

'all annual rents, profits and emoluments at any time within five years, employed, paid or bestowed, toward or for the maintenance, supportation or finding of any stipendiary priest, intended by any act or writing to have continuance for ever, should by the authority of the then Parliament, immediately after the Feast of Easter then next coming, be adjudged and deemed, and also be, in the very actual and real possession and seizin of the King and his heirs and successors for ever.'

It also enacted that Commissions should be appointed to ascertain the entitlement of the King under the Act. The Act was not quite as brutal as it might have been in that it provided for pensions to be given for life to all chantry priests displaced by its operation. As a result of their visitation to Sheffield, the Commissioners reported:[10]

SHEFELDE PARRYSHE

The Service or Perpetuall Stypend of III Priestes in the Paryshe Churche There

In the said paryshe of Shefeld, in circuite xxiij myles, dyvyded into dyvers hamletts and townes, is not priest founde for assistaunce in serving the cure, besydes the vicar, but the three stipendarie preistes founde ther for that purpose. The number of houslyng people is MM.

Alexander Bothe and William Hall, every one of theym, XL yeres of age, and Richard Booke, LX yeres of age, impotent, all incumbents, have none other lyving than the proffitts of the seyd service equally divided. Goods, nil. Plate, nil.

The yerely value of the freehold land to the seyd services belonging, in the occupacion of the burgesses of Shefelde, xvj li. xs. Coppiehold, nil. Whereof, Resolutes and deduccions by yere, nil.

Certen Obbites in the Parrishe Churche Aforeseid

The same were found to have contynuance for ever, and have landes for the mayntenance thereof, as apperith. The yerely value of the freehold land xijs. viijd. Coppiehold, nil. Whereof, Resolutes and deductions by yere, nil.

A Lampe in the Seyd Paryshe Churche

The same was found to have contynuance for ever, and have landes for the meytenance thereof. The yerely value of the freehold land belonging to the seyd lampe, in the tenure and occupacion of the seyd burgesses, vjs. viijd. Whereof, Resolutes and deductions by yere, nil.

The total income from the lands to be confiscated to the Crown amounted to £17.9s.4d.

Three things call for comment. The first is that the three assistant priests in Sheffield were not Chantry priests and should not have been included in a process aimed at suppressing 'superstitions and errors and phantasysing vain opinions of purgatory and masses.' True, the priests officiated at the altars of the Parish Church and were referred to, at times, as the Rood Priest, Our

Lady Priest and the St. Katherine Priest, but such duties were no more than was required of any priest officiating in a Parish Church. The substance of their duties was to serve the people of the parish, not to say masses for the dead. The Commissioners, zealous and, no doubt, ruthless in fulfilling their remit, would, presumably, have had little time, or inclination, to consider the balance of time and effort of individual priests. They seem to have been motivated more by the availability of property than by the proper administration of justice. So, all was confiscated.

Secondly, whilst it was clear that, since 1538 or thereabouts, income from the lands had supported three priests, this had come about as matter of either necessity or convenience, to maintain a service felt to be necessary by the community as a whole. The lands had not, generally, been given for such a purpose originally, unlike the usual bequests for chantries, although they had been given, for the most part, for Church purposes.

Thirdly, nothing much need have changed in the immediate aftermath of the implementation of the Commissioner's Report. The three assistant priests continued to be paid a stipend (albeit as an annual pension) but deserted their former duties in the parish. As the later Petition to Queen Mary puts it:

> 'the said three priests . . . now goynge abrode at their liberty, the churche beynge unserved to the gret discomefoorthe of the said inhabitaunce by reason of ye gret decaye of suche moste godlie service as heretofore hathe beyne used within the said churche.'[11]

The priests could, presumably, have chosen to continue to serve the people of the parish, but did not do so.

The matter was stirred up by the intervention of an informer. The use of informers to assist the implementation of unpopular measures of the Crown was not uncommon and, in this case, one, Henry Bayley, a Skinner of London, took it upon himself in 1551, to lay information in the Court of Augmentation against the town of Sheffield. It was unlikely that he was acting out of sheer public spiritedness. Bayley listed six properties which, he claimed, had been concealed from the Commissioners and were used for 'superstitious purposes'.[12] The lands were:

- A messuage called the George in the Old Change, London (which Bayley mistakenly claims was given by one Whitbread, for the finding of a Priest in the Parish Church of Sheffield to say mass for the soul of Whitbread. In fact, as we have seen, it was Felice Hyne, daughter of John Whitbread, citizen and fishmonger of London, who gave the George in trust for sale, the proceeds to be spent in buying a silver and

gilt cross for the Church.[13] (This trust for sale does not appear to have been executed.)
- 1 tenement and 2 acres of land in Sheffield in the tenure of James Heynde (then let for 10s.8d.)
- 1 meadow in Sheffield in the tenure of William Burrows (then let for 10s.0d.)
- 1 meadow in Sheffield in the tenure of Rylle's widow (then let for 10s.0d.)
- 1 tenement and 2 acres of land in Sheffield in the tenure of William Parlington (let for 10s.8d.)
- 6 acres of land at Red Hill in the tenure of John Goree.

All these, it was claimed by Bayley, were bequeathed to help find a priest and say mass and to keep a certain obit within the Parish Church. The statement of Bayley concludes by asking that the Court grant a commission, to the surveyors of the said County, authorising them to enquire into the matter, and asked that (here appears the self-interest), upon presenting His Majesty's title to the premises, the Commissioners would grant the said tenements to the Informer Henry Bayley, for 21 years, at the usual rent.'

A response to this Information was presented in the names of Robert Swyft and William Tailour and of the inhabitants of Sheffield,[14] claiming that the information was 'untrue, uncertain and insufficient in law . . . grounded on malice, to put the said inhabitants to expense, and chiefly with intent to get, either by lease or otherwise, the said messuage called the George in the Old Exchange, London.' The respondents were, we might say today, 'economical with the truth'. They claimed that:
- the rents and profits from the listed properties were used chiefly by the Church-graves for repairs of the Parish Church and of bridges and highways and for the relief of the indigent and needy, and not for finding and maintaining any priest or keeping an obit.
- nevertheless, with the depreciation and ultimate cessation of income from voluntary contributions and the May Games, money had been found for the three priests, but after making the charges for repairs, etc.
- they furthermore claimed that all the rents received had been fully disclosed to the Commissioners.

The Petition to Mary Tudor

When Queen Mary came to the throne in 1553, Swyft and Tailour acted quickly, presenting a Petition (reproduced on pp. 32 and 33) 'in the names of all other thenhabytance of the said parish' for the restitution of the lands confiscated by Edward.[15] Francis, the fifth Earl of Shrewsbury, probably gave his support. Although he had subscribed to an Order in Council of Queen Jane, dated six days after the death of Edward, he quickly saw which way the wind was blowing and seven days afterwards was a party to the proclamation of Queen Mary. He soon established himself at Court, his religious bias being more in keeping with Catholic Mary. Hunter states that Francis 'availed himself of his interest there to do an act of kindness, not to say of justice, to his tenantry and neighbours at Sheffield. In the late reign they had been deprived of certain public property, under pretence that the uses to which the income from it had been appropriated, came within the scope of the Act 1 Edward VI for the suppression of chantries, colleges and guilds. Of this he obtained for them restitution, and at the same time a royal patent declaring the future uses of the income of that property, and constituting a body corporate for its management and better protection.'[16] This petition for restitution is not unique. Pontefract petitioned in 1557 for restoration of what had been plundered earlier and Beverley secured restitution during Edwardian times.[17]

The clever drafting and diplomacy of the petition are worth noting. After a most undiplomatic reference to Henry Bayley ('of his moste covetus and ungodlye mynde sekynge only his owne pryvate gayne and lucre'), the petition skilfully states its arguments and persuasions:

1. That the confiscated lands (which did not, of course, include the properties referred to in Bayley's Information) did not fall within the compass of Edward's Act for Chantries Collegiate.

2. That the Crown has not benefited from the confiscation, since the three assistant priests continue to receive their stipend as an annual pension, for which they do nothing. The petitioners undertook to accept responsibility for the continued payment of these pensions, if their requests were granted.

3. That there are undoubted needs amongst the people of the parish which are currently not being met, to the detriment both of souls and bodies.

4. That whatever dispute there may have been about the purpose of bequeathed properties, the Queen is asked to restore the properties 'in the advancement of God's glory and His divine service.'

It is not possible to say whether the Petition was a strictly local reaction by those who felt genuinely aggrieved at the injustice of confiscation, or whether it reflected also, the resistance to the Edwardian 'reforms' which, as Duffy has shown, was common in many parts of the country.[18] It is worth noting that Mary's accession was widely welcomed in the North. A contemporary account records spontaneous rejoicing in Pontefract, Doncaster, Rotherham and many other market towns, 'wheratt tholle commonaltie in all places in the northe parttes grettlie reiocide, makynge grett fyers, drynkinge wyne and aylle, prayssing God.'[19]

Action upon the petition was speedy, whether because of the Earl's influence, or because it was a timely request, given the change in religious emphasis, we do not know. But within a matter of months, the petitioners' requests were granted. The response was not only speedy, it was comprehensive and final, in that it prescribes precisely the land and properties and the uses to which income shall be put and incorporates a Trust, in perpetuity, for the administration of the purposes of the Charter. The ultimate outcome was that both parties were satisfied. All the lands referred to in Bayley's Information were assigned to the Capital Burgesses and Bayley was granted his lease, though not until 1556, when the understandably tardy Burgesses were ordered by the Marquis of Winchester, the Queen's Lord High Treasurer, to grant the lease forthwith. The letter from the Marquis is dated 26 July 1556 and stated that

> 'In consideration of (Henry Bayley's) information and of his paynes, costs and continual trouble . . . there was granted to the said Henry Bayley . . . the preferment of the said concealed lands and tenements to have them in lease . . . Therefore as much as the Queen understanding the said travel (travail) taken for her benefit to be then altogether unrecompensed to his undoing, she had by him signified her pleasure that the said poor man have his lease promised him'.[20]

The Burgesses were required without delay to make him a lease of the two tenements in Old Change for 40 years.

Settlement of the petition and dispute was a costly business. £144.18s.2d was paid out to Swyft and Tailour for costs and journeys to London.

One immediate and lasting effect of the Charter was to divide the 'Town's property' into two. Prior to the confiscation by Edward, the total annual value of the 'public properties' in Sheffield appears to have been £27 (as stated in the Petition), to which must be added the income from the Old Change property (and also, probably from Aughton property). Of this, £17.9s.4d. (being the annual value of land and properties confiscated by Edward) went to the Twelve Capital Burgesses, the lion's share; leaving the remainder for the town's other purposes. That remainder was to form the nucleus of what ultimately became the Town Trust, incorporated in 1681.

Whatever the values of the land and properties in Edward's time, we know, from the earliest existing records, that in 1557 the rental income of the Capital Burgesses was £30.5s.5d. and in 1566 that of the 'Town Burgesses' was £7.11s.4d. There remains some mystery about these figures. It has been assumed by commentators[21] that the division was of property yielding £27 per annum, of which properties yielding £17.9s.4d were assigned in Mary's Charter to the Capital Burgesses and the remainder – £9.10s.8d. – remained with the 'Town Burgesses'. The discrepancies cannot be explained. We do not know the total rental income from the lands detailed in Henry Bayley's Information. Rental, excluding the Old Change property and the Red Hill land, was £2.1s.4d. This sum, added to the £17.9s.4d. already referred to, totals £19.10s.8d, which is far removed from the £30.5s.5d. recorded by the Church Burgesses in 1557. What is more likely is that the £27 referred to in the Petition is the total value of the income from lands referred to therein, which, together with the rental from the Old Change property, would bring the figure nearer to that recorded in the Burgesses accounts for 1557.

For centuries, the town's affairs were administered through two bodies – the 'Town's Burgesses' and the Twelve Capital (or Church) Burgesses, the latter having its priorities (but by no means all of its concerns) in ecclesiastical matters, and the former having responsibilities for 'civic' matters, notably the provision and maintenance of roads and bridges and, later, of street lighting and the Town Hall.

Disputes and Contention

Whatever differences or disputes there may have been between the two bodies and sets of interests (and there is no evidence of any dispute), no public concern emerges until well into the nineteenth century. The 'Trevor controversy' (an account of which is given in pp. 83-88) sparked off a stormy period for the Church Burgesses in the 1850s, in which Sheffield newspapers and the Town Council raised many questions about the manner in which the Trust performed its business and petitioned the Court for substantial changes. That controversy led to a Chancery suit and a new Scheme of Administration for the Trust in 1854 (p. 39). In 1906, the City Council returned to the attack and appointed a Special Committee to enquire into the constitution and administration of the Trust, and following upon the Report of that Committee, the Council proposed radical changes, claiming that the revenues of the Trust should be re-directed towards civic, rather than ecclesiastical purposes. The Council was still not reconciled to the Court's decision, handed down in the 1854 Scheme, and they persisted in their claim that a much higher proportion of the funds should be

The Author with the Election Book of the Sheffield Church Burgesses.

appropriated for secular purposes, viz. to repair bridges and highways and the relief of the poor. But there were to be no further petitions to the Court. Meetings took place in 1907 between the Burgesses and a deputation from the City Council, as a result of which differences remained but no further action was taken by the Council. Others also have cast doubt upon the Church Burgesses' title to the land and properties assigned to them in Queen Mary's Charter. J.D. Leader quotes S.O. Addy, who describes certain statements in the Petition to Queen Mary as a 'fictitious claim contrived by lawyers to make it appear that the lands did not properly come within the scope of the Statute.' (viz. the Act for Chantries Collegiate). That statement is reproduced in the Report of the Charity Commissioners of 1897.[22] As we have seen, R.L. Craig, the then Law Clerk to the Town Trustees in 1949, repeats the claim. Craig also makes the point that as a result of Queen Mary's Charter, the property confiscated under Edward VI was restored to the Town, but not to its rightful owners.

In 1906 there appears the suggestion, in the City Council Enquiry, that the Church Burgesses' title to their estate was flawed. Criticisms of the Burgesses, in the earlier Town Council proceedings in 1851,[23] were of lack of openness in the proceedings of the Burgesses and of too much concern with ecclesiastical matters rather than with wrongful appropriation of the Town's property in Queen Mary's time. The action of the Town Council in 1850, in seeking a new Scheme of Administration for the Trust, was concerned largely with ensuring that a larger proportion of the Trust's funds went to secular purposes and with securing greater public participation in the affairs of the Trust.

Let us now examine more closely the issue of title, always recognising that Mary Tudor's action in the Charter was undoubtedly fully legal. But there may be a case to answer that, in fairness to the inhabitants of Sheffield, the Queen might have been better advised to restore the confiscated lands to the Burgery, i.e. to the Town Burgesses (under whatever ad hoc arrangements had previously existed), rather than setting up a new incorporated body and, also, without specifying so closely the purposes to which the income was to be allocated.

Four issues appear to be crucial:

1. Was there in existence, prior to 1554, a body acting on behalf of the inhabitants of the township, allocating monies for public purposes?

2. Were the lands and properties assigned in Queen Mary's Charter to the Twelve Capital Burgesses and Commonalty misappropriated, viz. directed to be used for purposes which represented a radical departure from previous practice?

3. Was the Charter an Act of Incorporation of the Town of Sheffield?

4. Are there particular characteristics distinguishing the original Capital Burgesses named in the Charter?

Dealing with these questions in order:

1. Was there in existence, prior to 1554, a body, acting on behalf of the inhabitants of the township, allocating monies for public purposes?

The answer would appear to be – yes, in that funds were allocated for highways, bridges and for stipends of the three assistant priests. If, however, one asks about the constitution of that body and the powers under which it acted, then the answers that emerge, lacking in certainty though they may be, do not warrant a conclusion that Mary Tudor's Charter displaced a body of de facto, if not de jure, corporate status and replaced it with the newly incorporated Twelve Capital Burgesses and Commonalty. Evidence points to the Vicar and Church Graves (Churchwardens) as having control of allocation of public monies, an arrangement common in other towns at that time, if only because Church governance was at least legislated for, and in the Church's appointed and elected officers there resided some authority and some education. Indeed, Hey states that the Twelve Capital Burgesses were the successors of the twelve 'gravys of the kyrke of Sheffield' as they were known in 1499.[24] The Petition of Swyft and Tailour states:

> 'The issues and proffets of the said paryishe . . . were yerly by the Churchgraves of the said parish for the tyme beynge receyved and converted to the uses before remembered.'

Examination of deeds in the possession of the Church Burgesses dating from the 14th and 15th centuries, show that a number of them make grants to the Chaplain and Churchwardens. (See Appendix I). For example, an Indenture of 1499 is a form of lease from 'the Greve or Churche Maisters of the Churche of Sheffield.'[25] A Lease of 1549 relating to property in Old Change, London, names the Vicar and Churchwardens and Burgesses of the parish as owners.[26] Earlier deeds bequeath property to the Vicar of Sheffield.[27]

Ad hoc arrangements must have existed prior to Mary's Charter for the disbursement of monies for the public good. What cannot be substantiated is any claim that a recognised body existed for this purpose, other than that of the Vicar and Churchwardens. Leader's comment is clear enough: 'It has long been the opinion of the major part of the inhabitants of Sheffield that the Old Charter, commonly called Furnival's Grant, created the property which is vested in the hands of the Town Trustees for public use. This is, however, a mistake and perusal only of that instrument must convince any one that it has nothing to do with the matter'.[28] Samuel Mitchell had made the same point earlier:[29] 'Many have supposed that the lands now vested in the Burgesses (Town Trust) for public and charitable uses were the identical lands granted to the free tenants in 1297. This is not altogether the case. It was a grant in fee, to all the free tenants, of all the tofts, lands and tenements which they held of de Furnival at yearly rent of £3.8s.9¼d. But the Burgesses never paid any such rent, which they must have done if the tenements had fallen into their possession.'

It would appear that only after the 1554 Charter established the Twelve Capital Burgesses, was action taken to set up some formal body in the town to collect and administer the revenues of that portion of the Town's property not referred to in the 1554 Charter. Mitchell says; 'The property which, before the Reformation, had been in the hands of the Vicar and Churchwardens now transferred into the custody of some of the principal inhabitants calling themselves the Burgesses and Free Tenants of the Town of Sheffield. Whether by Royal Charter, Order in Chancery, or merely by common consent, I have not been able to determine.' It is highly likely that the action was taken by common consent, since the Town Trust was not incorporated until 1681 and there is no reference at that time (nor, indeed, in the Reports of the Charity Commissioners of 1828 and 1897, which summarised the history of the Trust) to any earlier documentation that might indicate anything as formal as a constitution. J.B. Wheat, referring to claims made from time to time that the Town Trust was founded by the Furnival Grant in 1297, notes: 'the claim will serve equally well for either (The Town Trust or the Church Burgesses) as they were of common origin, but in either case it is quite erroneous.'[30]

Certainly, there was a discontinuity in 1554, but not that of a 'rival' Trust set up with about three quarters of the assets stripped from a pre-existing Trust. In one sense, Queen Mary's Charter represented a simple act of restitution to the parish of what had been confiscated earlier by the Crown, but with a formal, recognised constitution for administering what was being returned, in place of former ad hoc arrangements. To secure the legal transfer, without having a recognised, constituted body to transfer to, would have been well-nigh impossible; and the only existing recognised body with a formal constitution would have been the Vicar and Churchwardens. Such a transfer might well have occasioned a protest from the Burgesses and Free Tenants. As it was, there seems to have been no protest.

As if to distinguish the administration under the 'Burgery of Sheffield' from that of the clearly stipulated purposes of administration by the Twelve Capital Burgesses and Commonalty, the first recorded rental of the Burgery in 1565 of £7.11s.4d. carries the description: 'to the use of all the said towne to be ymployed at the dyscreacyon of the sayde burgesses as hereafter shall ensu.'[31]

A formal constitution of the Town Trust followed two Commissions under much earlier legislation of 43 Queen Elizabeth I: 'An Act to Redress the Misemployment of Lands, Goods and Stocks of Money heretofore given to Charitable Uses.' The first Commission, issued on 16 May 1640, was interrupted by the Civil War. The second Commission reported in 1681.[32] Leader comments: 'The convenient fiction was set up that the lands and tenements were the gift of pious donors for charitable purposes, and thus came within the purview of the statute.' In Leader's words, the effect of the decree in 1681 was far-reaching: 'From a free commonalty of self-governing Burgesses, acting according to their unfettered discretion, it was changed into a quasi-charity with defined powers.'[33]

That it was not until 1640 that steps were taken to secure a formal incorporation of a body to administer the 'Town's properties' would seem to support a view that there was no local sense of injustice following Queen Mary's Charter. Certainly there does not seem to be anything to support what in the late nineteenth century was referred to as 'fictitious claims' and in the twentieth as 'perjured evidence and specious special pleading'. There would surely have been both protest and moves towards establishing the standing of what has been claimed by some as the prior body. The moves towards a formal constitution of what is now the Town Trust may well have been a result of changes after the death of Gilbert, 7th Earl of Shrewsbury, when subsequent Lords of the Manor ceased to reside, either regularly or frequently, at Sheffield Castle. As J.D. Leader puts it: 'It may well be that the loss of this paramount influence in the town was felt in some relaxation of the bonds that had hitherto held the community together.'[34] The cutlers of the town secured action rather more quickly to protect their interests. They saw the need for regulation of trade, 'now that there was no benevolent despot with whom they could discuss their troubles.'[35] A Bill was presented to Parliament by the cutlers in 1621 and was followed by a comprehensive Act in 1624, which established the Cutlers' Company.

We can now turn to the second question:

2. Were the land and properties assigned in Queen Mary's Charter to the Twelve Capital Burgesses and Commonalty misappropriated, viz. directed to be used for purposes which represented a radical departure from previous practice?

Was it, to be precise, a 'wrongful diversion of civic funds to Church uses?'[36] In particular, we have to note the priority afforded, in the Charter, to payment of the stipend of the three Assistant Priests. The other charitable objects are clearly secondary. The Town Council, through the Report of their Special Committee in 1906, claimed that there had, in effect, been a diversion and that the original purposes intended to be supported by income from 'the Town's properties' were those of repair of bridges and highways and the parish Church and the relief of the poor of the parish. J. Newton Coombe[37] has carefully reviewed the evidence relating to this claim and little can be added to his analysis. We should note:

i. There is, strictly speaking, no 'original purpose'. There are no records showing how the Free Tenants of the town determined the allocation of income from the Town's properties until 1566. The preamble to the first set of accounts for which records are available states that the proceeds of the rent income is 'to the use of all the sayde towne, to be ymployed at the dyscreacyon of the sayde Burgeses.'

ii. The petition to Queen Mary is the most direct evidence we have that bequests to the town were for the purpose of 'reparacion and amendment of severall briggs and wayes within the said parish of Sheffield; and to the reparacion of the churche there and to the releffe of the most nedye and indegent persones inhabytynge within the said parishe.' What is also clear from the Petition is that by some process of agreement, the stipends of the three assistant priests became a charge upon parish funds.

iii. It is also clear from deeds in the Church Burgesses' archives that bequests were made for specific purposes not connected with the maintenance of bridges and highways and relief of the poor, purposes that may be generally described as 'pious purposes'. Of 75 ancient deeds in the possession of the Church Burgesses, dating from 1304 to 1549, only one mentions bridges, highways or the poor. Many stipulate specific gifts for Church purposes, e.g. for altars, lamps, saying masses or for building work. Many of the deeds are grants by private individuals to the Chaplain and Church-maisters for the time being, viz. the Vicar and Churchwardens.[38] Examples are quoted in Appendix I.

iv. The lands confiscated under the Chantries Collegiate Act were undoubtedly given for pious purposes, if not for 'superstitious purposes'. As we have seen they gave an income equal to about three quarters of the total of the public monies of the town.

Coombe has categorised the lands specified in the Charter as falling into three categories:[39]

a. Lands granted to the Vicar and Churchwardens for the expressed object of providing religious ceremonies in the Parish Church for the benefit of the souls of donors and their relatives.

b. Lands granted to the Vicar and Churchwardens without condition or trust expressed in the deeds, but applied along with (a) in providing for religious services and ceremonies in the Parish Church, and (since about 1540) in payment of the stipends of the three priests appointed to assist the Vicar.

c. Lands granted to the Vicar and Churchwardens in some cases for the expressed object of providing religious ceremonies, and others without any condition or trust, and applied for the repair of the Parish Church and other Church expenses.

As he pointed out, (a) and (b) were confiscated to the Crown by the Chantry Commission and (c) were those lands disclosed by Bayley which were not confiscated and were subsequently included in the Charter. It would have been quite fair and appropriate, it would seem, for Queen Mary's Charter to have restricted the purposes of the Trust to the payment of the stipends of the three assistant priests and to aspects of the maintenance of the Parish Church, with emphasis perhaps upon the costs of divine worship, rather than the repair of the fabric. We may be led to one or both of two conclusions. Either there had been expenditure upon bridges, highways and the poor from the income from the town's lands, or Queen Mary's advisers and the petitioners were seeking to ensure, for the common good, a broad base of charitable giving. What, surely, cannot be concluded is that the Charter represents a radical discontinuity and an inversion (or, at least, a new direction) of priorities. The Charter enshrines priorities accepted and applied (with, it would seem, the general and deliberate approval of the Burgery) for many years before the grant of the Charter.

3. Was the Charter an Act of Incorporation of the Town of Sheffield? If this were so, then the general line of development pursued by the Church Burgesses in their emphasis upon ecclesiastical purposes might well have been misdirected. There is no doubt that the later record of the Trust in secular matters is substantial and significant, but it is true that ecclesiastical ends are dominant until the early nineteenth century. Addy has argued[40] that 'no competent person would now deny that the Twelve Capital Burgesses and Commonalty of Sheffield are the old governing body of the city.' Wheat[41] refers to, and dismisses, the possibility of regarding the Charter as an Act of Incorporation of the town, the Burgesses being the Aldermen of a Corporation. Other competent persons quickly made known their disagreement with Addy's assertion.[42] Partisanship may tend to take over from fact here. The Charity Commissioners in their 1897 Report had no doubt that a claim for incorporation of the town could not be entertained – 'it is not apparent how it can be claimed that the Church Burgesses were anything more than a corporation empowered to carry out the tasks mentioned in the Letters Patent.' That is the understanding of more recent administrators of the Trust.

Addy records[43] that other towns had Capital Burgesses and the number 12 or 24 was common as the unit of governance. In Ipswich in 1200, the whole community of the Borough elected 2 bailiffs, 4 convenors and 12 Capital Burgesses. As late as 1880, the Corporation of Oxford is described as consisting, 'as heretofore, of 8 portmen and 12 Capital Burgesses.' It was, no doubt, examples such as these which led Addy to claim a Charter of Incorporation for Sheffield. Mary, in her Charter, may have been following precedent that was well established of entrusting important affairs of the town to twelve Capital Burgesses, in this case appointed by Charter, and not elected by and from townspeople. But it is not possible to deduce that she was establishing the Incorporation of a town in so doing. A reading of the Charter will not support such contention. The Town Council, however, persisted in 1906 in their claim both that the Trust had wrongly given priority to ecclesiastical objects and that Sheffield Corporation should be regarded as the proper guardian of the assets then held by the Church Burgesses. This was in spite of the Charity Commissioners' views just quoted and the failure of the Town Council's petition in 1853 to pass muster in the Court of Chancery.

However, the reference to 'Commonalty' in the Charter might be held to carry with it the implication that the 12 Capital Burgesses should operate in a manner that not only would have regard to the public good (which no-one ever seems to have questioned) but would exhibit also a measure of accountability to the local population (which the Church Burgesses never established). Although the word 'Commonalty' is used in the Charter, the corporate body of the Burgesses is self-perpetuating, with no place for participation of the commonalty in the election of Burgesses. This stands in contrast to provision in the Town Trustees' Deed of Incorporation of 1681, which gives a voice in the nomination and appointment of Town Burgesses to 'the greater part of the inhabitants within the town.' The Church Burgesses, from time to time, have, indeed, displayed a reluctance to entertain openness in their affairs. Things might perhaps have gone another way. The first record we have of the accounts refers to their presentation on 2 November 1557 'before Robert Swyft and others, inhabitants of the said town.' Presentation of the annual accounts before public meeting continued year by year. In 1561, the reference is to presentation 'in the presence of the whole parish.' Reference to such 'public meetings' ceases at the end of the seventeenth century. Up until that time there are references to 'the Commonaltie', or 'with many of the Commonaltie', or, 'besides some of the Commonaltie.' A few of those attending are sometimes named, presumably the more prominent citizens of the town. For example, in 1573, the accounts were taken 'before the Rt. Hon. George, Earl of Shrewsbury and all ye Burgesses with many Inhabitants.'

In the intervening 300 years there is no evidence of any serious attempt being made to secure, for the Commonalty, a voice in the Burgesses' affairs, save for a request from the Vestry Meeting in 1808 that the annual accounts should be published. The response of the Burgesses (minuted on October 1808) is dignified, pained and firm, and offers only a crumb of comfort to the commonalty. Their letter is addressed to Thomas Sutton, Vicar of Sheffield:

> Reverend Sir:
>
> The Church Burgesses conceive that their conscientious conduct in the discharge of their duties should have prevented any such suspicion as the resolution of the Vestry Meeting seems to convey. And they are extremely sorry that when they endeavoured to conform to their Charter, and to correct those Encroachments upon it, which Counsel learned in the law had pointed out to them as having insensibly crept into the Trust, they should have been suspected of Mal Administration. They should rather have expected Credit for their Disinterested Conduct, when it is considered that as Individuals and Parishioners they are bringing upon themselves a certain part of the Expences which a Rate will lay upon the Parish. As to publishing their Accounts, it is such a Request as they cannot comply with, but a deputation of two or three Gentlemen from the Town may have a reasonable inspection of the accounts by calling at Mr. Wheat's Office.'

Only in the wake of the Trevor controversy (see p. 83) were voices again raised in criticism of lack of openness. In a debate in the Town Council on 6 January 1851, Alderman T. Dunn claimed that the Church Burgesses 'had never, so far as he was aware, made any statement to the public of their accounts or report of their proceedings. The whole of their business had been conducted in as close a manner as if it related to private property.'[44] An editorial in the *Sheffield Independent* of 11 January 1851 makes the strong comment:

> 'According to the Charter the commonalty have nothing to do with choosing the Burgesses. (They), therefore, are under no responsibility to the commonalty. And to inform the commonalty of what (they) do, would be to appeal to their judgement, and this creates a responsibility contrary to the Charter. With sophistry such as this the Capital Burgesses seem to have satisfied themselves for nearly 300 years. When, therefore, a public meeting requested them to publish their accounts, which their predecessors in the earlier days of the trust had done, they simply took no notice of such impertinence.'

These protestations reflect, to some extent, the views put forward in a little pamphlet of 1811, under the pseudonym of 'A Townsman'.[45] Printed at the time of the proposed Act of Parliament for lighting, cleaning and watching the Town, and addressed to one of the town's J.P.s, the author proposed sweeping changes. He attempted to show the 'practicability of uniting all parties in the application of the proposed Act of Parliament' and also 'how to obtain every object which has been suggested without paining the feelings of Individuals or of laying any great additional burdens upon the public.' He was dismissive of the purposes set out in the Burgesses' Charter, objecting to the provision made for the three assistant ministers on the grounds of 'its tendency to destroy, or at least lessen, the independence and consequent respectability, which are essential to the due discharge of the important office of the Ministers of God's word.' The clause relating to repair of the Parish Church is, he says, 'so indefinite as not to be understood' by (the Church Burgesses). And that relating to bridges and highways is 'completely nugatory, since they are now otherwise provided for.' Whereas the poor, he comments, 'have apparently been of late almost entirely overlooked or disregarded.'

Having dismissed the objects of the Charter, he goes on: 'the grand and radical defect appears to arise principally from the Burgesses being elected for life'; he opines that 'this has led to profound secrecy'. His remedy is to establish a single Trust – the 24 Capital Burgesses and Trustees of Sheffield, with very limited responsibilities for ecclesiastical matters and a substantial amount of local democracy. Nothing more seems to have been heard of the proposals.

In 1852, the Town Council presented a petition to the Court of Chancery proposing a Scheme for the administration of the Trust in which the assets of the Trust would be vested in the Town Council. The petition was dismissed by Vice-Chancellor Stuart in an Order dated 7 January 1853. Meanwhile, the Attorney-General had proposed a Scheme for consideration by the Court of Chancery which provided for publication and public inspection of Accounts and for the appointment of Burgesses to be made with the approval of the Court after public advertisement of nominations. The Court did not accept the Attorney-General's Scheme. As late as 1899, there is evidence to indicate that the Church Burgesses are under pressure to make known publicly their accounts. At their meeting held on 11 April of that year, a Minute refers to a letter received from the Charity Commissioners referring to the non-delivery of the yearly accounts of the Trust to the Churchwardens for presentation to the Vestry, in obedience to the provisions of the Charitable Trusts Amendments Act, 1855. The Burgesses resolved that a copy should be sent.

It does not appear from all this, that any convincing case can be made out in favour of a reading of the Charter as an Act of Incorporation of the Town of Sheffield. There is a difference of opinion amongst respected local historians, but the decisions of the Courts and the Charity Commissioners are at one. The Trust's Charter establishes a corporate body for the administration of the Trust, no more and no less. It also has to be said that the incorporation of the Town Trustees in 1681 is, likewise, not an act of incorporation of the town, although that Trust took upon itself some important functions of local government before later legislation conferred these responsibilities upon local authorities. As to the significance of 'the commonalty' in Queen Mary's Charter, it is clear that there is no provision for public involvement in the affairs of the Trust. The most that can be said is that the Burgesses should be regarded in some way as acting for the Commonalty in pursuing the objectives laid upon them in the Letters Patent.

4. Are there particular characteristics distinguishing the original twelve Capital Burgesses?

We have seen that, prior to the 1554 Charter, there was, so far as we are aware, no formalised administration for the Town's public monies. Such administration appears to have been in the hands of the Vicar and Churchwardens, together with some of the Burgesses of the town. We have no records to help us to understand how decisions were reached and implemented in relation to the Town's property. When the time came for restoration of the confiscated property, it could hardly be otherwise than as a legal conveyance to a formally constituted and incorporated body. We have noted that the body incorporated by Charter might be regarded as the natural successor to the 'twelve gravys of ye kirke of Sheffield.' (p. 15) The word 'Capital' can be taken to mean chief, leading, influential, prestigious. Presumably, the first Capital Burgesses were men of reputation in the town, but we have no means of knowing the basis of their selection. An Indenture of 1549-50,[46] being a lease from the Vicar and Churchwardens of property in the Old Change, London, lists 19 names other than the Vicar. Of these, 5 appear among the 12 original Capital Burgesses. They are: William Burrows, Robert Moore, Robert Smith, William Tailour, William Walton. It is not possible to pick out characteristics that differentiate them from what might have been expected of other prominent citizens. The same can be said of the other seven, although there were, clearly, influential and weighty people here. William Tailour (yeoman) of Holt House, Ecclesall, was cousin to Robert Swyft of Broomhall, the Principal Agent to the Earl of Shrewsbury. It was these two men who presented the Petition to Queen Mary. Robert Moore, a merchant, was a man of some substance, since in 1569 he was assessed at 8s. and helped to equip soldiers. William Walton, innkeeper, occupied Little

Gillcarr and his brother-in-law lived at Stannington Hall. Very little is known of Robert Smith except that he was the brother of Hugh, another Capital Burgess. There was a large and prominent family of Smiths, including Thomas Smith of Crowland, Lincolnshire, who later endowed the Grammar School in Sheffield. William Burrows, yeoman, lived at Shirecliffe Hall and had a brother Richard in Rotherham who was a wealthy lead miner.

Of the seven Capital Burgesses not named in the 1549 Indenture, we may note that Richard Fenton, merchant and gentleman, later of Doncaster and related by marriage to Swyft, appeared in recusant rolls of 1592-93 and was described as a 'dangerous recusant'. John Holland, tanner, of Greystones, was of a family closely connected with pre-Reformation chantries and William Burrowes made bequests to chantry priests.[47] But supporting chantries was not, at that time, indicative of a strong adherence to the Catholic cause. It may well have been no more than following the tradition of the times.

Perhaps all that one can say of the original twelve is that there was a deal of modest wealth, position and influence there, with no more, and no less of family interrelationships than one might have expected in a relatively small community. They would appear to be representative of weighty and respected citizens of the parish, but not of any particular Church party. R.E. Leader has commented that

> 'the most striking deduction from examination of the personality of the Capital Burgesses of 1554 is the exclusion from the Trust, as nominated by Queen Mary's advisers, of the townspeople themselves; and the predominance given to the landed class – to the gentry and yeomanry of the neighbourhood. This is pointedly shown if we contrast the first Capital Burgesses with the men of the Burgery, ultimately known as the Town Trust. The latter were essentially of the town, plain citizens, spending their lives in the daily work of the place. The former were of the country, remote from concern for the parish pump, aloof from the more democratic toilers and forming a sort of Upper House.'[48]

The contrast which Leader attempts to make cannot be sustained by any evidence. The Capital Burgesses were 'men of the Burgery'.

We cannot conclude that there are any particular distinguishing features of the original twelve in terms of factional interests. Whatever may have been the later bias of the Church Burgesses against Catholic tendencies or in favour of evangelical tendencies, it is not possible to discover amongst the original twelve any clear evidence that the basis of their selection was on grounds of churchmanship. One would expect, given the temper of the times, that some leanings in favour of the Catholicism of Mary might have been expected of those named in the Letters Patent. But only with Fenton and Holland might this have been the case. R.E. Leader in his article on the 1554 Burgesses, already alluded to, in referring to the exclusion of 'plain citizens' from office in the Trust, claims that 'it may be that the sturdy Protestant principles of the inhabitants made them impossible or unacceptable as Church administrators'. If this was so in 1554 (and there is no evidence to support the statement), then it must be said that, in later years, 'sturdy Protestant principles' were strongly in evidence amongst the Church Burgesses.

The Trust is launched

The Church Burgesses Trust was born out of Tudor turmoil. The responses in Sheffield to both threat and opportunity presented by Henry VIII, Edward VI and Mary I are proof of the vigour and independence of its people. What is remarkable is that the Trust should so quickly establish itself in an orderly and untroubled fashion. Given the factions and dissensions of the three or four decades from 1530 onwards, one might have expected some considerable local friction. There is no evidence of any such disturbance. This says as much for the good sense of the people of Sheffield as it does for the good judgment and integrity of the Church Burgesses. For the most part, over that period, the proceedings of the Trust are routine, relating only to a small canvas confined, very largely, to the Parish Church and its place in the community. Excursions into territory that had to do with relief for the poor and for education were of very limited compass. Not until the early nineteenth century do we see a broadening of interest and a surge of activity corresponding to the rapid development of the town of Sheffield at that time, a development both industrial and urban. During the whole of this period, the Burgesses exercised careful stewardship of their assets and extended these until their holdings of both land and property became significant. They could not rival the holdings of the successors to the Earls of Shrewsbury, the Dukes of Norfolk, but they were able, through their property, to make a mark upon the urban development of Sheffield in the nineteenth century. But before the Church Burgesses Trust could become the comprehensive charity that it is today, the instruments of administration had to change. The Charter, whilst remaining the source of authority and purpose, had to be supplemented by Schemes of Administration that permitted response to rapidly changing social circumstances. The successive Charity Schemes of the Trust, commencing with that of 1854, provided the means whereby the Church Burgesses could both consolidate and extend their assets and use their income to respond to changing social needs.

The Charter of Mary Tudor granted to the Church Burgesses 8 June 1554.

Anglie Francie et Hibernie

MARY BY THE GRACE OF GOD QUEEN

DEFENDER OF THE FAITH TO ALL TO WHOM THESE PRESENTS SHALL COME GREETING

WHEREAS our beloved subjects the Burgesses and Inhabitants of the Town and Parish of Sheffield in our County of York time out of mind were and have been seized in their Demesne as of fee of and in one yearly rent of eighteen pence issuing out of one Messuage or Tenement in Attercliff in the Parish of Sheffield aforesaid now or late in the Tenure of Ralph Bawnford, and of and in one other yearly Rent of two shillings issuing out of one Messuage in Little Sheffield in the Parish of Sheffield aforesaid now or late of Robert Taylor; and of and in one other yearly Rent of twenty one pence issuing out of one Messuage called Steel Bank in Sheffield aforesaid now or late in the Tenure of the Heirs of Stele; and of and in one other yearly rent of fourteen Shillings issuing out of one Messuage in Sheffield aforesaid called Grey Stones late in the Tenure of the Heirs of Christopher Eyre; and of and in one other yearly Rent of twenty one pence issuing out of one Messuage in Attercliff aforesaid lately in the Tenure of William Stanyforth; and of and in three Messuages Lands and Tenements with their Appurtenances in Attercliff aforesaid now in the several Tenures of Richard Savage Hugh Person and William Wood; also of and in One Messuage Lands and Tenements with their Appurtenances in Darnal in the Parish of Sheffield aforesaid now or late in the Tenure of Richard Borrows; also of and in one Cottage and one Croft of Land with the Appurtenances lying at the Brushes in Sheffield aforesaid now in the Tenure of Rowland Archdale; ALSO of and in two Cottages and two Crofts of Land with the Appurtenances in Owlerton within the Parish of Sheffield aforesaid now or late in the several Tenures of Thomas Mitchel and Nicholas Fox; also of and in one Cottage and two Closes of Land and Meadow in Walkley within the Parish of Sheffield aforesaid now in the Tenure of William Hale; ALSO of and in one Messuage and four Closes of Land and Meadow with the Appurtenances in Hallam within the Parish of Sheffield aforesaid now in the Tenure of the Widow Sele; also of and in divers closes Lands and Meadows in Little Sheffield aforesaid in the Tenure of John Parker or his Assigns; also of and in four Messuages with Lands and Tenements to the same belonging in Sheffield aforesaid now or late in the several Tenures of Alexander Clark William Parlington Robert Heptenstall and Thomas Mitchell Also of and in one Barn three Cottages and one Croft called Pincen Croft with the Appurtenances in Sheffield aforesaid in the Tenure of Humphrey Stafford or his assigns; ALSO of and in one Meadow with the Appurtenances in Sheffield aforesaid in the Tenure of William Burrows; Also of and in twenty five Cottages and all the Gardens and Crofts of Land with the Appurtenances to the same Cottages belonging in Sheffield aforesaid now or late in the several Tenures of William Burley, Thomas Trippitt, Gyles Greave, Wiliam Trickett, Thomas Bland, Richard Barley William Walton, Henry Ashley, Thomas Fox, Alexander Smith, Widow Hinchcliff, Godfrey Fulforth, Lawrence Bower, Richard Latham, Rodger Birley, James Taylor, Ralph Drake, Richard Lome, Thomas Arthur, John White, Thomas Clayton, William Trippit, Thomas Wilson, Henry Damme, and the Widow Gladwyn or their Assigns, ALSO of and in one Close of Land and Meadow with the Appurtenances in Sheffield aforesaid in the Tenure of Ralph Hollinhead, ALSO of and in three Crofts of Land with their Appurtenances in Sheffield aforesaid now or late in the several Tenures of William Spooner, Alice Jackson Widow, and William Hibbin, Also of and in two Messuages or Tenements and Lands and Meadow to the same belonging with the Appurtenances in Sheffield aforesaid now or late in the several possessions of Hugh Hawke and James Slatter, also of and in one Close of Land and Wood called Lady Spring and two Crofts called Malkin Crofts in Heeley in the Parish of Sheffield aforesaid now or late in the several Tenures of Thomas Blyth and James Taylor, Also of and in one Close of Land and certain Lands in Sheffield Town Fields now in the several Tenures of William Glete and Thomas Lewes; And of and in one Close of Land and Meadow called Redhill with the Appurtenances in Sheffield aforesaid now in the possession of Robert Bowre, Also of and in one Toft and divers Lands Meadows and Pastures with the Appurtenances in Aughton within the Parish of Aston in our said County of York in the Tenure or occupation of George West Gentleman or his Assigns; ALSO of and in two Messuages and Tenements with the Appurtenances situate and being in the Old Change in the Parish of Saint Augustin within our City of London now or late in the several Tenures or Occupations of Richard Sheppard and William Willoughby;

ALL AND SINGULAR which said Messuages, Cottages, Crofts, Meadows, Lands, Tenements and all other the Premises for several years past were given granted bequeathed and assigned to the said Burgesses and Inhabitants of Sheffield their Heirs and Successors by divers Persons for the Uses and Intents that the said Burgesses and Inhabitants of the Town aforesaid for the time being should convert and bestow all and singular the Issues Rents and Profits of the Premises yearly from time to time as well towards the Repairs of the Parish Church of Sheffield aforesaid and the Bridges and Common Ways and Passages within the said Parish as towards the maintenance and Relief of the Poor and Needy Inhabitants within the said Parish and to those Pious Uses and Intents the said Burgesses and Inhabitants of the Town of Sheffield aforesaid for the time being did bestow and convert all the Rents and Profits of the Premisses, ever since, until the thirtieth year of the reign of our dearest Father the late King Henry the eighth at which time by pious Gifts and Alms of the People and Inhabitants of the said Parish and by other Ways and Means three Priests were sustained to celebrate and Administer in the Parish Church aforesaid, so by degrees their Charity decreased, waxed cold and was utterly diminished and extinct so that the said Burgesses and Inhabitants of the Town and Parish aforesaid for the time being with parcel of the Rents and Profits of the said premisses were forced to support three Priests in the Parish Church aforesaid and to pay yearly the stipends and salleries of the same three Priests amounting to Sixteen pounds and ten shillings per annum Also they found and maintained one Lamp burning in the Parish Church aforesaid and annually one anniversary in the same Church and did expend for the maintaining of the said Lamp and Anniversary Nineteen shillings a year and the said Burgesses and Inhabitants of the said Town of Sheffield did persevere and continue in paying the aforesaid Stipends and maintaining the Lamp and Anniversary until the making of a certain Act of Parliament in the first year of the Reign of our dearest Brother the late King Edward the Sixth made and published concerning divers Colleges Chanteries and Gilds to be dissolved and abolished by virtue and under colour of the said Act, the said Burgesses and Inhabitants were obliged to render and pay yearly to the use of our said Brother out of the Issues Profits and Revenues of the Premisses for the Rents and Profits of the said Premisses so by them expended yearly in paying the Stipends of the said three Priests and maintaining the said Lamp and Anniversary the annual Rent of Seventeen pounds nine shillings and four pence; nevertheless since then certain questions and doubts concerning the right and title of the premisses have been moved and risen (to wit) whether the said messuages cottages and other premisses or the aforesaid rent of Seventeen pounds nine shillings and four pence by the said Burgesses and Inhabitants yearly expended to the uses aforesaid in manner aforesaid or neither of them ought to come to the hands of our said Brother or to the hands of US by virtue of the said Act of Parliament.

WE THEREFORE having considered the premisses and understanding that the said Town and Parish of Sheffield is of so large extent and so well peopled that the Vicar of the said Parish Church of Sheffield, without the help of some other Priests, by no means can, or is able to administer Sacraments and Sacramentals and other divine Services in the Parish Church aforesaid and to the said Parishioners, and being also willing and designing to take away and remove the said questions and doubts concerning the Right and Title of the Premises and that Sacraments and other divine Services may be administered and celebrated to the Glory of Almighty God in the Parish Church aforesaid and to the said Parishioners henceforth from time to time for ever as in times past to wit as has been accustomed in the time of our dearest Father and our other ancestors Kings of England aforetime, And also that this our Intent may take due effect our beloved Cosin and Councellor Francis Earl of Salop and our said beloved subjects the Burgesses and Inhabitants of the Town and Parish of Sheffield aforesaid have humbly desired and supplicated US that we would vouch safe to make create and establish the same Burgesses and Inhabitants into one body corporate and politick by the name of the Twelve Capital Burgesses and Commonalty of the Town and Parish aforesaid for ever and that we would vouchsafe to make and create the same Capital Burgesses and Commonalty and their successors fit persons and capable in the Law to receive and acquire to them and their successors within the Parish of Sheffield aforesaid Lands Tenements and Hereditaments in manner following and to the Uses and Intents under written

KNOW YE THEREFORE that we of our bounty inclining to their Requests of our special grace certain knowledge and our mere motion and also upon the considerations aforesaid and at the kind and special petition of our said beloved Cosin and Councellor Francis Earl of Salop and our said beloved subjects the Burgesses and Inhabitants of the Town and Parish of Sheffield aforesaid HAVE WILL'D and ordained appointed decreed and granted and by these presents for US our Heirs and Successors WE will ordain determine and appoint that the said Burgesses and Inhabitants of the Town and Parish of Sheffield aforesaid may and shall be incorporated by the name of the Twelve Capital Burgesses and Commonalty of the Town and Parish of Sheffield in the County of York realy in deed and name for ever and that the same Twelve Capital Burgesses and Commonalty from henceforth may and shall be one Body corporate and politick for ever and

Translation of the Charter.

OF ENGLAND FRANCE AND IRELAND

WE CREATE erect ordain make constitute declare and incorporate the same Twelve Capital Burgesses and Commonalty of the said Town and Parish of Sheffield one Body corporate and politick of themselves realy and fully by these Presents and that they may have a perpetual succession that by and under the same name they may be able to plead and be impleaded defend and be defended answer and be answered in all our Courts and Places both of US our Heirs and Successors and in all other Courts and Places whatsoever in all and singular Actions Suits Quarrels Causes and Demands real personal or mixt whatsoever and that the same Twelve Capital Burgesses and Commonalty and their Successors may and shall have a Common Seal to make grants and to do transact and seal all other things whatsoever touching and concerning the said messuages cottages lands tenements and other premisses or any of their hereditaments whatsoever and also that they the said Twelve Capital Burgesses and Commonalty by the name of the Twelve Capital Burgesses and Commonalty of the Town and Parish of Sheffield aforesaid may and shall be fit persons and capable in the Law to take and receive to themselves and their successors for ever the messuages lands tenements hereditaments and other the premisses aforesaid with all their appurtenances and that all and singular the premisses may have their due effect

WE OF OUR special Grace certain knowledge and our mere motion have assigned named made and ordained and by these Presents for US our heirs and successors DO name make and ordain our beloved Robert Swift Esquire, Hugh Smith, Richard Fenton, William Taylor, Robert Moore, William Walton, Robert Smith, Hugh Chawner, William Borrows, John Holland, Thomas Mitchell, and Thomas Parker of Attercliff Inhabitants of the Town and Parish of Sheffield aforesaid to be the first twelve principal Burgesses of the Town and Parish of Sheffield aforesaid

AND ALSO we will and for US our heirs and Successors by these Presents do grant to the aforesaid Twelve Capital Burgesses of the Town and Parish of Sheffield aforesaid and their Successors that as often and whensoever it shall happen that any of the said Twelve Capital Burgesses shall die or be removed from his Office of Capital Burgess of the Town and Parish aforesaid for any reasonable Cause that then and so often it may and shall be lawful for the rest of the Capital Burgesses remaining and surviving or the major part of the same when and as often as it shall please them and shall seem expedient within one Month next following the Death or removal of such Capital Burgess to name chuse and assign another of the said Inhabitants of the Town or Parish aforesaid being a discreet reputable and honest man to be a Capital Burgess of the Town and Parish aforesaid, who being so chosen and named shall from the time of such Election, be one of the Capital Burgesses of the Town and Parish of Sheffield aforesaid during his Life

AND FURTHER of our more abundant grace and of our certain knowledge and mere motion WE have given and granted and by these Presents for US our heirs and successors do give and grant to the said Twelve Capital Burgesses and Commonalty of the Town and Parish of Sheffield aforesaid all and singular the said Messuages Cottages Gardens Lands Tenements Meadows Feedings Pastures Rents Revenues Hereditaments and all and singular other the Premisses with all their Appurtenances in the said Town and Parish of Sheffield aforesaid and the aforesaid Tofts Lands Tenements Meadows Pastures and Hereditaments with their Appurtenances in Aughton aforesaid in the Parish of Aston aforesaid in our said County of York and the said two Messuages and Tenements with their appurtenances situate and being in the Old Change in the Parish of Saint Augustin within our said City of London AND ALSO the said Annual Rent of Seventeen Pounds nine shillings and fourpence by the said Burgesses and Inhabitants of the Town and Parish of Sheffield aforesaid annually paid to our said Brother the late King Edward the Sixth as is aforesaid AND the Reversion and Reversions of the said Messuages Lands Tenements Rents and other the Premises with all their Appurtenances; also the Rents and Annual profits whatsoever reserved on any Leases or Grants of the Premisses or any parcel thereof also all and singular our Woods Underwoods and Trees whatsoever growing and being in or upon the premisses or any parcel thereof and our whole Right Title Estate and Interest whatsoever of in and to all and singular the Premisses and every parcel thereof

TO HAVE HOLD AND ENJOY the said Messuages Cottages Lands Tenements Meadows Feedings Pastures Rents Revenues Woods Underwoods and all and singular other the Premisses and our whole Right Estate Title and Interest of and in the same with their and every of their Appurtenances to the said Twelve Capital Burgesses and Commonalty of the Town and Parish of Sheffield aforesaid and their Successors for ever TO THE USE and INTENT that the same Capital Burgesses and Commonalty and their Successors with Parcel of the Rents and Profits of the Premisses shall find and cause to be found from time to time for ever three Chaplains or Priests to celebrate and administer divine Services and Duties and the Sacraments and Sacramentals and other Things necessary to divine Worship in the Parish Church of Sheffield aforesaid and the Parish of the same which three Priests we will to be assisting and helping from time to time forever to the Vicar of the Parish Church of Sheffield aforesaid for the time being in the celebration and administration of the Sacraments and Sacramentals and in all other Things necessary to divine Worship to be administered in the Parish Church aforesaid and to the Parishioners thereof

AND ALSO TO THE USE and INTENT that the said Twelve Principal Burgesses and Commonalty of the said Town and Parish of Sheffield and their Successors may convert and bestow the whole surplus of the Rents and Profits of the Premisses over and above the several necessary and convenient Stipends and Salleries of the said three Priests and Chaplains from time to time as often as it may be needful and necessary towards the Repairs of the Parish Church of Sheffield aforesaid and the Bridges and Highways and the poor and needy Inhabitants within the said Parish

AND FURTHER of our further Grace we give License to and grant for use our Heirs and successors by these Presents to the said Burgesses and Commonalty of the Town and Parish of Sheffield aforesaid and their Successors that they and their Successors may be able to purchase and take to themselves and their Successors Lands Tenements and Hereditaments within the Parish of Sheffield aforesaid of the clear yearly value of Twenty Pounds to the Uses and Intents aforesaid so that the same Lands and Tenements be not held of us in Capite nor by Knight service nor of any other Person by Knight's Service And also with the leave of the Lord or Lords of which or of whom such Lands and Tenements have been held which Lands and Tenements shall not be put or subject to the Statute of Mortmain or any other Act Statute or Ordinance made or published to the contrary thereof in anywise notwithstanding

AND FURTHERMORE by these presents We will and grant that when and as often as any of the said three Chaplains for the time being shall happen to die or for some reasonable cause be removed from the Ministry aforesaid that then and so often it may and shall be lawful for the said Twelve Capital Burgesses and their successors or the major part of the same at what time and when they shall think fit and expedient within 6 weeks next following the death or removal of such Chaplain to name and assign another Chaplain to be one of the said three Chaplains in the Town of Sheffield aforesaid and which Chaplain being chosen shall be one of the said three Chaplains to administer their Sacraments and Sacramentals and to do and perform other services as the other two Chaplains there shall or ought to do PROVIDED ALWAYS and we will and ordain by these presents and the said Twelve Capital Burgesses and Commonalty of the Town and Parish of Sheffield aforesaid do grant for themselves and their successors that the said Burgesses and Commonalty and their successors shall acquit and discharge us our heirs and successors yearly from time to time for ever from and after the Feast of the Annunciation of the blessed Virgin Mary last past and from thenceforth free and discharge us from the several Pensions and Annuities following that were lately given and granted by our said Brother the late King Edward the Sixth to the Priests lately celebrating and serving in the Parish Church aforesaid (to wit) of and from a certain annual Pention or Annual Rent of Six pounds thirteen shillings and four pence given and granted to one Alexander Booth Clerk during his life, and of and from one other Annual Pention of five pounds to one Richard Bewick Clerk given and granted during his life And of and from one other Annual Pention of five pounds given and granted to one William Hall Clerk during his life

AND FURTHER we of our certain knowledge and mere motion by these presents do give and grant to the said Twelve Capital Burgesses and Commonalty of the Town and Parish of Sheffield aforesaid All and singular the Issues Rents Revenues and Profits of the said Messuages Lands and Tenements and the said Rent of Seventeen pounds nine shillings and four pence and of all other the premisses with all their appurtenances from the said Feast of the Annunciation of the blessed Virgin Mary last past thence arising accrewing or encreasing TO BE HELD by the same Twelve Capital Burgesses of our gift without any Account or anything else whatsoever to be paid rendered or done to us our heirs or successors in anywise howsoever although express in mention of the true and certain value and extent of the premisses or any of them or of the other Gifts or Grants by us or any of our Ancestors to the said Twelve Capital Burgesses and Commonalty before this time made in these presents be not fully expressed or any Statute Act Ordinance Provision or Restriction to the contrary thereof made published ordained or provided or any other cause or matter whatsoever in anywise notwithstanding

IN WITNESS whereof we have caused these our Letters to be made patent Witness ourself at Westminster the eighth day of June in the first year of our Reign.

UNDER our PRIVY SEAL &c.

MARY R.

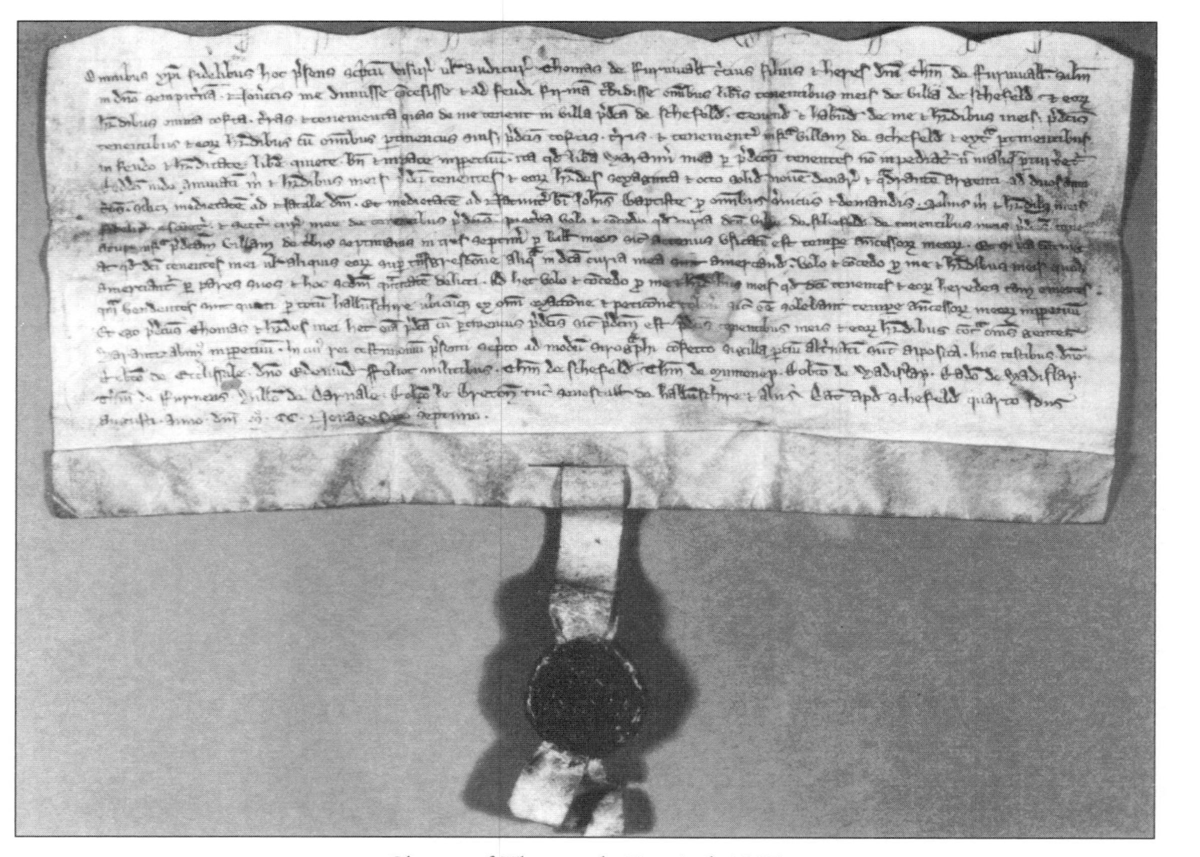

Charter of Thomas de Furnival 1297.

TRANSLATION

"To all the faithful of Christ who shall see or hear this present writing, Thomas of Furnivalle, the third, son and heir of Sir Thomas of Furnivalle, eternal salvation in the Lord.

Know ye that I have demised, granted, and delivered in fee farm to all my Free tenants of the town of Schefeld and their heirs all the tofts, lands, and holdings which they hold of me in the foresaid town of Schefeld, to hold and to have [the same] of me and my heirs to the foresaid tenants and their heirs with all their appurtenances belonging to the said tofts, lands, and holdings, within the town of Schefeld and outside, in fee and heredity, freely, quietly, well, and in peace, for ever, (provided that my free warren be not hindered by the said tenants or in any way disturbed), the said tenants and their heirs paying yearly therefor to me and my heirs £3. 8s. 9¼d. of silver, at the two terms of the year, namely, half at the Birthday of the Lord (Christmas), and half at the Nativity of Saint John Baptist, in discharge of all services and demands, reserving nevertheless to me and my heirs fealty, escheats, and suit of court of the said tenants.

Furthermore, I will and grant that the court of the said Town of Schefeld of my foresaid tenants shall be held within the foresaid town every three weeks by my Bailiffs, as hitherto has been accustomed in the time of my ancestors.

And if it should happen that my said tenants, or any of them, are to be fined for any trespass in my said court, I will and grant for myself and my heirs that they be fined by their peers, and that according to the measure of the offence.

Furthermore, I will and grant for myself and my heirs that the said tenants and their heirs, as well buyers as sellers, shall everywhere throughout all Hailamshire be quit from all exaction and demand of toll, as they were wont to be in the time of my ancestors, for ever.

And I, the aforesaid Thomas, and my heirs, will warrant all these matters aforesaid, with their aforesaid appurtenances, as is aforesaid, to my aforesaid tenants and their heirs, against all people for ever.

In witness whereof the seals of the parties are to the present writing, made in the manner of a chirograph, alternately affixed. Witnesses:— Sir Robert of Ecclissale, Sir Edemund Foliot, knights, Thomas of Schefeld, Thomas of Mounteney, Robert of Wadislay, Ralph of Wadislay, Thomas of Furneys, William of Darnale, Robert the Breton, then seneschal of Hallumshire, and others.

Given at Schefeld on the fourth of the Ides of August, in the year of the Lord 1297."

Translation of the Furnival Charter.

To the Quene our moste drad Soveraynge.

In moste lamentable wyse shewythe and cōplaynythe unto your ma^{tie} your trew faithfull and obedyent subiects Robert Swyft and Wm Taylor of the parishe of Sheffeld in the countie of Yorke and for and in the names of all other thenhabytance of the said parish, that wher your said orators together with others of the said parishe stand and be lawfullye seasyde in ther demaine as of fee, of and in certen lands tenem^{ts} and burgages set lyinge and beynge in the towne and parishe of Sheffeld aforesaid to the yerlye valew of xxvii^{li} and also of and in one messuage with appurtenances called the George set lyinge and beinge in the Olde Chaunge in your Grac's cytye of London w^{che} were gyven and assigned by dyvers persones of longe tyme paste to and for the reparacōn and amendm^{t} of several brygs and wayes w^{t}in the said parishe of Sheffeld; and to the reparacōn of the churche ther and to the releffe of the moste nedye and indegent persones inhabytynge w^{t}in the said parishe. The issues and proffets of all and singuler w^{che} premisses were yerlye by the churchegraves of the said parishe for the tyme beynge receyved and converted to the uses before remembred, unto abowte xiiiith yeres laste paste the inhabitaunts of the said parishe were enforced and cōstrayned for y^{t} ther said parishe was verey grett and populus haveynge w^{t}in the same xiiii. hamletts w^{che} for the moste parte are never woyd of plags and other evell deseases by reason of the gret nomber of poore and impotent persones inhabytynge w^{t}in the same to imparte and yerlye bestawe sume porchon of the reveneues of the said premises to and for the fyndynge of iii. prestes w^{t}in the said churche to helpe and assyste the vycare there as well in the vysytacōn of the said dissessed persones w^{t}in the said parishe from tyme to tyme as in the mynistracōn of devyne service and other sacram^{ts} w^{t}in the said churche. In w^{che} forme the same cōtynued untyll the makynge of the statute for dissolucōn of colegges and chauntrees. And for as moche as the cōmissioners appoynted for surveye of the said collygges and chauntres perceyvid that the inhabytants of the said parishe had in some one yere before the makynge of the said statute gyven and bestowed of the issues and profetts of the said premisses amongste the iii. severall prests the sume of xvii^{li} over and besyds ix^{s}. iiii^{d}. for an obyte, the said inhabytaunts were

Petition to Queen Mary Tudor from Robert Swyft and William Taylor.

cōpelled to certyfye before the said cōmissyoners the said yerly rent of xvii^{li}. ix^{s}. iiii^{d}. and accordynlye have ever synez answered and paid the same unto your m$^{tie's}$ receyvor of your grace's revenewes in the said countie of Yorke. Yet nevertheless one Henrye Bayleye of London skynner of his moste covetus and ungodlye mynde sekynge only his owne pryvate gayne and lucre hathe exebyted in your highnes courte of Augmentacōn a surmyssed informacōn cōserninge the said lands wherby he hathe cōtynually vexed and disquieted your said subiects and parishoners by the space of ii. hole yeres now laste paste and yet cōtynuythe the same to ther gret losse and impoverishment onles your hyghnes' accostomed clemencye and pytye be herin shewed. And for as moche moste drade soverayne ladye as the premisses were not gyven to the fyndynge of any preste or prestes to have cōtynuance for ever bot were fownde by the said parishoners of the said parishe of Sheffeld do think that the same were not w^{t}in the cōpasse of the estatute, so that your Grace is not justelye intituled to suche rent as was imployed in forme abovesaid to the fyndynge of the same prestes. And for that moste gracyous Ladye as the vycare of the said churche is not able w^{t}owte assystens to serve the cure, and to mynister the Sacraments and other devyne services w^{t}in the said parishe for the cōsyderacōn afore alegged; and also for that your highnes hathe no profett nor benefytte by the said rent by reason the same is paid furthe agen by the hands of your grace's receyvors unto the said iii. prestes for the yerlye pencōns now goynge abrode at their libertye, the churche beynge unserved to the gret discomefoorthe of the said inhabitaunce by reason of ye gret decaye of suche moste godlie service as heretofore hathe beyne used w^{t}in the said churche: Yt may therfor please your moste exilent ma^{tie} in the advancement of God's glorye and his devyne service to restore unto your said orators the said rent to be imployed and bestowed as heretofore it hathe beyne, your said orators dischargeinge your hyghnes of the said penchons; and your said subiects and all other the inhabitaunts of the said parishe and their posteryties shall have moste iuste cause for this charytable dede to pray unto God for the preservation of your moste royall estate longe to rayne and cōtynewe.

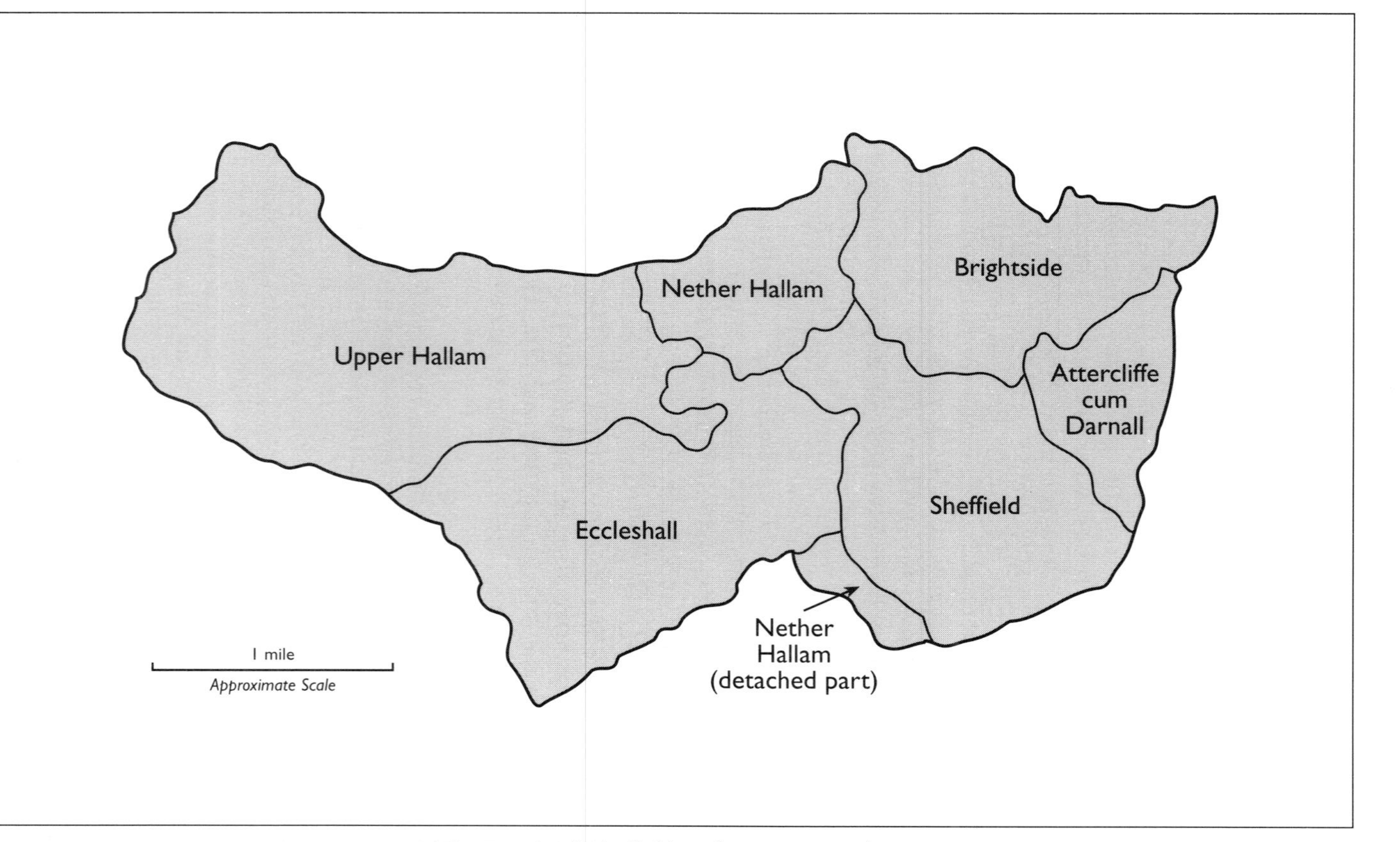

The Parish of Sheffield and its six Townships.

CHAPTER 2

The Charity Schemes

FOR 300 YEARS, the Church Burgesses operated solely under the authority of the 1554 Charter. They experienced difficulties of interpretation from time to time, but not until the Trevor controversy, and the difficulties that created, both amongst the Burgesses themselves and publicly, was it felt to be necessary to obtain a legal instrument (a Charity Scheme) to clarify and to delineate the powers of the Trust. Two things in particular required attention. One was the precise powers and responsibilities of the Burgesses in appointing the three assistant priests who operated from the Parish Church. Given that the Burgesses, under their Charter, could appoint the ministers without reference to the Vicar, it is surprising that the arrangement continued, without major upset, for so very long. As the town grew, the needs of the people in the townships made greater claims upon the ministers, creating some tension between the demands of the Parish Church and, initially, of the Chapels-at-Ease of Attercliffe and Ecclesall and, later, of the new Districts that were in due course to become parishes in their own right. If the resources of the parish of Sheffield were to be properly deployed and effectively managed, then an arrangement of dual control could not continue. The Vicar and Churchwardens had to be masters in their own house, and that meant that assistant clergy appointments and duties had to be formalised under the Vicar.

The second issue requiring clarification was that of the definition and disposal of expenditure for ecclesiastical and secular purposes. The Charter gave a broad brush description, useful perhaps for allowing discretion, but not helpful if particular items of expenditure were either claimed or challenged. Even without the Trevor controversy, with its sharp conflict between Burgesses, Assistant Minister and the Vicar, it would have been necessary to secure clarification at a time of rapidly changing needs and attitudes. The controversy, attracting public attention, including considerable newspaper coverage, meant that issues were sharpened and the pressures for change, and early change at that, were irresistible. Here, perhaps it is not too fanciful to suggest, is a Sheffield version of Barchester's Hiram's Hospital, with the *Sheffield and Rotherham Independent* cast in the role of the *Daily Jupiter*, but with no-one quite to identify with the Revd. Septimus Harding.

We must remember also the wider context of social change in these times. The mid- and late-18th century had seen a 'flowering of charitable effort' which, in the words of Owen, 'owed something to a vaguer, yet more pervasive, impulse than the Puritan ethic. Modern humanitarianism took its rise in the course of the century, and the benevolence and sensibility associated with it, though sometimes no more than emotions which it was fashionable to display, had a good deal to do with forming the social temper of the time.'[1] The rise of urban poverty in the nineteenth century brought further challenge, especially in a town like Sheffield, which grew so rapidly and became so heavily industrialised. The Burgesses could hardly ignore what was going on around them. They could not, in all conscience, profit from the increasing value of their estate in a time of rapid urban change and, at the same time, continue with a narrowly focussed charity, serving, very largely, the Parish Church. That way lay stagnation. The Burgesses were not looking merely for avoidance of problems with troublesome clergy. They were, it would seem, genuinely seeking a responsive instrument with which to work on a much wider canvas.

Questions and partial answers

Over the years, the Burgesses had been moved to seek the views of legal Counsel on interpretation of their powers under their Charter. The first reference to external opinion, by way, it would seem, of arbitration, was in 1619, to resolve a dispute concerning the stipend of the assistant ministers.[2] In 1605, Robert Rollinson had bequeathed two houses to the burgesses of Sheffield, to be used by two ministers of the Parish Church.[3] These were in Figtree Lane and, according to R.E. Leader, were referred to in 1625 as Figtree Hall.[4] Contention over rent and stipend led to arbitration in 1619 by Francis Coke and George Lascelles Esq. The decision was to award varying amounts to the three assistant ministers: 40 marks (£27) stipend plus 50s. rent annually; 20 marks (£13) stipend plus 40s. rent; and £10 stipend plus 40s. rent.

Issues relating to the assistant ministers were to be a recurring theme. In 1758 and 1759, the opinions of Serjeant Nares and Mr. Richard Wilson were sought.[5] Mr. Nares, on 30 June 1758, drew attention to the dangers of building up reserves 'for repairs to the Church, relief of the Poor in times of dearth and scarcity of the necessities of life, for defence of their rights and possessions and other contingencies', and pointed out that where there were surplus funds, the assistant ministers would be entitled to have their stipends increased. He commented upon the duties of the assistant ministers, that these ran beyond taking Divine Service and required care of souls in the parish and that the ministers were not subject to directions from the Archbishop. He pointed to the necessity of proving misconduct or incapacity if the Burgesses wished to remove a minister from office. Mr. Wilson responded on 7 March and 25 June 1759, largely confirming Mr. Nares' opinion, but stated that the maintenance of a large reserve was not justifiable. Indicating the complexity of deciding the duties and conditions of service of the assistant ministers, he averred that the 'Presbyters could not be compelled to preach, as preaching is no part of Divine Service, but if they preached, they must be licensed, but no license was necessary to entitle them to hold their office.' Contrary to Mr. Nares, his view was that the ministers could not be compelled to visit the sick or provide any other ministration to the inhabitants, other than in the Church.

Further opinions were sought on similar matters of Mr. William de Grey (30 December 1770) and Mr. Samuel Phipps (7 March 1771)[6]. The latter opined that the Burgesses were not responsible for providing surplices, Church books or wine for Communion.

In a comprehensive opinion of 1799, Mr. Hargraves must have set alarm bells ringing amongst the Burgesses. He was of the view that expenditure on wages of the Parish Clerk, the expenses of Visitations, Vestments, Church cloths, Communion wine, candles, Church utensils, removal of vagrants, clock and chimes, bells, organ, fire-buckets, were not allowed under the Charter. He warned against any expenditure on the Church building that went beyond what was strictly repair, and he advised against considering the idea of building Almshouses. As a result of this opinion the Burgesses decided, on 4 September 1799, that they could not contribute to substantial alterations then proposed for the Church.

In 1842, the Archdeacon, upon the instructions of the Archbishop of York, required the assistant ministers to obtain an Archbishop's licence to qualify them to fulfil the duties to which the Burgesses appointed them. Opinions from Sir William Follett and Dr. Adams were sought and, as a result, the Burgesses agreed to bear the cost of obtaining the licence, but only in that instance; in future, the cost would have to borne by the ministers or the Church.[7]

In 1845 the Burgesses, after consideration of relevant Acts of Parliament, agreed to grant a piece of land of about 1½ acres at Heeley as a site for the new Church and parsonage house. That decision was later questioned in the light of subsequent similar grants to other parishes and, in 1873, the opinion of Mr. H.F. Bristowe was sought, who pronounced that grants could be made, but under legislation other than that which the Burgesses had cited.

In 1879, Mr. Bristowe's opinion was again sought, on the question whether the Burgesses could contribute from their funds to support the Sheffield School Board, who had applied for a grant. His opinion, accepted by the Burgesses, was that funds from the Trust could only be used for Charity Schools (viz. those partly or wholly supported by voluntary subscriptions or by a charitable foundation) or for schools for the poor. Board Schools were held not to qualify under either heading.

On 30 May 1808 the Burgesses resolved to discontinue routine payments made to the Parish Church over many years.[8] Whether this was a result of lengthy pondering of Mr. Hargraves' opinion of 1799, or from a desire to save money, is not clear. It was, almost certainly, this decision which led the Vestry meeting later that year to request publication of the Burgesses' accounts. The list of items no longer covered by payments from the Church Burgesses was long:

Yearly rent of Barn in the Churchyard
Yearly payment of keeping the Boys in Order
Payment to the Sexton, for his attendance on Sunday evenings
Yearly salary of the Parish Clerk
Payment to Clerk for making transcriptions from the Parish register
Washing and repairing Surplices
Cleaning Church Pews
Candles for use in Church
Bread for the Sacraments
Wrappers to clean the Church
Wine for the Sacraments
Vestments for the Pulpit
Church Bibles and Prayerbooks
Parchments for the Register
Yearly payment for Bell Ropes.

Inevitably, the discontinuance of these payments caused difficulties for the Churchwardens and Parish. For more than a decade there was something of a minor war of attrition between the Church and the Burgesses, culminating in Counsel's Opinion (Mr. Peskell and Mr. Bell) being sought in February 1821. The opinions were not as clear-cut as the Burgesses might have wished and, indeed, suggested that the Charity would only properly be served by securing a legal instrument (a Scheme) stating precisely what its obligations were. The Burgesses were averse at that time to applying for a Scheme but they did, nevertheless, agree on 11 May 1821 to resume payments for bread and wine for Communion, bell ropes, washing surplices, trimmings for the pulpit, books for the reading desk, the parish register and copies therefrom and for rent for the Sexton's house – provided that the pew holders would pay for other items on the Churchwardens' list. Matters rumbled on unsatisfactorily. The redoubtable Mr. Hargraves, whose opinion in 1799 had perhaps led the Burgesses to their restrictions, was not supported by the Charity Commissioners in 1827, who were rather more relaxed and stated their opinion that Mr. Hargraves took too confined a view of the Charter and does not take into account the usage that formerly prevailed.'[9]

The Chancery Suit

It was against this background of unresolved questions, and with the much more pressing need to repair the serious breakdown in relationships between the Vicar, one of the assistant ministers (the Revd. George Trevor) and the Burgesses, that a friendly suit was instigated in the Court of Chancery in October 1850 by Joseph Wilson, the brother of Henry Wilson, the Capital Burgess at that time. The latter was undoubtedly the driving force in the business of securing reform and clear directions for the future. He, together with Richard Bayley, Thomas Creswick and Robert Younge were appointed as a committee on 27 August 1850 to prepare a draft Scheme. Indicative of dissension to come, Mr. Bayley declined to serve and his place was taken by George Hounsfield.

The Information laid before the Court by Joseph Wilson presented a summary of the changed circumstances in which the Trust was now called upon to operate. The relevance of the appointment of the three assistant ministers to current needs of the parish was questioned. Doubts were also expressed whether the Trust was properly fulfilling the objectives of the Charter in the pattern of its expenditure as it had developed over the years. The Informant suggested that uncertainties about the Burgesses' discretionary expenditure might perhaps best be resolved by the Court's approval of a Scheme which specified the future disposition of income. The Court was petitioned to ascertain from the Burgesses full details of their estates, income and expenditure and of all relevant documents. The Burgesses complied, with a full return of information, and on 8 May 1851 the Vice-Chancellor, Knight-Bruce, made a Decree referring the Case to the Master to approve a Scheme.

In his further information to the Court, the Relator, Joseph Wilson, described recent difficulties and disputes arising with the assistant ministers and suggested that stipendiary curates, under the full control of the Vicar, should be appointed. Information was also presented showing the changes in the old parish in which, since 1846, 25 Districts had been created and new Churches had been built. These changes, it was suggested, needed to be reflected in the responsibilities of the Burgesses. Detailed proposals for a new Scheme were presented by the Relator, prepared, we can safely assume, with the full knowledge and considerable help of his brother and other Burgesses. These proposals were accepted virtually unchanged by the Master and provided the essentials of the Scheme as it was finally approved.

As we have seen (p. 12), the Town Council took a close interest in what was afoot. In November 1850, they sought information from the Trust and it was refused them. The Council gave notice that they would make application to seek to remodel the Trust and they published Parliamentary notices of their intention to apply for alteration of the Charter in the *Sheffield and Rotherham Independent* of 16, 23 and 30 November 1850. They did, in fact, present their proposals, which were dismissed by the Court in 1853. On 8 December 1852, the Council resolved to present a Petition which was critical of the ecclesiastical nature of the Trust and of its alleged exclusiveness. The mode of election of Burgesses and of their exclusive allegiance to the established Church also came under fire. The Council opposed the proposals of Joseph Wilson and counter-proposed a Scheme which would vest all the Trust's assets in the Town Council and, in due course, when present obligations were fulfilled, would allocate one-third of income to ecclesiastical and two-thirds to secular purposes.

The draft observations of the Burgesses to this Petition went into some detail about the supposed claims of the 'commonalty' to participate in the affairs of the Trust and affirmed that it was only within the past few years that there had been any comment upon non-publication of the Accounts. The claim was made that since the Borough was incorporated only in 1843 (which Incorporation, it might be noted, was opposed by the Church Burgesses in a petition agreed at their meeting on 1 March 1838[10]), the Burgesses had, over a long period, ably protected the interests of the inhabitants. The Burgesses were not above making a fierce attack upon what they saw as the dangers of a newly emerging democracy. They challenged the claim that the Municipal Corporation 'fully and fairly represent the whole of the inhabitants of the parish . . . most of the persons of standing and respectability being totally unrepresented by the Municipality, there being very few members of the Church of England on the Council, almost the entire body being composed of Dissenters, and a considerable number of avowed infidels, the ruling party comprising Chartists, Socialists, and Democrats of the most ultra character.' The Burgesses also denied the Council's assertion that 'all the inhabitants are deeply interested in having the surplus of the income applied in repairing the bridges and highways and for the benefit of the poor.' The fury and indignation of the Burgesses can best be gauged perhaps from their comment that 'it was well-known that the Council had evinced every disposition to appropriate the Trust property in aid of their own empty coffers.'

The Attorney-General, no doubt taking account of the Town Council's action, and of public interest (including a public meeting in November 1850 which had produced its own proposals for change[11]), put forward his own recommendations to the Court of Chancery. The Burgesses, at their meetings on 20 July and 22 November 1853, considered his scheme and decided to oppose it. Neither was it accepted in toto by the Master in the Court of Chancery, but we should note that the Attorney-General had incorporated much of what had been included in the Burgesses' own proposals. The major differences were in respect of:

- the appointment of Burgesses, for which the Attorney-General proposed approval of nominees by the Court and public advertisement of nominations;
- publication of accounts, which should be open to inspection;
- the secular income to be applied five eighths to schools and one eighth to medical charities.

The 1854 Scheme

After nearly four years of deliberation, during which time local feelings had been stirred up, some long-standing prejudices well aired and much in-fighting indulged in, the considerable skill and organisation of the Church Burgesses was rewarded. The Master published his Report on 29 June 1854, almost exactly 300 years after the Charter, and on 1 August the Court made a final Decree ordering that the Scheme be brought into effect from 31 December 1854. The suit had been costly to the Burgesses. Total costs of £1439.17s.4d. were covered by a mortgage raised on Mr Huntsman's farm at Fulwood (he was Church Burgess from 1841 to 1854) and on part of the Burgesses' Attercliffe and Darnall estate.

The Scheme is reproduced in full in Appendix II. Its major provisions, which were to set the pattern of future responsibilities were:

1. 5/7 of the income to be applied to ecclesiastical and 2/7 to secular purposes;

2. The three Assistant Ministers to be replaced by two Chaplains, these to be Stipendiary Curates fully responsible to the Vicar;

3. Expenditure in maintaining and repairing the fabric of the Parish Church to be at the Burgesses' discretion;

4. Four Ecclesiastical Districts (when constituted), formed out of the old Parish, to be perpetually endowed, and as others are formed out of the

Netherthorpe, Porter Street, Broomhall and Gillcar Districts, these to be endowed at the discretion of the Burgesses;

5. The Burgesses were given powers to supplement the stipends of clergy in other parishes in Sheffield and to make contributions to the building of Churches and parsonage houses;

6. The expenses of Divine Worship for which the Burgesses are responsible at the Parish Church were listed;

7. Not more than £20 per annum to be contributed to the cost of repairing highways and bridges;

8. Of the secular income, 3/8 was to be expended in support of medical charities and 5/8 to educational charities for the poor.

The division of income between ecclesiastical and secular purposes (5/7 and 2/7) is, at first sight, somewhat peculiar. Yet it represents a faithful translation of the pattern of expenditure at the outset of the Trust. Precedent and tradition were followed meticulously by the Court of Chancery in apportioning the income.

In the first year for which accounts are available (1557), out of the total income of £30.5s.5d, the sum of £22.0s.11½d. was spent on Church expenses, including stipends of the three Assistant Ministers. 5/7 of £30.5s.5d is £21.12s.6d, and the Court could not get a more accurate rendering of expenditure without using a vulgar fraction even more unwieldy than 5/7. Furthermore, in 1850, whether by accident or design, about 70% (roughly 5/7) of income was still being expended for ecclesiastical purposes. The Court was, therefore, adhering closely to the practice of the Trust, both in the 1550s and the 1850s.

After 300 years, the Trust had an instrument of some precision which delineated its responsibilities and answered most of the questions requiring resolution. More importantly, the Chancery suit and its outcome had confirmed the able stewardship of the Church Burgesses over the long period of their history. It also confirmed and buttressed the independence of the Trust and demonstrated the robustness of the Burgesses and their ability to face both public criticism and the determined efforts of the Town Council to gain control of the Trust's assets. But, as we have seen (p. 12), public interest in the Burgesses affairs continued and the Town Council made one more attempt in 1906 to assert a measure of public control.

Subsequent Amendments

The Scheme of 1854 was soundly constructed and its essential provisions have proved equal to the demands generated by the unprecedented social and economic change of the succeeding 150 years. Inevitably, amendments proved to be necessary and these were made in:

4 March 1874	10 December 1953
16 February 1904	6 March 1959
6 January 1933	12 May 1970
8 October 1940	24 July 1978
12 May 1948	5 August 1992
2 January 1953	

A summary of the purport of the various amendments follows:

4 March 1874: Clause 3(O) amended: The surplus remaining, after payment of the stipends of the Ministers of the Districts already endowed by the Church Burgesses, may be applied in payment of an annual sum, not exceeding £200 in each case, for or towards the endowment of any legally created District in the Parish selected by the Church Burgesses with the approval of the Ecclesiastical Commissioners.

16 February 1904: The expenditure for educational purposes (5/8 of 2/7 of the net income after payment of the £20 towards highways and bridges) was allocated to the somewhat obscurely titled Church Burgesses Educational Foundation, without it being constituted as a separate entity. That came in 1953.

6 January 1933: Clause 3(C) amended: The words 'Bishop of Sheffield' are substituted for the words 'Archbishop of York' in paragraph C and the stipends of the First and Second Curates (henceforth to be called the First Chaplain and the Second Chaplain) shall be £350 and £250 annually respectively.

8 October 1940: Clause 3(K) amended: The income of the Infirmary Chaplain was allowed to be made up to £400 per annum instead of £150.

A Clause was inserted after 3(R): The Trustees may set apart and let in allotments in the manner prescribed by and subject to the Allotments Extension Act 1882 any portion of the land belonging to the Charity other than buildings and the appurtenances of buildings.

12 May 1948: The stipends of the First and Second Chaplain were increased to £450 and £350 respectively.

2 January 1953: The provisions of Clause 3(P) were extended: The Trustees shall be at liberty from time to time to apply all or part of any surplus of the Income applicable to Ecclesiastical Purposes remaining to be applied under Clause 3(P) in making occasional or recurrent and terminable payments at the discretion of the Trustees to or for the benefit of any clergyman of the Church of England in Priest's Orders filling or holding Ecclesiastical office or appointment in any district or parish within the area of the Ancient Parish of Sheffield.

Clause 3(R) was updated and extended, allowing grants to be made to the Board of Governors of the United Sheffield Hospitals and as follows:

- Grants to societies and organisations established or to be established in or near the City for application by them for any charitable purpose or purposes stipulated by the Trustees being a purpose or purposes conducive to:
  - (a) The assistance or welfare of the poor, sick or other needy inhabitants of the City; or
  - (b) The improvement of the physical, social or moral condition of the inhabitants, or of a substantial section or class of the inhabitants, of the City or of any particular district of the City.
- The Trustees may make grants for supplementing relief or assistance provided out of public funds . . . but no part of any grants shall be applied either directly or indirectly in relief of rates, taxes or other public funds.

10 December 1953: This develops the 1904 Scheme and constitutes the Church Burgesses Educational Foundation as a separate independent unincorporated Trust for the expenditure of the educational monies designated in that Scheme. The Foundation was established under a Scheme of the Ministry of Education as an independent Trust for the purposes of administering the educational part of the secular income of the Church Burgesses Trust.

The Trustees of the Foundation are specified as 8 persons, each appointed for a term of three years:

Five appointed by the Church Burgesses.

One appointed by Sheffield Education Committee.

One appointed by the Council of the University of Sheffield.

One appointed by the Sheffield Diocesan Council of Religious Education.

The application of income, for the benefit of boys and girls resident in the City of Sheffield, is given as:

- Exhibitions tenable at any school, college or University, to be awarded by rules made by the Trustees in consultation with Sheffield Education Committee.

- Financial assistance, outfits, clothing, instruments, tools or books to enable beneficiaries to prepare for entry into a profession, trade or calling.
- In otherwise promoting the education of beneficiaries.

6 March 1959: sets out the permissible investments of the Trust and states that competent financial advisers shall be employed.

12 May 1970: Clause 3(P) was amended by substitution of the word 'clergyman' with 'any priest or deacon of the Church of England.'

24 July 1978: Clause 3 of the 1854 Scheme was revoked, as was the extension to Clause 3(P) of the January 1953 revision. In their place was put a more flexible and discretionary provision for supplemental payments for stipends and for assistance to the wider work of the Church of England, and there was clearer definition of payments to be made to the Cathedral Council. This is the Scheme under which the Trustees currently disburse their ecclesiastical income.

5 August 1992: A revision and updating of the Scheme for the Church Burgesses Educational Foundation. The modifications, important in widening the discretionary powers of the Trustees, reflect the changes in educational and social provision since the previous amendments. Grants may be made in promoting the education of persons under the age of 25 years who are, or whose parents are, resident in the City of Sheffield and 'to any institution or organisation the objects of which include the promotion of the education (including social and physical training) of the aforesaid beneficiaries'.

Eleven amendments in just over 100 years, some of considerable significance for the Burgesses' policies, may be compared with the 300 years from 1554, operating under the original Charter. Clearly, the Trust has sought to ensure that it can respond to changing social and economic conditions. That having been said, the Charter remains the touchstone by which the purposes of the Trust, and any change therein, must be judged. It is significant that none of the amendments change the status of the Burgesses as an independent corporate body with a self-perpetuating trusteeship. Only in the turbulent mid-19th century does the method of appointment of Trustees appear to have been challenged. What could have been the dead hand of self-interest and isolation seems rather to have produced a commendable responsiveness. Not all ancient charities have sought to respond to changing circumstances as the Church Burgesses have done. The opinion, in a recent study,[12] that 'the craft unions and the church burgesses became ill-fitting archaic survivals in Sheffield' brings together two very different institutions not often linked together. Whatever may be the judgement on craft unions, it can hardly be maintained that the Church Burgesses Trust is archaic, considering its present range of activities. At one level, the various amendments to the Charity Schemes may be regarded (wrongly) as legal tinkering. At another level they are evidence of a desire to ensure that the Trust is both meeting the requirements of its founder and responding imaginatively and effectively to the changing needs of Church and people in a large, modern City.

CHAPTER 3

From Parish Church to Cathedral

FOR THE YEAR ENDING 31 March 1996, the Accounts of Sheffield Cathedral show that out of a total income of £420,000, the Church Burgesses contributed £195,000. Theirs was by far the largest single source of income; that from the Church Commissioners, the next largest, was £102,000. This is a far cry from 1557, the first year for which we have accounts for the Church Burgesses. In that year the Burgesses' contribution to the Parish Church (including the stipends of the three Assistant Priests) was £20.3s.8d. Growth of expenditure on this scale has been due, essentially, to the developments, over the centuries, that changed a middling to largish medieval parish church into a moderate-sized Cathedral.

Development of the building

The Church that the Burgesses assumed responsibility for in 1554 was essentially a modest medieval building in the Perpendicular style. The chancel, tower and Lady (Shrewsbury) Chapel remain of that building. In the early 1500s, the 4th Earl of Shrewsbury built a Chapel for private use by his family, probably building on an existing Lady Chapel. It remained a private chapel until 1933. The ancient Church had seven altars: the High Altar; Rood altar and altars dedicated to Our Lady, St. Katherine, St. Nicholas, St. Mary Magdalene and St. Clement. Bequests for the maintenance of services at these various altars occur in many wills of the 15th and 16th centuries. An Indenture of 1501 is directly relevant to later interests of the Church Burgesses.[1] Felice Hyne granted a tenement in Old Change, in the parish of St. Augustine in the City of London, to the Vicar and three others (one of whom, William Tailour, was one of the original Burgesses), with the instruction that, upon her death, the property was to be sold and the proceeds devoted to buying a Cross of silver and gilt, with the image of the crucifixion, Our Lady and St. John . . . 'the said Cross and other ornament thereto, to remain (in the Parish Church) for ever.'

Soon after the Charter was granted, the Reformation began to take effect, early in Elizabeth's reign. We see, in the Burgesses' accounts, some of the changes taking place. In 1559 6d. was paid to Ralph Hollingshead for wood for the Communion table. In 1560 4s.4d. was paid for 'powling down the auters'; and, again, in 1562 – 'paid at the taking downe of the alters for workmen and meate and drinke: 5s.4d.' And in 1570 the 'crosse in the Chirch yeard' was pulled down at a cost of 4d. and the cross stones sold to George Tynker for 12d. In 1566, 5s. was 'paid to Robert Swyft, the 13th Day of April, for makynge the communion table.'

But there was some tardiness in obeying Elizabeth's injunctions to remove rood and loft, as was the case in many other parishes in England. Old habits died hard.[2] Not until 1570 do we come across the entry: 'The 23rd day of June: Stufe sold by the Chyrche wardens, and tymber at the takeing downe of the loftes in the Church, as hereafter followeth:

One lofte on the North-side sold.

One stayre on the South-side.

One deyse in the rood quire.

Presumably, this would be the Rood loft constructed out of the bequest of John Wickersley of Broomhall, whose will of 24 April 1528 directed that part of the profits of lands were to be used 'to cause the loft in the Roods Chapel to be new rebuylded and to provide a set of vestments to be used at the Roods altar in the Chapel.'[3]

No significant structural changes appear to have been made to the Church until the late 18th century. An entry in the Burgesses Election Book for 20 March 1771 states that the Church was refaced, the outer walls being in a ruinous condition. There was a small addition to the North-east end in 1777. A two-storeyed extension was built there to replace a shed housing the fire engine. In area this matched the Shrewsbury Chapel at the South-east corner and provided a vestry on the ground floor with a room for the Church Burgesses over it. Prior to having their own room at the Church, the Burgesses had regularly used the Tontine Inn as a rendezvous. It is during the period of the 17th and 18th centuries that pews for rent took over the inside of the building. The earliest evidence of private pews appears in 1617 in a Grant from Tobit, Archbishop of York, to Edward Wood, Edward Sanders, Christopher Capper (Church Burgess) and Francis Moore of a 'loft erected by the grantees with the privity of the Vicar and Churchwardens of Sheffield for themselves and their families on the South side of the body of the Church there, the which their erection so made as it is of no prejudice to any of the parish so it is a comeliness and well beseeching that part of the Church where it is placed.'[4] And there are records of grants of pews in 1675 and 1692. A Grant dated 2 July 1792 records that a stall or pew on the south side of the Church was assigned by the Burgesses to Thomas Law for a consideration of £38. There is an added reference to recent alterations and additions to the Church providing extra pews: 'upon the said additional space of ground the said Burgesses and Commonalty at their own private expense have built and erected a number of stalls or pews on the said ground floor and gallery in the said Church and have lately made sale and disposition of the same pews at a public auction of what the said Thomas Law was the highest bidder for the pew granted to him.'

It was during the eighteenth century that the nave was swamped by an apparently insatiable demand for private pews. Things must have got completely out of hand, as Samuel Roberts' description of the Church towards the end of the eighteenth century shows.

> 'The church itself was then one of the most gloomy, irregularly paved places of worship in the kingdom. It seemed as if, after the work of pewing had begun, every person who chose had formed a pew for himself in his own way, to his own size, height and shape. There were several galleries, but all formed, as it seemed, in the same way as the pews; some of them on pillars, some hung on chains. The lord's closet was a gloomy structure.'[5]

Edward Goodwin, then Curate at Attercliffe, writing in 1764, and presenting the fair face of the Church, cannot avoid mentioning the seating:

> 'The Church is a very handsome structure, with a grand spire in the middle, has 8 very tuneable bells, an excellent clock, and a set of chimes . . . but it is very awkwardly seated.'[6]

Sketch plans drawn in 1798 by Fairbank at the instruction of the Burgesses show a veritable maze of seating both on the ground floor and in the galleries, even filling up a floor in the tower.[7]

Battles between the Burgesses and the seatholders continued over a long period. This was not because the Burgesses wished to abolish pew rents; far from it. They were men of their time who accepted private pews as a useful source of income for the church and, indeed, they regularly arranged auctions for the sale of the 'freehold' of pews. But they were strongly of the opinion that seatholders should make a contribution to meet the needs of the church, over and above the rents which they paid for pews. And they were also conscious of those who could not afford pew rents. They sought to ensure that free seats were provided for the poor and for pupils at the Boys' and Girls' Charity Schools. Surrounded by gloom and by ranks of box pews, it is little wonder that the boys in the congregation got out of hand from time to time. In 1764 the Account Book records the payment to the Churchwardens 'for finding 4 men to keep the boys in good behaviour during divine service', payments which continued for many years.

The 1805 alterations

The general disorder and gloom which Roberts depicts could not be allowed to continue. In 1802, the Burgesses and Vicar jointly agreed a statement that 'the seats, stalls, and pews in the body, and the lofts and other parts, are moulderous, rotten and decayed, and are moreover irregular and incommodious, and greatly unsuited to the rank, style and condition of life of the present owners and occupiers thereof.'[8] The Archdeacon, following his Visitation in 1800, had written a scathing report. The Burgesses minuted on 3 November 1800, following a public meeting with seatholders:

> 'The Archdeacon has lately visited the Church and on a view of the ruinous and disorderly state of the interior thereof, expressly signified to the Churchwardens that he should expect the whole of the Pews to be taken down and re-erected in a more uniform, commodious and handsome manner and that if those Persons who claimed Possession of the Pews did not come to an immediate agreement to defray the expenses of the same, he should forthwith issue his precept that it should be done by a Parish rate.'

The threat of a parish rate, from which Sheffield had been mercifully free due largely to the Burgesses' responsibility for maintaining the fabric of the Parish Church, must have speeded up action. But already, before the Archdeacon's Visitation, there were proposals afoot for significant change in the building. It was these proposals which led the Burgesses to seek Counsel's opinion (Mr. Hargraves) on the propriety of the Burgesses making a contribution to improvements, rather than repairs and maintenance. At their meeting on 4 September 1799, the Burgesses responded to the Churchwardens to the effect that they could not take upon themselves the cost of 'the alterations of the Church on the broad scale proposed', but they went on to offer a contribution: 'They consider themselves bound, and are immediately prepared to put the North side of the Church in as complete a repair as it was before the building of the North wall (estimated cost £200). But if the seatholders and proprietors should be willing to engage in such broad scale of general seating and ornamenting . . . the Trustees will give £600 . . . engaging to make accommodation for the Girls of the Charity School for the poor.' The seatholders took a lot of persuading. Later, the Burgesses were to increase the pressure upon seatholders to pay for the cost of cleaning the pews and other items. The discontinuance, in 1808, by the Burgesses of hitherto regular payments for many routine items of expenditure has already been referred to (p. 38). Resumption of some payments in 1821 was conditional upon the seatholders accepting responsibility for other items of expenditure, and it was not until 5 December 1826 that a

Minute appears indicating that the seatholders had finally concurred – 'capitulated' might be a better word.

The Burgesses had recognised that the structure of the nave required urgent and extensive repair, and agreed with the Vicar that

> 'the Parish Church of Sheffield has become ruinous and in decay in the walls, arches, pews, roofs and other parts of the fabric all need immediate reparation and amendment.'[9]

On 3 November 1800, they agreed 'to pay for the pulling down the Pillars and Arches in the Body of the Church, raising them higher, altering the roof of the Church over the North and South Isles and in short for whatever alterations appertain to the Fabrick of the Church.' There was, however, an important rider . . .

> 'only in this express and indispensible condition viz. that the seatholders do consent to defray the expenses of new pewing in the Church. That whatever pews and vacant spaces for Benches remain at the extreme parts of the Church over and above after satisfying the Claims of the present seatholders shall be allotted to the Burgesses to be by them appropriated to the use of the Poor and for their sole benefit without paying any rent.'

The total cost of this building work to the Burgesses was a little under £3000, including a sum of £32.0s.6d,

> 'to Mason's Carpenters employed at the rising of the roof of the Church as a customary gratuity.'

The old nave was demolished and the new nave widened to the width of the transepts and its height extended considerably, to include clerestories. The increase in height seemed to be provided largely to take galleries of pews, for these obscured the clerestories. The restored Church was dedicated on 6 October 1805 and the recently appointed Vicar, Thomas Sutton, preached. Joseph Hunter, writing in 1819, was duly impressed:

> 'On entering by the principal door we are now therefore presented with a view of a spacious, lofty, and well-pewed church, capable of accommodating from two thousand five hundred to three thousand persons, which number it is supposed usually attended the late Sunday evening services. Here are no fantastical or ostentatious ornaments, but nothing seems to be wanting for the decent performance of all the sacred ordinances, and for the comfort of the parishioners while attending divine ministrations.'[10]

The new nave was not to stand for long without extensive alteration, but it provided the essential scale of the nave as it now is, in terms of height and

Sheffield Parish Church, 1829 (courtesy of the Sheffield City Libraries).

breadth. The widening of the nave destroyed the earlier cruciform shape of the church. Also erected in 1805 at a cost of £60 was the King's Arms, set above the western arch of the tower. The Burgesses minuted on 7 May 1805: 'that the King's Arms be placed in the centre of the Span, both ways', and on 6 August 1805, 'that the Colour of the King's Arms be a few shades lighter than the Colour of the wall and that the Letters be gilt.' Samuel Roberts, in his autobiography, recalls the effect upon him: 'High under the lofty centre arch, spanned from side to side, the massive Rood Loft, behind which, filling up the apex of the arch, were the King's Arms, painted most gloriously and magnificently large.' With the nave extension, the Church seated 2,700 persons. Apart from benches for boys and girls from the Charity Schools, there were about 100 free seats, none of them in positions allowing good visibility. One later change must have made a great impression inside the Church, and that was the introduction of gas lighting in 1823. The installation cost the Burgesses £362.9s.4d. Shortly after the nave reconstruction in 1805, the Duke of Norfolk paid the Burgesses £210 in 1809 for repair work carried out to the Shrewsbury Chapel, but only after a dispute on cost. Repairs to the roof and the interior of the Chancel cost £386, the work being carried out by the Burgesses on behalf of the Duke. Mr. Eyre, the Duke's Agent, clearly thought the work could have been done for less and offered to pay two thirds of the repair costs and one third of the architect's fees, an offer the Burgesses accepted with reluctance. Settlement of the account was tardy, however, and the Burgesses sought in November 1809 to hurry things along. They agreed that in future the Duke could be responsible for his own repairs.

A small, but significant, change was made in 1840 with the erection of a screen between the nave and the chancel, for which the Burgesses agreed a maximum payment of £300. Even after the substantial re-pewing of 1805, the search continued for still more pews. On 26 January 1837, the Burgesses minuted: 'that the Vicar had suggested that a gallery over the West end, or some other means, be constructed to provide room for extra pews. Trustees, after viewing the interior, concluded that there does not seem to be any feasible plan for providing the additional accommodation required.' Again, on 5 November 1853, the Vicar submitted plans for proposed alterations in internal arrangements and sought a grant from the Burgesses, who resolved that they did not feel empowered to contribute. There was only one way to resolve the pew problem, and that was to get rid of it by abolishing pew rents and clearing out box pews. Which is what happened in the next substantial piece of rebuilding.

The 1880 Extension

Canon Rowley Hill was appointed Vicar on 24 December 1873, and in just under four years he ensured a transformation of the building. The time was right for an energetic reforming Vicar. Three factors came together in his time, more or less forcing change:

- With the considerable population growth in Sheffield, new parishes had been created and new Churches built. There was no longer the same intense pressure on the old Parish Church. In economic terms, pew-holders were going elsewhere.
- Pew rents, in any case, were rapidly going out of fashion. They had come to be regarded by many as a contradiction of the tasks of the Church to get the Christian message to all people. And Tractarian liturgical change was also bringing about changes in the internal geography of churches inimical to dominance of space by box pews.
- And, thirdly, a ruling in the Sheffield Court (Broomhead v. Oates, 1856) declared that 'no person could have such a title in a pew as would give him the right to let it and sue for the rent.' The days of the pew-renting freeholder were over. The tyranny of the seatholders was broken and the way was open to clear away the clutter.

Canon Hill had raised a substantial part of the money required to carry out the substantial changes that were proposed, but he moved before the work was done, leaving his successor, Archdeacon Blakeney (appointed

26 September 1877) to carry it through. The newly ordered Church was dedicated on 26 October 1880. The nave had been extended by 25 feet; North and South transepts were built; the church floor was raised and retiled; the organ was moved from just north of the tower into what is now St. Katherine's Chapel; and a new Vestry and Burgesses' Room were built at the north-east corner. Most significantly, perhaps, the old pews were swept away and replaced with oak bench pews, reducing the seating to 1,400. In all these far-reaching changes, it might appear that the Burgesses were more interested in their own meeting room. On 4 July 1877, they resolved that before giving up their present rights in the Vestry Chamber, satisfactory arrangements must be made for legally vesting in them the rights to the new chamber proposed to be provided. The Vicar gave them the necessary assurance on 3 May 1880 and on 27 January 1881, Thomas Flockton, Surveyor to the Burgesses, reported that the new room had been built on the ground floor – 'not yet quite finished, but your safe has been refixed in it.' The cost of furnishing the new room was £183.6s.0d.

Nearly 70 years were to elapse before stained glass windows were installed in the room, giving a clear indication of its purpose. Christopher Webb visited in May 1946 and produced designs in June 1948, but these were not proceeded with. Then Albert Harland, a Church Burgess, made a gift of £500 in January 1950 specifically for stained glass for the Burgesses' Room. John Baker was commissioned and the installed glass was dedicated in February 1952. The windows incorporate the seal of the Trust; the Good Samaritan representing healing and charity; and a poor scholar, representing the work of the Burgesses in education. One window has the symbols of the four Gospels. The borders of the windows incorporate the monogram MR in honour of Mary Tudor, founder of the Trust.

From Parish Church to Cathedral

The Church remained unaltered until the upheavals of the 1930s, by which time the Parish Church had become the Cathedral Church of the Diocese of Sheffield, created in 1914. Sir Charles Nicholson began work in 1921 to make a Cathedral out of a parish church. The lack of commitment and motive power behind the concept and its fulfilment might be judged by noting that the Executive Committee charged with planning the changes met in 1921 and then stood adjourned for 14 years. Nicholson's plans were grandiose and revolutionary. He proposed almost to double the size of the building and to turn its axis round to north-south. Work began on the first stage of the Nicholson building in 1937. Inevitably, building was interrupted by the War and the Nicholson plans were finally abandoned in the

Sheffield Cathedral, 1996 (Derek Richards).

mid-1950s. By then, the Chapter House, Crypt Chapel, Chapel of the Holy Spirit, St. George's Chapel, Sacristry, Vestry and Song School had all been completed. But there was no longer the will, nor the money, to proceed with a great new Gothic Cathedral for Sheffield. However things could hardly stay as they were. Sir Charles Nicholson having died in 1949, George Pace was engaged as Architect to produce revised plans. However the cost of building Pace's proposals was at least twice what the Cathedral had bargained for. So, in 1961, the architect Arthur Bailey was given the remit of extending the West end of the nave and providing a Hall. The additions, dedicated on 15 November 1966, extended the nave by 28 feet, gave a new South Porch, Narthex, and Lantern and a new St. George's Chapel to replace that built in 1937, which was taken over by a new organ.

Maintaining the Fabric

The Burgesses' responsibilities are for repair and maintenance of the fabric of the Church, not for enlargement and enhancement. But at each successive stage of enlargement the Burgesses have accepted the inevitable consequences of having to maintain a larger building. The beneficial and commendable contributions of the Church Burgesses over the centuries have been, not so much in substantial donations to major development and restoration (although there have been such donations), but to the constant funding of the maintenance operation, week by week, year by year. One may have doubts about their stewardship in the late 18th century, which could allow the Church to become 'ruinous and in decay', but that was an exceptional observation, and, in respect of the fabric of the Church, probably overstated. The complete reliance of the Vicar and Churchwardens (and therefore of the people of the parish) upon the Church Burgesses to ensure a good sound fabric has not been misplaced. The challenge for the Burgesses has been two-fold. Firstly, so to manage and increase their assets that income is sufficient to meet ever-growing demands made upon them. Secondly, to maintain a harmonious, constructive relationship with the Church (and latterly the Cathedral) authorities, in which the independence of each party is respected by the other, with both parties sharing a common understanding of needs and objectives. There have been times when the delicate balance necessary to preserve the independence and integrity of both parties has been upset, but such occasions have been rare.

For almost 200 years, from the granting of the Charter, entries in the Account Books consist mostly of regular, routine payments for maintenance. For example:

1557: Delivered to Thomas Clayton and others his Fellow Churchwardens for the Church needs for iron to make a Church Gate withall: 6d.
1561: Paid to a waller for mending ye church yarde wall: 15s.9d.
1562: To the Plumber for 22 pounds of Sawther (solder) to the Leades and for his Workmanship and his Boye for 4 days the Sawther at 8d. the pound: £1.2s.0d.
1564: In rewarde to my Lord's Plumber for his pains to look at the Steple: 2s.0d
1565: Payment for pointing the Church Steeple and Battlements: £10 0s.0d.
In part of payment of a more sum for pointing the Church Steeple: £5.0s.0d.
For felling and hewing 3 Loades tymber that was gotten in oure Ladye Spring, to make ladders for the Church and for Leading the same, with ale: 3s.1d.
For egges and gathering blood to make morther 12d.
For making the Wether Cocke 13s.0d.
For drink to the Mason's man the same day he took down the Weather Cocke 2d.

In Elizabethan times, walls of the Church would have been decorated and there are several references to necessary work having been carried out:

1565: Payd to William Goodroyd of Darbye for his paynes for comyng to loke on owr church, to have whytlymed hyt, and to have sete on the screpture; towards his charges for money 16d., and for his dyner 4d.
1566: Paid to John the paynter for whashinge above the hyghe alter: 3d.
Paid to Benyt Bridges the 29th daye of May for whytlyminge the churche and wyrtynge the scryptures: £1.19s.10d.
To Richard Roberts for teaching the Painter to settle the Scripture and reading over Letter by Letter Daye: 8d.
1567: For keeping the church walls clean: 1s.0d.

(In Victorian times, the fashion grew of removing wall decorations and plaster and exposing the stone underneath. The 1880 alterations included the scraping of the walls down to the stone; this was after the chancel walls and pillars had been painted afresh in 1865.)

Repairs to the nave were undertaken in 1797, with the payment of £300 to John Beevers for taking down and rebuilding part of the north-west side of the Church. Carpenter's work in the roof cost an extra £76.19s.9½d. In 1803, a further contribution of £200 was made. The new pewing cost the Burgesses £410.17s.4d. In 1841, £300 was paid for the new chancel screen, plus £300 for the Organ Case Gallery. In the following year, £83.10s. was paid for a stained glass window. Regular maintenance of the stained glass had long been a concern of the Burgesses. On 6 November 1667, an agreement was made 'to uphold and maintain in good repair all the glass wyndowes belonging to the Church of Sheffield att 40s. the year from Martinmas next ensueinge for 10 years at the Burgesses pleasure and he is to leave ym in good repaire when the Agreement ends.'

For the 1776-77 alterations, the Burgesses spent about £300 on mason's and carpenter's work. By the 1850s they were redecorating the church after the substantial repairs. 50 years earlier, and in 1861, about £300 was spent on masonry repairs. New carved oak stalls were made in 1868 at a cost of £84.15s. and choir stalls were installed in 1872.

In 1880 £960 was spent on gas heating equipment, the gas bill the following year being £61.5s.11d., with coke costing £15.16s.4d. Gas lighting had been installed in 1823 and in January 1887 the decision was taken to install electric light at a cost of £420, 'provided that the Vicar and Churchwardens undertake to pay in excess of £70 annual cost', which they agreed. They were, however, rather 'choosy' in their specification, making it clear that they 'wished to vary the degree of light so as to be able to have full light, half light and skeleton light', presumably with the intention, at least in part, of being able to economise on electricity consumption.

On 29 January 1903, the Burgesses minuted that 'an application by the National Telephone Company to erect an Electrophone on the Pulpit was not entertained.' They might move with the times in respect of gas and electricity installations, but an 'Electrophone' was clearly too much for them.

Maintenance of the fabric of a building, parts of which date back to the 15th century, does not get easier with the passage of time and newer additions to the building can be more troublesome than the ancient structure. Always there is the risk of escalation of the cost of repair and restoration. In October 1827, repairs to the roof were initially estimated as costing £320. By January 1829, £780 had been spent and by June 1829, the total cost of repairs to eradicate death watch beetle damage and to carry out inside repairs to the roof and tower had escalated to £2461, almost an eight-fold increase on the original estimate. But these figures are small when set alongside the current levels of routine expenditure on masonry and related maintenance, of the order of £40,000-50,000 per annum.

In 1883, the Burgesses contributed £350 to the restoration fund, going beyond their responsibility for maintenance of the fabric. Not that the Burgesses were a 'soft touch' by any means. They knew when to 'pass the buck'. The Archdeacon complained, in 1838, about the state of the Church (notwithstanding the extensive alterations 35 years earlier) and the 'want of more books'. The Burgesses ordered that the Churchwardens be informed

Sheffield Cathedral, Choir and Sanctuary (Derek Richards).

and that the Archdeacon's representations be attended to. In July 1856, the Churchwardens asked the Trust to provide drainage to carry off water from the roof and spouts of the Church; to which the Burgesses responded that they 'conceive they are not empowered to apply any portion of their funds to that object'; which reads oddly, coming so soon after the granting of the new Charity Scheme two years earlier.

The Burgesses had to contend with more than the effects of weather and fair wear and tear. On 10 March 1831, a minute reads:

> 'The grave digger having again encroached on the Fabric of the Church by digging a grave under the foundations at the South east corner of the building, Ordered that Mr. Sutton's attention be called to the Subject requesting him to give directions for preventing a similar encroachment in the future.'

The Costs of Divine Worship

The Charter directs that the Burgesses, inter alia, 'shall find and cause to be found from time to time . . . other things necessary to divine worship in the Parish Church of Sheffield.' It is a broad provision and it is not surprising that there has been some contention about what should be included as 'things necessary to divine worship.'

In Elizabethan times, before these things were banned, the cost of setting up the Easter tomb was an accepted charge:

1557: Paid to Sir Richarde Bewecke for a painted cloth: 8d.
1558: For a clothe to ye Sepulcres house, conteynynge 12 yards at 8d. ye yerd: 8s.0d.
To Hugh Paynter for painting ye Sepulchre clothe: 4s. 0d.
For setting up of ye Resurecon: 7d.
1559: For settynge uppe ye Resurrection: 1s.10d.
For nails that they had at the Resurrection: 3d.
For ale at the mending of the bells and for the resurrection: 11d.

Some of the earliest entries in the Account Books refer to books for worship and for instruction:

1564: For the second part of the Homilies: 5s.0d.
To Robert Spooner for his costs to Doncaster for the book of Homilies: 10d
For the Paraphrases of Erasmus in English and the Queen's Injunctions: 15s. 4d.

(The English translation of Erasmus' paraphrases upon the New Testament was published in 1548)

A Booke called Thanksgiving for the Plague and the Salter in English: 1s 8d.
1565: For mending the Bible: 2s. 8d.
1567: For the Book of the Articles: 4d.
(The Articles of the Church of England were first issued in 1549 and again in 1552. Elizabeth promulgated them in 1559).
1569: For bringing the new Bible from London: 1s. 9d.
Paid for the same Bible, Communion Book and a Psalter:
1570: For carrying the Communion Book from London: 4d.
For a Homilies Book and the Articles: 1s. 0d.
For 4 Song Books of Genevies Psalms: 3s. 0d.
(Containing the Geneva Psalms of Calvin).
1571: A Psalter for the Church in metre: 2s. 4d.

It is interesting to note that *Foxe's Book of Martyrs*, that pillar of Protestantism, published in 1563, was still much in evidence in the Parish Church in 1730, when 2s.6d. was paid to Mr. Hanby for lettering and gilding the book.

It would appear that the Burgesses paid, not only for a Surplice for Mr. Pavey, the Parish Clerk (4s.6d. in 1560), but also for surplices for the assistant ministers. 5s.0d was paid in 1559 (for One surplice) and in 1568, 8 yards of Linnen to make the Parish Priest a Surplice cost 8s. 0d.

In 1745 there is an item of £25.19s.0d. for a new velvet pulpit cloth with gold fringes. And also accepted as an expense of divine worship was the cost of shrouding the pulpit for mourning, e.g.:

1832: On the occasion of the Death of the Duke of York: £1 8s. 7d.
1847: On the occasion of Mr. Edward Goodwin's death (he was Curate at Attercliffe): £5. 19s. 0d.
1851: Black cloth and fringe for pulpit: £12 16s. 5d.

One essential item of pulpit furniture of the 17th and 18th centuries was not forgotten:

1672: For an Howre Glasse for the Church: 1s. 0d.

Items for altar and sacramental use figure regularly in the Accounts:

1569: Paid for a Box to put the singing Breade in: 4d.
(i.e. the bread consecrated by the Priest singing the prayer of consecration).
1571: Delivered to Mr. Vicar and the Churchwardens the 1st of May to go to Yorke to change the Chalice and make a cup upon it: £1.
1599: For 2 pewter cuppes and one Tyne bottell for the Church use: 3s. 9d.
1605: For 2 silver cups and 2 patens in weight 38 ozs. and a halfe at 5s. 5d. the Ounce the some is £10 18s. 0d.
For a Box to carrie them in and a yeard of fustian to keepe them in and the carriage: 3s. 4d.

(To commemorate their Quarter Centenary, in 1954, the Burgesses presented to the Cathedral a Charles II silver alms dish.)

1606: 5 yeardes of lynn clothe at 2s. 0d. the yeard for the Communion table and for seweing and fryngeing the same: 11s. 0d.

We first read of supplies for Communion in 1574, when 4d. was paid for a 'Quart of Wyne for ye Communion' upon Whit Sunday. In 1587 an entry reads: 'Communyon at New Year's Day 14d.; at Easter 31s. 8d.; at Wydsun 2s. 8d. and at Mighalmas 2s. 3d.'

The cost of communion wine is caught up with wine for the use of clergy, both resident and visiting, and for other hospitality. The Election Book has several entries indicating the attention paid by the Burgesses to the supply of wine:

15 October 1708: That the Communion Wine be equally had at Mrs. Pegg's and Mr. Pearson's so long as they supply ye Church with good wine, and those that supply bad wine then no more to be had at that place.

Charles II Silver Dish, presented to the Cathedral by the Burgesses in commemoration of their 400th year, 1954.

Liberality seemed much in evidence at that time, in spite of careful accounting being insisted upon:

> 9 November 1709: At a Publick Meeting Ordered that for ye future ye Churchwardens give an account how much wine they take up for ye Sacrament, and how much ye Capitall to pay for, and that for each stranger that preaches have one bottel of wine, whether he preach once or twice – that the Vicar have a bottel of saik at Easter, and Whitsuntide and Christmass and a bottel of wine every Sacrament day, besides the 3 Assistants to have each a bottel of wine at Easter Whitsuntide and Christmass – the Churchwardens to have each a bottel of wine at Easter.

But there must have been some contention, because we read a following minute:

> 8 December 1710: Agreed that all the Sacrament wine this year for the Church be had at Mrs. Pegg's provided she send good wine, and the year following to be had at Mr. Pearson's on the same proviso, and that the Capitall Burgess for the time being take up the Sacrament wine or order it to be taken up. And that the Churchwardens for the time being meddle not in taking up the wine. And a particular account to be taken by those the Wine is bought off and by them delivered to the Capitall (viz) how much to the Sacraments and how much to the Vicar and Assistant p'suant to the late Order.'

In 1735, austerity was the order of the day:

> 5 November 1735: That the Capitall Burgesses shall for the future only be allowed to give 6 bottles of wine to the Church and Chappell Wardens, that is each one a bottle.

We have already noted (p. 38) the action of the Burgesses in 1808 in stopping the payment for items that had long been regarded as allowable expenses of divine worship. But these minutes show that, long before then, there had been room for questioning, if not dispute.

Preachers and visiting dignitaries were accustomed to being treated well, as appears from the Account books:

> 1647: Mr. Metcalfe, for his panes coming to Sheffield being sent for by the Burgesses £2. Also, wine and sugar 12s.
>
> 1711: More wine paid Mrs. Pegg, the same being had when the Bishop was here viz. 3 gallons red wine £1; 6 quarts of Canary 15s.; 3 gallons of sherry £1 8s.; 3 gallons of white wine £1. (No stinting here!)

Bells and Clocks

It is only too apparent from the Accounts of the Church Burgesses that Church bells require constant and unremitting maintenance. It is rare in any one year for there to be no entry relating to the care of bells and some of the incidental expenses are revealing, as, for example in 1566, when 4s.2d. was paid for making the Great Bell Clapper, plus 1d. for a Boy for going to Ecclesfield to see whether the 'Clapper was reddy or not of Richard Byrley's.' R.E. Leader's comment[11] upon the expenses of the bells is understandable:

> 'The amounts paid through all the centuries for bell-ringing would, if capitalised, make a very considerable increase in the town's estate, but it is evident that our ancestors rejoiced in strident peals from the church belfry

more than their degenerate descendants, one of whom expressed the pious wish that the rascal ringers, those foes of repose for the good of the land, had round their necks what they pull with their hand.'

The Burgesses had paid those 'rascal ringers' from a very early date. The Accounts for 1559 include: 'Item pd. to ryngers yt dyd ringe for Sr. Thomas Twell, at the recyvynge of certen stuf gevyn by hym to the church, wth xd. to the priestes and clerke for deyrge: xvid.'

Apart from constant maintenance, the Burgesses paid for new bells from time to time:

1619: Taking down and hanging the bell: 8s. 0d.
Carrying of the bell to Chesterfield and back again: £1 5s. 0d.
Casting of the bell: £7 0s. 0d.
Metal added to the same: £4 12s. 0d.

In 1688, £19.8s.0d. was paid to Homfray Wilkinson, Bellfounder, for casting the No. 3 Bell.

In 1732/33, two new bells were recast and installed, several entries in the Accounts referring to this work:

1732: Pd. Geo. Heward for carrying ye 2 old Bells from Sheffield to Aldwarth 17s.; paid him more £1 0s. 0d. for bringing ye 2 new Bells from Deneby to Sheffd.
Pd. for freight and dues for 2 old bells to York and 2 new bells coming back from York: £3 0s. 0d.
Pd. a Messenger for going down below Doncaster to seek ye new bells 2s. 6d. & for hanging ye little bell in one of the Steeple Windows: 1s. 4d.

1733: To Mr. Sellers of York for recasting the 1st and 6th Bells, 25-0-24 of mettle at 20s. per £25. 0s. 3d. & for 4.1.16 of Mettle added to ye weight of ye said bells at 13d. a pound £26 13s. 0d. a Clapper 2.19 at 6d. a pound £1 17s. 6d. deduct towards the charges of two Bells returned to York yt were not tunable £1 0s. 9d. £52 10s. 0d.

The 8 new bells cast in this year cost the Burgesses over £375.

In 1799 a new peal of 10 bells was installed. The Burgesses contributed £50 initially to the public appeal launched to cover the cost. But in 1801, there was deficiency of £193.19s.1d., of which the Burgesses paid half. There was a dispute between a Mr. Mears, who supplied the bells, and John Greaves, the Town Collector, and the Burgesses met one half of the cost of the law suit (£21.15s). The accounts for this new peal were finally cleared in 1805, with the Burgesses making a final contribution of £103.17s., plus £24.11s. solicitor's costs. Of the 1799 peal, Gatty records that the tenor bell was cast in a barn 'which stood on the site of what is now an auction room, at the east end of the churchyard, in what was called York Street, when the townspeople threw into the fused metal their silver mugs, and other pieces of silver, in order to sweeten the tone.'[12] In 1922, two bells were recast and the whole peal retuned and rehung at a cost to the Burgesses of over £2000.

By some arrangement, never explained, it was the Town Burgesses (who continue to pay annual grants), not the Church Burgesses, who came to accept responsibility for making payments to the bell ringers. There are many entries in the Account Books of the Town Trust referring to such payments.[13] One explanation for the acceptance by the Town Trust of this responsibility might be that the ringing of the bells could be regarded as a service to the town by way of marking important public occasions or even, should there be cause, of raising a public alarm or warning. As recently as 1967, in the Cathedral Statutes approved at that time, there is a reference to the Town Trustees, discharging them from any previous liabilities. Statute XIV reads:

> 'St. Peter's Company of Change Ringers: The Provost shall maintain all usages and relationships hitherto existing from ancient times between the Vicar and the St. Peter's Company of Change Ringers. Nothing in this Statute shall impose any obligation upon the Town Trustees of Sheffield.'

There is a number of entries relating to the Clock in the 16th century. 1564 must have been a troublesome year, with payment for mending the clock being made on three occasions. In 1571, there is a payment 'to Robert Burgen and his 2 servants for working 12 days about the Clock taking it down and setting it up: 12s.', with a further 3½ days 'Worke to sawe Timber for the Clocke and his coming to the Towne: 2s. 6d.' Also: 'for 3 days about the Stairs making to the Clock and for their Borde to Harry Swift Wife: 6s.4d.' In 1630 a new clock was installed at a cost of £12 and replaced in 1678 at a cost of £20.19s.6d. This clock had chimes, which were replaced in 1733. The new set of chimes and new timepiece on the North side of the church were installed at a cost of £130 and the two dials of the clock painted and gilded for £21.2s.4d. A clock house was built in 1750 and a new clock placed in it costing £96.10s. and a new set of chimes was provided at a cost of £63, with £20 to pay for the painting of the Sun and Clock dials.

By 1773, however, both clock and chimes had 'gone into decay' and the Church Burgesses were petitioned by the Free Burgesses, gentlemen, merchants and other inhabitants of Sheffield and, after considering the petition, the Burgesses ordered that the Clerk obtain an estimate from Mr.

Whitehurst, clockmaker of Derby. Mr. Whitehurst attended their next meeting on 18 March 1773 and proposed to 'make and erect in the old Church a complete sett of chimes to change themselves every day and play 7 tunes six times over at 5, 9 and 12 o'clock daily.' This cost £120 plus painting of the dial at £10. In 1867, a new clock was installed in its present position, the Burgesses contributing something over £150 towards the cost.

Organs and Organists: Harmony and Discord

There was an organ in the Parish Church in 1528. The will of John Wickersley of Broomhall dated 24 April in that year states: 'I will that my executors cause the loft in the Rood Chapel where the organnes now stande to be new builded.'[14] For a number of years until 1620 there were regular entries in the Burgesses' accounts for payments for work done to the Organs (referred to in the plural, as was customary during that period), e.g.:

1560: Payd to John Howe ye organe maker for a full acquytance the some of 10s.
1567: Paid to John Tysdale for mendynge ye organs and for stuff: 3s. 4d.
1570: Paid to John Tysdale for mendynge ye organs . . . and for meals and drink: 20s. 4d.
1572: A lock and bolt for ye organes: 6d.

Hunter says that the organ that was in the Church at the time of Queen Elizabeth was 'silenced by the puritan spirit which prevailed in the parish in the middle of the seventeenth century, nor was another erected till the period of the late great repairs of the Church'.[15] He would be referring here to the rebuilding of the nave undertaken around 1800. Mackerness has written a most useful account of the organs and music, which may be referred to for more detail on the instruments and organists.[16]

The 1805 organ built by G.P. England at a cost of £770 was brought into use in October 1805, the Burgesses contributing £105. This organ came into being on the back of a Press campaign, the Burgesses minuting on 22 February 1802:

> 'The Trustees do consider an Organ as extremely desirable and approve of the Situation marked out for it on the plans and therefore agree to give their Countenance to the proposals published in the *Sheffield Iris* of the 18th for immediately procuring the Means of building it.'

There were great occasions on 9th, 10th and 11th October, 1805 with oratorio performances, this festival being underwritten jointly by the Church Burgesses, Town Trustees and the Cutlers Company. This organ was reconstructed in 1841 and the Burgesses paid £300 for a new case and gallery and £20.10s.6d. for 25 new front pipes. In 1857, the organ was moved to the shallow north transept by the tower and in 1872 was once again on the move, being renewed by Brindley and Foster and installed in what is now the sanctuary of St. Katherine's Chapel. In 1888 it was enlarged and again rebuilt and moved to the north choir aisle, for which the Burgesses paid £740, with a further £500 spent on building work. When, in the mid-1960s, a new organ was built, the Burgesses contributed something over £4500.

Regular small contributions from the Burgesses to the 'Church singers' begin in 1821, with £2.2s.0d, increased to £5.5s.0d. in 1826. These contributions continued for many years, steadily increasing over the years. In 1933, a grant of £100 was made to the Choir, the Burgesses carefully considering whether the choir was 'a necessity of Divine Worship', and, whilst making the grant, they disclaimed any legal liability to continue such contributions. But the contributions continued until 1943, when the amount was increased from £225 to £285 per annum.

We have already noted that in 1571 a 'psalter in metre' was purchased. It is fair to assume, therefore, that at that time psalms were being sung in the Parish Church. The funerals of the 5th and 6th Earls of Shrewsbury were most grand occasions with a choir with surplices for the former and singing men and six trumpets for the latter.[17]

Mackerness records a report of 1848 to the effect that 'the choir of four attempted ambitious services and neglected the anthem; recourse was had to the frothiest and most inane of chants.' This was during the term of Joseph Bottomley, who was Organist from 1820 to 1860. Bottomley's long tenure spanned a period of great change. He was a musician of some distinction and the author of a Dictionary of Music. But his performance in the office to which he had been appointed was a matter of some considerable concern to his employers. The Burgesses' Minute Book is liberally embellished with references to what was clearly something of a saga, commencing on 31 January 1828, when the Burgesses resolved that 'the subscription towards the Choir singers be discontinued, the Choir being conducted at present in a manner by no means satisfactory to the Trust.' A few months later, on 24 July, Mr. Bottomley took the full force of criticism:

> 'In consequence of numerous complaints of the bad playing of the organ in the parish church for some Sundays past, the Burgesses feel themselves called upon to express to Mr. Bottomley their regret at his having so long absented himself from the duties of this office, and that without any application to the

> Trust for leave for that purpose, contrary to his terms of agreement with them.'

By November of the following year, there was more to find fault with:

> 'It having been represented to the Burgesses that the Organ in the parish church has suffered from the Admission of Persons to practice upon it for their improvement, they do request Mr. Bottomley as Organist will not allow such permission to any person in future without the sanction of the Burgesses.'

And so it continued, with the Burgesses working themselves up into a state of some indignation, minuted ten years later, on 4 January 1838:

> 'The Grounds of Complaint as to the manner of playing the Organ not having been removed notwithstanding the professions some time ago of Mr. Bottomley, ordered that our Clerk inform him that unless these complaints be remedied forthwith the Trust will be under the necessity of taking measures which they would gladly avoid which could not but be disagreeable to Mr. Bottomley.'

But Mr. Bottomley continued as Organist, although all was not well; the Burgesses from time to time showing their irritation by refusing to pay for organ tuning or the odd, necessary repair. And then, on 3 February 1853, Mr. Bottomley submitted his letter of resignation. But, inexplicably, he was still there in 1860 when the end finally came. On 5 January of that year we read in the Minute Book:

> 'Letter from Mr. Bottomley resigning as Organist, Resolved: Consideration be deferred to the next meeting. Mr. Bottomley to be informed that in all probability his resignation will be accepted and a new appointment made.'

And the following day (the Burgesses could act very quickly at times), there is the laconic note: 'Resignation of Mr. Bottomley accepted from Christmas last. Mr. George Henry Smith appointed in his place.'

The Burgesses' differences with Organists did not end with Mr. Bottomley's leaving. Trouble surfaced again in 1936. At a meeting on 24 November a Burgess 'complained of the continued excessive use of powerful stops which made it impossible to hear the singing of the Choir and congregation.' He went on: 'in Sheffield Churches as a whole there was good congregational singing, but in the Cathedral there was not. The Organist's performance on the organ confused the Choir.' The Burgesses resolved unanimously to terminate the Organist's appointment when he reached his 70th birthday the following March, later extended until June, when he was provided with a pension of £200, a generous provision compared with his salary of £350.

An Assessment of the Burgesses' contribution to the Parish Church and the Cathedral

In 1557, just over 70% of the Burgesses' income was spent on the Parish Church, including the stipends of the three Assistant Ministers, which was, indeed, the major item of expenditure. By the 1850s, routine expenditure on the maintenance of the Parish Church amounted to about 27% of the Burgesses' expenditure. As demands grew, with the establishment of other parishes carved out of the old Parish of Sheffield, and with the requirements of the new Charity Scheme, the Parish Church became, proportionately, less of a charge on Burgesses' expenditure. By 1900, routine expenditure on the Parish Church was less than 25% of total expenditure and by 1920, it was down to 13%. These figures exclude, of course, any significant capital contributions, of which there were many, to alterations and improvements. In the 1990s, the proportion has fluctuated between 30% and 55%.

One direct result of the Burgesses' contribution to the Parish Church and to the new parishes was noted on p. 50, viz. the avoidance of a parish rate for Sheffield. In many other towns there were bitter clashes with Dissenters over the levying of Church rates. Understandably, Dissenters objected strongly to having to pay for the maintenance of the Established Church. Their own churches were totally dependent upon pew rents and voluntary collections. They saw no reason why the Established Church should differ. There were discussions from time to time in Sheffield over the levying of a church rate. In 1818 and 1819, for example, Vestry Meetings considered the need for a rate and in 1819 a resolution for the levying of a 2d. rate was lost, an amendment being approved to the effect that pew holders in the Parish Church should pay more for their privileges.[18] One factor in the absence of a church rate was undoubtedly the strength of non-conformism in Sheffield. But the other factor was no less strong, and that was the Burgesses' payments for the cost of maintaining both the fabric and running costs of the Parish Church. That Sheffield was free from the bitterness, and sometimes the violence, occasioned by disputes over church rates was due, in no small measure, to the fact that the Parish Church could depend upon the Burgesses meeting its expenses. It is ironic that a 16th century Charter granted to preserve the Catholic traditions of the Established Church should have eased the lot of non-conformists two and three centuries later.

We cannot compare directly later spending with the 16th century, when most of the expenditure went on clergy stipends. It is clear that the pattern of spending has changed radically down the centuries. Yet the Cathedral, as it now is, remains the single most important responsibility of the Church Burgesses and they accept that, within the terms of their Charter, there is a priority attached to the Cathedral which takes precedence over other responsibilities. Their financial strategy must take account of two factors. Firstly, the inexorable increase of running costs of the Cathedral and, secondly, that the responsibilities laid upon them in their Charter, and subsequently delineated in the Charity Schemes, relate to the whole of the old Parish of Sheffield, which now, of course, comprises many parishes created out of the ancient Parish. These new parishes, almost all of them 19th and 20th century creations, are endowed and helped in many ways by the Burgesses. This is not a matter of taking away resources from the old Parish Church and redistributing them. It has been more a matter of expanding the assets of the Trust so that many demands can be met.

But, nevertheless, the Burgesses' responsibility for the Old Parish Church (now the Cathedral) is quite different to any responsibilities the Trust may have towards other churches and parishes. For the specific responsibility of maintaining the fabric and the costs of Divine Worship is unique to the Cathedral. It is this responsibility which creates the special relationship between the Burgesses and the Cathedral. It might perhaps be thought remarkable that the responsibility of maintaining a medieval Church could be sustained as that Church grew and was transformed into a modern Cathedral in the centre of a great City. Yet it has been so sustained, as other activities of the Trust have been similarly expanded and developed.

The growth of expenditure on the Cathedral has been especially large post-war. From £3288 in 1946 to about £200,000 in 1996 is a rate of growth well in excess of inflation, and reflects both the increased activity of the Cathedral and higher standards of maintenance of a larger building. In addition to the costs of regular ongoing maintenance, the Burgesses must be ready to meet urgent major expenses. In the 1960s an attempt was made to build up a reserve for such items in a Cathedral Deferred Repairs Account and a sum of £20,000 was paid into this account over a period of five years. That was soon swallowed up in general expenditure. In 1971, roof repairs cost £26,000 over and above regular maintenance. In 1994, when the Cathedral Square was being laid out, the Burgesses' contribution of £50,000 was a major part of the total cost.

The questions have to be asked whether, over the long period of growth and change, the Burgesses have been effectively supportive of the tasks and mission of the Parish Church, and whether the arrangement is one which can meet the demands of the future. Clearly, in the past, there have been tensions from time to time between the Burgesses and the Vicar and Churchwardens. Notably, one may record friction which continued from 1808 until 1821 over payments for Church requisites. And, in 1850, the

Vicar of the day stood firm against the injudicious appointment, by the Burgesses, of the Revd. George Trevor as Assistant Minister. But, for the most part, there have been relatively infrequent and minor differences of opinion and misunderstandings, rather than major upsets. The record in the Minutes in 1922 might be typical of the level of disagreement. The Burgesses were considering the use of the Burgesses' Room by unauthorised persons, the Clerk expressing the view that the Burgesses had exclusive and indefeasible rights in the Room. There was some exchange with the Churchwardens and on 29 August 1922, the laconic entry: 'It was left to the Capital to explain the position to the new Vicar.' One may imagine a tutorial explaining the traditions and how best to work with them.

The Burgesses' Room has, clearly, from time to time, been something of an irritant to Provosts, who may have regarded the territorial claim of the Burgesses as an unwelcome symbol of their power. The issue surfaced again in a letter to the Capital Burgess from Provost Jarvis on 30 December 1932:

> 'I am sending you an advance copy of the Form of Service for my Installation. You will see that on page 12 I have to lay claim to the keys of the several Chambers of the Cathedral. This raises in a rather awkward form the question of the Church Burgesses' Room. I feel this is the occasion when, if the Burgesses wish to assert their claim to exclusive use, a public statement ought to be made.'

The Burgesses' Room, Sheffield Cathedral.

Either, this was a genuine and innocent attempt to secure absolute clarity within a formal and solemn setting, or, perhaps more likely, an attempt to force the hands of the Burgesses. The Provost may have concluded that the Burgesses would not wish to go as far as having to make a public declaration of ownership of their Room. The Capital Burgess thought otherwise: 'It is my duty formally to uphold the right of the Church Burgesses to their Room.' and he went on to suggest a form of words that the Provost could use as he made his claim to the keys . . . 'excepting those of that room known as the Church Burgesses' Room of which the Church Burgesses lay claim to the exclusive use.'

Surprisingly, perhaps, the matter was not laid to rest. The Bishop returned to the issue when Provost Cruse was appointed in 1949. He requested that the Burgesses hand over the key to the Provost. A meeting was arranged at which it was agreed that there would be no handover, the precedent of 1932 being quoted and also Statute IX of the Constitution and Statutes of the Cathedral, which recognises the Burgesses' exclusive rights to their room.

All this might be regarded as a petty business, unworthy of the parties concerned, but it is perhaps indicative of some deeper feeling of a Provost wishing to be totally master in his own house. Only once in the long history of the Burgesses does there appear to have been a serious breakdown in relationships and that, surprisingly, with Provost Jarvis, a man of exemplary qualities with a great record as Provost. The dispute followed, however, a most stressful period for him, culminating in the terrible air raids of December 1940. We know that he had a serious breakdown in health at that time. He can be fully excused any apparent over-reaction. The episode was sparked off by what the Provost, in a letter of 12 February 1941, called an 'unpleasant incident', in which two Burgesses had intervened to stop repair work being done on the organ, work already sanctioned by their Surveyor. Feelings were inflamed by some intemperate language on both sides, with accusations from the Provost of bad feeling and a claim that an impasse had been reached. The Provost went on to make an attack on the Burgesses' Charity Scheme as a bad one and he proposed to go to the Courts to seek amendment. The Provost had a meeting with the Chief Charity Commissioner from which he (mistakenly) drew comfort and encouragement, only to have the ground cut from under him when the Charity Commissioners wrote to say that he had misunderstood the position. What the Provost and the Cathedral Council wanted was a block grant, with no strings attached, calculated either as a fixed proportion of the Burgesses' income, or based upon average expenditure on the Cathedral over a period of time.

At no other time does there appear to have been any real threat amounting to a breakdown in relationships and no evidence can be found to suggest that any moves have been taken by Vicar, Churchwardens or others to question the stewardship of the Burgesses or to attempt to formalise procedures by way of protocols or memoranda of agreements. Good sense and a sense of common purpose appear to have prevailed. It could have been otherwise. There might have developed a master-servant relationship, with underlying resentment against the master. And, if that was unlikely, given the authoritative position of the Vicar in his own parish and the standing of the individuals concerned, there might have been bitter battles between equals. One may venture the opinion that, given the relative tranquillity of the relationship, the Vicar and Churchwardens have been generally satisfied with the support given by the Burgesses.

But has that support been adequate? Has the Church, and its Divine Offices, been maintained in a satisfactory manner? One might be tempted to use as evidence against the Burgesses the Archdiaconal Visitation in 1800 with its 'ruinous and in decay . . . moulderous, rotten and decayed . . . flooring and pavement broken, interrupted, ruinous . . . ' Yet, it is difficult to square this with the Burgesses' regular spending on maintenance and it all seems to have come about remarkably quickly, since no previous Visitation by the Archdeacon expresses a view of impending dereliction. David Lunn, Bishop of Sheffield, has said: 'I smell collusion.' And he should know![19] James Wilkinson, the Vicar at that time, presumably wanted change, especially in the pewing arrangements (and so, it would seem, did the Burgesses) and, indeed, drastic changes were made. But it is difficult to conclude that the 1805 rebuilding of the nave was necessary because of serious neglect of the fabric. One telling fact about the Burgesses' stewardship is that at no time since 1554 has the Parish Church or Cathedral found it necessary to engage in a public appeal for funds to restore the fabric of the Church. Appeals have been made for money to enlarge the Church, but the common, almost obligatory, appeals, typical of other Cathedrals, to counter severe dry rot, falling towers, leaking roofs, death watch beetle, or whatever, have been notably absent in Sheffield. It is reasonable to conclude that the Burgesses have fulfilled, to the satisfaction of the Church authorities, the responsibilities placed upon them. Had this not been so, dissatisfaction would surely have been expressed. This is not an attempt to present an unblemished record by a group of all-wise men. It has to be said that, amongst successive Vicars of Sheffield, have been some very able, determined men, well able to carry their case and to negotiate skilfully. But it has been a partnership, in which the Burgesses have had regard to the

Church's ministry in the town and City. It has to be said, however, that this partnership has, in recent years, been greatly assisted by English Heritage, whose financial support has strengthened and complemented the work of the Burgesses.

Since 1914, when the Diocese and Cathedral of Sheffield were created, the demands upon the Church, in respect of both City and Diocese, have increased enormously. That a Tudor Charter should have weathered 80 years of Cathedral growth and change is, in many ways, remarkable. Is the instrument sufficiently robust to cope with future demands? That is a question for the Burgesses and for the Cathedral authorities. Commencing afresh, one might not think of a system of dual control containing an apparent potential for serious breakdown. And yet, the fact that it has worked well and has survived the period of enormous growth and change of the 19th and 20th centuries, might give some grounds for confidence about the future.

Yet, the challenges that lie ahead are enormous. The work of the Cathedrals' Fabric Commission for England will mean new procedures and perhaps more demanding standards. The Church Commissioners are steadily reducing their grant to the Diocese. New Statutes will soon be in place for the Cathedral, with a new Chapter, a new Council, new systems of accountability and new working relationships. And over all looms the tremendous challenge of the mission of the Cathedral for the 21st century in a City and Diocese that are seeking regeneration. The next 100 years could be the most testing in the history of the Church Burgesses.

From the Very Revd. W.F. Curtis, Provost of Sheffield: 1974-1988

When I became Provost in 1974, I was given an outline of the history and relationship between the Trust and the Cathedral. With that background, I have been especially glad to read these chapters, filling out, as they do, the information I already had and putting it into perspective.

I was greatly intrigued to see references to the seating in the Parish Church early in the last century. Roberts refers to 2,750, whilst Hunter in 1819 referred to the Church as being capable of accommodating 2,500 to 3,000 persons and he comments that this is the number usually attending the late Sunday evening service. For the enthronement of Bishop David Lunn in 1980, we provided seating for 1,330 or thereabouts, and regarded this as the absolute maximum!

But, whether the seating is 3,000 or 1,330, the fact is that we have been provided with a fine building on a prime site in the City centre. Part of that provision has been through the contribution made by the Burgesses since

1554. Over those years the Church Burgesses on the one hand and the Parish Church/Cathedral on the other have endeavoured by the grace of God to be good stewards of what has been entrusted to them. Having served as Provost for 14 years I would like to acknowledge the time and effort so generously given by the Burgesses in fulfilling their responsibilities.

Our Cathedral is well placed to engage in its mission locally and within the City and Diocese. It has a good range of accommodation for worship and other activities. It has public transport within a stone's throw – a facility which may have greater significance in the future.

However, in the near future changes are certain to take place. Very shortly a whole range of maintenance work will need to be undertaken and modest re-ordering of the interior and enlargement of the Hall will be necessary. These changes will, I am confident, be completed through the mutual trust of all concerned and with a sense of partnership.

Perhaps a Provost retired for upwards of nine years is not the best person to engage in prophecy! But one thing I can write with confidence is that changes – great changes – lie ahead if we are to engage relevantly and faithfully with people and communities in the inner City and to serve both the City and the Diocese.

We, whether Church Burgesses, Cathedral authorities, or amongst those associated with the life and work of the Cathedral, have God-given responsibilities. My prayer is that all concerned will be enabled to respond with faith and confidence to undertake new tasks and seize new opportunities in the mission of the Church to which our Cathedral is being called.

From the Rt. Revd. John Gladwin, Bishop of Guildford, Provost of Sheffield, 1988-1994:

As the local guru says to the visiting and lost stranger: 'If I were attempting to go there, I wouldn't start from here!' No one in their right mind would set up a relationship such as has existed between the Church Burgesses and the Parish Church, now Cathedral Church, of Sheffield. It invites those endless and energy-sapping border disputes about who actually runs the place.

Yet for all its potential difficulty (which has sometimes become actual in periods of the history), the thing has worked. That is probably rooted in the reality that the good citizens of Sheffield who are the Church Burgesses, and those responsible for the Parish Church ministry, are on the same side. This is Sheffield's Church and these are responsible for a trust which benefits Sheffield and its people. A civic town centre, and now Cathedral Church

The Burgesses' Room, Sheffield Cathedral, showing the windows.

sustained by the historic trust managed by the city's leading citizens. Well, as near as damn it!

When you look at Sheffield Cathedral you either view the extraordinary building as problem or as opportunity. Complex and baffling – yes, indeed. But is it problem, or is it opportunity? Those who succeed see it as opportunity. The same is true of the unique bond between the Burgesses and the Cathedral (Parish Church). Those who see it as opportunity – unique as it is – succeed.

Fortunately, for most of the history, it has been opportunity. May that paradoxical reality of the gift of our most Catholic Queen sustaining one of the most Protestant and Evangelical of parish church Cathedrals add a further dimension which gives cause both for smiles and thanksgiving.

CHAPTER 4

Clergy Matters: Conflict and Commitment

FROM 1554 UNTIL 1854, the first responsibility of the Church Burgesses was that of providing the stipends of the three Assistant Ministers at the Parish Church. The Charity Scheme of 1854 altered this, as already described in Chapter II. Thereafter, the Burgesses were responsible for funding two Chaplains at the Parish Church and for providing perpetual endowments for parishes formed out of the old parish of Sheffield. So the Scheme opened the way for very considerable growth in funding of clergy. It was not, however, until 30 years later that the payment of Assistant Ministers' stipends was finally phased out with the death, in 1888, of the Revd. Samuel Earnshaw, the last remaining Minister. His stipend of £400 per annum was redistributed amongst the new Sheffield parishes (see p. 89). The discontinuance of the payment of stipends for the three Assistant Ministers (the petition for which payment had led to the foundation of the Trust) did not mean any diminution of clergy support by the Burgesses. Quite the contrary; the new provisions were a recognition of the needs of a rapidly growing urban population. Through support both for clergy stipends and for church building, the Burgesses made a considerable contribution to enable the Anglican Church to face the enormous challenges of population growth and social change in the 19th and 20th centuries.

The Assistant Ministers' Stipends

The Account Book for 1557 has the entries:

Furst to Sir Alexander bothe for his holle yeres wages endyt at wyt sondaye last past before the daye of date herof the som of:	vjli xiijs iiijd
Itm pd to Sir Rycharde Beweke for his wages endyt in lykewise ye some of:	vli
Itm pd to Sir Willm Hanbe for his yeres wages endyt in lykewise the some of:	vli

('Sir' was commonly used as a term of address for clergy before the adoption of the title 'Reverend').

The movement, in cash terms, over the years of the Assistant Ministers' stipends is shown in Table 1. The figures include various 'augmentation' fees which began to be paid in 1750 and continued thereafter but exclude any payment of rents.

Table 1: Stipends of Assistant Ministers

1557	£16	13s.	4d.	1725	£116	0s.	0d.
1600	40	0	0	1750	136	0	0
1625	50	0	0	1775	221	10	0
1650	115	0	0	1800	360	0	0
1675	112	0	0	1825	750	0	0
1700	116	0	0	1850	1064	0	0

As we shall see later, there were disputes from time to time about the precise duties required of an Assistant Minister. The Burgesses were slow to introduce a contract or detailed job specification and, since the Vicar had limited control only over the Ministers, and some inducement seemed to be necessary, additional payments were introduced for certain duties. Initially, payments of £10.0s.0d. p.a. were made for reading Evening Prayer on Sundays. In 1789, an additional £15.0s.0d. was paid as a 'gratuity' and a further £10.0s.0d. for 'lectures on Sunday evenings.' The 'augmentation' grew until it was ultimately about half of the basic stipend.

We have referred earlier (p. 36) to the Rollinson bequest of two houses for use by the Assistant Ministers and to payments made by the Burgesses for the rent of these. As things developed, the total emoluments of the Assistant Priests must have made the office very attractive, additionally so when the very considerable freedom associated with the posts is taken into consideration. In addition to generous augmentations of stipend for duties which other clergymen would have accepted as part of normal duties, the Burgesses were considerate, even generous, employers. The Election Book records on 16 January 1730: 'Agreed that the Capital make Mr. Hemingway a present of £10 towards defraying the expenses he has lately been at in going to the Bath for the remedy of his health.' (Mr. Hemingway died on 3 March in that year.) And the Minute Book has an entry for 20 January 1800: 'resolved that in Consideration of the present high price of Bread and other necessaries of Life the addition of £15 per annum be made to the salary of Revd. Matthew Preston whose large Family and Situation seem particularly to demand addition and the Addition of £10 per annum to the Salaries of each of the two other Assistant Ministers, Revd. G. Bayliff and Revd. E. Goodwin, during the pleasure of the Trustees.' On 3 June 1811, the

Burgesses minuted: 'In consideration of the severe sickness with which the Revd. George Smith has been afflicted . . . and his large family, ordered that £31.10s. be paid to him as a donation.'

We may note that the stipends of the Assistant Ministers compared very favourably, for a long period, with that of the Vicar. In 1545, the living was worth £13.6s.8d; in 1649, £22 (compared with £50 for the senior Assistant Minister); in 1700, £75. By 1750, the stipend of the senior Assistant Minister, including augmentation, had risen to £80 and to £140 by 1800. The Town Trustees took pity, as it were, upon the Vicar, or were persuaded to do so, for in 1688 they made a collection to augment his stipend.[1] This was voluntary 'by way of entreaty'. In 1706, a two years' gratuity of £20 was paid, 'the same being carried by a majority of Freeholders.' It was James Wilkinson, Vicar 1754-1805, who substantially raised the value of the living by developing the Vicarage glebe during his incumbency. He took on the living at a stipend of £75 and left it at a value of £500.

The Burgesses' generosity showed itself also in their payment to candidates presenting themselves for consideration for appointment as Assistant Minister. They required a sermon from each candidate, in addition to interview. In 1766 they gave a total of 16 guineas to 'the several gentlemen in consideration of their trouble and expence in offering themselves as Candidates for the late Assistant Minister's place.' Such payments were repeated on future similar occasions. The labour of critically assessing the 'trial' sermons of six or eight aspiring candidates (in the days when long sermons were a point of honour) must have been considerable. Regrettably, the Burgesses have left no records of such assessment.

We should note that the Burgesses also paid the wages and expenses of the Parish Clerk. At the time of the establishment of the Trust, Edward Pavye was Clerk and received wages of 13s.4d. In addition, various other payments were made to him from time to time:

1557: For waschinge of the churche clothes and candyls: 3s. 4d.
1559: To Sir James Angel and Edward Pavye about the Church business before the Visitation and at Rotherham at the Visitation, their charges: 8s.
To Edward Pavye and Hugh Spooner for their pains about the Church business: 4s 6d.
1560: For a surplice for Edward Pavye: 4s. 6d.
1570: To Edward Pavye serving Hibberte during ye time he Kept to his House: 2s.
1572: To Edward Pavye for his Annuity: £1 13s. 4.

Pavye's name as Parish Clerk appears for the last time in the Annual Accounts for 1583, so he must have held office for 30 years or so.

Duties of Assistant Ministers

Although the Assistant Ministers may be regarded as the successors to the three medieval priests serving the altars of The Rood, Our Lady and St. Katherine,[2] their duties involved the whole of the parish. One served the Parish Church, one the Chapel-at-Ease at Ecclesall and the other the Chapel at Attercliffe. In 1684, there is a reference to an additional payment being made to the chaplain at Ecclesall Chapel:

> 'thirtie shillings more yearly which was given by John Crooke to Ecclesall Chapel over and above his stypend, and that the Inhabitants of Ecclesall Byerley doe alsoe pay unto him yearely what can be raised within the byerley, so as it be not less than Nine poundes and ten shillings.'

(Ecclesall Byerley is now referred to as The Ancient Township of Ecclesall Bierlow.)

It is clear that each Assistant performed some duties at the Parish Church, for specific payments were made for 'reading evening service.' A minute in the Election Book dated 5 December 1764 ordered that Evening Prayers were to be read in the Old Church every evening weekly by the three Ministers alternately. Fifty years later we read in the Minute Book for 7 October 1819:

> 'As it appears from reference to the proceedings of the Trust on 5 December 1764 and to the accounts of 31 December 1787, that the Evening Service was introduced by the Burgesses and salaries paid by them for the due performance of such services by the Ministers, in order that the poor might be able to attend Divine Service in the evenings in the Parish Church, the Trust do resolve that the expences of lighting the Church for such services under their direction be defrayed out of Church funds, part of which are by their Charter intended for the use of the poor.'

Duties within the areas served by the Chapels-at-Ease must also have been required of the Ministers. From 27 January 1774 each Assistant Minister was required to enter into a specific contract with the Burgesses, duly entered in the Election Book. By that time the Burgesses had learned, to their cost, that there was ample room for dispute between Assistant Minister and Vicar, from which the Burgesses could not stand aloof. Hunter's comment[3] was somewhat wide of the mark:

> 'The placing in the same church of three clergymen possessing a co-ordinate authority with the Vicar appears contrary to the monarchical spirit of the English establishment, yet it may be observed that the experiment seems here to have succeeded. No unedifying rivalries and contentions have sprung up among them, but all striving together in the work and labour of love.'

Most, but not all, of the Burgesses were caught up in 1743 with the unseemly dispute between the Vicar of Sheffield, John Dossie, and the Revd. John Downes, who was not an Assistant Minister at the Parish Church, but Curate at St. Paul's.[4] In 1715, William Birley had bequeathed £900 to the town, and interest from £300 of this was to be paid to the Chaplain at the Shrewsbury Hospital. The 12 Trustees of the Charity were drawn from the Church Burgesses, the Town Trust and the Grammar School Governors. At the time of the dispute, 9 of the 12 Trustees were Church Burgesses. John Downes, the Curate at St. Paul's (who was the nephew of Robert Downes who had paid for the building of St. Paul's), laid claim to the Hospital Chaplain's stipend of £16 a year, which was being paid to the Vicar of Sheffield. Downes' claim was based upon his interpretation of the clause in Birley's will which read: '(payment to) perform Divine Service in the Chapel of the Hospital, or in any other place that shall be regularly appointed to that use.' He claimed that, since the building of St. Paul's Church, the money should have been diverted from the Hospital to that Church. In an extended correspondence with the Archbishop of York, neither side gave quarter and, at one stage, there was even a counterfeit letter from one of the Trustees of the Birley Charity to the Archbishop. In a testy letter to the Vicar, the Archbishop attempted to wash his hands of the affair:

> 'It is high time that this ugly dispute between yourself and the Preacher was ended and if you should see reason on reconsidering this Affair to give up the point in debate, for the sake of Peace, as a matter of doubtful right, for such most certainly it is, it would be proper it should be done of your own motion. For I desire no other share in the business.'[5]

Ten of the twelve Trustees who voted the continuation of payment to the Vicar were Church Burgesses and they were incensed by the counterfeit letter and the impugning of their motives of support for the Vicar. With their support the Vicar stuck to his guns and kept the money.

John Dossie was unfortunate with his Curates. In 1752, he had to accept the Revd. John Dickinson as one of his Assistant Ministers. Of the manner of this appointment it would be preferable to say nothing, for it suggests some manipulation of the Burgesses.[6] Yet it must be supposed that it represents but a mild form of 18th century wire-pulling. John Dickinson went from the Grammar School to St. John's College, Cambridge,and in 1749 became the incumbent of the chapelry of Levington in Lincolnshire and was licensed also as preacher at St. Peter's, Wisbech. He maintained contact with Sheffield and made a favourable impression in preaching the Cutlers' Feast sermon in 1748, so much so that moves began to secure for him the appointment as Assistant Minister, in the expectation and belief that one of the existing Assistants was near to death. Gilbert Dixon, Law Clerk to the Cutler's Company, started the wheel turning by organising a canvas on Dickinson's behalf.

> Dixon wrote to Dickinson: 'Jerry Hancock (uncle of Dickinson) has set his wheels awork for you. Mr. Nodder (one of the Church Burgesses) has given him a list of the Burgesses and he has buzz'd about a day or two, which had made some sport . . . If you will condescend to ask for this little thing (and, without asking, the Burgesses will not think themselves properly complimented), you ought to set about it immediately, and your friends here will be doing everything in their power for your service.'

Mr. Dixon was certain the wire-pulling would succeed: 'In short, sir, you are as sure of the succession to Ecclesall as ye Prince of Wales to the Crown of England.' And: 'Mrs. Dixon will get some new china against your coming, and she hopes to have many a dish of tea and chat with you.' And, in 1752, John Dickinson was duly appointed, the great problem being, however, that he had no intention of moving to Sheffield and proposed to retain his Lincolnshire appointment. He came to Sheffield in 1752 to preach another Cutler's' Feast sermon, and again in 1754, when he preached two sermons in the Parish Church. Apart from this, nothing. The redoubtable James Wilkinson, who succeeded John Dossie as Vicar of Sheffield in September 1754, took action in 1756, charging Dickinson with neglect of duty. He refused either to go or to reside in Sheffield and fulfil properly the duties of his office. The Vicar, Archdeacon and Archbishop were powerless to remove him and the Burgesses found that, whilst it was easy to appoint an Assistant Minister, it was exceedingly difficult to remove him. Minuting in the Election Book on 24 September 1756, that the Assistant Minister should 'either reside or resign' and threatening suspension of payment of his stipend were words that had to be eaten. Not until 1763 did Dickinson relinquish his appointment and he was paid the full arrears of his salary.

All this was a remarkable foreshadowing of the dispute with George Trevor a hundred years later. The circumstances were very different, but the outcome was very similar. The Burgesses found that their powers of appointment and their direct employment of Assistant Ministers put them in a position of weakness, not strength, when faced with contumacious clergy. Church discipline and Church procedures would have been more effective in controlling waywardness and non co-operation. It was the Canon Trevor dispute which forced the Burgesses to give up the appointment of Assistant Ministers. To that dispute we now turn.

Canon George Trevor: Standing firm on principle

Hunter gives a succinct summary of the Trevor affair.[7] Wheat goes into more detail.[8] Indeed, J. Newton Coombe, the Church Burgess who wrote the admirable, if formal, 'Memorandum', published in 1913, was alarmed by what he read in Wheat's draft. Writing to him on 15 September 1914, he says: 'There is of course a great deal of controversy in the Book which it would not be wise to make public.'[9] He obviously disapproved of any public disclosure of what he regarded as a controversial matter, which might show the Burgesses in a poor light. Because Wheat's monograph is available only in typescript, and also because of the significance of the Trevor affair in bringing about far-reaching changes in the administration of the Trust, the essentials of the dispute will be recounted here in some detail.

On 3 April 1850, the Revd. William Harris, one of the Assistant Ministers, died. At that time the Vicar, Dr. Thomas Sutton, was incapacitated and not able fully to perform the duties of his office. (He died, in fact, on 15 January, 1851). The Revd. John Gibson, an Assistant Minister, had for some years been suffering from a mental breakdown and was no longer resident in Sheffield. The third Minister, Revd. Samuel Earnshaw, was also, at that time, suffering a temporary breakdown. It appears to have been a time of severe clergy stress in Sheffield!

The Burgesses filled the vacancy in the usual way, by initial public advertisement and selection of a short list of 6 candidates, from over 80 applications. Having interviewed and heard the candidates preach, the Burgesses decided in favour of George Trevor, then Vicar of All Saints', York and a Canon of York, a man of undoubted ability and impressive achievement. Upon submission of the six names to Dr. Sutton, he indicated an objection to Trevor, whom he had previously refused to allow to preach in the Parish Church. It seems that Canon Trevor was an advocate and supporter of the Society for the Propagation of the Gospel in Foreign Parts, a body considered much 'too high church' by the evangelically minded Dr. Sutton. The Burgesses, firm in their views that they had chosen the best candidate, and after allowing for his alleged Tractarian views, confirmed the appointment, although by only a bare majority of 7 to 5. Dr. Sutton also remained firm and was quickly supported in his resolve by a statement from 26 Sheffield clergymen backing his stand. The Burgesses chose to disregard both the Vicar and the solid support from Sheffield clergy. Instead, they took note, amongst other things, of a testimonial in favour of Canon Trevor written by George Spencer, the former Bishop of Madras; a somewhat unconvincing counterweight, one might have thought, to the strong local objections. Spencer, then resident in the Diocese of Bath and Wells, was, however, a prominent Evangelical, and unlikely to give his support to anyone inclined to high church practices. Canon Trevor was duly appointed by the Burgesses at their meeting on 13 May 1850 and in due course was licensed by the Archbishop, notwithstanding the Vicar's appeal that he be refused a license. Canon Trevor made it clear to the Vicar and the Burgesses that he was ready and available to take up his post and perform the duties required of him, but to no avail. Without the Vicar's authorisation he could not perform in the parish. Both the Vicar and the Burgesses took Counsel's opinion upon the issues. The matter, in law, was clear enough – Dr. Adams of Doctor's Commons gave the Burgesses an unmistakable directive: 'the absolute right of election is with the Burgesses', but, 'the license, without the consent of the Vicar . . . is of no avail.'

It is difficult not to side with the Vicar in this quarrel. Whatever the reason for his not wanting the Revd. George Trevor, the Vicar's views had been made very clear to the Burgesses and one might have expected them to have accepted his veto. To impose someone in these circumstances was not only folly, but was bound to cause deep resentment. The rapid deterioration of the situation is apparent from two letters which the Vicar sent to the Burgesses. Dr. Sutton's initial letter of 30 April 1850 whilst firm, is eirenic:

> 'In 1846 I refused my pulpit to Mr. Trevor and regret that further knowledge of his Sentiments has not led me to alter my determination. The subject has been much in my prayerful thoughts and I trust to Him who ordereth all things as seemeth best to his Godly wisdom, to guide you by his spirit to the man most calculated to 'win souls for Christ.' He that winneth souls is wise. That your choice may rest on one whose great object may be to humble the sinner and exalt the Saviour is the earnest prayer of . . . Yours, & etc'.

Three weeks later, in a letter to the Law Clerk of 20 May, the tone was very different and Dr. Sutton's anger and determination are only too apparent: 'Will you make my compliments to the Trust and say that the Pulpit is mine and that I shall not require the services of the Revd. George Trevor to officiate therein.'

An impasse having been created, how to get out of it? Canon Trevor himself suggested that he might be allowed to exercise pastoral charge and even that he might perform service in the Town Hall, but the Vicar would not agree. The Burgesses chose the worst possible way to break the deadlock. On 3 October 1850, they agreed a resolution, passed on the casting vote of the Chairman: 'that under existing circumstances no salary or allowance be paid . . . to the Revd. George Trevor, who retains his Incumbency at York, does not reside within three-quarters of a mile of the

Parish Church of Sheffield, and who has not yet been admitted by the Vicar of the Parish of Sheffield to enter upon or perform . . . the duties of the Office of one of the Assistant Ministers or Chaplains of the Parish Church of Sheffield.' Again, after the event, the Burgesses sought Counsel's opinion, who categorically advised that the stipend could not be withheld and that the use of a casting vote by the Chairman was invalid. By this time, disagreement in the Trust had led Richard Bayley to resign, which occasioned another Counsel's opinion on the validity of resignation. The Burgesses paid one quarter's salary to Canon Trevor, but after yet another adverse Counsel's opinion, met on 9 December 1850 and resolved, by 6 votes to 5, to stop further payments to Trevor, until such time as he could perform the duties required of him. The Burgesses who had voted against this action took the most unusual step of handing to the Law Clerk a letter of protest, disclaiming any participation in withholding the stipend and for any consequent liability.

Canon Trevor now moved to the attack and filed a case in Chancery against the Burgesses. The outcome of the Decree made in Court was read at their meeting on 22 September 1851. The result was a clear victory for Trevor and the Burgesses had no option but to continue paying his salary. The suit cost the Burgesses £213.17s.4d., but much much more than that in goodwill and reputation.

Meanwhile, Dr. Sutton, the 'aged clergyman', in Canon Trevor's phrase, had died. However, his successor, Dr. Thomas Sale, cast in the same mould of churchmanship as his predecessor, did not soften the stance towards Trevor and maintained the veto. Efforts continued to try to find some modus vivendi that would satisfy honour and principles on all sides. At their meeting on 5 January 1852, the Burgesses noted a letter from the Archbishop asking whether 'some sphere of labour may not be found in the parish where Mr. Trevor's time and talents might be usefully and honourably employed.' Several possibilities were explored, involving pastoral charge of one of the Districts of Sheffield, and it seemed that agreement was very near on one occasion. Duties in the Netherthorpe and Porter Street districts were considered. In April 1852, the Burgesses minuted that Canon Trevor 'had concluded an agreement with the Vicar for spiritual charge of the Gilcar District.' But that agreement fell through. At one stage, it was proposed to form a new District of Broomhall and to build a large new Church of 1,000 sittings, with Trevor as Incumbent. The proposals were discussed in some detail, locally, and with the Archbishop of York and his staff. Canon Trevor declined to participate in this arrangement when it was made clear to him that he would not be permitted to hold that appointment together with the

Chaplaincy at the Parish Church and his living at York. As a consequence of that proposal falling through, a small 'iron' church was erected at Broomhall. One is left with the feeling that Canon Trevor was ultimately reluctant to accept any arrangement, perhaps because he could foresee controversy continuing or, maybe, because he preferred an arrangement which allowed him the benefits of his York living and a handsome Sheffield stipend for which no duties were necessary.

In December 1853, Trevor agreed that the Revd. James Chadwick should serve as Curate in his place in Sheffield, an arrangement accepted by the Vicar. So the duties were assigned to the Curate, who received a stipend of 100 guineas, paid by Canon Trevor out of his salary of £400. If honour is the right word to use, then we may say that honour was satisfied all round. But not until July 1873 did Canon Trevor resign his office as Assistant Minister. His letter of resignation to the Law Clerk at that time demonstrates his lasting sense of grievance and firm conviction, bordering on the self-righteous, that he was in the right:

Beeford Rectory, Hull.

'The time has come at which I have contemplated the resignation of my Chaplaincy at Sheffield.

In selecting me for the appointment in preference to more than 80 candidates (some of whom had strong private claims on their patronage) at a time when I had not a single acquaintance in the Trust or in the Town, the Burgesses exhibited a sense of public duty which was honourable alike to themselves and to the object of their choice. It would answer no good purpose to recall the unhappy circumstances which defeated their hopes and mine and compelled me after five years residence to leave the duties to a Curate nominated by the Vicar but paid by myself. The arrangement was recommended to me by the Diocesan (Archbishop Musgrave) as the best that under the circumstances could be adopted for the Spiritual good of the Parish. I acquiesced in it most reluctantly and always reserving the right to cancel it whenever the obstacles to my personal service could be removed.

That contingency has now been finally recluded by my appointment to this Benefice, and in accepting the offer of it I intimated to the Archbishop my intention of relinquishing the right which the law still gives me to the Chaplaincy. In consultation with his Grace the present month was fixed for the date of my resignation; and if you would be good enough to send me the proper document for giving legal effect to that determination from the 1st July instant I am prepared to sign it.

In requesting you to lay this communication before the Church Burgesses, I will only further express my deep regret that I have been prevented from rendering the aid which I desired to the spiritual needs of your great population and my earnest hope that the funds which I now return to their disposition may be more profitably bestowed under God's good blessing in promoting the religious welfare of a town in which I cannot cease to feel a peculiar interest.'

This episode, almost bizarre in its demonstration of capricious defence of principle, would hardly be worth commenting upon at this length were it not for two things in particular:

1. The publicity surrounding the case, which was almost wholly unsympathetic and, at times, downright antagonistic, to the Burgesses. It soon became very clear that the organs of the public voice much preferred to side with the human face of the Vicar and the Parish Church, than to give a hearing to what was seen by many as a secretive, manipulative, self-appointed body. The *Sheffield and Rotherham Independent* of 11 January 1851 is not untypical of the tone of the attacks mounted upon the Trust:

'It is deeply to be regretted that the last year of Dr. Sutton's incumbency should have been disturbed by the Trevor controversy. The original error was the election, by the Capital Burgesses, of a man to whom they knew that the Vicar had decided and conscientious objections. That error was more than doubled by the machinations afterwards resorted to, and disclosed in the letters of the parties subsequently published. It is revolting to read the schemes for 'blistering' the good old man, and for 'starving the Vicar into compliance', which were discussed and concocted. Nor can the smooth words by which it has been attempted to gloss over these schemes, nor the pseudo-virtuous indignation hurled at the author of these awkward disclosures, ever efface the litterae scriptae. Many imputations were made upon Dr. Sutton in reference to his rejection of Mr. Trevor. It was insinuated that he was in a state of mental incapacity, and that he was under the influence of others. We are assured by those who knew him well, and had access to him, that these insinuations are totally groundless.'

The Burgesses were forced to face the fact, unwelcome to some of them no doubt, that a public trust must be prepared to face up to public scrutiny. In the last resort, there is always a public accountability which has to be discharged. And such public accountability cannot be effectively rendered if the Trustees are deeply divided amongst themselves.

2. More importantly perhaps, the Trevor case proved that it was necessary to change the relationship between Burgesses and the Vicar in respect of staff whom he must control if the ministry of the Parish Church was to be effectively fulfilled. It says much for the Burgesses that in making that change, they were also ready to face up to the task of making the 1554 Charter into an instrument capable of meeting the challenges of the late

19th century and beyond. It is hardly conceivable that the Trust could have continued in its ancient ways, faced with the upheavals of 19th century urban change. But the Trevor case undoubtedly provided the spur for rapid and drastic action.

Alongside Downes, Dickinson and Trevor, other instances of problems with Assistant Ministers are but minor aberrations, but two entries from the Minute Books are worth reproducing, showing the extent to which the Burgesses were involved, from time to time, in matters which, one might have expected, would have been resolved by the Vicar as a matter of everyday working relationships. On 13 February 1817, the Minute Book records that representations had been made by various parishioners 'that the Assistant Ministers perform the duty of visiting the sick and baptising children by alternate weeks, whereas their conditions of appointment require performance of these duties at all reasonable times. The Church Burgesses call upon the Ministers to give up such arrangements and hope they will always be ready to do these important duties whenever properly applied to.' And, on 4 March 1858:

> 'Complaints having been made to the Trust that on Friday morning 19 February last no service had been performed in the Church and on Friday morning 26 February the service had been performed by a stranger, casually present, and that the Burgesses being informed that the Duty on both occasions ought in the ordinary rotation to have devolved upon the Revd. Samuel Earnshaw. Resolved to ask Mr. Earnshaw for an explanation.'

It would appear from a subsequent minute of 6 May 1858, that Mr. Earnshaw provided a satisfactory explanation.

Stipends for Clergy in Sheffield Parishes

The 1854 Scheme opened the way for the Burgesses to endow the new parishes that were being carved out of the old parish of Sheffield. Subsequent amendments to the Scheme extended the powers of endowment and widened the Burgesses' discretion. As the number of parishes and Churches in Sheffield grew, so did the Burgesses' contributions to clergy stipends.

The first payment of a stipend, other than to the Assistant Ministers at the Parish Church, was made in 1867 to the parish of St. Silas, Gilcar, when £145.19s.8d. was granted to the Incumbent, the Revd. Charles Wright. In the following year, payment was also made to St. Mark's, Broomhill. These payments to these two parishes continued until 1878, when St. Barnabas, Highfield, was added. In 1879, All Saints', Ecclesall, St. George's, St. Mary's,

Bramall Lane and Fulwood, were added and in that year, total payments towards stipends in these seven parishes amounted to £587. After the death of the Revd. Samuel Earnshaw, the last surviving Assistant Minister, his stipend of £400 became available for allocation to new parishes and was divided as follows: Owlerton £30; Walkley £50; St. Mary's £40; St. George's £30; St. Philip's £40; Pitsmoor £50; Wicker £30; Neepsend £50; Emmanuel £50; St. Simon £30.

The rapid growth of the Burgesses' contributions to stipends is shown in Table 2. These figures exclude the annual grant, made over many years, towards the stipend of the Chaplain of the Infirmary. This commenced in 1856 with payment of £50, quickly increased to £100.

Table 2: Burgesses' Contributions to Clergy Stipends

Year	£	s	d
1875	£1039	5s	0d
1900	£2854	19s	9d
1925	£6018	6s	0d
1950	£7733	2s	10d
1975	£23,351.00		
1990	£136,660.00		

Although the fiction is maintained that the Burgesses contribute to stipends and curacy grants in individual parishes, in fact, a block grant is paid to the Diocese for their apportionment to parishes in the four Sheffield Deaneries. It is of interest to note the significance of the Burgesses' total contribution. In 1995, the total of grants for stipends was £111,665. The stipends bill for clergy in the four Sheffield Deaneries in that year was £925,014, so the Burgesses contributed 12% of stipends. For 1996, the Burgesses' contribution was £134,000, making up about 14% of the stipends in the four Deaneries. In 1996, stipendiary grants were paid in respect of the following parishes:-

St. Mark, Broomhill
Netherthorpe
St. Cuthbert, Fir Vale
St. Timothy, Crookes
All Saints', Ecclesall
Christ Church, Fulwood
St. Mary, Walkley
St. Leonard, Doncaster
St. Catherine, Richmond Rd
St. Leonard, Norwood
Sheffield Manor
St. Silas & St. Jude
St. Peter, Abbeydale
St. Clement, Attercliffe
St. Thomas & St. Margaret (Brightside)
Pitsmoor with Ellesmere
St, Thomas, Crookes
St. Hilda, Shiregreen
St. Matthew, Carver St
St. Andrew, Sharrow
St. George
St. Mary's, Bramall Lane
St. Augustine, Endcliffe
St. Oswald, Millhouses
St. John, Park
Holy Trinity, Millhouses
St. John, Owlerton
Christ Church, Heeley
Shiregreen: St. James and St. Christopher
St. Lawrence, Tinsley

For these parishes, in 1996, the Burgesses were funding about 28% of the stipends.

It is not possible to compare directly the current value of the Burgesses' contribution to clergy stipends with their endowments during the heyday of Victorian development. A rough approximation shows that they have not quite maintained their proportionate contribution to total stipends; but that was hardly to be expected, given the variable effects of inflation, changes in the methods of funding clergy, and the increased number of churches. At the beginning of the 20th century, the Burgesses were providing endowments for clergy stipends to 30 out of the 42 new churches in the old parish of Sheffield. These endowments amounted to 43% of the stipends of clergy in the 30 endowed churches and to 32% of stipends of clergy in all 42 churches. If adjustment were made to take account of the phasing out of the Easter offering and of different methods of dealing with fees for occasional services, the figures for current and past spending would probably be quite close to each other. But, whatever the precise proportionate contribution, it is clear that the Burgesses' support for stipends remains substantial.

Patronage: The Parish Church

Patronage – the right to present a new Incumbent to a living – used to be a matter of considerable power and privilege. It is hardly that any longer, but does allow the patrons of a living, if they are so minded, to exercise a certain influence in the choice of a new Vicar. At the very least, and this is a matter of significance, the patrons of the living can ensure that the process of selection is carried through with scrupulous regard to fairness, with thorough and effective consultation, and that the best possible candidate is secured for the appointment. For the Burgesses, patronage is important also in that it involves the continuation of a supportive role for Vicar and parish, a role which is generally regarded very highly. There must be few such patrons as the Burgesses who maintain such close contact with their parishes and who are ready to help in practical ways as the need arises.

The Burgesses' patronage of the old Parish Church did not come their way until 1890, after they had accepted the patronage of the new parishes they had endowed. The manner of their obtaining the patronage, through purchase of the advowson, is a complicated little story. A presentative advowson – the right of presenting to the Bishop a nominee for a living – goes back to feudal times, and is treated in English law as property which can be transferred by gift or purchase. The advowson of the Parish Church of Sheffield passed through a number of hands.[10] The Canons of Worksop Priory had the right of appointment until the dissolution of the Priory in

1538. Francis, 5th Earl of Shrewsbury, sought the advowson in a grant of Edward VI of 1552, but this grant was in error, since an earlier grant of Henry VIII in 1544 had conveyed to Robert and William Swyft of Broom Hall tithes for Ecclesall, Upper and Nether Hallam townships, together with the advowson of the Parish Church. Robert's daughter married Richard Jessop, who acquired the Broom Hall inheritance and the advowson. In 1734, there was no male heir of the Jessop line and the property passed to four daughters as co-heirs. Two died unmarried. The eldest daughter married Andrew Wilkinson of Boroughbridge. The second daughter married John Eyre, who changed his name to Gell. The advowson was thus split between the Wilkinsons and the Gells, who presented alternately.

The Wilkinsons of Boroughbridge had seven sons, all of whom died childless (one of whom was James Wilkinson, Vicar of Sheffield, 1754-1805). When James died he bequeathed his half-share of the advowson to a cousin Barbara, who was a grand-daughter of Elizabeth Jessop. Barbara Wilkinson married Marmaduke Lawson, and their son Andrew inherited the half-share. He sold it to Revd Matthew Preston, a former Assistant Minister of Sheffield. David Lunn states this was brought about 'in order to secure the succession of an evangelical ministry.'[11] The Simeon Trustees subsequently bought this half-share. The other half-share, originally in the hands of Philip Gell of Hopton, Derbyshire, was purchased by Henry Wilson of Westbrook (Church Burgess 1832-1880) who passed it on to his son Alfred, who, in his will of 4 October 1890, devised it to the Church Burgesses. So, the right of presentation alternates today between the Church Burgesses and the Simeon Trust. If, however, the Incumbent should be appointed a Diocesan Bishop, the vacancy is filled by the Crown. This has happened three times: in 1897 when Canon Rowley Hill became Bishop of Sodor and Man; in 1922 when the Very Revd. Charles Carr became Bishop of Coventry and in 1994 when the Very Revd. John Gladwin became Bishop of Guildford. One technicality should be noted. The advowson gives the right of presentation of the Vicar of the parish of Sheffield, who is now also the Provost of Sheffield, but the right of presentation does not acknowledge the Cathedral of Sheffield.

Patronage: Other Parishes

The Burgesses generally assumed the patronage of the livings of new parishes as they endowed them. Endowment was regarded as constituting a purchase of the advowson, although it was not expressed formally in this way. With the changes in parishes, especially in recent years, with much parochial reorganisation, the number of parishes of which the Burgesses are patrons has declined, but is still significant. The current list of parishes of which the Burgesses are patrons is:

The Cathedral and Parish Church of Sheffield: Alternating with the Simeon Trustees.

Attercliffe Deanery

St. John, Park
Sheffield Manor: member of Patronage Board
Attercliffe, Darnall and Tinsley: member of Patronage Board

Ecclesall Deanery

St. Augustine, Endcliffe
St. Peter, Abbeydale
St. Mary, Bramall Lane: Alternating with the Provost of Sheffield
St. Oswald, Millhouses
St. Silas, Broomhall

Ecclesfield Deanery

St. Margaret, Brightside and St. Thomas, Wincobank: Alternating with the Crown.
St. Cuthbert, Fir Vale

Hallam Deanery

St. Timothy, Crookes
St. Stephen, Netherthorpe: Jointly with the Church Patronage Trust
St. Mark, Broomhill
St. Bartholomew: Jointly with Church Patronage Trust.

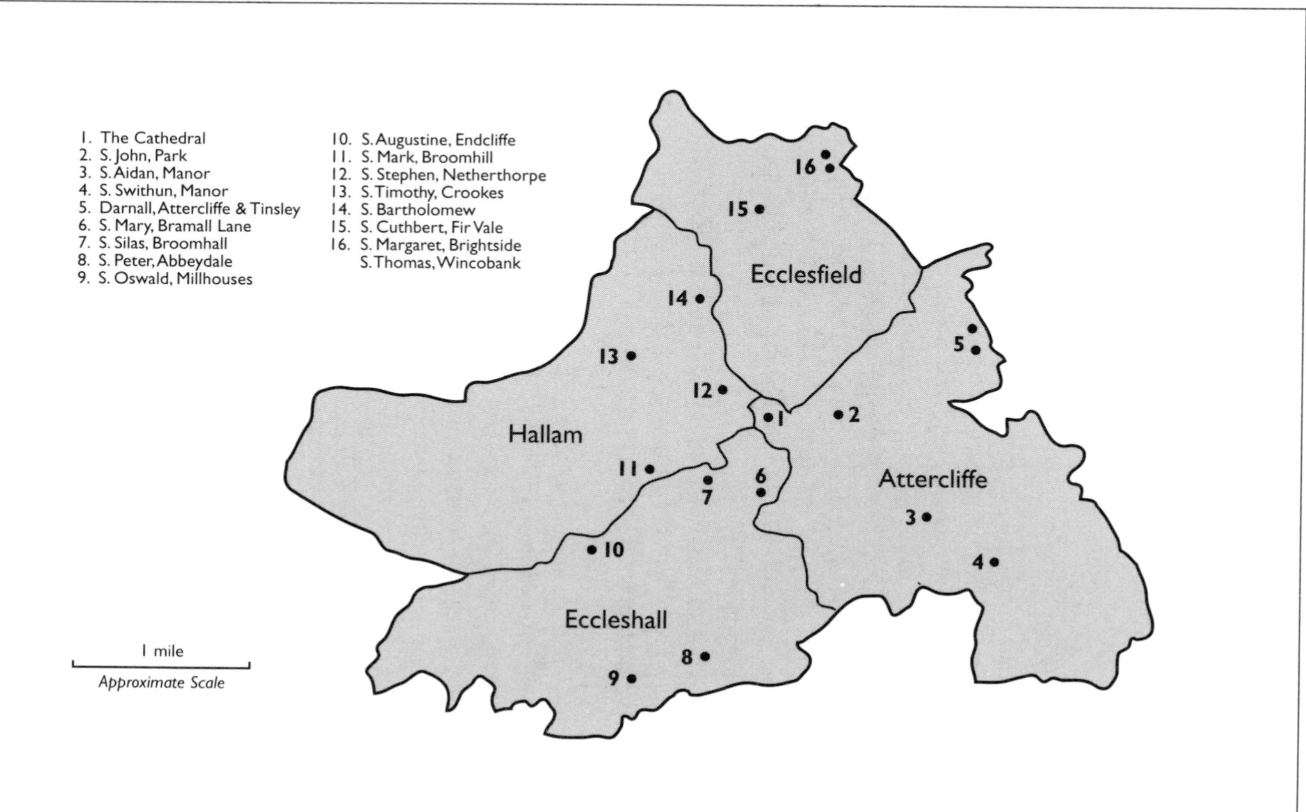

Churches in the Patronage of the Church Burgesses.

CHAPTER 5

The Building of Churches

THE VICTORIAN YEARS were a time of great expansion of Church provision in Sheffield, as elsewhere. The Church Burgesses' contribution to Church building during this period was limited but, as their resources grew, they provided a useful and timely support to new parishes as these were created. Initially, as we have seen in Chapter IV, that support was by way of endowment to provide clergy stipends. Then, at the turn of the century, grants for the building of churches began to be made. Although but a small part of the total sum invested in buildings for the Established Church, the grants were, nevertheless, of significance in individual parishes, often in the poorer parts of the city.

The first record of a grant for a church building, other than for the Parish Church, is in 1630, when the sum of £8 was paid 'towards the building of a Chappell at Attercliffe.' There was no further church building grant until 1821.

The Victorian Momentum

Until May 1740, when St. Paul's was consecrated, the Established Church had but three places of worship in the parish of Sheffield – the Parish Church itself and the chapels-at-ease at Attercliffe and Ecclesall. The population at that time was about 14,000. St. Paul's, built as a result of the generosity of a private benefactor, Robert Downes, was completed in 1721, but a dispute over patronage delayed its opening for 19 years. The Burgesses had a census of the parish taken in 1736 in an effort to speed up the opening of the church.[1] There were, at that time, lively and flourishing nonconformist congregations in Sheffield (Upper and Nether Chapel, Fulwood Chapel, Quaker Meeting House), but the Established Church had by no means kept pace with the growth of population. St. James's was consecrated in 1789 and that church, together with St. Paul's, added about 2,000 sittings to the 4,000 or so sittings in the other established churches. The Dissenting chapels provided 4,300 sittings between 1700 and 1790.

By 1820, the population of the parish was about 65,000 and by then it had been recognised nationally that the Established Church needed to undertake a massive programme of building new churches in order to reach out to the urban masses.[2] In 1818 Parliament voted £1m. for new buildings of the Church of England in populous areas not adequately served by existing churches. In 1824 a further £0.5m. was voted. Sheffield profited from four of these 'Million Act' churches: St. George's, 1825; Christ Church, Attercliffe, 1826; St. Philip's, 1828; St. Mary's, Bramall Lane, 1830. This was the start of the Victorian surge in church building. Where the Government had led, others followed in a concern for souls and good social order.

The munificence of private benefactors and the assiduity and acumen of Church Extension Societies and of public subscription schemes kept the momentum rolling. The first Sheffield Church Extension Society was formed in 1865, with the object of building seven new churches in five years. This was followed in 1877 by a second such Society. In 1869, the Sheffield Church Conference and Parochial Aid Society was founded. Eight churches were built by private benefactors, of whom two were Church Burgesses: Henry Wilson, who built St. Stephen's and St. Silas, Gilcar, and Sir John Brown, who built All Saints', Brightside.

Sir Robert Peel's Church Building Act of 1843 had cleared the way for the easier creation of new parishes. Stipends had to be found, of course, in addition to the provision of buildings, and the Ecclesiastical Commissioners were empowered to borrow up to £600,000 from Queen Anne's Bounty for this purpose. In Sheffield, the Church Burgesses and the Ecclesiastical Commissioners provided the bulk of the money for new stipends. Dr. Thomas Sutton, the Vicar of Sheffield, was indefatigable in creating new parishes carved out of his own empire. He used the provisions of the new Act to establish ten new parishes in addition to the Ecclesiastical Districts of Attercliffe, Darnall, Brightside, Wicker and Pitsmoor, created under previously existing legislation.

The momentum of building is striking, especially when it is remembered that the new churches were, for the most part, large buildings with seating capacities which would now be considered greatly excessive for modern congregations. The 1881 census shows that the number of sittings in established churches stood at 30,551, compared with 4,640 before the commencement of the building of the 'Million Act' churches. The number of new Anglican churches built during the Victorian period was:

1821-30:	4	1861-70:	4
1831-40:	4	1871-80:	7
1841-50:	4	1881-90:	3
1851-60:	6	1891-1900:	5

In addition, there were mission churches, vicarages and church schools, for building activity was by no means confined to parish churches. During these 80 years, population increased from just under 70,000 to about 380,000, so accommodation in the established churches was increasing at a slightly faster rate than the growth of the population. The total cost of all this building activity was not less than £165,000. (These were the days when St John's, Ranmoor, in all its Gothic grandeur, was built for £16,000). The Burgesses' contribution was but a token, at almost £5,000 over the eighty years. But, in addition, the Burgesses provided the sites for church and vicarage for Christ Church, Heeley and for St. Jude's, Eldon Street and for a vicarage for St. Barnabas, Highfield. More significant contributions were to come later, as we shall see. But it is worth remembering that this was a time when money for building churches was readily available. No doubt a good deal of energy had to be expended in raising the sums necessary to provide church buildings, but the cause was regarded, almost universally, as a worthy one and support came from many quarters. More difficult was finding the means to meet the regular, ongoing commitment of paying the stipends of the clergy. It was in helping to meet this recurrent cost that the Burgesses made their most valuable contribution in the Victorian boom years. There was another, entirely practical, reason for limited Burgesses' support for church building at this time. They had not built up sufficient capital reserves to allow them to dispense largesse on a significant scale. The following 40 years showed a somewhat different picture.

The Forty Years to World War II

Wickham, in his *Church and People in an Industrial City*, categorises 1850-1900 as the years of religious boom and, thereafter, we move into decline and fall. It is true that church attendance declined significantly in the inter-war years and thereafter. Yet, the demand for new church buildings continued, despite falling congregations. Either the people or the churches were not in the right place at the right time, or there was a conviction that the activity of church building would somehow bring back the people. Walton, in her *History of the Diocese of Sheffield*, paints a picture of Church leaders determined to maintain the living presence of the Church throughout the Diocese and especially in areas of new housing.[3] In November 1930, the Bishop of Sheffield launched an appeal to raise 100,000 guineas in three years to build 12 new churches, 10 or 12 new mission churches, and additional facilities for 30 parishes. The money was raised within the stipulated period, but only just. The Burgesses contributed £4,000, but only after some wrangling about how the money would be spent.

Part of the reredos in the Shrewsbury Chapel, Sheffield Cathedral, showing the Seal of the Church Burgesses.

Decline and fall there may have been over the 40 year period, but 25 new churches were built in Sheffield during this time, matching quite surprisingly the heyday of Victorian building, although fashion, and necessity, had moved towards the provision of somewhat smaller buildings. The scale of grants by the Burgesses during this period was much greater than previously, as follows:

	£	
1901-05:	2467	
1906-10:	9334	
1911-15:	4592	
1916-20:	300	
1921-25:	9360	
1926-30:	13,535	
1931-35:	14,875	
1936-40:	4162	Total: £58,625

Some grants to individual parishes were very substantial and went towards the cost of both new church buildings and parsonage houses. (There must have been some very substantial vicarages built during this period!) We may note the most significant grants:

	£
St. Aidan, Park:	7085
St. Alban, Darnall:	9372
St. Barnabas, Highfield:	1990
St. Cuthbert, Fir Vale:	2760
St. Margaret, Brightside:	7865
St. Nathanael, Crookesmoor:	2202
St. Oswald, Millhouses:	3179
St. Peter, Abbeydale:	2611
St. Simon, Eyre Street:	1550
St. Swithun, Manor:	9433
St. Timothy, Crookes:	3346

The majority of these churches, built with such high hopes in the inter-war years, are either no longer functioning or face enormous difficulties in maintaining a Christian ministry in areas of desperate need and vestigial Christian allegiance.

Post-War building

The 1940 air raids caused considerable damage to church property in Sheffield. Two churches, St. Mark's, Broomhill and St. Alban's, Darnall were a total loss. Almost a complete loss were Christ Church, Attercliffe; Emmanuel, Attercliffe; St. James'; St. Simon, Eyre Street; St. Philip's, Netherthorpe and St. Luke's, Dyers Hill. Another 10 churches and 40 vicarages were badly damaged. It was decided that St. Anne's, Hoyle Street and St. Mary's, Bramall Lane should be urgently repaired; the rest could only be left largely as they were. Of these churches, all but three (Christ Church and Emmanuel, Attercliffe; and St. James') were endowed by the Burgesses. In Attercliffe and Darnall, war damage hastened the rationalisation of church buildings and it was decided, early in 1942, to unite the Attercliffe parishes and to centralise worship at St. Bartholomew's, Carbrook. By February 1945, the Diocese had produced a comprehensive plan, under the title 'Church in Action', for new buildings and refurbishment of church plant throughout the Diocese. A target of £750,000 was announced. Two and a half years later over £200,000 had been raised; a magnificent achievement, all things considered, but far short of what was required.

The Burgesses' contribution was slow in developing momentum, although substantial grants were made in the 50s and 60s. In the mid-50s, £12,500 went to the new church of St. Columba, Crosspool; £2000 to

William Temple church, Manor, and £2500 to the new tower of St. Cuthbert's. But it is in the late 70s and subsequently that Burgessess' spending on churches becomes very significant, as shown in the following table:

	Total Grants £	
1956-60	19,693	
61-65	21,376	
66-70	36,149	
71-75	47,861	
76-80	190,607	
81-85	260,558	
86-90	683,498	
91-95	872,494	Total: £2,132,235

Major beneficiaries of Burgesses' grants have included: Christ Church, Heeley: £56,000; Christ Church, Pitsmoor: £70,000; St. John's, Park: £75,000; St. Polycarp's, Malin Bridge: £50,000; St. Mary's, Bramall Lane: £74,000; St. Leonard's, Norwood: £63,500; St. Bartholomew's: £240,000; St. Swithun's: £150,000; Whirlow Grange Conference Centre: £85,000; St. Catherine of Siena: £90,000; St. Gabriel's, Greystones: £100,000; All Saints', Ecclesall: £125,000.

The Burgesses' contribution in retrospect

The Church Burgesses' impact upon church building has not been as great as that of the individual benefactors of the late 19th century, but their influence and effect have been steady and significant. In some cases, major grants for new buildings might well have made the difference between success and failure of a building appeal. In many more cases, the rapid response of the Burgesses to the need for urgent, major repairs, has been of enormous help to parishes. The vogue in recent years for reordering, rather than refurbishment, of churches has undoubtedly benefitted from some substantial grants. In many cases the timeliness of the promise of a grant has enabled an appeal to get off to a good and successful start. It is impossible to say what all this adds up to in terms of a contribution to the effective ministry of the church. But church buildings are important, both as symbols and as necessary plant, and it is fair to claim, for some inner city parishes especially, that Burgesses' support has been of significance in maintaining a Church presence. It is not only substantial grants towards new buildings, or major, costly, repairs, which have made an impact, although there have been many of these. It is also in responding quickly to a host of smaller needs that the Burgesses have made a significant contribution. Putting a new roof on an old building or eradicating the hidden devastation of dry rot, do not often generate enthusiastic giving, even from the church-going public. Yet, for many congregations, such expenses are well beyond their means and in such cases Burgesses' support has at least boosted morale, if not guaranteed survival.

The battle with buildings is constant; to maintain, to improve and, as occasion demands, to build anew. It is difficult to know which presents the greater challenge, an old, vast Victorian building, or a compact, modern church, subject, so often it would seem, to structural defect or heavy maintenance costs. Yet, the effort to maintain buildings is not, in itself, a diversion from Christian ministry but, again and again, is a spur, forcing re-assessment of priorities and of strategy for parish ministry as a whole. The Burgesses' contribution to ministry through church building is not confined to building grants. In assessing need and determining their own priorities, the Burgesses bring a wealth of experience which is also of value to the parishes. Their advice is sought often. They are not a faceless, grant-making body; but neither are they desirous of seeking to make policy decisions which properly belong to the parish and the Diocese, though the knowledge of the significance of their resource gives them an increasing right to demand better central planning. Their role has been one, essentially, of encouragement; encouraging Sheffield parishes in the maintenance and development of their ministry and encouraging the Diocese in respect of its Sheffield churches, by providing a useful resource in areas of priority need.

The considerable and continuing expenditure on buildings, of which the Burgesses' contribution is but a fraction, has to be set against a massive decline in church-going over the past one hundred years or so. The 1881 Census[4] gave a total Church of England attendance in Sheffield of 33,835. This figure may well have been inflated above the average attendance, and no direct comparison is possible with figures for current attendance. But direct and accurate comparison is not needed. The decline is all too evident. The total population of Sheffield has grown considerably during the past one hundred years and the proportion of church-going population has decreased considerably. For the four Sheffield Deaneries in 1995, the figure for average Sunday attendance is about 9,000, less than 30% of the 1881 figure. There is some evidence to indicate that the decline, seemingly so inexorable during the past century, has been stemmed, but there is no indication of any massive revival of church-going. It is, however, undoubtedly the case that in some parishes there is clear evidence of growth and renewal; a growth seen not only in numbers, but in the purposefulness and energy of the Christian ministry in these places. It would be reassuring, perhaps, to be able to say that investment in church building, both by way of refurbishment and of new building, has been a prime factor in such renewal. But no such conclusive statement can be made. The Burgesses' contribution to church building continues to be an act of faith in the continuing presence of the church in a parish, rather than an investment with a guaranteed return. And that, in retrospect, is probably the most valuable aspect of their contribution.

CHAPTER 6

The Church Burgesses and Education

THE CHURCH BURGESSES' support for education in Sheffield, though neither munificent nor spectacular, has been regular and consistent. As individuals, also, Burgesses have figured prominently in the establishment and governance of the Grammar School, the Boys' and Girls' Charity Schools, the Free Writing School and the University. With the development in the nineteenth century of denominational Day and Sunday Schools and of the Ragged Schools, the Trust developed a pattern of annual grants which continued over many years. The concern of the Burgesses for education derives from the provision in their Charter for assisting the poor and needy. Very early entries in their Accounts refer to help for 'pore scholers'. The Election Book has an entry for 13 August 1668 'that there be wood sett out in Ladye Spring for the erecting of a Schooll house on Sharramoor which is to be paid for by the Inhabitants of Ecclesall Byerly.' Although the 1854 Scheme broadened the activities of the Trust, expenditure upon education still had to relate to to the poor of the parish. Since the establishment of the Church Burgesses Educational Foundation in 1904 (which was given the status of an Independent Trust in 1953), support for educational activities and interests has been steadily broadened under successive changes to the instruments of administration of the Trust (see Chapter II), so that the Trust now operates, in respect of income applied for secular purposes, as a general educational charity. From 13s.4d. for a 'poore Scholler' in 1573 to a grant expenditure of £160,000 by the Church Burgesses Educational Foundation in 1995, is a transformation indeed. Yet a common thread runs through it all – a concern that worthy individuals shall be provided with educational opportunity by means of personal grants and that schools and other institutions shall be assisted in the maintenance and furtherance of their work. There has been another consistent interest in the educational work of the Burgesses over the past 150 years, reflecting the origins of the Trust as a body having prime responsibility for the Parish Church and its clergy. That interest lies in education by and for the Church of England. The Church Burgesses Educational Foundation is by no means an exclusive denominational body, and only about a quarter of its expenditure is currently directed specifically towards Church schools, support for clergy children and other Church interests. But the Foundation accepts that it has a particular relationship with the Established Church in Sheffield and seeks ways of strengthening that relationship.

We will trace, first of all, the Burgesses' support for the Grammar School, the Charity Schools and the Free Writing School and then go on to the wider canvas of the 19th and 20th centuries.

The Grammar School

The 'Free Grammar School of James, King of England', was founded by Letters Patent dated 6 May 1604, following a Petition by the inhabitants of Sheffield.[1] The foundation was made possible by the benefaction of Thomas Smith of Crowland, Lincolnshire (who had family connections with Sheffield), in his will of 2 July 1603.[2] Although a new foundation in 1604, the Grammar School took over a building in which there had been a school for some 40 years. That school may have been set up in response to an 'Homily against Idleness', preached by the Revd. Richard Haward, Vicar of Sheffield 1559-1567, in which he emphasised the value of 'godly learning'.[3] The Burgesses had not totally maintained the earlier school, but had made grants to it for specific purposes, including the payment of the Master's wages. The earliest reference to a payment to the school appears in the Burgesses' accounts for 1567:

Item paid to Mr. Yonge the scole mr. for the accomplyment of
his wages at Chrystmas: xis. viijd.
Item paid also to the sayd scole mr. at our Lady Daye: xiijs. jd.
Item paid also to the scole mr. for makinge upp his wages: xiijs. iiijd.

And in 1568:

Item gevyn to Mr. Yonge for the obteyninge of a Lycence
to kepe the schole: xs.
The pore Schollers iijd.

In 1573, there is the oft-quoted entry indicating that the Burgesses were prepared to give a grant for what we would now call 'higher education':[4]

Item gyven to Willm Lee a poore Scholler in Sheaffeld towards
the settynge him to the Universytie of Chambrydge and byinge him
bookes and other ffurnyture: xiijs. iiijd.

And William Lee has another mention in 1575:

Item gyven to Willm. Lee poore scholler towards his
exhibisyon at Cambridge. xiijs. iiijd.

There are other entries in the Accounts which show that the Burgesses made contributions towards the work of the school:

1593:	Item payd to Mr. Sampson ye Curate for his qrtes wages the third of June 1593 being ye first yt ever he was payd:	xxxvijs. vjd.
	Item more payd to sayd Mr. Sampson for helping to teach poore schollers under Mr. Craweshawe this first of Oct 1593:	xxs.
	Item payd to Mr. Craweshawe ye xvijth of June 1593 xvs. ye first yt ever he had payd of this accompt:	xvs.
1594:	Paid more to ye sayd Sr. Wm. Sampson for teaching xx poore schollers for iij quarter wages endyd at Penticost last:	iijli.
	Item gyven towards ye slating of ye School house	xiijs. iiijd.
1595:	Sr. Wm. Sampson vijli. xs. and for teaching xx poore schollers:	iijli.

(William Sampson was one of the three Assistant Ministers at the Parish Church. Another was John Machon, who, in 1596, was a tenant of 'ye Scholehouse and ye Croft at ye Townhead' for which he paid a rent of 6s. 8d.)

1598:	Item given to John Hall for teaching of poore children:	ijs.

Hunter quotes a survey of lands of the Church Burgesses taken in 1594 which has the following entry: 'The Schole house containeth 3 baies and a Cole-house all slated, which together with a croft and garden, orchard and a court containeth 0a. 3r. 0p. The rent is 12d.' It would appear that the new Grammar School took over this property. An indenture of 3 March 1619 granted a lease of the property to the Grammar School Governors. So the Burgesses supported the school through grant of the site for a nominal rent. The Burgesses continued paying for the maintenance of the school premises after the granting of the Patent for the foundation of the Grammar school e.g:

1604:	Item pd for Repayring of the Church house wherein the schollers are taught:	vs. viijd.
1605:	Item to John Belfeld for Repayring of the scholehouse:	xijd.
	Item pd towards the Charges of the free schole until such tyme as it can be collected in the town and parish and be repaid again:	iijli.
	Item pd to John Rodes for workmanship at the scholehouse:	vjs.
1606:	Item pd for makeing a seat for ye scholemr. and for nayles:	iiijd.

The Letters Patent stipulate that the governance of the school is to be in the hands of 13 Governors, one of whom is to be the Vicar of the Parish. The other 12 were initially nominated by the Earl of Shrewsbury and thereafter, as vacancies occurred, the surviving Governors elected replacements. Seven of the twelve foundation Governors (other than the Vicar) were Church Burgesses at the time of the foundation and William Dickenson, a foundation Governor, was elected a Burgess in 1606. The Church Burgesses continued to take a proprietorial interest in the school. Individual Burgesses, as Governors, made up deficiencies in the school's accounts from time to time, as, for example, in 1620, when Malin Stacie loaned £3.17s.2d., for which he was paid back £3.5s.2d. To meet running costs, an assessment was made in 1606 upon householders of the town, raising £103.18s.3d. Whereas Sheffield avoided a Church Rate (because the Church Burgesses met the expenses of the Parish Church), the town experienced an education rate very soon after the foundation of the Grammar School.

In 1644, the school house was described as 'not habitable' by the Governors in a petition to Lord Fairfax. The scholars were temporarily moved out of the old building into the workhouse in West Bar Green while a new school was being built. The new building was erected in 1648 on the site of the old school, the Burgesses continuing their lease at a nominal rent of 1/-s. In 1647 the Burgesses made a loan of £100 towards the new building. Thereafter, contributions from the Burgesses' funds are rare. In 1794, they made a loan of £100. But in 1802, the Governors of the Grammar School, having received £800 from the Duke of Norfolk, were loaning £700 to the Burgesses, repaid in 1818.

There is a report in 1764 of the School 'being in a flourishing state.'[5] But in 1828 the Charity Commissioners reported a 'reduced condition' with only 21 boys, due to 'the preference of the inhabitants for a mercantile education.'[6] The minutes of the Church Burgesses and of the Governors of the Grammar School were not formally separated until the beginning of the nineteenth century; the proprietorial interest of the Burgesses had remained strong. In a minute of 17 February 1809 it was resolved that a letter should be sent to the Revd. Charles Chadwick, the Headmaster, expressing concern about reports in circulation conveying reflections on the School. 'The Burgesses would not wish to interfere', they wrote, but 'as Guardians of the School, they expect the Headmaster to take proper steps for vindicating its character.' The Headmaster wrote back to reassure, but pointed out that his own recent illness had been very troublesome and he implied that the Burgesses should have held back their criticism. The Burgesses replied on 6 April in a repentant response, but with a slight sting in the tail:

> 'The Governors of the Grammar School have that respect for themselves that they would not have their own feelings by Reflections on those Visitations of Providence which all are trouble to. So far as the Master of the Grammar School suffers such Afflictions, the Trustees feel great sympathy and offer their best wishes for his recovery . . . The Governors have heard of unnecessary severity and want of Authority in the inferior department.'

By 1823, the Townhead buildings were dilapidated and a new building was erected by public subscription. The Burgesses exchanged the old lease for a new lease of 595 years of a site in St. George's Square, still at a nominal rent of 1/0s. This new building was in use until 1885, when the Grammar School amalgamated with Sheffield Collegiate School, ultimately to be incorporated in the King Edward VII School. In June 1886, the old Grammar School premises and two adjoining corners of land were conveyed to the Technical School Committee, the forerunner of Sheffield University, whose Mappin Street buildings now stand where the former Grammar School was. The Grammar School merger with the Collegiate School was effected under a Scheme of 1888. The Governing Body of the merged school consisted of 15 Governors, plus the Vicar of Sheffield. Surprisingly, perhaps, the Church Burgesses were not one of the bodies having the right to appoint Representative Governors. However, of the 15 Governors appointed initially, seven were either Church Burgesses at the time or were elected to the Trust within a year or two following. The remaining assets of the old Grammar School foundation are now administered as a charity through the Grammar School Trust.

It is odd that the King James Free Grammar School of Sheffield never developed the strength and reputation which one finds in so many other Royal Grammar School foundations. One might have expected, in such a populous town as Sheffield, that a Grammar School would have prospered well beyond what was achieved in the only moderately successful and chequered history of the town's Royal foundation. True, it had some notable, even distinguished, alumni, whom Moore-Smith in his paper describes.[7] But the flowering of excellence, so typical of many Royal foundations, was lacking here in Sheffield. The passing of the Royal Grammar School seems to have occasioned no great public concern. It sank without trace, except for the continuing Grammar School Trust. In the definitive *History of the City of Sheffield, 1843-1993* it rates barely a mention.[8] The Grammar School in the mid-nineteenth century does not stand out as a beacon of learning. Sheffield's educational provision at that time was poor. Thomas Sutton, the Vicar of Sheffield, had in 1839 stated that school provision was totally inadequate for the poorest classes in the parish and Holland's statistics of 1840 confirmed Sutton's views.[9]

Although the Grammar School was an independent foundation, the Church Burgesses, individually and collectively, were undoubtedly of substantial influence. If we have here a school of insufficient vigour and excellence to survive the educational upheavals of the 19th and 20th centuries, it is fair to ask whether some of the failings of the school may be laid at the door of the Church Burgesses. It is possible only to express an opinion; a detailed assessment of the causes of failure to establish a flourishing school of continued high reputation would take us into much wider territory. But some pointers may be given:

1. Close identification of the Church Burgesses with the Established Church (the Vicar also being an ex-officio Governor) may not have been helpful. The radical Non-Conformity of Sheffield may well have tended to categorise the Grammar School as a creation of the Established Church. There are towns where such an identification would have been a strong commendation, but that would not be the case with many Sheffield inhabitants. Furthermore, the arrangement for the selection of the Free Scholars, whereby individual Governors nominated in turn as vacancies arose, may well have contributed to a view that here was a school controlled by a coterie of the Established Church.

2. Very few former pupils of the Grammar School became Burgesses. Moore-Smith lists 106 notable alumni between 1621 and 1829. Of these, only six were elected Church Burgess. R.E. Leader lists a further 27 former pupils who attended the school in the mid-19th century. Of these, only two were elected Burgess.[10] At no time, therefore, was there a strong contingent of former pupils present as Burgesses. One does not have to be a former pupil of a school to have a strong commitment to the office of Governor of that school, but it is noteworthy that so very few Burgesses had direct experience of being taught in the school they were governing.

3. The comment of the Charity Commissioners in 1828 that the reduced condition of the school could be ascribed to the preference of the inhabitants for a mercantile education is revealing. The emphasis upon trade skills in the early 19th century was particularly strong in Sheffield. Early to work meant early to earn, and an academic education would have been regarded by many as a distraction from the business of fitting oneself to earn a living. But it is strange that Sheffield differed from so many other towns dependent upon trade and commerce, where grammar schools flourished alongside other means of training young people for work.

But, when all these factors are considered, there is a sense of opportunity missed, perhaps because of lack of civic pride and civic endeavour. Sheffield lacked the municipal grandeur of Birmingham or Manchester. And the Church Burgesses and the Grammar School Governors seem to have lacked the will to create a school of eminence to stand on a par with other ancient foundations. Their concern was with dispensing charity rather than with creating excellence.

The Boys' and Girls' Charity Schools[11]

The Boys' Charity School for orphan boys was founded in 1706, largely at the initiative of the Revd. Nathan Drake, Vicar of Sheffield, and Robert Turie, one of his Assistant Ministers. The school started with ten boys and a few girls taught in a room in the Shrewsbury Hospital. Generous subscriptions enabled an early start to be made upon a purpose-built building. The Duke of Norfolk gave £30 per annum. Joseph Banks (a Church Burgess) gave £100 and the land at the north-east corner of the Churchyard (now East Parade) upon which the school was erected, coming into use in 1710. Later, Thomas Hanby bequeathed £3000, from which interest payments began to be made to the school in 1787. Around 1830 Thomas Watson (another Church Burgess) gave £2000 to the school. A new building, which still stands, was erected in 1825, which the Charity Commissioners referred to in 1879 as externally resembling 'a superior town residence of the early part of the century.' There was a further enlargement in 1899. A playground was provided on the roof (paid for by Samuel Roberts), following complaints of the behaviour of the boys, who had been accustomed to use the churchyard as their playground. The Trustees of the school convinced themselves that in this new playground the boys 'were in less danger of accidents and of confrontation from depraved characters without'. At the time of the 1895 Enquiry by the Charity Commissioners, 8 of the 12 Governors of the school were Church Burgesses. The school moved in September 1911 to much larger premises in Psalter Lane and it changed its name in 1922 to The Bluecoat School, just about the time that the old Bluecoat uniform was phased out in favour of nondescript grey.

Initially clothing, feeding and instructing 20 poor boys, with the dress of a blue uniform, after the fashion of Christ's Hospital, London, the school had 100 boys in 1845 and was still at that number at the time of the move to Psalter Lane. With the outbreak of war in September 1939, the Bluecoat School building was taken over by the Army and the school never resumed its activities, its assets ultimately being transferred in 1954 to the Bluecoat Foundation.

The Girls' Charity School was founded in 1786; the Revd. Edward

Goodwin, an Assistant Minister at the Parish Church and Curate of Attercliffe, being one of the prime movers in its foundation. A handsome building, opposite the Boys' Charity School, was built at that time at a cost of £1500 to house 60 girls. The school still stands, now used as solicitor's offices, but still bearing the inscribed stone in its facade proclaiming its original purpose. On 15 May 1872, the Burgesses minuted that the Treasurer of the School had enquired whether the Burgesses would sell the freehold of the site. In response, the suggestion was made that, instead of erecting a new school on the old site, the possibility should be explored of a more open site in the country. This course was followed and in 1875 the school moved to Mount Pleasant, Highfield, to occupy the house originally built by Francis Hurt Sitwell in 1786. It is a well-proportioned, imposing red brick structure, built in what was then a most salubrious neighbourhood. The school closed around 1960, and in 1962 its assets were added to those of the Bluecoat School to form the Sheffield Bluecoat and Mount Pleasant Educational Foundation, which still continues as a charity.

Whilst the Church Burgesses Trust did not have direct responsibility for the affairs of the Charity Schools, their contributions to the upkeep of the schools were regular and were maintained over a long period. The Burgesses were also concerned that the pupils of the Schools should have appropriate religious and moral instruction. Following the 1805 alterations to the Parish Church, they commenced negotiations to ensure that pupils from the Schools should have an allocation of pews. Some complicated negotiations with the Boys' School broke down in July 1806, with the Governors apparently virtually walking out of the discussions. The Burgesses minuted that the negotiations were abruptly broken off by the Boys' School. 'The Burgesses do discharge the Boys from sitting in the Pews in the Open Gallery. Ordered that notice be sent to the Girls' Charity School that the Girls can be allowed (during the pleasure of the Burgesses) to occupy the Pews alluded to.'

In 1804, the boys of the Charity School were paid £1 as a year's payment for keeping the churchyard clean, a very modest sum, one might think, for such a duty. That, of course, was before they were barred from using the churchyard as a playground.

The first regular subscription to the Charity Schools began in 1828, with a sum of £5.5s.0d. being paid to the Girls' School. Thereafter, contributions to both Schools were paid on an annual basis, with an interruption of payment between 1850 and 1869. In the 1840s, the subscription was increased to £10.10s.0d. and to £100 in 1870. A summary of the pattern of grants follows:

	Total Grant £	
1828	5: 5:0	(Girls' School only)
1830	10:10:0	
1850	5: 5:0	(Girls' School only)
1870	150: 0:0	
1880	300: 0:0	
1890	290: 0:0	
1900	325: 0:0	
1905	375: 0:0	
1910	365: 0:0	
1920	600: 0:0	
1930	350: 0:0	
1935	500: 0:0	
1939	920: 0:0	(including special grant of £250 to Boys' School)

By 1830, the total cost of running the Boys' School was about £1000, so the Burgesses' contribution was not much more than a mere token at that time, and at no time did the Burgesses' contributions to either school represent a substantial part of the Schools' budget, but were, no doubt, useful in providing supplementation of income and indication of support from an influential quarter.

The Free Writing School[12]

In his will of 1715, William Birley bequeathed the sum of £900 to the town, to be split three ways: £300 for 'encouraging writing and arithmetic', to be taught at the free school (viz. the Grammar School) or such proper place, by a fit person; £300 for the stipend of a minister at the Shrewsbury Hospital; and £300 to old and indigent tradesmen or their widows. A schoolhouse for the Free Writing School (which followed on from the Birley will), with Master's house attached, was built by the Burgesses in 1721 on land adjoining the site of the Grammar School. In 1746, Goodwin notes that 60 boys were being taught there.[13] In the early days, the Writing Master at the School also taught at the Grammar School. Ralph Gosling, the map-maker, was a master at the Free Writing School, probably until 1755. Henry Coward (the distinguished musician, later knighted), was Master at the School from 1879 until the School closed in 1888. He thereafter devoted himself to music.

Not all the Masters were as distinguished as Coward or Gosling. In 1821, we read in the minutes:

> 'Owing to the gross negligence of the Master, the School and School House and Fences are in a ruinous state of dilapidation. It is evident that Mr. Job

Cawood the present Writing Master is imprisoned for debt and has given notice . . . of his intention to take the benefit of the Insolvent Act. Resolved that Mr. Cawood, having appeared in custody before the meeting and requested that he would be able to open the School on Monday and intended to put it in proper order – he be allowed to occupy the premises till Christmas on condition of living in the House and keeping that part of the property in order which it is incumbent upon him to do and on condition that he conduct himself in a regular and orderly manner.'

With the Grammar School buildings being dilapidated in the 1820s, and a new road (School Croft) being made through the site, the Free Writing School was rebuilt in approximately its old position. The Town Trustees contributed £200 towards the new building and the Burgesses paid bills totalling £670 in 1827 and 1828. The School was extended in 1847 as a result of what appears to be some gentle arm-twisting by Mr. Henry Wild, the Master at that time. The Burgesses minuted on 21 March 1847:

'Mr. Henry Wild, the master of the Free Writing School, having intimated to several of the Burgesses he had been offered a Government Appointment for life as Schoolmaster to the Convicts at Woolwich with a salary of £100 a year, and they, having stated he would remain in Sheffield if a Class Room were added to the present School Building and which was found too small for the accommodation of the Scholars – Resolved: that in order to retain the valuable services of Mr. Wild . . . it is the opinion of this meeting that the School Building be enlarged by the addition of a Class Room thereto, that the outlay should not exceed £100 and that this Trust contribute one third thereof.'

The enlargement was duly completed, the Burgesses purchasing in June 1847 a small piece of land adjoining School Croft for £150 and, in 1848, contributing £33.6s.8d. towards the cost of the building.

In 1880, the Trustees of the Grammar School, needing funds for their removal to St. George's Square, sought to take over the assets of the Free Writing School. The Charity Commissioners produced a Draft Scheme in 1885, which the Burgesses opposed. In a very full minute of 20 April of that year the Burgesses recorded that they viewed with alarm the proposal to appropriate the Free Writing School premises for the benefit of the Grammar School. In that minute is set out the history of the implementation of William Birley's charity, demonstrating the independence of the Free Writing School. In June 1886 the Charity Commissioners responded and amended the Draft Scheme in the light of the Burgesses' representations. Whilst the Birley endowment of the Free Writing School was handed over to the Grammar School Governors, the premises remained with the Burgesses. But they were poor premises. In 1885, Mr. A.F. Leach, an Assistant Commissioner under the Endowed Schools Act, had visited, in connection with the proposed takeover by the Grammar School, and had reported that, with 60 pupils on the books, he found an 'an old, dirty-looking, draughty building with one large room and a small classroom and no lavatory'.

In December 1888, an application was received to use the now disused Free Writing School premises as a place of worship for poor Jews. Thomas Flockton, the Surveyor, reported in January 1889 that 'the property appears to be suitable for adaptation for a small manufactory or other similar purposes and I recommend it be advertised and let on a 99 year lease', which recommendation the Burgesses accepted. The area around School Croft, a collection of poor housing, small workshops and ale houses, all very congested and insanitary, deteriorated into a bad slum area and in the late 19th century was known as 'The Plague Spot'. A slum clearance scheme was drawn up by the Town Council and in 1896 the Free Writing School was purchased by the Health Committee of the Council and was demolished in 1900 to make way for new developments.

Aid to Church Schools

By the late 18th century, the pace of industrial development in Sheffield, with consequent growth of population, was exceedingly rapid. But of social advance for the masses there was little sign. Moral stagnation went hand in hand with dreadfully poor housing, lack of education and churches that made little impact upon areas of greatest need. To help combat the great nuisance of undisciplined, truculent and lawless children, the first Sunday School was established in a private house in 1785 by a Mrs. Loftus. Denominational Sunday Schools quickly followed, with a Methodist foundation in 1798.[14] The Denominational Sunday Schools gave priority to religious instruction, but reading and writing were also taught, although there was much dispute about the propriety of such secular instruction being given on the Sabbath. Jabez Bunting, the Wesleyan minister, did his utmost to stamp out this practice.[15] When, in 1808, during his Sheffield ministry, Bunting's eye 'fell upon children in Sunday School being taught to write, his indignation knew no bounds. Here was an awful abuse of the Sabbath'.[16]

By 1840, Sunday School attendance in Sheffield was about 13,000 at 100 schools, of which about 4,000 attended 38 Church of England Sunday Schools.[17] At that time the population of the parish was 112,000. Ward has said: 'Sunday Schools were the only religious institution which the nineteenth century public in the mass had any intention of using.'[18] Opinion is deeply divided as to the merits of this institution, which developed so rapidly in the 19th century. Salt quotes a local wit who once said that the early Sheffield Sunday schools were like the sperm oil lamps that were used to light the town's streets before the introduction of gas lighting: 'they shed little light, but drew attention to the surrounding darkness.' R.E. Leader[19] is much more positive: 'Another beneficent legacy handed down from the dying eighteenth century to the nineteenth and appearing as a ray of light streaming through black clouds, was the establishment of Sunday Schools.' E.P. Thompson[20] is not persuaded, and uses Lecky's blunt description, 'religious terrorism', to describe some of the denominational excursions into education.

Where the Sunday Schools had led, the day schools followed, with the Churches being prominent in founding schools which would provide for the working classes a minimum of instruction coupled with moral precept. The National Schools of the Church of England for Promoting the Education of the Poor in the Principles of the Established Church (founded in 1811) raised substantial sums voluntarily and took the lion's share of the money voted by the Government, after 1833, for education. The British Schools of the Non-Conformists (supported by the British and Foreign Schools Society, founded 1814), followed on. In 1825, there were in Sheffield, 6 National day Schools, 2 Lancasterian Schools and 35 (mostly small) private academies. By 1840, the picture was one of rapid growth and varied provision:

		Schools	Pupils
Schools:	Endowed	8	407
	Church of England	24	3345
	Wesleyan Methodist	5	700
	Lancasterian	2	1114
	Roman Catholic	2	133
	Total	41	5699

In 1848, the Ragged School was founded, to reach out to the very poorest, and ultimately attracted considerable numbers.

In spite of burgeoning activity, educational provision in Sheffield in the mid-19th century was meagre. Although Samuel Roberts, in his autobiography, was writing of the turn of the 18th century, we can catch something of the atmosphere of schools at that time from his description, which is worthy of Dickens:

> 'The teacher . . . a gentlemanly personage, his name was Quinn . . . I remember him the best by his sitting with a plate of cherries before him, eating them slowly, one by one, and when he had done, proclaiming a scramble for the stones upon the floor, most of which stones found their way down our little

throats . . . The old gentleman had about 500 scholars, crowded under different teachers, into five separate rooms.'

In 1840, not more than 50% of the school-aged population regularly attended school and only one third appeared to be able to 'read fairly.'[21]

It was against this background of growing, yet very inadequate, provision in education that the Church Burgesses began to make their contribution, small though it was, to education in Sheffield. Their first grant of £5 was made in 1832 to Ecclesall. This was followed, in 1836, by a grant of £20 to Pitsmoor and of £5.5s.0d. to the Parish Church for their Sunday School. Then, in 1840 and subsequent years, a number of grants:

1840: Towards the erection of Schools for the poor at Crookes: £50.
St. Mary's National Schools: £50.
Fulwood Schools: £30.
1841: St. Mary's Schools: £30.
1842: Attercliffe School: £30.
Owlerton School: £30.
Eldon Street Infants and Sunday Schools: £30.
1843: Crookes School: £20.
1844: St. George's School: £100.
1850: Attercliffe National and Infants Schools: £10.

After that, a twenty-year period in which no grants were made to education. Grants resumed in 1870 and continued regularly thereafter. These grants were made, almost wholly, to Church of England schools, although there were occasional grants to the Ragged Schools (ranging from £75 to £150 over the period 1870 to 1874) and to Lancasterian Schools. Total annual grants made to Church Schools are shown in the Table following. For the most part, annual grants paid to individual schools were small, usually of the order of £30-£50.

Grants to Church Schools

	£		£
1840	130	1920	1406
1850	10	1925	2772
1860	Nil	1930	1969
1870	150	1935	1796
1880	241	1939	1135
1890	532	1945	1316
1900	793	1950	1008*
1915	1230		

*Payments in each of the two previous years were over £3000.

The Church Burgesses Educational Foundation.

The Church Burgesses Educational Foundation was constituted as an independent Trust on 10 December 1953. Some reference to the work of the Foundation is necessary to complete an account of the Burgesses' interest in education. Under the Scheme establishing the Foundation, the main Trust assigns five-eighths of two-sevenths of its income (i.e. about 18%) for educational purposes, the application of this income being decided solely by the Educational Foundation. Five of the Foundation's Trustees are appointed by the Church Burgesses Trust and one each appointed by Sheffield Education Committee, the University of Sheffield and the Sheffield Diocese.

From the outset, grants made by the Foundation have fallen into four main categories:

i. *Schools:* these are made to Church of England Schools in Sheffield, mostly for educational equipment and books.

ii. *Special Grants:* for educational activities by organisations. These include grants to Independent and Local Authority Schools and organisations which provide or encourage, for example, theatre; outdoor pursuits; music. There may sometimes be an overlap of interest here with the secular grants of the main Trust.

iii. *Youth Organisations:* such as, Scouts and Guides, the YMCA and YWCA, Youth Clubs and the Cutlery Apprentices' Scheme.

iv. *Individual Grants:* mostly to children at school, including clergy children for costs of tuition at independent and boarding schools, but also for further education, for music tuition and instruments, for special educational needs and for overseas and adventure expeditions.

From time to time, grants have also been made for other education-related activities, such as Bibles and hymn books for schools and, for the period 1958-74, towards the cost of salaries, such as those for the Diocesan Youth Chaplain and Diocesan Drama Director.

Grants to individuals have always figured strongly, amounting to 30% to 45% of total expenditure, and may involve substantial investment in children at boarding schools. Grants to youth organisations have usually been as significant sums paid to a relatively small number of organisations each year. Of interest is the growth over the years in allocations to Church Schools. For many years varying between only 3% to 5% of the Foundation's total expenditure, this has moved up, in recent years, to around 15%; that is, about £20,000 per year. Grants made to individual schools cover the cost, for example, of computers, audio-visual and science equipment, as well as books.

Of interest also is the Foundation's support for music in the City. The Burgesses have, over a very long period, supported music at the Cathedral, through contributions for the choir, the organ and organists, and, in addition, there have been grants to promising young musicians (for tuition and instruments) and for choral and orchestral activities involving children and young people. Recently, with the severe cutbacks in Local Authority funding for music, the Foundation has increased its grants in support of music tuition and orchestras.

CHAPTER 7

A Charity For All Seasons

> 'The said twelve Principal Burgesses and Commonalty of the said Town and Parish of Sheffield and their Successors may convert and bestow the whole Surplus of the Rents and Profits of the Premisses over and above the several necessary and convenient Stipends and Sallaries of the said three Priests and Chaplains from time to time as often as it may be needful and necessary towards the Repairs of the Parish Church of Sheffield aforesaid and the Bridges and highways and the poor and needy inhabitants within the said Parish.'

SO READS THE CHARTER. We must note that, whilst there is an obligation upon the Burgesses to pay the stipends of the three priests, other payments are discretionary. From the outset, however, it is clear that an order of priority was established by the Burgesses. First in that order came repairs to the Parish Church and then came relief of the poor of the parish and, thirdly, contributions to highways and bridges. That order of priority continued unchanged for 300 years and, following the 1854 Charity Scheme, the only change introduced thereafter was that contributions for the poor were channelled wholly into hospitals, education and the like. Whilst payments for highways and bridges have rarely been little more than a token, those for relief of the poor have been rather more than that and represent a genuine attempt by the Burgesses to allocate their limited resources so as to have some effect within a broad area of considerable need. Within the last 100 years the secular activities of the Trust have considerably broadened in scope, so that it now functions as a general purpose charity. What was a prior call upon resources for ecclesiastical purposes has now been changed into fixed proportions of income allocated to ecclesiastical and secular purposes.

Highways and Bridges

Clause 4[Q] of the 1854 Scheme (which is still in force) stipulates that the Burgesses shall contribute no more than £20 a year towards repairing the bridges and highways of the parish. This requirement is currently discharged by payment to the City Council of £5 a year – a token, and no more, of an ancient responsibility. But it has not always been so. The Burgesses' contributions to repairs of highways and bridges in the 16th and 17th centuries were rather more than a token and must have made some difference to travel in and around the parish. But at no time does it appear that the Burgesses accepted major responsibility for such repair. The Town Trust was more active in this regard.

In the 16th century there is a number of ad hoc payments for construction and repair of bridges:

1562: For mending Heely Bridge: £1 0s. 0d
1566: Given towards the making of Brightside Bridge: £1 6s. 8d.
Towards the making of Heeley Bridge: £1 0s. 0d.
1568: Mending Attercliffe Bridge: 6s.
Building of Owlerton Bridge: £1 0s. 0d.
1580: Brightside Bridge: £1 10s. 0d.
1583: Newe Bridge: £3 6s. 8d.

During this period, some of the Burgesses had responsibility for oversight of bridge repairs. Richard Jessop in 1580 for Heeley Bridge, Hugh Rawson for Attercliffe Bridge and James Rawson, who provided timber for Sheffield Bridge.

In the 17th century, regular payments for highways begin, in addition to contributions towards bridge repair and construction. £6 was paid for repair of Brightside Bridge in 1619 and a further £1 in 1647. The Burgesses provided timber for the repair of Heeley Bridge in 1662 and in 1667 a tree from 'Cold Pit Lane' was felled for the repair of Little Sheffield Bridge. The first 'block grant' for highways came in 1621, £7 being paid 'for amending highways in Sheffield, Brightside, Attercliffe and Darnall, Ecclesall and Hallam'. £9 was paid for highways and bridges in 1622, £7 in 1628, £9 in 1629 and £2.10s.0d. in 1631. There was no further contribution until 1647, when £1 was paid for repair of highways. In 1665, the first combined payment for 'highways and the poor' was made, a sum of £25, repeated in 1666, with £20 paid in 1668. Thereafter sums varying between £4 and £25 were paid for poor and highways until 1704.

Payments for highways begin again in 1708, when £2.10s.0d. was given. Very occasionally there is reference to payment for specific work undertaken, e.g.:

1707: Yt ye Overseers of ye High wayes of ye towne and parish have 50s. given them as hereafter menconed (vizt) 20s. thereof for repaireing ye cawsey & way betwixt Sheffeild Bridge & West forth Bridge, 15s. for repaireing Sheffield moor cawsey and 15s. for repaireing and Raileing hill foote Banke.

1724: Attercliffe haveing made a new Cowsey Cross their Moor at a Great expense ye Burgesses for their encouragemt have pd into Mr. Speight's hands to be appleyd at his discretion for the further Improvemt & bettering ye Cawsey & wayes there ye sum of £2 which ye collector payes now.

1727: Yt fifty shillings be given to nether Hallam to make a Cawsey with betwixt Owlerton Hall and ye Smithey by ye River and also twenty shillings for Mr. Speight to finish Attercliff Cawsey with.

1735: Ordered that £5 be paid to finish the Wicker Causeway and 50s. towards repairing Cowpit Lane.

1764: Ordered that 10 guineas be paid towards the building or repairing of the bridge over the Don between Colson Crofts and the Bridge Houses.

After 1708, payments for highways were made annually to 1854, the sums varying between £1 and £10. For the last 50 years of this period, annual donations are mostly around £1.5s.0d. to £3. Sometimes a breakdown is given by township as, for example, for 1728: Sheffield: £1.10s.0d.; Brightside: £1.13s.4d.; Ecclesall: £1.5s.0d.; Attercliffe: 16s. 8d.; Hallam, Nether and Upper: 5s.0d.; Heeley: 5s. 0d. It is not possible to discover any pattern in these annual payments. They do not seem to be related to the funds available to the Burgesses. Yet, the fact that the payments are regularly continued demonstrates that the Burgesses accepted some responsibility to make at least a token payment in fulfilment of their Charter. Reference to a highways 'gratuity' of £1.10s.0d. in 1819 and to a three years' 'donation' in 1830 indicates the charitable, rather than the obligatory, nature of the payments. The payments are not even round sums. One wonders how £3.1s.8d. for 1844 was arrived at. It was, of course, the Town Trust and its predecessor body which was the more important contributor to highways and bridges over the whole period from the 16th century until the establishment of local authority responsibility in the 19th century. Their records have many entries indicating that the Burgesses' contributions were quite minor. Of course, as the 19th century development of the town began in earnest, the Burgesses were called upon to pay substantial sums for road development, as this affected their estates. Subsequent maintenance of new roads became the responsibility of the local authority.

Hospitals

Well before the 1854 Scheme made specific provision for payments 'towards the maintenance and support of the Sheffield General Infirmary, the Sheffield Public Dispensary and such other Medical and Surgical Charities for the time being existing within the parish of Sheffield', the Burgesses had made contributions for the support of hospitals. The first record of a payment is 'To the Treasurer of the General Infirmary lately erected at Sheffield the Burgesses' subscription for 1798: £52.10s.0d.' Owen[1] has commented: 'In the realm of secular philanthropy the 18th century accomplished nothing of more ultimate importance than to lay the foundation of the voluntary hospital system.' It is interesting to note the Burgesses' early support for the first hospital in Sheffield and to remember that it was Dr. William Younge (Church Burgess, 1791-1838) who campaigned effectively for its foundation and was its physician from 1797 to 1838. Regrettably, the Burgesses minuted in April 1806 their decision that 'the Subscription to the Sheffield General Infirmary be discontinued because of the present low state of funds of the Trust.' A subscription of £60.10s.0d. was made to the Sheffield Public Dispensary in 1838. These contributions marked the beginning of regular payments by the Burgesses to hospitals in Sheffield. These were almost entirely annual grants for running expenses, although a donation of £210 was made for the Infirmary Fever Ward in 1839. Subsequently, as the Hospital for Women and the Childrens' Hospital were built, contributions were made also to those institutions. Payments for the Chaplain of the Infirmary began in 1856 with £50, increasing as the years went by.

There is a gap in hospital payments from the 1850s until 1870. Thereafter, annual contributions are regular until 1953. The pattern of hospital grants over this period was as follows:

	£		£
1870	180	1920	1455
1880	325	1930	1391
1890	407	1939	1532
1900	671	1945	1567
1910	881	1950	1780

Whilst not major benefactions, these payments must have been both welcome and useful as a part of the pattern of voluntary contributions which did so much to maintain hospital provision until the establishment of the National Health Service.

The Poor

In fulfilment of the Charter requirements to make payments from their surplus for the poor and needy inhabitants of the parish, the Burgesses' contributions fall into four categories:

1. Contributions towards general relief of the indigent population, as appears from the sums paid 'to the poor of the parish.'
2. Relief at times of particular distress, as with severely cold winters or when the price of bread has soared, following a bad harvest.
3. Contributions to individuals in response to particular personal circumstances.
4. Indirect contributions to those in need, paid to charitable organisations. These have included support for the Charity Schools and hospitals.

During the 450 years of the Burgesses' history, views on the poor have changed significantly. In Tudor times, the general view was of two classes of poor, the impotent poor and vagabonds. The former comprised the 'deserving poor'; the latter were not only undesirable, they were feared as a potential source of serious civil disorder and were not merely to be discouraged, but were to be suppressed. Hence the harsh penalties for vagrancy. Jordan[2] writes:

> 'The notion persisted that hungry men were idle men and that poverty was a consequence of a moral fault. Perhaps the most significant of all the social gains of the late 16th and early 17th centuries was when it came to be understood that not all who were forced to beg were actually or potentially vagrants of immoral disposition.'

It was in Tudor times that the statutory framework of the Poor Law was laid down. In 1597 a comprehensive Act for the relief of the poor was passed and, with slight amendment, remained in force for 250 years. Under this Act overseers of the poor were to be appointed with wide-ranging powers: to raise taxes; commit children to apprenticeship; to build poor houses. In the 17th century Puritan piety softened some of the harshness of earlier times, yet did not overcome it completely, but paved the way for the relative benevolence of the 18th century, when modern humanitarianism begins to emerge. True, that benevolence often had a hard, sharp edge to it; the poor were to be instructed and trained, put to work, to make themselves useful. As urban poverty grew in the 19th century, philanthropy flowered, combined with the working of the Poor Law, which still reflected the harshness and fears of former times.

The Burgesses, for their part, always seem to have operated a policy combining the two elements of relieving the deserving poor and providing opportunities for improvement. They both fed and clothed the poor and educated the children. Both elements are present from the very earliest records. The first reference to gifts to the poor appears in 1568, recording a payment of £1.6s.8d. to the poor inhabitants of Sheffield. The names of 59 recipients are listed, receiving gifts, mostly of 4d. and 6d, but one of 1s. and one 2s. It is also recorded: 'likewise, on the same day to the poor of the parish: Ecclesall: 3s.4d.; Hallam: 5s.0d.; Brightside: 4s.0d.' In the same year 3d. was given to 'three poor schollers'. Also recorded are payments for a boy being placed in service, which are worth stating in full:

1569: Item paid to John Sheldon on the viii day of March for Thomas Yowles sone, setting forthe to servis. First for iii yards and a halfe russet friese: iiis. Item paid for a yearde of carsaie for the said Yowlles boye xxiid. Item paid for a yeard lynen clothe to make hym a doblet: xd. Item paid for a yearde of canvasse to lyne the said dublet and a dossyne buttons for the same viid. Item paid for a shirt clothe and a coller for the said boye xvid. Item paid for halfe a yearde of whytte pleyne clothe for the said boye viid. Item paide for a paire of showes for the said boye: xd. Item for his aparel makinge xiiid.

Also, in the same year:

Given to Thomas Woodes wife for helping to set two of her children to service: 6s.8d.

Other early entries illustrate the general relief of impotent poor and specific help to individuals:

1570: For poor Robert Crook and Margt, Bright being poor people: 3s. 4d.
For cloth to set poor Lancelot Daughter to service to London: 5s.
Given to the poor of the Towne and Pishe of Sheffield: £3 10s. 0d.

This was a plague year, as several entries indicate:

For the charge of Antonie Hibbert and his wife . . . keeping in their home for 1 month for fear of the plague: £1 7s. 11d.
Paid for keeping of Hoole wife suspected of plague: 4s.
Towards his loss in plague time: 4s.
To Edward Pavye (Parish Clerk) serving Hibbert during the time he kept to his home: 2s.

1571: To poor Sick people at the Commandment of the Capital Burgesses as doth appear by our particular Book: 11s. 4d.
Money given unto the poor People of the Town and Parish of Sheffield Anno 1571 in every Byerlow as followethe: Hallam: 7s. 2d.; Ecclesall: 6s. 8d.; Brightside: 8s.; Attercliffe and Darnall: 10s. 2d.; Sheffielde: £1 8s. 4d.

1572: For ye Burial of ye poor Boye called Brodebent: 1s.

1573: To Robert Crosbye daughter at her setting forth into the Country: 2s.
To Harrye Steel when he laid sick at sundry times: 2s. 4d.
To Thomas Trippett when he was sick: 6d.

To the setting forth of two children to London: 5s.
To John Townened wife for to keep her husband that lyeth sick: 1s.
To the poor people within the Towne and pish. of Sheffield; £5 6s. 8d.

By the early 17th century annual grants had increased considerably, e.g.:

1619: To the poor: £10. 0s. 0d.

Individual grants still continued: To a blinde man: 2s. 6d.
To another poor man: 1s. 0d.

Thereafter, annual grants of £10 to £20 continue for over 200 years, supplemented by special grants from time to time. Sometimes, as for 1571, the amounts given to the various townships are recorded as e.g.:

1621: To the poor of Brightside and Attercliffe and Darnall: 10s. 0d.
1679: To the poor: Ecclesall: £1 16s. 0d.; Brightside: £1 13s. 4d.; Attercliffe: £5 6s. 8d.; Hallam: £1 16s. 8d.; Sheffield: £5 16s. 8d.

In 1630, the Burgesses gave £12 towards the building of the Workhouse. This was built on Burgesses' land in West Bar. A lease for 800 years was granted in 1665 and in 1825 a ground rent of 10s. was being paid.

The first combined payment for the poor and highways (£25) appears in 1665, and the first reference to overseers of the poor and highways comes in the following year. Entries relating to special and individual grants include:

1731: To overseers of the poor a years' rent of Thomas Spooner's house being Mr. Rollinson's gift to put out a poor child as apprentice: £1 0s. 0d. (this is a regular payment for many years).
1740: Last Winter the Accountant gave to the poor and indigent persons of the town and parish of Sheffield by order of the Burgesses on account of the Badness of trade and the extreme severity of the season: £30 0s. 0d.
1757: Paid William Broadbent the Town Collector to be laid out in Corn to be sold at under value to the poor inhabitants of the Town on account of the extraordinary dearness of Corn: £50.
Also paid to the several hamlets following the same account: Attercliffe and Darnall: £5; Ecclesall: £5; Upper Hallam: £2. 10s.; Nether Hallam: £1 10s.; Brightside: £5;
1760: Paid to the overseers of the poor over and above the payment of £15: £99 10s.
1761: Paid to the overseers of the poor over and besides the usual payment: £49 15s.
1773: To the poor of several districts buying corn to be ground and sold to the poor at the reduced price of 5s. per load: £99 10s 0d.; and the same again for 1774.

1785: £25 bequeathed by John Swann for a Sermon to be preached on 24 June yearly (St. John the Baptist's Day) and for bread to be given to the poor: Paid Mr. Bayliff (for the sermon) 10s. 6d. John Ash for bread to the poor: 9s 6d.

1789: To the poor of the several Districts in consideration of the inclemency of the season: £99 10s 0d.

1795: Paid to the poor of several districts in consideration of the inclemency of the season and in the same proportion as was paid to the poor on like occasion in 1773 and 1789: £99 10s 0d.
Also a further donation in consideration of the high price of Corn: £99 10s 0d.

1800: To Anthony Hufton the Burgesses' donation towards supplying the poor of Sheffield with soup: £10 10s. 0d.
To Gamaliel Milner to the poor of Attercliffe for the same purpose: £5.

1801: Donation to public subscriptions raised for relief of the poor of Sheffield in consideration of the dearness of provisions: £200.

In 1811 appears the interesting entry:

To overseers of the poor for labour at levelling and forming the street at the bottom of the new burial ground: £34 13s. 1½d.

– a form of outdoor relief it would seem.

In addition to normal annual grants of £5 to £18 in the early 1800s, additional gratuities of £50 were paid (£105 in 1812). And, for 1821, we read: Paid to Isaac Drabble, your subscription towards cloathing 60 poor men on the Coronation: £52 10s.

Also, in 1819, a donation of 20 guineas was made to the Society for Bettering the Condition of the Poor, followed by further donations of £25 in 1821 and £40 in 1827. The Society was founded in Sheffield in 1803, a response in part to the widespread distress, national as well as local, which followed the bad harvests and rising prices of the late 1790s. It was particularly active during the bad winters of 1816-17.[3]

In 1826, £50 was paid to the fund for relieving distressed manufacturers.

From 1825 until 1854 payments were made for clothing for 36 poor people. These provided hats and coats for men and bonnets and cloaks for women. Typical entries read:

1826: Battye and Sykes – cloth for the poor being 107¼ yds at 4s. 6d. less discount: £23 0s 4d.

1829: 36 hats and bonnets for the poor: £7 4s 0d.
36 cloaks and coats: £11 14s. 0d.
Cloth for making up: £20 19s. 0d.

In addition to the clothing, each of the 36 poor persons received a cash gift of £1. These distributions were made around Christmas time, on St. Thomas's Day. A minute of 29 November 1826 reads:

> 'Resolved that the persons to whom a coat and hat may be given by the Trust at Christmas shall be resident within the Parish but not necessarily Housekeepers, and that they be required to assemble at the Cutlers' Hall before going to Church on Easter Sunday.'

In 1838, 20 poor women were provided with bonnets 'at the Coronation of Queen Victoria', at a cost of £3.15s.0d. In that year also £150 was given for relief of distress of the poor, in addition to the regular annual subscription. In 1842, there was a contribution of £50 for blankets for the poor and £100 'for relief of the distressed poor on the occasion of the christening of the Prince of Wales.'

After 1854, payments to the poor cease. The new Charity Scheme which came into force in that year stipulated that the secular income of the Trust should be divided amongst hospitals and schools (three-eighths to the former, five-eighths to the latter). So ended 300 years of direct charitable relief of the poor.

Current charitable giving

Whilst there is no longer any direct payment to 'the poor', the Burgesses' charitable giving is on a considerable scale, through payments made, for the most part, to other charitable bodies working directly with and for those in need. The Burgesses are now able to make grants to societies and organisations whose purpose is the welfare of the sick and needy of the City or the improvement of the conditions of inhabitants. Such support has grown steadily over the years and for 1996 the total sum given to societies and organisations was just over £120,000. A list of organisations supported in 1996 follows. This is given, not to commend the largesse of the Burgesses, but to illustrate the range of voluntary activity under way at any one time within the City. The list exemplifies the vigour of the voluntary sector and the range of needs which fall outside the network and the capacity of statutory provision. That network may be extensive, but years of welfare state provision, however massive and costly, have served to prove the necessity and the value of a vigorous, responsive voluntary sector. The Church Burgesses remain very supportive of that sector.

Adult Feasibility Study
Age Concern
Angleton Youth
C.H.R.I.S. Fund
Child Helpline
Christ Church, Pitsmoor, Community Vehicle

Christian Action Network
Community Accounting Service
Darnall Welfare Rights and Advice Centre
Elim Pentecostal Church
Family Conciliation Service
Five Loaves Helping Hands
Grenoside Park Bowling Club
Hallam Diocesan Caring Service
House of Help
In the Boat
Lower Don Valley Forum
Manor Befriending Project
Manor Training and Resource Centre
Message
Netherthorpe After School Club
North Sheffield Disabled Help Groups
Phoenix House
Relate
S.A.F.A.R. Project
Sheffield Area Bereavement Forum
Sheffield Association for Teaching English
Sheffield Citizens Advocacy
Sheffield Family Service Unit
Sheffield Mencap
Sheffield Oratorio Chorus
Sheffield Samaritans
Sheffield Somali Special Needs Scheme
South Yorkshire Probationary Service
Spinkhill Senior Citizens Group
St. Mary's Community Centre
United Response
Victim Support
WEA South Yorkshire
Whirlow Hall Farm Trust
Woodseats Neighbourhood Centre

Citizen's Advice Bureau
C.R.U.S.E.
Dial a Ride Club
Ethel Trust
Firth Park Advice Centre
Five Weirs Walk Trust
Greystones Community Association
Ken Hawley Collection Appeal
Impact
Jigsaw
McMurphy's Drop In
Manor Community Association
Maypole
MIND
Norfolk Park Playwork Alliance
Parent Lifeline
Pitsmoor Adventure Playground
SADACCA Day Centre
Share (Contact Group Trust)
Sheffield Association for Cerebral Palsy
Sheffield Autistic Society
Sheffield Family Holiday Fund
Sheffield Homestart
Sheffield NSPCC
Sheffield Portage Project
Sheffield Victim Offender Mediation Project
South Yorkshire Counselling Centre
South West Area Sitting Service
St. Luke's Hospice
Trinity Day Care Trust
Unity
Voluntary Action Sheffield
Westbourne House
Work
Wybourn Basement Association

CHAPTER 8

The Burgesses' Estates

FOUR LANDOWNERS have been of particular importance in the history of the development of Sheffield. The Earls of Shrewsbury, whose estates passed to the Dukes of Norfolk; the Town Trust; the Church Burgesses and, latterly, dwarfing the others, the City Council. In the 16th century, the estates of the Burgesses were minuscule by comparison with those of the Earl of Shrewsbury. In 1519, the gross rental of all the English estates of George, the Sixth Earl, was £5500 and, later, of Gilbert, the Seventh Earl, £7500. In 1581, the rentals of the Shrewsbury estates in Sheffield totalled £555 per annum.[1] At that time, the rental of the Burgesses' property in Sheffield was about £40 per annum. Yet this relatively small rental represented some strategically valuable holdings of land, crucial to the later development of urban Sheffield.

In the late 16th century, the town of Sheffield, with a population of about 2,000, would be dominated topographically by the Castle, the Park, the Parish Church, the Market place, the Rivers Sheaf and Don with their bridges, and the natural hills and valleys, still very much in evidence. There would be two major streets converging on the market place and then leading on to Lady's Bridge across the River Don. The main features of the town's development are apparent from a succession of maps: Ralph Gosling's in 1736, and the views of the town by Thomas Oughtibridge (1737) and Samuel and Nathaniel Buck (1745); William Fairbank's maps of 1771 and 1797 and of John Leather in 1823. Gosling's map, which gives a population of 9695 (a slight understatement), still shows plenty of open space in what is now the densely developed City Centre. Immediately to the south-west of the Parish Church was Brelsforth Orchards; in the south-east lay Alsop Fields. To the west, barely a quarter of a mile from the Parish Church, began the open moor. Fifty years later, all open space in the centre of the town had been developed and expansion westwards was well under way. Much of this development involved Burgesses' land.

For nearly 250 years, the Burgesses' management of their estates was uneventful. Arrears of rent were chased, the occasional eviction threatened, necessary repairs of property were carried out and fences maintained. Maintenance of an agricultural economy was at least as important as responding to industrial developments, as these occurred. The Burgesses were conservation-minded well before the 'green movement' became fashionable. In administering the Birley estates, we read of decisions taken on 3 July 1806 in respect of the Neepsend woodlands:

> 'Ordered that Larches be planted amongst the young Elms, Ash, Sycamores, towards the west end of the Wood where they are much exposed to the wind, thinking it necessary for the Encouragement of the Growth of that Part of the Wood.'

They received the Surveyor's report that

> 'the Young plantation is very flourishing except in one part between the Woods of the Trust and the Duke of Devonshire's Wood, where the fence was broken down by Trespassers. Ordered that a Broad Ditch be made to prevent such Inroad.'

It was in the late 18th and early 19th centuries that all this changed as urban and industrial development proceeded apace. The first building lease for 800 years was to John Cooper, a shearsmith in 1737, requiring him to build one or more dwelling houses of value £60 on each of three plots of land in Pinson Crofts.[2] Thereafter, and especially towards the end of the century, many more building leases followed.

The early holdings

Most of the original holdings referred to in the Charter cannot be precisely identified. Clearly, there were significant areas of land in the Burgesses' ownership in Attercliffe and Darnall, in Sheffield Town Fields and Little Sheffield (the open land to the south-west). Lady's Spring, a wood in Meersbrook, features often in the Account and Minute Books and was carefully husbanded by the Burgesses. It was exchanged in 1800 for a farm of 23 acres at Fulwood. 'The Brushes' is probably Hinde House, adjoining Hinde Common Lane, developed in the early 20th century alongside Firth Park Estate. Pinson Crofts is the area which now comprises Union Street, Burgess Street, Cambridge Street. Part of the land at Walkley was sold in 1856 to the Waterworks Company and the remainder to Sheffield Corporation in 1906. There is something of a mystery about the land at Aughton, which is shown in very early accounts as giving a rent of 14s. per annum. But there is no record of any rent being received after 1580 and in 1642 an entry in the Account Book reads: 'Agreed that the arrearage for the land at Aughton should be struck out being £41.12s.0d. at 14s. per annum.' No further account of the land appears and it may well be that there was an exchange for land elsewhere.

The Old Change property is well documented. Originally, this comprised two houses near Cheapside known by the sign of 'The George'. William Fairbank describes it in 1768 as 'a tenement formerly known by the sign of the "Three Sugar Loaves", now inhabited by John Sandford and containing 36 square yards and 7 feet, and a tenement formerly known by the sign of the "Three Morris Dancers" and now inhabited by Henry Penn containing 121 square yards.' After a series of lets it went on a building lease in 1904 for a term of 80 years. In 1904 also a small adjoining property 32a Old Change was purchased for £3,500 and let at a rent of £550. In 1953, the Old Change property was acquired by the City of London Corporation for £10,300.

Over the 400-year period to 1950, the income from rents from holdings, which changed considerably during that period, increased 400-fold. Table 1, at the end of this Chapter, gives the figures. Throughout this period income from rent has remained the major source of income for the Burgesses. Commencing as a property-based Trust, they have so remained, but with a considerable widening of the base of their investment portfolio in recent years.

The Nineteenth-century development

In the earliest years of the Trust leases were generally granted for 21 years. Such changes as were made in the estates were largely by way of exchanges, many of which are recorded in the accounts. Sales and purchases began in earnest in the late 18th century. Leases, which had previously been short term, were, from 1731, granted as building leases, in appropriate cases for a term of 800 years. This continued for 50 years or so, when they were superseded by 99-year leases. Disposed of under 800-year leases were Pinson Crofts, Brelsforth Orchards (Leopold Street; Orchard Street); the Townfield Close (Gibraltar Street; Trinity Street).

The disposition of the Burgesses' property in central Sheffield around 1780 is shown in a sketch map in J.D. Leader's *Records of the Burgery of Sheffield*. This is reproduced as on p. 142. The property delineated may well correspond largely with original holdings referred to in the Charter. The map does not, of course, show holdings outside the immediate town centre, which included estates in Attercliffe and Darnall, Walkley, Heeley, Owlerton, nor the important central properties in Leavygreave and Portobello. In his 1768 plans of the Burgesses' estates[3], Fairbank gives the areas of all the holdings. In summary, these were:

	acres	rods	perches	
Attercliffe and Darnall	40	2	37	(40.73 acres)
Grimethorpe	1	3	36	(1.98)
Owlerton	1	2	34	(1.71)
Walkley and Hallam Liberty	19	3	5	(19.78)
Heeley	12	3	2	(12.76)
Leavygreave	16	3	13	(16.83)
Broad Lane	22	0	37	(22.23)
Broomhall Lane	4	2	15	(4.59)
Little Sheffield	6	1	10	(6.32)
Total	126	3	29	(126.93)

Significant changes occurred in the nineteenth century, both in the distribution of holdings and, more importantly, in the usage of land owned by the Burgesses in various parts of the parish. (see page 143) The changing value (mostly by considerable appreciation) of the Burgesses' property during the 19th century can be seen by comparing figures for 1825 and 1895 taken from the Reports of the Charity Commissioners in 1829 and 1898. Tables at the end of this Chapter compare areas and rentals of holdings and list acquisitions and disposals during this period. Of interest is the static value of land in Attercliffe and Darnall, Gell Street and Trinity Street. Land which rapidly appreciated in value over that time was in what are now the prime areas of the city centre: Fargate, Paradise Street, Burgess Street. A little further out, Broad Lane and Leavygreave also showed considerable appreciation. The Burgesses, with a clear eye on future residential and commercial development, invested heavily towards the end of the 19th century in the Glossop Road, Devonshire Street and Wilkinson Street areas. A very rough comparison shows where the valuable investments lay. Land in Attercliffe and Darnall in 1895 was returning under £3 an acre; that in Fargate £850 an acre. Between these extremes, Broad Lane yielded £175, Glossop Road £72 and Leavygreave £63 an acre.

The Burgesses' portfolio was a mixed bag. Not all, by any means, was high quality residential holdings. Some of the worst slums in Sheffield were, in the early 19th century, in the area around the old Grammar School, now Townhead and Campo Lane. On 25 January 1849, a deputation of tenants from Leicester Street (where there were some 90 dwellings on Burgesses' land) waited upon the Burgesses, and we read in the Minute Book that they

> 'stated that they had been required by the Sanitary Commissioners to remove the filth &c. which had accumulated in the Street in consequence of not having been either drained or pitched and having requested the Burgesses to bear a Part of the expense of properly pitching and draining the above Street.

Resolved: that the Trust contribute the sum of £10 as soon as the Street shall have been certified by the Magistrates as fit for the use of the public.'

In the latter part of the 19th and early 20th centuries some considerable changes in the Burgesses' estates were due to the wholesale development of the city centre and land was taken, sometimes by compulsory purchase, for new streets, street widening or for rationalisation required by the City Council. But the Burgesses pursued their own development interests, notably in the westward growth of the town up West Bar and Brook Hill to Leavygreave and Portobello and from Barker's Pool to Devonshire Street. The Burgesses' interests in building development began, as already noted, in the mid-18th century, with 800-year leases. In 1778, 99-year leases were introduced and these became standard for the westward development which began shortly thereafter. In 1825, there were 79 leases for 800 years, about 30% of all the leases in force at that time. By 1895, the number of 800-year leases had fallen to 38, comprising less than 10% of all leases. Practically all the new leases granted in this 70-year period were for 99 years.

Postles[4] has pointed out how, well in advance of statutory building regulations, the Burgesses imposed their own building controls through their leases. The covenants required of the lessee specify, not only the number and value of houses to be built upon each plot, but also the number of storeys and, in many cases, the materials of the building. A plan and elevation were required for each house and these had to be approved by the Surveyor to the Burgesses. Some of the materials' specifications are very detailed. A typical lease is that granted in 1803 to James Kirkby, silver plater, for a plot in Leavygreave.[5] The lessee is required

'at his own expense within a space of three years to make, build, erect and finish . . . according to a plan and elevation approved by the Burgesses two good and substantial Dwelling Houses of well-burnt brick and with Timbers of suitable strength and thickness to front Wilkinson Street, with the sum of £300 each at least, such dwelling Houses to be entirely of new materials, to be only two storeys high, to be faced with the best Stock brick, to be set back 66' from Wilkinson Street and to be fenced off therefrom by a brick wall with stone coping surmounted by Cast Metal or Iron Palisades...Trades excluded: soap boiler, sugar Baker, Distiller, Dyer, Melting and Tallow Chandler or any other business which shall be deemed offensive to the Neighbourhood... including Workshop, Steel Furnace, Warehouse, Manufactory, Cast Iron Foundry or Steam Engine, Slaughter House.'

The Burgesses were strict in requiring observance of the conditions laid down in covenants. We read that at their meeting on 26 April 1820, it was

> 'ordered that all persons who have not performed their building covenants be peremptorily required to do so by the Spring of 1821 or that proceedings do then be taken to eject them from their premises without further notice.'

The Burgesses were, however, prepared to change the conditions of a covenant where good reason was presented. On 5 July 1849, for example, they decided that 'John Fearn may have a new lease and that instead of the present Covenant to erect buildings thereon of the value of £300 he shall be required to lay out £100 only, which buildings however shall be not more than 9' high.'

On 11 March 1830, the Burgesses minuted:

> 'In future a clause to be inserted in building leases requiring the tenants to lay down a flagged causeway adjoining the streets and to pitch to the middle of the street with Bolders to the extent of their respective lots.'

In 1856, general principles were laid down for developments at Leavygreave:

> The houses to front Glossop Road to be set back 9' and those to front the new Hounsfield Road to be set back 6'.
> The houses to be three storeys high, neither more nor less.
> The premises not to be used as Workshops or Manufactories of any kind or for the purpose of any trade or business whatever which shall be considered objectionable by the Burgesses, with special restriction against Public Houses, Beershops or other places of public entertainment.
> No goods to be exposed in front of the buildings.

However, these principles proved to be too restrictive in their application, for the Surveyor reported on 6 January 1860: 'after your judicious alteration in the resolution stipulating three storey houses at Leavygreave, I have found no difficulty in letting off a considerable portion of the land.'

The properties in Glossop Road still constitute a fine example of late Georgian town buildings, the whole development being improved and upgraded in the 1990s.

What had been a rural estate in the mid-18th century became rapidly urbanised. Mostly, new leases were granted for building modest houses and small workshops or warehouses. William Fowler's Directory of the Burgesses' Estates, prepared in 1851, shows that there were at least 2000 houses on Burgesses' land at that time, with scores of workshops, public houses and warehouses. The investors who fuelled this urban development of the Burgesses' estates fall essentially into two categories. There were local builders who built and leased their properties, and the second category comprised cutlers and allied tradesmen – shearsmiths, scissorsmiths, filesmiths, and the like. Commonly, a cutler would take a lease on a plot of land, build a workshop, and then several other small houses around it. Profits from the business were ploughed into real estate, not into the business itself. This pattern of investment may well explain why so many 'mesters' remained 'little mesters'. As Postles has indicated, such investment may well have been regarded as the best hedge against the cyclical nature of business, but it remains true that profits invested in property diluted the capital available for business.

We may note that, whilst the Burgesses sought to preserve confidentiality in so much of their decision-making, they were much more open in their property dealings. They minuted on 18 September 1799:

> 'Resolved that no person shall hereafter be considered as tenant to any lot of land, whether for building purposes or otherwise, until he shall have had the consent of the Burgesses at a public meeting.'

They were also keen to learn from others, as appears from a minute of 20 August 1849.

> 'Mr. Fowler (the Surveyor) sought to establish a general rule relating to renewal of leases. After considerable discussion it was resolved to ascertain the practice which obtained amongst large owners of property in other towns.'

Mr. Fowler had to report on 4 October that no general principles appeared to be established.

Urban and residential development

Urban development westwards out of the town centre was the key to the growth in value of the assets of the Burgesses in the late 19th century. Holdings around 1900 are shown on p. 143. It was not a smooth and easy development. The Leavygreave development exercised the Burgesses not a little. In 1862, Mr. Flockton, their Surveyor, was reporting that 'the time is generally unfavourable for building operations.' But, on 31 January 1867, he could, with satisfaction, report that 'the Leavygreave land is nearly all disposed of at a rental of £230.0s.1½d. plus £74.11s.11d for which proposals are agreed.'

Comprehensive development was undertaken in the area bordered by Upper Allen Street and Devonshire Street and, further to the west, between Brook Hill and Wilkinson Street. The extent of the landholding in this area at the end of the 19th century can be seen from Table 2. The developments would have been still more extensive had not the Burgesses been generous and self-denying in granting land for the new St. George's Church and

Schools and, later, to the emerging University. In 1817, $2^{1}/_{2}$ acres between Broad Lane and Portobello Lane were given for the St. George's Church, in exchange for 15 acres at Attercliffe; not a good bargain for the Burgesses. Later, what was then the Technical College acquired the old Grammar School premises at St. George's and the Burgesses sold off to the College and its successor, the University, land between Charlotte Street and Abney Street and Broad Lane and Portobello Street. This made possible the provision of a single, large site for University development. Partially to compensate for the loss of this prime, central block of land, the Burgesses extended their holdings in Brook Hill, and in 1860 bought the old Water Works Company in Leavygreave and built Hounsfield Road.

Also, five acres of land between Devonshire Street and Fitzwilliam Street, known as the Blacklands, was developed between 1820 and 1840 by constructing Wellington Street, Trafalgar Street, Chester Street and Eldon Street and the whole of this area was very quickly fully built up.

Many of the holdings shown on the 1780 map are no longer in the Burgesses' ownership. Queen Street properties were sold to the Town Trust at the end of the 19th century for road widening and, on the north side, sold to the Trustees of the Queen Street Chapel. Snig Hill, Water Lane and Newhall Street freeholds were acquired by the Sheffield Corporation in 1902. Castle Street properties were exchanged in 1856 for land at Crosspool. Plots in Bullstake (now the Haymarket) were sold in 1866 to the Midland Railway Company and the remainder in 1871 for the construction of Commercial Street. Market Place properties were sold at the end of the 19th century either to the leaseholders or were compulsorily acquired by the Corporation for road widening. In Fargate, a parcel of land was acquired by the Council in 1882 and a further plot in 1894 and the large plot at the junction of Fargate and High Street was leased to John Walsh for building purposes. But other land in Fargate was retained for development. In 1875, a 99-years' lease was agreed with Truswell's Brewery at 3s. 6d. per square yard, subject to a minimum of £4000 being spent on development within five years, later revised to seven years.

Attercliffe and Darnall

The Burgesses' largest holdings in area were, for many years, in Attercliffe and Darnall. Originally, as an agricultural holding, it was made up of a collection of strips. From the mid-18th century various exchanges were made to consolidate the holding. A number of these exchanges was with the Staniforth family, several of whom, in earlier days, had been Burgesses. By this process of exchanges, the number of plots was reduced from about 30 to 8 or 9. So the land became manageable for development purposes. But the transition from agricultural land to industrial and residential use was not an easy one. The Surveyor repeatedly refers in his reports to problems in managing this substantial part of the Burgesses' estates. We get a sense of the frustration in managing the transition from a minute of 30 January 1873:

> 'I am sorry to have to report unfavourably of your property at Attercliffe and Darnall as agricultural land. The increase of the works and smoke and the great number of trespassers in that locality render farming there a very undesirable occupation. Fences are down in all directions and it seems impossible to maintain them . . .
>
> Against this discouraging account of the land from an agricultural point of view must be set the fact that the changes to which it is due have been at the same time in converting some of it into building land and that probably a much greater income may be eventually derived from letting this on a building lease than is provided by the whole estate at present.'

The Burgesses appointed a committee to report back upon proposals for future development. In January 1875, the Surveyor was reporting that 'considerable expenditure in road making may be necessary if the Darnall estates are to be let for building.' And, in July 1883, the Surveyor was still very cautious: 'I am unable to report favourably on the condition of present prospects of the remainder of your estate at Attercliffe or rather Darnall. It is a transition state.'

The Burgesses faced a problem common to so many developers – how to realise the potential of their assets when they lacked the capital required for the initial infra-structure. Not only was road building necessary, but much of the land needed making up before any development could take place. Fortunately, the availability of waste from nearby works resolved the problem. Hard core from the Atlas Works of Sir John Brown (then a Church Burgess) was extensively tipped over a number of years, which not only levelled and consolidated the land, but provided a useful source of income. By the end of January 1885, the tipping from the John Brown works was approaching termination. A Total of 109,000 cubic yards had been tipped, yielding £2040 to the Burgesses. The final account for tipping was presented in January 1889, with total income amounting to £3125.

The Burgesses did almost as well out of the proceeds of tipping on their land as they did out of coal. We first read of receipts from coal in 1750:

> 'Received £100 from Joseph Alsebrook and Joseph Swift to get Coals on Church Lands in Darnall called the Little Leylands and Great Leylands.'

Receipts over the next 50 years from this source totalled just over £1800, ranging from £42 to £130 per year. As late as August 1872, a new lease for getting coal was being granted to Thomas Jeffcock, agent of Thomas Staniforth, 'whose lands are intermixed with those of the Trust.' A further lease was agreed in July 1873 of land in what was referred to as 'the Darnall Coal Field'.

Coal was found elsewhere on the Burgesses' estates, but royalties were meagre. £30 came from Leavygreave in each of the two years, 1753 and 1755. Broad Lane yielded £278 between 1757 and 1759 and the Black Lands of Little Sheffield gave total receipts of £223 between 1764 and 1769. In 1756, the Burgesses were doing their own surveying, for they paid David Jonathan Smith £15.4s.4d. for 'boring, sinking and trying the Coal in the Church Lands near Sheffield.' In 1767 there is an entry in the account book: 'Samuel Jeffcock on account of the purchase monies for the liberty of getting coal in the Church Lands near Little Sheffield Moor now in the possession of James Kirkby £30.' In 1760, disused machinery from coal operations was being sold off: 'Received of Messrs. Binks for Engines, Utensils and other Materials sold them from the Church Coal Pitts £36.17s.9d. Received of Mr. Clay £13 for an old Engine sold him from the same Coal Pitts.'

At the beginning of the 20th century, there was some further income from coal. During the period 1899-1912, the Nunnery Colliery yielded just over £6000 in royalties and rents.

Outlook for the future

Investment in property has always been regarded by charities, in the past, as sound and safe, providing a reasonably assured income and preserving the value of capital assets. In more recent times, that policy has come under increasing pressure and scrutiny. Although there may be greater risks involved in the stock market, there are also distinct possibilities of better returns, both as income and capital appreciation. Furthermore, the preservation of a capital base in property now demands much more by way of active management than used to be the case.

Properties that were once prime City centre sites become quickly blighted by out-of-town developments. Enhancing the development potential of a property demands, more and more, a policy of active consolidation to give larger sites. Maintenance can now rarely be a matter of merely keeping a property in good repair, but is much more likely to call for substantial, costly improvement in order to keep abreast of the market.

All these pressures mean that the Burgesses are unlikely in the future to make the sort of impact upon city centre development that they made in the 19th century. Holdings in property are likely to decline in favour of investment in equities. Small scattered properties will, presumably, either be sold off or retained only where consolidation with neighbouring sites is possible. Any prime city-centre properties must be assessed in terms of their future yield and not as historic holdings. None of this should mean a change in the ethical stance of the Burgesses in relation to their investment, but it will almost certainly mean that the era of being beneficent landlords is past and investment management has taken over.

Table 1: Income from Rents

Year	Total Rent £			Year	Total Rent £		
1557	30	5	5	1750	296	12	2
1565	30	9	5	1775	382	16	6
1575	30	11	2	1800	797	17	4
1600	48	13	4	1825	1210	1	2
1625	100	5	3	1850	2178	13	1
1650	148	8	2	1875	2487	7	6
1675	178	0	0	1900	6004	17	11
1700	183	7	4	1925	10981	8	8
1725	221	10	5	1950	12206	10	1

Table 2: Holdings in 1825 and 1895

	1825				1895			
	Area: acres	Annual Rent £			Area: acres	Annual Rent £		
Attercliffe and Darnall	66.14	203	14	3	65.15	194	17	4
Allen Street	2.89	53	0	5	0.78	51	13	7
Balm Green	0.33	17	5	0	–	–		
Bell Hagg	14.29	21	19	4	–	–		
Beet Street	–	–			1.14	45	11	1
Brelsforth Orchards	1.57	20	2	10	0.25	106	3	9
Bridge Street	–	–			0.29	267	0	0
Bright Street	0.04		10	0	0.04	12	0	0
Broad Lane	3.54	112	17	11	1.28	224	15	6
Brook Hill	–	–			0.84	65	13	0
Broomhall Lane	3.81	27	4	3	–	–		
Broomhall Street	–	–			0.28	12	4	0
Burgess Street	2.53	25	7	6	0.03	50	8	4
Button Lane	2.63	36	0	0	0.50	29	8	2
Cambridge Street	–	–			0.15	75	8	4
Castle Green	0.10	5	5	0	–	–		

	1825		1895	
	Area: acres	Annual Rent £	Area: acres	Annual Rent £
Castle Street	0.15	12 12 0	0.08	100 0 0
Charlotte Street	0.71	1 0	0.46	30 12 10
Chester Street	–	–	1.57	89 18 0
Church Street	0.17	13 16 10	–	–
Coal Pit Lane	0.80	5 2 3	–	–
Cornhill	0.44	9 11 6	0.20	24 18 0
Dee Street	–	–	0.18	10 14 4
Devonshire Street	–	–	1.52	65 14 10
Edward Street	1.28	31 7 6	1.00	43 3 1
Eldon Street	–	–	1.00	64 2 8
Fargate	0.81	66 12 0	0.59	498 11 0
Figtree Lane	0.07	13 13 0	–	–
Fulwood	23.08	40 0 0	23.08	50 0 0
Gell Street	1.31	27 15 6	1.15	19 1 5
Glossop Road	–	–	3.45	254 14 8
Grimesthorpe	2.73	16 19 0	0.07	35 15 0
Hallam	54.61	141 14 4	–	–
Hanover Street	–	–	0.37	45 13 4
Harrison Street	0.40	17 1 4	–	–
Haymarket	0.17	16 7 6	–	–
Heeley	4.09	29 4 0	2.08	93 17 10
Hinde House	2.68	9 9 0	2.88	16 9 0
Leavygreave	5.84	104 18 6	3.63	219 7 3
Leicester Street	–	–	1.13	53 15 7
Loxley	0.47	10 0	0.26	10 0
Market Place	0.13	13 12 0	0.07	131 0 0
North Street	0.22	9 2 6	0.49	114 16 6
Owlerton	1.77	11 5 0	1.10	9 9 0
Paradise Street	0.52	15 7 10	0.15	125 0 0
Pinstone Street	0.96	7 6 5	0.20	15 5 0
Portobello	–	–	0.59	29 9 7
Queen Street	0.79	53 7 7	0.73	213 18 4
Ratten Row	0.03	8 4	–	–
Red Hill	0.21	4 6 6	0.45	68 10 0
School Croft	0.97	9 11 5	0.70	64 7 2
Scotland Street	0.41	4 0 8	0.59	5 15 2
Sims Croft	0.79	7 5 2	0.90	8 2 4
Snig Hill	0.19	13 17 0	0.18	190 0 0
Solly Street	1.37	27 15 3	1.34	114 7 0
Spring Lane	0.80	8 0 0	–	–
St. Philip's Road	–	–	0.22	22 3 6

	1825		1895	
	Area: acres	Annual Rent £	Area: acres	Annual Rent £
Stephen Hill	–	–	14.55	62 13 0
Stud Field	0.25	5 0	0.13	1 0 0
Tenter Street	0.04	13 17 0	–	–
Townhead Street	0.13	8 8 4	–	–
Trafalgar Street	–	–	1.77	86 5 6
Trinity Street	1.26	19 1 6	1.05	16 0 4
Tudor Street	0.04	18 0	0.04	18 0
Under-the-water	0.16	10 8 0	–	–
Union Street	0.14	1 0 9	–	–
Walkley	17.42	79 15 0	14.92	33 15 6
Water Lane	0.16	8 1 0	–	–
Wellington Street	–	–	1.55	75 15 2
West Bar	0.67	37 2 6	0.58	82 5 6
West John Street	–	–	0.28	15 10 2
Wheeldon Street	0.32	6 8 4	0.32	34 13 4
Wilkinson Street	0.20	2 6 0	2.24	82 19 6

Table 3: Acquisitions between 1825 and 1895

	Area: acres	Annual Rent: £
Beet Street	1.14	45 11 1
Bridge Street	0.29	267 0 0
Brook Hill	0.84	65 13 0
Broomhall Street	0.28	12 4 0
Cambridge Street	0.15	75 8 4
Chester Street	1.57	95 1 10
Dee Street	0.18	10 14 4
Devonshire Street	1.52	65 14 10
Eldon Street	1.00	64 2 8
Glossop Road	3.45	254 14 8
Hanover Street	0.37	45 13 4
Leicester Street	1.13	53 15 7
Portobello	0.59	28 9 7
St. Philip's Road	0.22	22 3 6
Stephen Hill	14.55	62 13 0
Trafalgar Street	1.77	86 5 6
Wellington Sreet	1.55	75 15 2
West John Street	0.28	15 10 2

Table 4: Disposals between 1825 and 1895

	Area: acres	Annual Rent: £		
Balm Green	0.33	17	5	0
Bell Hagg	14.29	21	19	4
Broomhall Lane	3.81	27	4	3
Castle Green	0.10	5	5	0
Church Street	0.17	13	16	10
Coal Pit Lane	0.80	5	2	3
Fig Tree Lane	0.07	13	13	0
Hallam	54.61	141	14	4
Harrison Street	0.40	17	1	4
Haymarket	0.17	16	17	6
Ratten Row	0.03		8	4
Spring Lane	0.80	8	0	0
Tenter Street	0.04	13	17	0
Townhead Street	0.13	8	8	4
Under-the-water	0.16	10	8	0
Union Street	0.14	1	0	9
Water Lane	0.16	8	1	0

Chapel of the Holy Spirit, Sheffield Cathedral, looking North.

Church Burgesses' lands marked

Church Burgesses' lands in Central Sheffield about 1780.

Church Burgesses' lands in Central Sheffield about 1900.

CHAPTER 9

The Men of the Trust

(Note: In writing this chapter, the *Biographical Register of Burgesses* prepared by P.J. Wallis has been invaluable. This was originally published in the *Transactions of the Hunter Archaeological Society*, Vol.7: 1952, 51-62; 1953-54, 144-157; 1955, 194-199; 1957, 344-360. It was revised and expanded in 1986 by S.E. Fowl, and by David C. Wilson in 1997. In referring to individual Burgesses, the reference number in the Register is given, followed by the dates of service as a Burgess. For example, Edward Rawson (12.3, 1594-7), indicates that this Burgess is the third in line of succession to the Burgess listed 12th in the Charter and he served as a Burgess during the dates stated.)

The Biographical Register is reproduced as Appendix VII and contains a complete list of Church Burgesses, with dates and order of succession.)

THE CURRENT MEMBERSHIP of the Church Burgesses Trust provides a fair indication of the pattern of interests, influence and connections, not untypical of the Trust over the long period of its history. Of the current Burgesses, two have held office as Master Cutler, two as High Sheriff and two have strong family connections with previous Burgesses. There are two solicitors, one judge, one accountant and one chartered surveyor. One is in the steel industry, one in engineering and two are chief executives of commercial enterprises. One was formerly a Vice-Chancellor. Unusually, one is a clergyman. They are staunch Anglicans, to a man.

It is stipulated in the Charter, that to be elected, a Church Burgess must be an inhabitant of the town or parish of Sheffield and a discreet, reputable and honest man. There is nothing here about Church membership. In practice, with but few exceptions, Church Burgesses have been members of the Church of England. They have also, for the most part, been prominent in the town's affairs in different ways, with many inter-connections with the Cutlers' Company and the Town Trust. Of the 288 men who have served as Church Burgesses since the inception of the Trust, 25 have held office as Master Cutler, 9 as High Sheriff and 7 as Mayor or Lord Mayor. 68 have served as Town Trustees. As we shall see, some prominent families have been very well represented on the Trust, with extensive networks created through

Charles I, three Burgesses, James Bright (9.5), Stephen Bright (4.3) and Malin Stacey (5.4), had demonstrated that they were not the King's men when they refused knighthoods and were fined for this refusal. Sir John Bright (4.4),depicted as a member of the Commonwealth Army in the Firth memorial window in the old North transept of the Cathedral, was 'the most active in Sheffield for the Parliament.' He had earlier protested against the King's intention of raising forces in the county without the authorisation of Parliament.[1] He was a Colonel in the Commonwealth Army, Military Governor of the City of York and was involved in the siege of Pontefract Castle. He was, for a time, Governor of Sheffield Castle. In 1643 he was made a Parliamentary sequestrator for the estates of delinquents. His religious sympathies are evident in his appointment of the Puritan Revd. William Bagshaw as his domestic chaplain and he patronised ejected ministers who refused to assent to the 1662 Act of Uniformity. Another member of the family, Revd. John Bright (2.8), succeeded Thomas Toller as Vicar of Sheffield and maintained Toller's strong Puritan tradition. The Brights were not alone amongst the Burgesses in their Parliamentary sympathies. James Creswick (7.7), also a Parliamentary sequestrator, is described as a 'most zealous Commonwealth man.' He had strong connections with Puritans and Presbyterians. His daughter, Sarah, married Thomas Birbeck, son of the Presbyterian Thomas, who was ejected from his Ackworth living after earlier appointment as Assistant Minister in Sheffield and Curate of Attercliffe. James Creswick's nephew, also James, was ejected from the living of Freshwater. Edward Saunderson (8.3) was another Burgess appointed as Parliamentary sequestrator. William Spencer (10.6), a Lieutenant Colonel in the Parliamentary Army, was imprisoned for a while by the Duke of Newcastle and had to pay £350 for his release. He married Elizabeth, daughter of Edward Gill, a Parliamentary Commander and Governor of Sheffield Castle, 1645-46. Wickham[2] has summarised succinctly: 'The Jessops, Brights and Spencers were decidedly parliamentarian in politics and puritan in piety.'

Allegiance to the Parliamentary cause and Puritan leaning commonly went together. The Brights – Sir John and the Revd. John – have already been mentioned, but there must have been a majority of Burgesses at that time of the Puritan persuasion. The mid-17th century saw a clutch of Puritans appointed as Assistant Minister of Sheffield. They included Thomas Birbeck (or Birkbeck), John Bright, William Bagshaw and even Thomas Toller, following his retirement as Vicar of Sheffield. Bagshaw was ordained in the Presbyterian manner and pursued a well-regarded ministry at Glossop until his refusal to assent to the Act of Uniformity led to his ejection from the living. He then adopted a wider ministry, becoming known as 'The Apostle of the Peak', and established dissenting congregations in various parts of Derbyshire. John Crooke (1.7), a Parliamentary sequestrator, had a son John who, when Vicar of Denby, was ejected in 1662.

The power-base for Parliament and for Puritanism in Sheffield in the 17th century must have been considerable. Wickham sums it up: 'The three most opulent families of the parish were the Jessops of Broom Hall who were patrons of the living of Sheffield, the Brights of Carbrook and the Spencers of Attercliffe, . . . of like mind to the clergy whom they appointed and with whom they were related and intermarried.'[3] These were the families present in strength as Church Burgesses. It was William Jessop (3.2; 12.5) who, when patron of the living, presented Thomas Toller as Vicar of Sheffield in 1597/8 and thereby established the Puritan tradition at the Parish Church. His son, also William (2.7), in the same tradition, presented John Bright as Vicar, who later became a Burgess.

The Commonwealth and Restoration periods in Sheffield parish were confused, to say the least. John Bright the Vicar died in 1643, and in his place was appointed a Royalist Vicar, Edward Browne, whilst the Duke of Newcastle was in Sheffield with his army. When the Parliamentary forces took control of Sheffield the following year, Thomas Birbeck, formerly an Assistant Minister and a Parliamentarian, was appointed and, when he moved in 1646, James Fisher (brother-in-law of Stephen Bright (4.3)) became Vicar. David Lunn[4] states that James Fisher 'marks a crossroads in the religious history of Sheffield.' For, in addition to serving as Vicar of Sheffield, he also ministered to a 'gathered church of the truly faithful.' When Fisher was ejected in 1662 (along with all three Assistant Ministers), his 'other congregation' was not dispersed, but in fact was strengthened and James Fisher can properly be called the founder of the first Dissenting congregation in Sheffield. A contemporary diarist writes of Fisher: 'He deigns separation and courts all apostates', but a 20th-century assessment is very different: 'A man of great piety and worth, an excellent preacher and an instrument of much good.'[5] Thomas Birbeck, after his ejection from the living of Ackworth, returned to Sheffield. Dale records: 'He was a very worthy divine and a solid, substantial preacher; one of cheerful spirit, but much afflicted with the stone and did much good.'[6] Matthew Bloom, after his ejection as Assistant Minister, continued in Sheffield and had a licence as a Presbyterian to preach. He later joined forces with Rowland Hancock to form the Dissenting congregation at Shirecliffe Hall and, on division of that congregation, moved to Attercliffe Hall congregation. In the latter part of his life he carried on business as a maltster. Edward Prime, also an ejected

Assistant Minister, preached in his own house in Sheffield as a Presbyterian. So those clergy appointed by the Church Burgesses provided a solid base for the development of Dissenting congregations in Sheffield.

Writing of those who refused to assent to the Act of Uniformity in 1662, who were holding firm to their Presbyterian and/or Puritan convictions by refusing episcopal ordination and the use of the Prayer Book, Hunter has this to say:

> 'These men had doubtless their faults and their weaknesses. They cavilled about trifles. They were credulous about possessions. Their piety was for the most part of a severe and gloomy character. The frequency and the length of their religious exercises give great reason to suppose that many of them confounded the instrumental means with the ends of religion. Their notions of religious liberty were of the most confined description . . . But they had real, in-wrought piety; a deep sense of the importance of their pastoral office; many of them were persons of extensive reading and real learning; and their conduct was unimpeachably correct.'[7]

The Church Burgesses down the centuries have been staunch Anglicans, but, as the Church of England is a broad Church, so the Trust has had its non-conformists. William Staniforth (4.2, 1587-1621) seems to have fathered a line of non-conformity. One of his sons was formally reported for not using the Book of Common Prayer and three of his other sons were non-conformist ministers. John Staniforth (4.5, 1688-1704) was a member, first of the Shirecliffe Hall and then of the Attercliffe Dissenting congregations. Thomas Britland (6.9, 1659-96) was said to be a non-conformist. His second wife was the daughter of the Puritan Rector of Handsworth and widow of Robert Hoole, a member of the family which helped establish the Shirecliffe Hall congregation. Joseph Nicholson (2.13, 1671-93), with his wife, was a member of the same Dissenting congregation and then moved to the Attercliffe congregation. Joseph's elder brother, James (2.12, 1669-71), was closely connected with other dissenters: Robert Hoole, William Spencer, Matthew Bloom (former Assistant Minister in the Parish and subsequently Minister at Shirecliffe) and his widow; all these were founder members of the Shirecliffe congregation. The Spencers were a staunch dissenting family. William Spencer (10.7, 1667-86), a member first of Shirecliffe and then of Attercliffe Dissenters, sent his son Thomas (7.10, 1688-1703) to be admitted as the first pupil at the non-conformist academy in Attercliffe. Thomas Marriott (12.11, 1682-1706), a celebrated Parliamentarian, was active at Stannington Chapel, encouraging non-conformist ministers, and was executor for William Bagshaw. Joseph Banks (6.10, 1697-1726), whilst not himself a non-conformist, 'had his finger in every local pie' and was agent for the Dukes of Norfolk, Leeds and Newcastle. Hunter notes, 'He got a fortune very rapidly.'[8] He married Mary the daughter of Rowland Hancock, who was ejected as Curate of Ecclesall and became Minister to the Dissenting congregation at Shirecliffe Hall. Thomas Handley (4.7, 1713-46) faced opposition when he was elected a Church Burgess, it being held by some that he was 'not a good Churchman.' He had some of his children baptised at the Presbyterian Upper Chapel.

The Jessops of Broom Hall had an impeccable Anglican pedigree, but were not ill-disposed to Dissenters. William Ronksley, the schoolmaster, left a bequest in his will for the erection of a Dissenting chapel at Fulwood (built in 1728) and William Jessop (3.8, 1691-1734) and his heirs were appointed Trustees. They appointed the pastors of this chapel until the mid-19th century.[9] And just to show how broad a Church the Church Burgesses Trust can be, Thomas Heaton (9.9, 1729-1734) described on his memorial as being 'easy and agreeable . . . and died greatly lamented', is supposed in his correspondence to have expressed 'strong Jacobite sympathies.'

Perhaps it is only in the 17th century that allegiance to a party by the Church Burgesses comes through strongly. There was then evident support for the Parliamentary-Presbyterian-Puritan causes. Later, in the 19th century, there was a strong evangelical cast to the Vicars of Sheffield, but it cannot be said that the Burgesses were as committed to the evangelical ascendancy as they had been to the Puritan cause in the 17th century. The Burgesses did not assume any responsibility for patronage of the living until Henry Wilson's bequest of 1890. Their influence lay with the appointment of the Assistant Ministers until 1854. Thomas Sutton laid firm evangelical foundations during his long ministry of 46 years as Vicar. Yet it was during his time that the Burgesses appointed George Trevor, definitely not an evangelical. Either the Burgesses were seeking through his appointment to counteract evangelical tendencies (which seems unlikely), or they were genuinely persuaded that Trevor's abilities, rather than his churchmanship, should be given weight. And Samuel Earnshaw, appointed Assistant Minister in 1848, was again not an evangelical. Wickham states, he was:

> '. . . certainly one of the most distinguished ministers that ever adorned the pulpit of the parish, not only as a theologian of broad views, stoutly defending the humanities over against his narrow Evangelical brethren, but as a mathematician who could write on such abstruse subjects as the Sine and Cosine of an Infinite Angle, the Mathematical Theory of Sound, and the Molecular Forces of the Luminiferous Ether! One wonders which is the more impressive, his scientific capabilities or his length of service as assistant minister in Sheffield.'[10]

He must be, perhaps, the only clergyman in Sheffield to have had extracts from one of his sermons published by a Sheffield theatre on its bill-boards.

In the exercise of their patronage in the new parishes from the mid-19th century, the Church Burgesses were Low Church, rather than positively Evangelical. In this they reflected the prevailing Sheffield ethos. Father Ommaney at St. Matthew's, Carver Street (not a Burgesses' living), a firm, even perhaps a crusading, Tractarian, was an aberration in Sheffield (but a successful, even brilliant aberration). The Church Burgesses showed no wish to move in that direction in any of their appointments. They had, in 1843, addressed a memorial to the Heads of the Oxford Colleges, expressing disagreement with 'Puseyite principles.' They were quick off the mark with their protest; it was in that year that Pusey was suspended by the Vice-Chancellor for his Tractarian views. Earlier, on 21 February 1833, they had resolved to approve a petition to Parliament for the better observance of the Sabbath. For the Church Burgesses, this meant Sunday Schools and church going, but not High Church ritual. Low Church leanings were still evident in the late 20th century. James Merryweather (6.26, 1945-66), son of the distinguished Vicar of Carbrook, St. Phillip's and Fulwood, strongly maintained, whilst Churchwarden of St. Andrew's, Sharrow, that there would be no candles on the altar whilst he attended the church. None appeared until after his death. This was notwithstanding the rather splendid and prominent Rood cross atop the chancel screen.

Social standing, trade and profession

David Hey[11] has written of 'the Governors' of Sheffield (the men who served the highest offices in local society) in the 17th and 18th centuries. He has shown that the leading position of a few families, whilst evident over a period of time, was not maintained. Election to the office of Church Burgess was regarded as a high honour, 'but strangely, some of the most prominent tradesmen were never called to serve.' Perhaps the test of churchmanship was failed by some prominent citizens. Yet some of the wealthiest people of the town were amongst the early Burgesses.[12] In 1571, the three most affluent inhabitants of Sheffield township were Nicholas Stanyfforde, Widow Braye and Thomas Scargell. Thomas Braye, who died in 1569, was a Burgess (1.2). Thomas Scargell, also a Church Burgess (7.2), was perhaps the wealthiest man in Sheffield. The wealthiest inhabitants of other townships included: John Hoole, shearsmith of Brightside; William Burrows of Shirecliffe Hall and Hugh Chalnor, all Church Burgesses. But we must note that the wealthiest Sheffield citizens were not at all affluent by comparison with the Lords of the Manor with their vast estates.

Relatively modest wealth combined with sound social standing were therefore evident from the outset. The Jessops and the Brights were the most notable dynasties from the 'great houses' of Broom Hall and Banner Cross Hall. Starting with Robert Swyft (1.1) of Broom Hall, one of the original Burgesses, his daughter Anne married Robert Jessop, who inherited and gave rise to a line of Jessop Burgesses. In all, five successive Jessop generations followed Robert Swyft, covering the period (but not quite continuously) from 1554 to 1734. The Jessops were considerable landowners in Sheffield and elsewhere. Richard inherited some of Robert Swyft's estates through his wife Anne and was subsequently associated with interests in land recovery near Worksop. Richard's son William (3.2 and 2.5) lived at Worksop, and also at North Lees, Hathersage (with connections with the Eyre and Fenton families). William's grandson, Francis (3.7) married Robert Eyre's daughter, Barbara.

A total of 13 Brights have served as Church Burgess, four of these comprising the 'Banner Cross Hall' dynasty of father-son successions, continuous from 1636-1722. Robert (5.5, 1636-67), the first of the dynasty, owned at his death in 1667, 60 acres of land at Banner Cross and Millhouses. John, his grandson (5.7, 1686-1703), moved to Chesterfield whilst retaining Banner Cross Hall and became Mayor of that town and also High Sheriff of Derbyshire. Robert's great-grandson, another John (5.8, 1703-22), married Barbara, daughter of Francis Jessop of Broom Hall. This John had substantial holdings in Derbyshire lead mines as well as property and land at Bolsover and Rawmarsh.

Banner Cross Hall came back into the Burgesses' picture in the 19th and 20th centuries, but this time there was no dynasty of landed gentry. Five occupiers of the Hall served as Church Burgess: Samuel Butcher (9.21, 1855-69); Henry Greaves (4.12, 1856-59); George Wilson (6.20, 1884-85); William Esam (7.18, 1901-32); Sir Henry Kenyon Stephenson (1.19), who lived there for a while before moving to Hassop Hall near Bakewell. His father, Sir Henry (1.18, 1887-1904), founded the typefounders, Stephenson Blake with William Blake (6.22, 1896-1904). Sir Henry Kenyon Stephenson, who was created Baronet in 1936, followed his father as Chairman of the family firm. He graced a remarkable number of important offices: Treasurer and Pro-Chancellor of the University of Sheffield; Mayor of Sheffield (twice); M.P. for the Park Division; High Sheriff of Derbyshire. Like his father before him, he received the Freedom of the City.

In the 16th and 17th centuries, Shirecliffe Hall and Fulwood Hall also provided Burgesses, but with none of the continuity of Broom Hall and Banner Cross. William Burrows (1.3, 1570-87), probably a kinsman of the original Burgess (9.1) of the same or similar name, rented Shirecliffe Hall. Joseph Banks (6.10, 1697-1726), that man of many parts. Here he spent the early part of his married life, in non-conformist surroundings, his children probably being born here. He lived at Shirecliffe Hall, having married Mary, the daughter of Rowland Hancock of the Hall. Later he bought Hoyle House, became part-owner of Handsworth Colliery, and moved to Scofton, Worksop. 150 years later, Sir Henry Watson (2.22, 1880-1901) of Shirecliffe Hall, an attorney and partner of William Esam (7.18) and a Director of Charles Cammell Ltd., served as Burgess.

The Foxes of Fulwood Hall make an appearance in the 17th century. William (11.3, 1642-48), his son Ulysses (11.5, 1617-49) and his grandson William (6.7, 1642-48) came from a family long resident in Fulwood. Solid gentry, they appear to have played their part in local affairs, leaving no great mark upon the town, but, like so many Burgesses, contributing in quiet, unspectacular ways to its economic and social health.

Some 'great houses' figure in the 19th and 20th centuries amongst the Burgesses, evidence, not of ancient position and privilege, but of successful entrepreneurs establishing themselves visibly in the community. No dynasties issued from these Victorian mansions and, tellingly, not one now remains as a private residence.

Westbrook, built by Henry Wilson (2.21, 1832-90) of Sharrow Snuff Mills, was until recently the headquarters of the Health Authority. Henry was the moving force behind the 1854 Charity Scheme and also bought the half-share of the Parish Church advowson from the Gell family and bequeathed it to the Burgesses. He was a prominent supporter of the Collegiate School and a Church benefactor on a large scale. The house was still owned by the family when Henry Wilson's grandson, Albert Harland (9.27, 1921-57), was elected a Burgess.

Sir John Brown (12.20, 1864-96), the son of a slater, founded a great steel empire and built Endcliffe Hall, now the Headquarters of the York and Lancaster Regiment. Samuel Roberts (4.13, 1859-87) lived in Queen's Tower, which had been built by his father, a silver plater, as a commemoration of Mary, Queen of Scots. The grandson, another Samuel (3.16, 1885-1926), also occupied the house and was one of the few Members of Parliament amongst Burgesses, being member for Ecclesall, 1902-23. Queen's Tower is now surrounded by the Norfolk Park Council estate and has had a variety of uses in recent years, but not as a private residence.

These few examples, ancient and modern, illustrate well the calibre and standing of people that the Church Burgesses have called upon in their long history. They are examples which could be multiplied many times; they are not isolated stars in the firmament. But it would be wrong to imagine that the Burgesses have always sought to recruit the most notable, prominent citizens to serve the Trust. Discretion, reputation, honesty – these are the qualities stipulated in the Charter. These qualities, together with being a good Churchman, have mattered; not just wealth and position. But Sheffield has been, for centuries, a town of trades and manufactures and of those professions necessary for a thriving economic community. How have these trades and professions been represented in the Church Burgesses Trust? Surprisingly, perhaps, only 27 Church Burgesses have been cutlers, 12 in the 17th and 8 in the 19th centuries. In the 17th century, the Creswicks, father, son (probably) and nephew, were all cutlers, and father and son held office as Master Cutler. Robert Sorsby (10.9), Master Cutler in 1669, was a noted cutler. His father, Malin, Master Cutler in 1649 was the son of Robert, the first Master Cutler, in 1624. The tanners are almost as well represented in the 16th and 17th centuries as the cutlers; 4 in the 16th century and 8 in the 17th. The Hollands and the Rawsons were successful tanning tradesmen. John Holland (10.1, 1554-71), one of the original twelve Burgesses, was a member of the extensive Holland family with four main branches, one having Robert, Vicar of Sheffield, 1569-97. The other branches were at Dove House, Greystones, Button Hill and Hallam. The Rawsons were present in strength in the 16th and 17th centuries. John (12.2, 1563-94), his brother James (9.3, 1573-1603) and his son Edward (12.3, 1594-1607), were followed by the sons of James and Edward. The Rawsons were connected through marriage to the Brights, the Sorsbys and the Creswicks.[13]

The rise and fall of trades and manufactures in Sheffield are well reflected in the membership of the Trust:

	Century				
	16th	17th	18th	19th	20th
Tanning	4	8	–	–	–
Mercer	3	3	2	1	–
Lead production and merchants	–	1	7	–	–
Silver and silver plate	–	–	3	7	2
Steel	–	–	2	8	19
The law has been consistently represented:					
	2	2	5	6	12

Only one architect has served as a Burgess: John Webster (9.25, 1904-13). He has many Sheffield buildings to his credit, including the Jessop and Children's Hospitals and many churches, including St. Bartholomew's, St. Cuthbert's, St. Anne's, St. Clement's and St. Augustine's.

The Burgesses have been graced by two Fellows of the Royal Society: Francis Jessop (3.7, 1661-91) and John M. Whittaker (11.23, 1956-71).

Benefactors

The great public benefactors of Sheffield (names such as Goodwin, Graves, Mappin, Thomas Jessop, Edgar Allen) have not been numbered amongst the Church Burgesses. Neither has the Trust benefited from substantial bequests akin to that of the £111,000 or so bequeathed to the Town Trust in 1860 by Samuel Bailey. But Sir William Ellis (5.17, 1920-45) was very generous to the Burgesses. He bequeathed four seventeenths of his residuary estate to the Church Burgesses, subject to a prior life interest for his daughter, Dorothy. Upon her death, the annual income arising from the bequest was to be used by the Burgesses 'in making grants to such Incumbents of benefices within the ancient Ecclesiastical Parish of Sheffield as the Church Burgesses think fit . . .' The current capital value of the Sir William Ellis Bequest stands at about £85,000. Philanthropic activities by Burgesses have not generally been associated with large public bequests, although there have been some of these. For the most part we see a smattering of smallish benefactions, reflecting, to some extent, the modest wealth of the Burgesses. Sir John Brown, with his Endcliffe Hall ostentation, is not at all typical of the Sheffield Church Burgesses.

In the 16th century, William Burrows (1.3), one of the original Burgesses, was following the tradition of the day in making provision for chantry priests to remember his soul. Richard Jessop (10.2) made bequests to the poor and William Sylvester (7.3) left £10 for Sheffield poor and smaller bequests to the poor of Bradfield, Ecclesfield, Handsworth, Norton and some other parishes. The Accounts for 1572 record:

> 'Note that Francis Swift in the year of our Lord God 1572 did bequeathe by his last will and testament to the Twelve Capital Burgesses one House with the Appurtanences in the Tenure and Occupation of one, Thomas Birley, Cutler, nigh unto the Barker Poole, after the natural death of his two Sisters.'

Robert Rollinson (7.5) in the 17th century left two houses as residences for the Assistant Ministers of Sheffield and also left land and money for the School, £1 per annum for the Parish Church and £10 to the workhouse. He also enlarged and improved the public water supply at Barker's Pool. Roger Lee (9.6, 1653-83) left the largish sum for that time of £50 for 12 poor and aged persons in Ecclesall. In 1638, a number of Burgesses made personal contributions towards the cost of the new Cutlers' Hall. These varied between 4s. and £1, hardly an enthusiastic endorsement of the new venture. In 1709 there was something in the nature of a subscription list amongst the Burgesses for contributions to the Grammar School Master's new house. Mostly, the contributions were 10s. or £1 and the total sum raised in this way was £9. 8s.; not a munificent gift, but rather better than the support for Cutlers' Hall 60 years earlier. On the other hand, the considerable problems of poverty in 1795, after failure of the harvest and consequent high prices for corn, were taken on board by the Burgesses. The Trust donated some £200 and 8 individual Burgesses personally guaranteed a total of £2300 for the Corn Committee. John Turner (9.12, 1777-96) left £100 to each of the Boys' and Girls' Charity Schools. Dr. John Waterhouse (1.10, 1702-14) left £50 to the Grammar School.

In 1823, when the new Grammar School was being built in St. George's Square, most of the Burgesses at that time made small subscriptions of five or ten guineas, but there were no large donations. Presumably, the Burgesses felt that the Trust was being very supportive in giving land for the building. But the 19th century, with its generation of wealth in Sheffield as elsewhere, saw benefactions on a larger scale than hitherto. Thomas Watson (2.20, 1809-32), silver plater, left bequests to the Infirmary, the Girls' Charity School and National Schools and gave £2000 to the Boys' Charity School for the support of ten boys at the School. George Hounsfield's (8.19, 1841-70) bequests in his will of 1866 benefited the Infirmary and the Charity Schools and his wife established the Hounsfield Pensions in his name in 1870, leaving over £21,000 for the Burgesses to administer for the benefit of 'men, unmarried women or widows not under 50 years, of good character and sober life and conversation, members of the Established Church of England, in reduced, needy or poor circumstances.' William Horn (11.18, 1854-73), manufacturer of files, saws and edge tools, left £17,500 to various charities.

But it is for philanthropy to new churches that the 19th century is particularly notable and a number of Burgesses were prominent in this regard. Sir Samuel Roberts (3.16, 1885-1926), of whom Odom records: 'his name recalls nothing but what is pure and unselfish and good',[14] and who throughout his life was a decided Evangelical Churchman, gave £2000 to the Church Extension Scheme, £2000 to St. Barnabas and £1000 to St. Paul's. He also supported Firth College with a donation of £1000. Sir John Brown, in his lifetime, built All Saints' Church, Ellesmere Road. Henry Wilson (2.21) was a munificent benefactor of churches. He gave £1000 for building St. Matthew's, Carver Street and bore the entire cost of site, building and fittings of St. Stephen's (£5700) and similarly for St. Silas, Gilcar (£8000). His other gifts included £1000 and the site for St. Barnabas, the site and £2000 for St. Matthias. For a number of years from 1852, he sustained the Grammar School over a difficult period and he built Napier Street Day and Sunday Schools at a cost of £4500. He was active also in funding the Church Missionary Society for its missionary work in Central Africa, giving £5000 in 1876. In all, he probably gave at least £60,000 for a range of activities in Sheffield during his lifetime and some £10,000 for activities outside Sheffield.

Sir Henry Stephenson (1.18), was also a great supporter of new church building, contributing to the Church Extension Societies and making donations to individual churches, including £1000 to St. Anne's, Hoyle Street and £750 to St. Augustine's. But his major contributions were to education. His £10,000 for the buildings of the new University College undoubtedly assured a successful venture. The Hall of Residence named after him was funded by his wife (£10,000) in 1912 in his memory.

These individual Burgesses, in their philanthropy, more than matched the totality of spending by the Church Burgesses Trust on church building during this period. Together, individual Burgesses and the Trust made a most significant contribution in shaping the Church of England in Victorian Sheffield.

Philanthropy is demonstrated, not only in gifts of money for worthy purposes, but in personal labour for good causes. Four Burgesses who left their mark upon Sheffield for good made lasting contributions to the public health of the town. Robert Rollinson in the 17th century has already been referred to as being instrumental in reconstructing Barker's Pool to provide a supply of water which greatly helped in keeping streets clean. Joseph Matthewman (11.14, 1773-91) was one of the prime movers in the town for securing a supply of clean water for the growing population. And it was the initiative and energy of Dr. William Younge (11.15, 1791-1838) which resulted in the building of the Infirmary and he served as its first physician for a number of years. And John Dodsley Webster was instrumental, along with William Jackson Cleaver, surgeon, and Henry Vickers, solicitor, in the establishment of the Children's Hospital. In his professional capacity as an architect, he designed the buildings of the Hospital and served as its Chairman for some years.

Prudent, discreet and cautious

Trustees of public charities are not in the business of taking risks with their inheritance. They have a prime responsibility to ensure that the assets of their Trust are not only wisely and effectively applied to fulfil the declared purposes of the Trust, but are also sound and secure for the use of future generations. They will act cautiously and with prudence. The Church Burgesses would surely have concurred with Thomas Fuller, a Church historian writing in 1643:

> 'God's work must not be done lazily, but leisurely; haste maketh waste in this kind. In reformations of great importance, the violent driving in of the nail will either break the head or bow the point thereof, or rive and split that which should be fastened therewith. That may be insensibly screwed which may not be knocked into people. Fair and softly goeth far; but alas! we have too many fiery spirits, who, like Jehu, drive on so furiously, they will overturn all in church and state, if their fierceness be not seasonably entrenched.'[15]

The contrast between the entrepreneurial risk-taking of individual Burgesses and the collective caution of the corporate body is stark. Robert Swyft (1.1) was a land dealer on a large scale, skilfully operating in the scheming, turbulent world of post-Dissolution property sales, providing well for the subsequent Broom Hall dynasty. Sir John Brown built up from scratch one of the largest steel complexes in Europe. John Kenyon (2.19, 1784-1809) opened up Europe for trade with Sheffield. Sir Henry Stephenson established, with his partner William Blake, the internationally known type-founders. Henry Wilson developed his father's snuff business in Sharrow to provide the wherewithal for his munificent philanthropy. In the 1730s, eight of the Burgesses were amongst the original list of shareholders of the Don Navigation Company – the merchant adventurers of Sheffield. There are many others one could mention, the movers and shakers of Sheffield trade and commerce. But the Burgesses collectively displayed none of these traits of initiative and risk-taking. Theirs was a responsibility of exercising a public trust cautiously and prudently, although, as we have seen (Chapter VIII), they were successful in the management of their not inconsiderable estates.

True, they were supportive of moves to ensure the development of Sheffield commerce, but from the sidelines. We find them on 21 March 1833 affixing their Seal to a Petition to the Post-Master General for accelerating the arrival of the Leeds and Birmingham mails to Sheffield, and in 1836 they took the lead in proposing a Petition from public bodies of the town for the establishment of a new day mail between Sheffield and London. In 1844, another Petition was prepared in favour of the proposed railway between Sheffield and Chesterfield. But in March 1838, the Burgesses were moved to present a Petition against the proposed Charter of Incorporation of the Borough of Sheffield. In this, perhaps, they were demonstrating a distrust of the growth of democracy and a fear of encroachment by local bureaucracy. The Town Trust, at the same time, was indicating its ambivalence on the issue. At their meeting in February 1838, they had before them a resolution expressing full support for the Charter, but adopted an amendment that 'this Trust remains neuter in respect thereto.'

Any fears about the growth of democracy which the Burgesses may have entertained would have been heightened by the growth of Chartism following the Reform Act of 1832. Chartist disturbances in Sheffield in 1839 led to violence.[16] There were demonstrations and marches upon the Parish Church with demands that the Vicar preach upon selected texts. On Sunday, 15 September 1839, the police were at the church gates armed with cutlasses to provide safe conduct for regular church-goers. On 2 April 1840, the Minute Book records that the Churchwardens asked for £12.17s.6d. as the cost of 'keeping the Peace during recent Chartist Excitements.' The Burgesses agreed to contribute £5 and asked that the Seatholders contribute their portion.

In 1847, the Burgesses were moved to express their displeasure at what they saw as an attempt at intimidation of a Justice of the Peace. They minuted on 3 May:

> 'A section of the Working Classes of the Borough of Sheffield having announced their intention of presenting to Parliament a petition reflecting upon the Character and Conduct of Wilson Overend Esquire, one of Her Majesty's Justices of the Peace for the West Riding of Yorkshire, in regard to certain Decisions and Convictions under the Combination Act. Resolved: That without offering any Opinion as to the Decisions, this Meeting is firmly convinced that Mr. Overend, in arriving at such Conclusions, acted with the strictest honesty and Impartiality and according to the best of his knowledge and Judgment . . . They regret to learn that any Section of the Inhabitants should thus proceed to impeach the Conduct and Character of Mr. Overend or attempt to intimidate him in the discharge of his Magisterial Duties.'

As to suspicions of local bureaucracy, we have seen in Chapter III that the Town Council in the 1850s was in opposition to the Trust. With the substantial developments in the Burgesses' property in the late 19th century, the Trust and the Council were involved in frequent negotiations. One can detect a certain tetchiness from time to time amongst the Burgesses, although, for the most part, there was, it would seem, harmonious and constructive collaboration. We read, however, on 29 May 1902: 'The Clerk and the Surveyor reported upon the matter of the sewer recently made under the footpath over Charity land at Walkley Bank. Resolved: that the

Church Burgesses protest against the arbitrary action of the City Surveyor in proceeding to make the sewer without giving formal notice or obtaining the Church Burgesses' previous consent and notwithstanding the remonstrance of their Surveyor, and are of the opinion that so hostile a method of carrying out the stringent powers vested in the City Council is not likely to conduce to harmonious working between two public bodies.' But in the following month, the Burgesses beat a hasty retreat: 'There now appears to have been a misapprehension of the facts of the case and more minute investigation is found to justify a withdrawal of the protest.'

The Burgesses have, from time to time, demonstrated a reluctance to subject themselves to scrutiny by the commonalty. In this, no doubt, they were taking the view that prudence, good judgement and wisdom would be better secured through discreet and measured discussion in the Burgesses' chamber, rather than by public debate. They have preferred to exercise their own discretion, rather than to put their faith in democratic involvement. That reluctance to involve the commonalty – a belief that accountability is best secured through appointed Trustees rather than by public meetings – led to charges of secretive behaviour. And yet, it may be said that the Burgesses collectively have been self-effacing, rather than secretive. Whatever may have been the public profile of individual Burgesses – and this has been considerable with many Burgesses – the Trust collectively has shunned the limelight. There is no monument or memorial within the Cathedral which carries a reference to the Church Burgesses. One has to look hard around the Cathedral for evidence of their existence. Two pews in the nave have small plates bearing the inscription 'Church Burgesses'. The seal of the Burgesses appears on the reredos in the Lady Chapel and in the Pye-Smith memorial window in St. Katherine's Chapel. One of the stained glass windows in the Chapter House depicts the granting of the Charter by Mary Tudor, but, surprisingly, does not have the seal of the Burgesses. An oversight or mistake, perhaps, by the designer.

The Burgesses, in the exercise of their public trust, have reflected the dictum of Charles Lamb: 'The greatest pleasure I know is to do a good action by stealth, and have it found out by accident.' The Burgesses have nothing to hide. Their self-effacement reflects a deeply ingrained belief that public trust is best guaranteed through personal integrity. Eyebrows might now be raised if individual Burgesses borrowed money from the Trust, yet when Joseph Clay and John Young did that in the 1790s (at the same rate as Consols), it was not thought in any way improper, but regarded as a safe investment.

When, in 1839, Samuel Roberts drew the attention of the Burgesses to the fact that they were in breach of the conditions of William Hanby's will by not paying certain contributions to the Boys' Charity School, the oversight (and it was just that) was quickly remedied. Their concern about the consequences of such maladministration bringing the name of the Trust into disrepute is evident from their minute of 24 April:

> 'The Church Burgesses having duly considered the statement submitted to them by Mr. Samuel Roberts and the Extract from Mr. Hanby's Will with which he has since supplied them, and looking at the consequences which possibly might result from a close Investigation into the past, deem it more prudent not to enter upon such an Enquiry, especially as they understand that the Error complained of has been set right for the future and that the Trustees of the Boy's Charity School generally are satisfied at this arrangement.'

Least said, soonest mended.

Characteristics of the Trust

In looking back over the years at the composition of the Trust, five things stand out:

1. Continuity. There are two factors here – length of service and family succession. 30 years' service on the Trust is very common and several Burgesses served for over 40 years. This longevity, combined with family succession, must have guaranteed a stability which could have meant stagnation. In fact, as is clear from the effective management of the development and disposition of the Trust's assets, the Trust has not stagnated. It has kept, not only in touch with, but abreast of, and has been responsive to, the demands of successive generations of change. But length of service can only be secured by appointing young men as Trustees and this has been done repeatedly. Great length of service means that, at any one time, the Trust has had elderly men as Trustees. The leavening of the experience of age with the freshness of youth must have been significant in maintaining responsiveness to change. The fact that there is no age limit for Burgesses, and that very many have remained as members until their death, carries with it a considerable risk of inertia and passivity. That this seems to have been avoided says something for the quality of intellect and energy of those appointed.

2. Local eminence. The experience of men of position and standing in the community has brought to the Trust, not only authority and gravitas, but a practical understanding of the responsibility which rests upon the Trust. Men of local eminence have brought into the Trust's affairs the powers of judgment they exercised in their business and professional affairs.

Their business acumen has been applied in the interests of the Trust in conserving and strengthening for future generations the value of its assets. It has been vitally important that Burgesses have not been appointed to be mere figure-heads, gracing the Trust with their name and remaining essentially inactive. However eminent, each Burgess seems to have been, almost without exception, a committed, active member of the Trust. Local eminence has brought with it experience that has been put to use, not mere patronage.

3. Balance. Whether by design or accident, there has always been a balance in the range of professional and commercial interests represented amongst Burgesses. And when, from time to time, there appeared to be some danger of membership being handed down as a sort of family possession, this has been averted by bringing in new blood. But balance is relative and many might wish to see a rather wider representation of interests. The Trust has still to appoint its first woman or black person. But we must be careful to have regard to the nature of the Trust. It is not a representative body charged with representing all shades of opinion (despite the inclusion of the word 'Commonalty' in its title); it is a body of Trustees each individually and collectively accountable for fulfilling the conditions laid down in its Charter and Charity Schemes. Variety and balance of membership is important, not so much to bring a range of opinions and views, but to provide diversity of relevant experience in administering the Trust. It is notable how, down the years, such a diversity has been continued.

4. Consensus. Apart from the Trevor affair, which generated deep divisions in the Trust, its business has been carried on with a high degree of mutual agreement. Very few occasions are recorded in the minutes in which there has been a vote. Furthermore, no one Burgess seems, at any one time, to have dominated proceedings. Perhaps only with Henry Wilson, the architect of the 1854 Scheme, do we see a dominant position being taken by an individual Burgess. Presumably, this has much to do with the quality of the individual Burgesses, each capable of making their views known and standing up for themselves. But often, in such cases, in many other organisations, deep divisions are rife and long-standing harmony difficult to achieve. A contributory factor to consensus could well be the tradition of electing the Capital Burgess to serve for one year only. Each Burgess in turn accepts the responsibility of chairmanship. This has provided an element of democracy, contributing to the ethos of consensus, and has ensured that each Burgess gains a thorough knowledge of the workings of the Trust across the whole range of its activities.

5. Christian commitment. For 300 years from 1554 the Trust could well

have been regarded as an arm of the Parish Church. But, since 1854, the Trust, whilst maintaining a central commitment to the Parish Church, has taken on an ever-widening ecclesiastical and secular role. Despite the broadening of responsibilities of the Trust, Christian commitment remains the hallmark of the Church Burgesses. It is, perhaps, this quality, more than any other, which has undergirded the work of the Trust during its history. There remains a firm commitment to the ministry of the Church, a ministry which the Trust regards as having to be exercised well beyond the confines of the institutionalised Church. The Christian commitment of the Burgesses would seem to bring with it, not only a dedicated membership of the Church of England, but a Christian faith which is worked out in the demanding setting of an urban community. To that extent, the work of the Church Burgesses, through the Trust, is faith in action.

Chapel of the Holy Spirit, Sheffield Cathedral, looking South.

APPENDIX I

Ancient Deeds Relating to Grants to the Parish Church

(Note: References: Hall (5) refers to the document numbered (5) in T.W. Hall, *A Catalogue of the Ancient Deeds belonging to the Twelve Capital Burgesses and Commonalty of Sheffield* (Northend, Sheffield, 1913). E.B. (2) refers to the document numbered (2) in the 'Schedule and Abstracts of all the Deeds belonging to the Church Estate from 1304 to the granting of the Charter of Incorporation in the first year of Queen Mary'. This appears on pages 86-90 of the *Burgesses' Election Book*. No date is given, but the list appears between the Minutes of a meeting held on 19 March 1766 and the rental account for 1767. At the end of the list there is the statement: 'Examined with the original deeds in the Church Chest' signed by James Wheat, Clerk to the Burgesses.)

1. 1320: Grant from Adam Drake of Attercliffe to the service of the Virgin Mary in the Church of Sheffield, a rood and a half of land in a field at Attercliffe called Leyland. (E.B. 2)

2. 1332: Grant from Henry de Tapton and others to John de Elcliff, chaplain, of a life estate in a croft and an acre of arable land in the town of Sheffield, the said croft lying in the Balne. (Hall (5) – who notes that the Balne is that part of Sheffield now known as Balm Green.)

3. 1333: Charter confirming the grant by John del Wood del Brome to John Elcliff, chaplain, of the lands referred to in 2. (Hall (6))

4. 1338: Charter confirming a grant from William Moton to John de Elcliffe, chaplain of Sheffield of all lands and tenements which William Moton held in the town and interior of Sheffield. (Hall (12)).

5. 1338: Release and Quit Claim by William Moton to John de Elcliffe of Sheffield, chaplain, of all his right and claim in all his land with a building thereon lying in the interior of Sheffield. (Hall (13)).

6. 1345: Charter confirming grant by William Moton to John de Elclif of Sheffield, chaplain, a toft with a building thereon lying in that part of Sheffield called Balne; and an acre and a half of arable land with its appurtenances lying above the Kirktoftes of Sheffield. (Hall (17)).

7. 1349: Release and Quit Claim by Isabelle wife of the then late William Motun to John de Elclif of Sheffield, chaplain, of all right and claim in a toft

with buildings and all other appurtenances in the same town, which is called Lambekyntoft. (Hall (19)).

8. 1349: Grant by John de Elclyff, chaplain, to Isabelle Moton of a life estate in a toft with buildings in Sheffield called Lambekyntoft. (Hall (20).

9. 1383: Charter confirming a grant from Alan Lambarde, chaplain and others to Joan Costenoght wife of John de Walkmylne of a tenement. (Hall (32)).

10. 1393: Grant from Henry de Alseby, chaplain of Sheffield, to Agnes formerly wife of William Hancock of Darnall for her life of Lands in the Fields of Darnall. Remainder to Richard Hancock in Tail. (E.B. (39)).

11. 1499: Indenture of Lease from the Greve or Church Maisters of the parish Churche of Sheffeld to Geoffrey Buttery one of their body of four tenements lying in Sheffield beneath the Irish Cross there at an annual rent of 33s. 4d. payable half-yearly (Hall (69)).

12. 1500: Release and Quit Claim by Thomas Stubbe to John Pleasaunce, vicar of Sheffield of all right of and in all those three tenements with three gardens lying in Sheffield at the north end of a lane there called Water Lane. (Hall (70)).

13. 1508: Release from William son of John Stangfordson of Richard Staniford to Robert Hudson, Bayliff of Sheffield and others of one yearly rent of 21s. out of Lands and Tenements in the Village and Fields of Attercliffe to be received out of the said Lands and Tenements. To the use of God the Blessed Mary and sustaining of the Guild of the Blessed Virgin Mary . . . of the Annual Rents given by Adam Copley, deceased. (E.B. (80).

14. 1525: Bond from William Newman, Leatherseller and another to William Taylor and others, keepers of Sheffield Church, in 10 marks to perform Covenants. (E.B. (82)).

15. 1551: Counterpart Lease from the Churchwardens and Burgesses to Rowland Sheperd, Citizen and Merchant Taylor of London, of a Messuage in the Old Change London for 40 years under the yearly rent of 45s. 4d. (E.B. (83)).

APPENDIX II

The Charity Scheme of 1854

[PUBLISHED BY AUTHORITY]

IN CHANCERY
THE ATTORNEY GENERAL -v- THE TWELVE CAPITAL BURGESSES AND COMMONALITY OF THE TOWN AND PARISH OF SHEFFIELD, IN THE COUNTY OF YORK, AND ANOTHER

SCHEME for the future application of the Income of the Trust Property, pursuant to the Report of WILLIAM HENRY TINNEY, ESQUIRE, one of the Masters of the High Court of Chancery, confirmed by the said Court by an Order, dated the 1st day of August 1854.

1. The Twelve Capital Burgesses and Commonalty of Sheffield shall pay and dispose of the surplus Rents, Revenues, and Profits of the Charity Estates and Property, after deducting the necessary Expenses of care and management and repairs thereof, according to the Provisions hereinafter mentioned.
2. Out of the surplus Rents, Revenues, and Profits, £1,600 per annum, being a sum about equal to the amount at present annually applied to Ecclesiastical Purposes, shall be applied to the Ecclesiastical Purposes hereinafter mentioned, and the remainder shall be applied to the Secular Purposes hereinafter mentioned until the sum annually applicable to Secular Purposes shall, by the increase of the Income of the Trust Property or otherwise, amount to £640, being two-fifths of the said sum of £1,600; and thence forward the Net Annual Income of the said Trust Property shall be divided into seven equal parts, five of which shall be applied to the Ecclesiastical Purposes hereinafter mentioned, and the remainder to the Secular Purposes hereinafter mentioned.
3. The portion of the Income applicable to Ecclesiastical Purposes shall be applied as follows:
   - [A.] The Twelve Capital Burgesses and Commonalty of Sheffield shall pay thereout £400 per year to each of the present Chaplains or Assistant Ministers, so long as he shall continue to fill the office of Chaplain or Assistant Minister.
   - [B.] On the resignation or removal, by death or otherwise, of the present Chaplains or Assistant Ministers, or any of them, the vacancy or vacancies created by such removal shall not be filled up, but in the place of two of such Chaplains or Assistant Ministers the Vicar for the time being of the Parish and Parish Church of Sheffield shall, from time to time, appoint Stipendiary Curates, being respectively Clergymen of the Church of

England, in Priest's Orders, to assist him in the performance of his clerical duties in the Parish and Parish Church of Sheffield, such Curates to be respectively called the First and Second Curate of the Parish and Parish Church of Sheffield.

[C.] When, and so often as any vacancy shall occur in the said curacies respectively, the Vicar for the time being of the Parish and Parish Church of Sheffield shall appoint a proper person to fill the curacy or curacies so becoming vacant; and in the case the said Vicar, for the time being, shall not within three months after any such vacancy fill up the same, by nominating such Curate as aforesaid, the nomination shall be made by the Archbishop of York, for the time being.

[D.] When, and so soon as the first vacancy in the office of Chaplain or Assistant Minster shall have occurred, the First Curate shall be appointed in the manner hereinbefore mentioned; and when he shall have been appointed, and duly licensed, the said Twelve Capital Burgesses and Commonalty shall, out of the portion of the aforesaid Income applicable to Ecclesiastical Purposes, pay to such First Curate and his successors, as First Curate, the sum of £200 a year.

[E.] When a second vacancy in the office of Chaplain or Assistant Minister shall have occurred, the Second Curate shall be appointed in manner hereinbefore mentioned; and when he shall have been appointed, and duly licensed, the said Twelve Capital Burgesses and Commonalty shall, out of the portion of the aforesaid Income applicable to Ecclesiastical Purposes, pay to such Second Curate and his successors, as Second Curate, the sum of £150 a year.

[F.] The said Annual Sums shall be paid, as well to the said Chaplains or Assistant Ministers as to the said Curates, quarterly, on the 25th day of March, the 24th day of June, the 29th day of September, and the 25th day of December, in every year; and any Curate appointed between two Quarterly Days shall be entitled to be paid a proportion only up to the Quarterly Day next following his entering on his duties; while upon the resignation or removal of any Chaplain, Assistant Minister, or Curate, he or his executors or administrators, as the case may be, shall be entitled to a proportionate part of the accruing Quarter's Payment up to the time of his ceasing to be such Chaplain, Assistant Minister, or Curate.

[G.] The Curates so to be appointed shall be deemed, in all respects, Stipendiary Curates, and removable as such, and their appointments shall cease or determine upon the death, resignation, or removal of the Vicar for the time being of the said Parish and Parish Church.

[H.] The clergyman filling the office of Second Curate for the time being, shall not have any preferential claim to the office of First Curate on any vacancy happening therein.

[I.] The said Twelve Capital Burgesses and Commonalty shall also expend, out of the proportion of the said Income applicable to Ecclesiastical Purposes, such amount as they shall in their discretion consider to be necessary for the purpose of substantially and effectually supporting and repairing the fabric of the Parish Church of Sheffield; and shall keep the said Church insured against Fire in some Insurance Office, for a sum not less than £2,000.

[J.] The said Twelve Capital Burgesses and Commonalty shall annually, out of the portion of the said Income applicable to Ecclesiastical Purposes, pay in like manner as they have usually paid the same the ordinary expenses attending on the celebration of Divine Worship in the said Parish Church; (that is to say) the Salaries of the Organist, Organ Blower, and the Sexton; and the expenses of Warming, Lighting, Painting, and Cleansing the Church; and keeping the Bells, Bell Ropes, and Clock in a sufficient condition; and the costs of Washing the Surplices of the Clergymen, and providing the Sacramental Bread and Wine, and all incidental expenses.

[K.] The said Burgesses and Commonalty shall also pay thereout such sum, not exceeding £100 in any one year, as to them shall seem meet, in or towards payment of the Salary of the Chaplain of the Infirmary of Sheffield, provided that no such payment shall be made as together with the Income of the said Chaplain, as such Chaplain, derived from other sources shall amount to more than £150 per annum.

[L.] The residue of the Net Income applicable to Ecclesiastical Purposes shall, from time to time, be applied in the manner hereinafter mentioned; and the objects hereinafter declared shall be carried into effect in the order in which they are hereinafter mentioned.

[M.] When and as any Ecclesiastical District shall be constituted out of the districts in the Parish of Sheffield now known as Netherthorpe, Porter Street, Broomhall, and Gillcar, such districts, not exceeding four in number, shall be respectively endowed by the said Twelve Capital Burgesses and Commonalty with a perpetual annual sum of £150, chargeable upon the Income of the said Trust Property, or some sufficient part thereof, as soon as it can be ascertained that the Income of the said Property shall be sufficient to answer the same; such annual sum to be applied in payment of the Salary or Stipend of the Curates or Ministers of such districts respectively, by Four Quarterly Payments on the usual Quarter Days hereinbefore mentioned; and any clergyman appointed during the interval between two Quarterly Days shall be entitled to be paid in proportion up to the Quarter Day next following his entering on his duty, provided that no such endowment shall be made unless the right of presentation to the district shall, at or immediately after the same shall be made, be assured to the said Twelve Capital Burgesses and their successors for ever.

[N.] The said districts, when so created as aforesaid, shall be respectively endowed in such order as the said Twelve Capital Burgesses and Commonalty shall, with the approval of the Ecclesiastical Commissioners, determine: and if more than four Ecclesiastical Districts should be constructed out of Netherthorpe, Porter Street, Broomhall, and Gillcar, the said Twelve Capital Burgesses and Commonalty shall select for endowment such four thereof as they may, with the like approbation, think fit.

[O.] The surplus, if any, of the Income applicable to Ecclesiastical purposes which shall remain after providing for the objects hereinbefore mentioned, shall be applied, at the discretion of the said Burgesses and Commonalty, in increasing the Salaries of the Incumbents of the Districts or District Churches in the parish of Sheffield, other than the said Netherthorpe, Porter Street, Broomhall, and Gillcar Districts, provided that none of the said Salaries or Stipends shall be so increased by the said Burgesses and Commonalty, as to amount in the whole to more than £150 a year exclusive of Pew Rents.

[P.] If any surplus of the Income applicable to Ecclesiastical purposes shall at any time remain after making and providing for the payments hereinbefore mentioned, the said Burgesses and Commonalty shall at their discretion apply such surplus in building or contributing to build any additional Churches or Parsonage Houses within the parish of Sheffield, or in endowing or contributing to endow any additional Districts or Churches which may be constituted or erected therein.

4. The Portion of the Income applicable to Secular Purposes shall be applied as follows:

[A.] The Burgesses and Commonalty shall thereout contribute such annual sum as they in their discretion shall think fit, not exceeding £20 a year, towards repairing the Bridges and Highways of the parish.

[B.] The Burgesses and Commonalty shall apply three-eighth parts of the Income applicable to secular purposes, after deducting the payment mentioned in the last preceding clause, towards the maintenance and support of the Sheffield General Infirmary, the Sheffield Public Dispensary, and such other Medical and Surgical Charities for the time being existing within the parish of Sheffield, particularly District Dispensaries and Ophthalmic Hospitals, or Institutions, as the Burgesses and Commonalty may think proper.

[C.] The other five-eighths of the Income applicable to secular purposes after deducting the payment towards repairing Bridges and Highways shall be distributed by the said Twelve Capital Burgesses amongst the Boys' and Girls' Charity Schools, the Lancasterian Schools, the National Schools, and all other the Public Day Schools for the time being existing in the parish of Sheffield for the education of the Poor, which shall be under Government Inspection, or in connection with the National Society, or the British and Foreign School Society, or such of them as shall apply for such aid, the distributions to be in proportion, as nearly as conveniently may be, to the number of Scholars attending such Schools and their means of support for the time being, provided that all applications for aid to any such School shall be made in writing, and transmitted to the Capital Burgesses in the month of January in each year, and shall be accompanied by a Certificate under the hand of the Treasurer or other proper officer of the School on behalf of which application shall be made, of the average number of Scholars attending the same during the preceding year ending the 31st of December, and of the Income applicable during the preceding year ending as aforesaid, to the maintenance of such School.

5. This Scheme shall be printed at the expense of the said Charity, and a copy thereof given to every person who is now or may hereafter be appointed a Capital Burgess of the said Charity, and a copy thereof shall also be supplied to every person who shall be willing to pay the sum of one shilling for the same, and all monies received for such copies shall be paid half-yearly to the said Capital Burgesses.

APPENDIX III

Miscellanea

DOWN THE YEARS, there have been many interesting, odd or quaint entries in the various records of the Church Burgesses which, whilst not greatly significant for the conduct of their business, are nevertheless sometimes revealing of attitudes or circumstances of the time. Some of these are reproduced here, in no particular order. They are no more than a miscellany of items, but it seems a pity not to include them for amusement, curiosity or edification.

First of all, a comment upon the convention followed by the Burgesses in their use of the term 'Capital Burgess', which has come to be used to describe the person holding office as Chairman. The Chairman of the Trust, from earliest times, was appointed to hold that office for a limited period and was referred to as the 'Collector of the Church Rents' for many years. But there is an entry in the Election Book for 28 August 1673: 'that Mr. Browne's bill of disbursement for his house be paid by Mr. Jessop, Capitall.' This appears to be the first use of that term to describe the Chairman of the Trustees, although the term Collector continued to be used also for a long time after that.

A system in which a newly elected Burgess became Chairman (Capital) in the year following his election was adopted quite early. Whilst the responsibility so placed upon a new Burgess is daunting, the tradition ensures that a newly elected Trustee shall quickly gain a knowledge of all the Trust's business. Recognising that it is possible to thrust office too quickly upon inexperienced shoulders, the Minute Book records on 18 June 1798: 'Ordered that in future no Gentleman elected a Burgess shall execute the office of Capital Burgess until he shall have been twelve months one of the Body.'

Another tradition is that the office of Capital is handed on by seniority, excepting when a newly elected Burgess takes office. But a process of election from three members nominated by the retiring Capital used to be in operation, as is clear from a minute in the Election Book for 8 December 1741, which describes an exception to that process: 'Paul Meyer was elected a Burgess in the place of Thos. Wright Gent. late Collector who dyed 17th Nov. last before he had entered on the Collectorship. Therefore for want of a Head or Collector to nominate 3 persons for one to be chosed thereout as is usual the said Election was made in the following manner, to whit, each of the said Burgesses nominated and voted for such one person as he thought proper by writing down the name of such person privately on a scrap of paper and putting the same into a hat, whereupon the said Paul Meyer was found to have 6 votes and was declared duly chosen.'

Concern about non-attendance of Burgesses at regular meetings appears in an entry in the Account Book dated 27 January 1688: 'If any of the Burgesses having sufficient warning of a meeting and absents himself therefrom without reasonable cause to be allowed by the rest of the Burgesses, he shall pay 2s.6d. to the Capital Burgess for the time being'. And, again, in a minute 4 June 1857: 'Resolved that in future the names of Burgesses be called over 15 minutes after the time for which the meeting is convened and that any member of the Trust not then present be fined 2s.6d. and the fine be increased to 5s. if the member had not given notice of his intention not to be present.'

Conflicts of interest must undoubtedly have arisen from time to time as Burgesses with so many interests in the town have had to make decisions having some relationship with those interests. But in 1820, a rather different conflict of interest arose. On 6 April, the Burgesses minuted: 'Consequent upon a Burgess being elected Churchwarden. Resolved: that the two roles are incompatible.' In the July following there was a further resolution: 'to seek Counsel's opinion on the matter.' But we have no further record of views upon the alleged incompatibility.

Some of the very early entries in the accounts give a new depth of meaning to the term creative accounting.

1558: Item there was in the Boxe 1s.11½d.

The Churchwardens clearly had difficulty sometimes in accounting for the money they had dealt with:

1560: Item there was lost by the fall of money in their hands: 1s.8½d. (presumably through carelessness, rather than by currency speculation.)

The Reste of Edward Thelwall was as appeareth by the fact of this Accompt in anno 1560 and did hang of his Head: 11s.11d.

Item lost ut alligatur: 9d.

1561: Lost in money 6d.

1564: Item 2s. there is surplus in the books who hath it I know not.

It is not always possible to dispense charity at arm's length. The Burgesses have found, on more than one occasion, that payment of a grant is not the end of the matter. We might well, from the following entries in the Election Book, conclude that there was something of a saga with the Lee family and that the bare bones only appear in the minutes:

13 December 1718: 'At a Church Burgesses Meeting this day 'tis agreed that out of the rents and profitts of the houseing and land late in James Lee's possession belonging to the Church Burgesses that £25 be advanced to pay Charles Symon in full for young James Lee's board goale fees and all other demands and also £18 to Mr. Richard Booth of York who hath the said James Lee in custody at the said Charles Symon's . . . and that when the houseing and land late in James Lee's possession is sold (the rent whereof was now agreed to be £6 per. ann.) that out of the money by the sale thereof James Lee's widow shall have £43 and that money be paid unto some person or persons that the Church Burgesses shall approve for her use.'

23 December 1719: 'Mr. Thomas Handley agrees to take into his hands £50 parte of the money the late James Lee's house and land was sold for And to pay Widd. Lee 30s. a quarter till the whole be run up if she soe long live And if she die before the whole be run up the remainder thereof to be paid into the Burgesses' hands . . . Memo: £116 part of the money was paid into the hands of Mr. Clay who pays the £50 to Mr. Handley as above And the rest (viz.) £66 is to remaine in the hands of Mr. Clay And he to pay interest for it And give due notice to the Burgesses before he pays the same.'

15 May 1729: 'Memo: the Account is discharged thus (to whitt) Mr. Handley paid the Widdow in her lifetime £43 10s. 0d. and the remainder being £6 10s. 0d. be this day paid over to Mr. Denis Nevile ye present Capitall so he is discharged . . . And Memo: it now appears Mr. Clay has paid to Jos. Butler and Barbary his wife (the said Barbary being a daughter of the said James Lee) £30 by the Burgesses Order and £2 more to James Lee Junr. and £4 more to John Lee Barber for the use of James Lee Junr. to buy him a Bedd and other necessaries so Mr. Clay hath paid in the whole £36 which deducted from the £66 above there now only remains in Mr. Clay's hands £30 which £30 is ordered to be paid into the hands of Mr. Nevile the present Capitall.'

The Burgesses are not the only landlords to find that disputatious tenants can be a trial:

18 January 1684: 'That John and Thomas Hale shall hold each their own parcells as the same is now divided till Martinmas next without Lease att ye old rent And if it be made appear that either of them doo disturb the other dureing that tyme or wrong or abuse each other then the whold be taken from the wrongdoer and a lease made of it to the other.'

We are apt to think that church property was sacrosanct in former times, except in times of war or civil disturbance. But 18th century alms boxes and Church chests had their attractions for thieves as appears in the Accounts:

1744: Paid to the Bellman for crying a reward for a discovery of the person who broak into the Church Burgesses Chest: 1s. 0d.

1745: Paid to the Bellman for crying the Church broke open: 1s. 0d.

R.E. Leader has referred to umbrellas in one of his Talks of the Town.[1] In 1765, £2 15s. 0d. was paid for an umbrella for church use. Leader writes: 'manifestly this means for the protection of clergy when conducting funerals. The Churchyard was clearly a privileged place, for many years elapsed before anyone could show himself in the streets with an umbrella without being subjected to the scurrilous jibes of a ribald populace.' In 1785 15s. was paid to Joseph Salthouse for an umbrella for the use of clergy. And in 1795, 7s. 6d. was paid to Hannah Cocker for repairing an Umbrella'; perhaps the same that was bought ten years earlier. Then a gap of 50 years to 1844 before another entry: Umbrella for the use of the Clergy: £10; the increase in price perhaps due to a combination of inflation and a better quality product.

An interesting little sidelight upon the habits and practices of workmen is cast by the number of entries in the Accounts relating to drink bought for those who did jobs at the Parish Church:

1557: Pd. Wm. Walton wife for ale: 1s. 0d.

1559: For ale at the mending of the bells and for the resurrection: 11d.

For bread and ale to Pavye (the Parish Clerk): 4d.

1562: For mending of the Church walls and other Things finding themselves Meate and Drinke:

For Drinke to the Masons man the same day he took down the Weather Cocke: 2d.

For a Cann to serve the Mason withal 2d.

Pd. for Drinke at John Sheldon's for 1 man that helped downe with the ladders of the church: 2d.

And hospitality extended beyond the provision of drink for labouring men:

1561: Item paid to 2 priests to drink: 2s.

1568: Item given for the Dinner of certain men at the Exchange of certain Lands with Robt. More by estimation a Roode: 2s.

1572: For the Supper of Christopher Wilson, Wm. Cudworth and Richd. Greaves and for the Breakfast in the Morning and Horse Meat two nights: 2s. 10d.

Item paid for the Dinner of Robt. Urton and Robt. Bowie and their Horse Meyte and to the Summonary Clerk his duety at the sd. visitation: 1s. 7d.

An item in 1566 could be either for the refreshments of helpers or for the Burgesses themselves: Item paid for Ale when we made the Books: 6d

The long-standing tradition continues of a Rent Audit Dinner around Martinmas, but no longer for the purpose of mustering tenants to pay their dues. Nowadays, it is an occasion still of business (albeit a pleasant social event) allowing Burgesses opportunity to meet, in a small gathering, clergy from their parishes or the Diocese. The first reference to a Rent Dinner is in the accounts for 1566: Item pd. for the Dinner of the 12 Capital Burgesses the Day of the Reckoning: 4s. No one could accuse the Burgesses of over-indulging themselves on that occasion. The cost per head is similar to what they paid for a workman's ale. Other entries appear with regularity:

1568: For the Burgesses Dinner the Reckoning Day with Drinkes for Neighbours: 5s. 4d.

1571: For Dinners of the Twelve Capital Burgesses with others to the number 24 with Drinks at after Dinner: 9s.

For the Church Burgesses Dinner at ye searching of ye Evidence: 4s.

1572: For the Church Burgesses Dinner and others that viewed the Church Land being 16 persons and for Drinke when they came home: 6s.8d.

For the charges of the Capital Burgesses meeting 2 sevl. Days for this Reckoning making and other needful business at. Wm. Walton's the sume of 9s.0d.

We referred in Chapter VIII to the wood at Lady's Spring and to the attention paid by the Burgesses to their woodland. There are several entries in the Election Book which illustrate careful management of this renewable resource:

15 June 1674: Then agreed at a publique Meeting of the Burgesses and Cominaltie that noo wood be felled in the Ladie Spring or elsewhere att any tyme but such as shall be sett out by two or more of the Burgesses and they to be appointed by the said Burgesses or major pte of them att a publique Meeting.

28 June 1681: That such wood as shall be necessarie for the repairs of the vicarrige house att Sheffield shall be sett out and appointed in the Ladies Spring and Carrwood and to be chosen such as is on the decaying land and to be vallued att a reasonable pryce to be paid by the Parish for the same.

In 1697 an agreement was made with John Fell that he was to have 70 trees marked and one unmarked from Ladies Spring which he was to pay for the felling of and to stub the same for which he was to pay before Martimas £75 and if he did not clear £15 he was to have another tree added worth 50s.

And in the Accounts for 1733: Henry Wilkinson for planting upwards of 200 ash plants in Lady's Spring: 11s. 0d.

In the Election Book for 7 November 1733, we read: 'that Mr. Fell is to pay the principal money of £140 mentioned in his Bond and no interest he having a very hard bargain of the wood he bought of the Burgesses in ye Lady Spring.'

In 1670 land in Attercliffe was being opened up for agriculture for two men had 20 months allowed them to 'stubb cut down carry away and convert to their own use all the oaks and ash trees in the Carr Wood in Attercliffe and 3 hedgerows near unto the same, and also 3 oakes in the square meadow adjoining, the trees were to be stubbed up by the roots and the land made plowable' – for which they agreed to pay £50.

Estates have their problems from time to time as appears from an entry in the Election Book for 22 March 1727: 'Ordered that the Clerk to prepare a letter for the Burgesses to signe to send to Esq. Bright in order to secure and amend the ways on Little Sheffield Common to the land of the Burgerry there the Brick makers there haveing very much spoyld the wayes by digging of clay to make bricks of.'

Dubious grants are very rare in the Burgesses' accounts, but a minute of 18 June 1799 appears to indicate that enthusiasm for encouraging public order led them into an error of judgement: 'Proposals for raising an armed association of Infantry and a Corps of Cavalry for the defence of the Town of Sheffield. Resolved that as such a Corps, in case of any actual disturbance or Insurrection to the Neighbourhood might be essentially serviceable for the preservation of the Church and its estates, as well as of property in general, this Body do think themselves called upon to contribute towards the Encouragement of such a Corps and do therefore order that the sum of £50 be paid to the Committee for the Management of the Funds of such a Corps.'

It is interesting that the justification of such a payment is set out in terms, as it were, of insurance for the Burgesses' property. However, in 1803 they were forced, with regret, to reconsider this decision after taking account of the opinion of Counsel: 29 August 1803: 'On consideration of the affair of Subscription to the proposed Volunteer Corps of Sheffield that the State of the Funds of the Charity and the opinion of Mr. Hargeaves respecting such application of the Moneys, do strongly oppose it however willing the Trustees feel themselves to promote the Subscription.'

In 1825, at the time of the demolition of the Old Grammar School appears the entry: 'To Samuel Wingfield, for watching the Old Grammar School 11 nights: £1 2s. 0d.'

An entry in the accounts for 1808 demonstrates the high regard the Burgesses had for the Revd. James Wilkinson and also must represent something of a bargain: 'Paid to F. Chantrey: bust of Revd. James Wilkinson: £10 10s.'

A minute of 26 April 1837 reads: Ordered that the Trust decline contributing to the fund for the destruction of mad dogs as not coming within the meaning of the Trust.

In 1848, we have the curious case of the missing plans. On 6 July William Fowler was appointed Surveyor to the Trust in place of the late Mr. Fairbank. There was great difficulty in getting hold of plans of the Burgesses' estates from Fairbank's office. At a meeting on 25 June 1849 the Burgesses resolved: 'that Mr. Robert Younge be requested to hand over as soon as practicable the several plans, papers and other documents belonging to the Trust which were in the hands of the late Mr. Fairbank at the time of his death.' This was followed by minutes for 5 April and 25 April indicating that Younge was being pressed hard to secure the handover of documents, but he stated that all the documents to which the Burgesses were entitled had been handed over. Two Burgesses, George Hounsfield and Henry Wilson were deputed to have discussions with Younge, who agreed that James Wheat, the Law Clerk, could examine the Fairbank's papers. In July, Wheat reported that only a portion of the plans had been handed over, but there was a willingness to hand over the remainder, that willingness being tempered by a requirement that they be paid for. The Law Clerk and the Surveyor were authorised to negotiate with Fairbank's representatives and in August the sum of £40 was paid. Since Fairbank had been paid to do the work in the first place, it seems hardly fair that the Burgeses should have to pay a second time for their own property.

APPENDIX IV

Law Clerks and Surveyors

Law Clerks

THE ELECTION BOOK records that on 3 December 1652, James Lee 'shall have and receive the sum of 20s. yearly for attending and entering of the several orders of the Burgery.' This is the first reference to a named person undertaking such duties. The last mention of James Lee is in the Accounts for 1663. Thereafter, until 1735, references in the Accounts are to payments made to un-named persons, 'the Clerk', or 'our Clerk', for duties of attending meetings and making up the accounts. In 1673, however, there is a payment to John Styring for 'his attendance and for drawing the Rentall', and a further reference to Mr. Styring – a payment for his salary and attendance – in 1697. It is possible therefore that John Styring served as Law Clerk for a number of years. But it is not until William Battie's appointment on 27 May 1735 that we can make a confident record of the sequence of Law Clerks of the Trust. That sequence is as follows:

William BATTIE:	1735-1766
James WHEAT (the Younger):	1805-1848
John James WHEAT:	1848-1911
John Bristowe WHEAT:	1911-1936
Brian PYE -SMITH:	1936-1966
Peter S. NEWTON:	1966*
Martin P.W. LEE:	1968-1997
Godfrey J. SMALLMAN:	1997-

Surveyors

The first reference to a named surveyor is in the Accounts for 1739, as a payment to William Fairbank for surveying Pinson Crofts. Thereafter, there are records of payments for surveys undertaken by Fairbank. In 1784, appears a payment to William Fairbank (who would be the son of the William referred to in 1739) 'for business done by him as surveyor to the Trust.' This is the first reference to the office of Surveyor. The Fairbanks continued in this capacity until the death of William Fairbank Fairbank in

*Note 1: Peter Newton became seriously ill shortly after his appointment and died in February, 1968. Brian Pye-Smith took over the administration of the Trust in an honorary capacity until the appointment of Martin Lee.

1848. William Fowler was appointed Surveyor on 6 July 1848. It is likely therefore that four generations of the Fairbank family officiated as Surveyor to the Trust between 1739 and 1848. Appointments thereafter were:

William FOWLER:	1848-1858
Thomas J. FLOCKTON:	1858-1899
Charles B. FLOCKTON:	1899-1945
Sidney Eric SHEPHERD	1945-1964
Charles Richard Stephen SANDFORD	1964-1982
Nicholas R.B. ROBINSON:	1982-

APPENDIX V

A Note on the Value of Money

IN 1557, the disposable income of the Church Burgesses was slightly more than £30. Four hundred years later it was approaching £20,000 and currently stands slightly in excess of £1m. Do these increases represent, only or largely, the inexorable effects of inflation, or has there been a real increase in the resources of the Trust? The answers to these questions will reflect upon the stewardship exercised by the Trust and upon the expectations of the recipients of the Trust's financial support.

It is exceptionally difficult, if not impossible, to express, in directly relevant terms, the changing value of money over a long period of time. A national Cost of Living Index has been in use for barely 80 years and the relationship between that Index and 'the value of money' remains a matter for debate. It is just not possible to agree a single national indicator which would adequately reflect the changing value of money over a period of some 450 years. Nevertheless, some rough guidance may be attempted which must, however, carry the considerable caveat that it is a rough-and-ready guidance only and cannot be used to determine, with any sort of accuracy, precise comparisons of the value of the Trust's income during its long history.

The work of Sir Henry Phelps Brown and Sheila Hopkins provide the basis upon which others have worked. (See: Henry Phelps Brown and Sheila Hopkins: *A perspective of wages and prices*, Methuen, 1981) In meticulous studies, making use of much original material and the findings of previous workers in the field (notably Thorold Rogers, Steffen, Meredith and Beveridge), Phelps Brown and Hopkins have given data showing the variations in prices of consumables and in wage rates of building craftsmen and labourers over 7 centuries, from about 1250 to 1950. They have published tables and graphs of the movement of both prices and wages. But they, too, have entered their important caveat that it is not possible to attach much meaning to the cost of maintaining a constant standard of living through seven centuries of social change.

Tables of the Retail Price Index and the Purchasing Power of the Pound are published regularly by the Central Statistical Office and the Bank of England. Published tables on the purchasing power of the pound purport to present a complete run of data from the 13th century to the present day. We would do well, however, to heed the caveats already mentioned. There are variations between the various published tables and it would be pointless to attempt here a reconciliation of various sets of figures. In any event, it is quite clear that, whatever the basis upon which national statistics are produced, they are not directly relevant to the local situation we have to consider.

The following Table has been compiled by selecting information from the movement of the Retail Price Index and the Purchasing Power of the Pound. The figure for 1995 could vary by up to 25%, depending upon which data are used. The figure quoted here is deliberately on the high side.

Table showing comparative value of money

1550	£10
1650	£28
1750	£32
1850	£55
1950	£200
1995	£5,000

(viz., what was purchased with £10 in 1557 would now require £5,000)

On this basis, the £30 income of the Burgesses in 1557 would now represent something like £15,000 in current money. But one has only to glance at what the Burgesses did with £30 in 1557 to realise the invalidity of this comparison. From this income, the Burgesses paid the stipends of three priests (which would now amount to not less than £45,000-£50,000); the wages of the Parish Clerk; maintenance and running costs of the Parish Church; and also paid off substantial legal costs.

In total, the outgoings in 1557 must represent an expenditure of not less than £75,000 in today's money. This sum is five times greater than that derived from Retail Price Index/Purchasing Power of the Pound Tables.

What is clear is that the Church Burgesses, in the stewardship of their resources, have generated income which has greatly exceeded any measure of the effects of inflation.

APPENDIX VI

A Note on the Terms: Burgess, Capital Burgess and Burgery

IN ANCIENT TIMES, a Burgess was a free-man of a town, whether incorporated or unincorporated; viz. a man who was not under obligation to fulfil feudal duties required by the lord of the manor. Such freedom was granted by the lord upon payment, either as commuted capital or regular payments of rent for property or land of which the free-man would, in effect be the freeholder. The Furnival Charter of 1297 established the rights of those who, in the Charter, are referred to as 'the Free Tenants of the town of Sheffield'. Later, in Sheffield, as in other towns, the free-man, i.e. Burgess, came to accept responsibilities for ordering the necessities of community life; they provided the slowly emerging framework of what ultimately was legislated for as local government. The Charter of Incorporation of the borough of Sheffield, granted in 1843, states: 'the body corporate shall be called the Mayor, Aldermen and Burgesses of the borough of Sheffield'. By that time, Burgesses were those who had the right to vote, based upon their status as householder and ratepayer.

Burgesses, and other citizens, comprised the Burgery, the community of the town. J.D. Leader, in writing the history of the Town Trust, called his book: *The Records of the Burgery of Sheffield*. Well before the incorporation of the town, one could speak of the Burgery of Sheffield, comprising all those activities carried on under formal and informal regulation within the extensive parish of Sheffield. The word 'Burgery' has the same root as 'burgh', 'borough' and 'burghers'. In the late 16th and 17th centuries, the Town Trust granted leases in the name of 'the Burghers, or major part of the Burghers, of Sheffield', or 'the Burghers, or major part of the Burghers and Free Tenants of Sheffield', purporting therefore to act on behalf of the Burgery of Sheffield. The Church Burgesses, too, used the term in 1652, in referring to their Clerk, James Lee, 'attending and entering several orders of the Burgery'. In short, he and they were attending to the town's business.

It is clear that, well before there were 'Church Burgesses' or a 'Town Trust', there were Burgesses, freeholders in modern parlance, who, whether men of substance or of more modest means, would be responsible for maintaining the essential infra-structure of the community, as we might now put it. From their number some would be appointed to hold public office as church wardens, sheriff and in other capacities. Bequests were made to the town in the care and trust of the Burgesses, as, for example, in the William Hyne will of 1498, which bequeathed property to pay for masses in the Parish Church, but, if these services were not performed, the proceeds were 'for the use of the freeholders of Sheffield called the Burgesses', to be disposed of 'in mending bridges, causeys and highways . . .'

When, in 1554, Queen Mary Tudor granted her Charter, she formally established a Trust with a clearly defined constitution and membership. In naming the Trust as 'The Twelve Capital Burgesses and Commonalty of Sheffield', she, or her advisers, were following a practice already established in other towns in which governance was in the hands of 'Capital Burgesses', viz. Burgesses who had been selected or elected to undertake important local duties. In Sheffield, the first Capital Burgesses were appointed by the Queen and the Trust was to be self-perpetuating, in contrast to arrangements in other towns in which the Capital Burgesses were elected by other Burgesses.

The Twelve Capital Burgesses seem to have adopted the name 'Church Burgesses' by the early 17th century; the terms 'School Burgesses' being used for the Governors of the Grammar School and 'Town's Burgesses' for those who administered the proceeds of the town's lands. The chairman, for the time being, of the Trust was, from earliest times, known as 'the Collector' and he was, literally, the person who received rents in person from tenants who attended, at the appointed times to make their payments. The adoption of the term 'Capital Burgess' in its current meaning of the chairman for the time being of the Trust came into use from 1673. This convention can be confusing. 'Capital Burgesses', in the plural refers to the whole Trust. In the singular, the Capital Burgess means the Trustee who currently serves as chairman.

APPENDIX VII

A Biographical Register of the Sheffield Church Burgesses 1554-1997

Compiled by P.J. Wallis
Revised and Expanded by S.E. Fowl (1986) and D.C. Wilson (1997)

(The Register prepared by P.J. Wallis was originally published in the *Transactions of the Hunter Archaeological Society*: Vol. 7, 1952, 51-62; 1953-54, 144-157; 1955, 194-199; 1957, 344-360)

A summary chart of succession is first given, followed by biographical entries for each Burgess, who is identified by reference to the chart of succession. The original Burgesses are numbered in the order in which they are mentioned in the Charter and later members follow in order of succession. For example, George Hounsfield is numbered 8.19, viz. he is 19th in order of succession to Hugh Chalnor, who was the 8th named Burgess in the Charter.

Abbrevations Used

S.	Sheffield	F.	Freedom of the Cutlers' Company
A.	Attercliffe	app.	apprentice(d)
B.	Brightside	sh.	shearsmith
Bd.	Bradfield	yeo.	yeoman
D.	Darnall	t.	tailor
E.	Ecclesall	bn.	born
Fd.	Fulwood	bap.	baptised
H.	Hallam	m.	married
N.	Norton	d.	died
C.	Curate	bur.	buried
M.	Assistant Minister	(e).s.	(eldest) son
V.	Vicar	(o.)d.	(only) daughter
CB.	Church Burgess	c.	child
CW.	Church Warden	c.h.	co-heir(ess)
GS(G).	Grammar School (Governor)	s.p.	without issue
TT.	Town Trust(ee) [This term is used before the incorporation]	w.d.	will dated
		w.p.	will proved (usually at York)
TC.	Town Collector	MI	monumental inscription
Ald.	Alderman	wid.	widow
MC.	Master Cutler	bro.	brother

1

1 Robert Swift
1554-8/9
2 Thomas Braye
1558/9-70
3 William Burrowes
1570-87
4 William Hoole
1587-1627/8
5 Nicholas Saunderson
1627/8-164?
6 William Rawson
164?-8/9
7 John Crooke
1648/9-68/9
8 William Cooke
1668/9-73
9 Zachary Wilson
1673-1702
10 John Waterhouse
1702-14
11 Thomas Wright
1714-41
12 Paul Meyer
1741-43
13 Isaac Nodder
1743/4-68
14 Thomas Younge
1768-84
15 Francis Fenton
1785-1835
16 Richard Bayley
1825-50
17 Edward Hudson
1850-87
18 Henry Stephenson
1887-1904
19 Henry Kenyon Stephenson
1904-47
20 Samuel Eric Osborn
1947-51
21 John Philip Hunt
1951-57
22 Bertram Harold Barber
1957-80
23 Rev Canon Dr George Tolley
1980-

2

1 Hugh Smith
1554-60
2 James Turner
1560-83
3 William Dickenson
1583-1606
4 William Creswick
1606-13
5 William Jessop
1613-17
6 George Jessop
1623-5?
7 William Jessop
1630-41
8 John Bright
1641-43
9 James Moseley
1643-47
10 Humphrey Shemeld
1647-57
11 Edward Rawson
1657-69
12 James Nicholson
1669-71
13 Joseph Nicholson
1671-93/4
14 Thomas Chappell
1693/4-1703
15 Arthur Palmer
1703-22
16 Joseph Bright
1722-43
17 John Nodder
1743-72
18 Thomas Gunning
1772-84
19 John Kenyon
1784-1809
20 Thomas Watson
1809-32
21 Henry Wilson
1832-80
22 Henry Edmund Watson
1880-1901
23 James Dixon
1901-25
24 Reginald Thorp Wilson
1925-53
25 Ralph Macro Wilson
1953-58
26 David Clement Wilson
1958-

3

1 Richard Fenton
1554-79
2 William Jessop
1579-84
3 John Hyley
1585-1604
4 Nicholas Turton
1604-26
5 John Wilson
1626-164?
6 James Moseley
164?-61
7 Francis Jessop
1661-91
8 William Jessop
1691-1734
9 John Ellison
1734-41
10 Wharton Bridden
1741-2
11 Matthew Lambert
1742-70
12 Thomas Smith
1770-74
13 Gamaliel Milner
1774-1825
14 Henry Newbould
1825-71
15 Thomas Austin Sorby
1871-85
16 Samuel Roberts
1885-1926
17 Thomas Kingsford Wilson
1926-37
18 Alfred Henry Winston
1937-52
19 Ambrose Firth
1952-62
20 Percy James Clarke Bovill
1962-67
21 Thomas Norman Boddy
1967-84
22 Professor Geoffrey D Sims
1984-

4

1 William Taylor
1554-87
2 William Staniforth
1587-1620/1
3 Stephen Bright
1620/1-42
4 John Bright
1642-88
5 John Staniforth
1688-1704
6 William Hawley
1704-13
7 Thomas Handley
1713-46
8 John Shirecliffe
1746/7-89
9 Thomas Smith
1789-98
10 Robert Turner
1798-1822
11 John Porter
1822-56
12 Henry Marwood Greaves
1856-59
13 Samuel Roberts
1859-87
14 Charles Macro Wilson
1887-1902
15 John Newton Coombe
1902-20
16 Frederic Markham Tindall
1920-32
17 Arthur Wallace Pickard-Cambridge
1932-39
18 Henry Swift Levick
1939-52
19 Philip Neill
1952-77
20 Peter Wilton Lee
1977-

5

1 Robert Moore
1554-83
2 George Moore
1583-95
3 William Lee
1595-1609
4 Malin Stacey
1609-36
5 Robert Bright
1636-67
6 John Bright
1667-86
7 John Bright
1686-1703
8 John Bright
1703-22
9 Arthur Speight
1722-38/9
10 Joseph Clay
1739-97
11 Benjamin Wainwright
1797-1819
12 James Drabble
1819-41
13 Henry Furniss
1841-72
14 Henry Unwin
1871-9
15 Walter Brown
1879-1901
16 William Chesterman
1901-20
17 Sir William Henry Ellis
1920-45
18 Carl Eric Holmstrom
1945-68
19 Howard Poulsom Forder
1968-84
20 Stewart McKee Hamilton
1984-

6

1 William Walton
1554-73
2 James Haldsworth
1573-96/7
3 William Scargell
1597-1602
4 Roger Lee
1602-14
5 Christopher Capper
1614-36
6 George Dodson
1636-42
7 William Fox
1642-8
8 Robert Hoole
1648-58/9
9 Thomas Britland
1659-96
10 Joseph Banks
1697-1726
11 George Steer
1726-38
12 Samuel Staniforth
1738-48
13 Walter Osborne
1749-78
14 James Wheat
1778-1805
15 William Wilson
1805-29
16 Samuel Revill
1829-60
17 George Walker
1860-74
18 Henry Rodgers
1874-82
19 Arthur Thomas
1882-84
20 George Wilson
1884-85
21 Arthur Jackson
1885-95
22 William Greaves Blake
1886-1904
23 Henry Barlow Sandford
1904-30
24 James Henry Doncaster
1930-40
25 Sir Alan John Grant
1940-45
26 James White Merryweather
1945-66
27 Brian Charles Pye-Smith
1966-81
28 John Frank William Peters
1981-

7

1 Robert Smith
1554-56
2 Thomas Scargell
1559-75
3 William Sylvester
1575-93/4
4 Leonard Bamforth
1594
5 Robert Rollinson
1594-1631
6 James Creswick
1631-42
7 James Creswick
1642-52
8 Henry Bright
1652-73
9 George Wylde
1673-88
10 Thomas Spencer
1688-1703
11 Robert Clay
1703-37
12 Gamaliel Milner
1737-48
13 John Trevers Younge
1748-1807
14 Samuel Younge
1807-40
15 Robert Younge
1840-74
16 Thomas Turner
1874-95
17 William Smith
1895-1901
18 William Burnett Esam
1901-32
19 Victor Henry Sandford
1932-77
20 Paul Terence Ward
1977-1998

8

1 Hugh Chalnor
1554-1603
2 Jasper Fisher
1603-34
3 Edward Saunderson
1634-72/3
4 Edward Barlow
1672/3-75/6
5 Joseph Sturtevant
1675/6-85
6 William Fenton
1685-96
7 Stephen Bright
1696-?
8 Thomas Diston
?-1702
9 William Sitwell
1703
10 Hugh Spooner
1703-12
11 George Bamforth
1712-30
12 John Nodder
1730-32/3
13 John Fell
1732/3-62
14 Robert Waterhouse
1762-4
15 Thomas Bright
1764-78
16 Samuel Staniforth
1778-1820
17 Charles Younge
1820-31
18 Bartholomew Hounsfield
1831-41
19 George Hounsfield
1841-70
20 Thomas Wilson
1870-95
21 Samuel Gray Richardson
1895-1930
22 David Flather
1930-44
23 Alfred Edward Bassett
1944-46
24 John Basil Peile
1946-1988
25 Nicholas James Anthony Hutton
1988-

9

1 William Burrowes
1554-58
2 John Hoole
1558-72/3
3 James Rawson
1573-1603
4 Hugh Rawson
1603-28
5 James Bright
1628-53
6 Roger Lee
1653-83
7 Jonathan Lee
1683-1713
8 Christopher Broomhead
1713-29
9 Thomas Heaton
1729-34
10 William Burton
1734/5-64
11 John Fenton
1764-76
12 John Turner
1777-96
13 Richard Swallow
1796-1801
14 Richard Swallow
1801
15 John Rawson
1801-19
16 Henry Limbrey Toll
1819-22
17 Ralph Blakelock Esam
1822-27
18 Charles Brownell
1827-40
19 James Creswick
1840-54
20 Nathaniel Creswick
1854-55
21 Samuel Butcher
1855-69
22 John Jobson Smith
1869-78
23 James William Harrison
1878-97
24 Charles Belk
1897-1904
25 John Dodsley Webster
1904-13
26 James Rossiter Hoyle
1913-21
27 Albert Harland
1921-57
28 Charles Graham Murray
1957-

10

1 John Holland
1554-71
2 Richard Jessop
1571-80
3 John Bright
1580-87
4 John Holland
1587-1641
5 George Ludlam
1642-51
6 William Spencer
1651-67
7 William Spencer
1667-86
8 Francis Barlow
1686-89/90
9 Robert Sorsby
1690-1700/01
10 John Fell
1701-24
11 Joseph Steer
1724-44
12 Thomas Waterhouse
1744-60
13 William Staniforth
1760-68
14 James Allott
1768-76
15 George Greaves
1776
16 John Winter
1776-92
17 John Parsons
1792-95
18 Thomas Ruddiman Stewart
1795-98
19 John Greaves
1798-1828
20 John Sorby
1828-44
21 Charles Frederick Younge
1844-64
22 Henry Isaac Dixon
1864-1901
23 Harry Parker Marsh
1901-33
24 Edward Wilfred Pye-Smith
1933-48
25 Charles Clifford Everard
1948-75
26 James Peter Rees Holt
1975-1997

11

1 Thomas Mitchell
1554-63/4
2 Robert Mitchell
1564-1609/10
3 William Fox
1610
4 Edward Saunderson
1610-17
5 Ulysses Fox
1617-49
6 William Unwen
1649-62/3
7 Alexander Ashton
1663-82
8 George Bamforth
1682-1701
9 Robert Sorsby
1701-17
10 George Lee
1717-20
11 Denis Neville
1720-32
12 John Fenton
1732-61
13 John Hussey
1761-73
14 Joseph Matthewman
1773-91
15 William Younge
1791-1838
16 Laurence Potts
1838-41
17 Francis Huntsman
1841-54
18 William Ibbotson Horn
1854-73
19 Francis Hobson
1873-1902
20 Edward Willoughby Firth
1902-35
21 John Henry W Laverick
1935-51
22 Gerald Steel
1951-56
23 John Macnaughton Whittaker
1956-71
24 William Herbert Olivier
1971-80
25 Douglas Leslie Fletcher
1980-

12

1 Thomas Parker
1554-?
2 John Rawson
1563-94
3 Edward Rawson
1594-7
4 John Shemeld
1597-1603
5 Thomas Creswick
1603-11-?
6 Francis Barlow
161?-16
7 John Hoole
1616-21
8 Richard Shemeld
1622-45
9 William Creswick
1645-66
10 Richard Woodgrove
1666-82
11 Thomas Marriott
1682-1706
12 Thomas Parkin
1706-29
13 John Battie
1729/30-47/8
14 William Battie
1748-74
15 William Burton
1774-98
16 Joseph Ibberson
1798
17 Simon Andrews Younge
1798-1811
18 Thomas Newbould
1811-44
19 Thomas Creswick
1844-63
20 John Brown
1864-96
21 Charles Edmund Vickers
1896-1925
22 Sir Ronald Wilfred Matthews
1925-39
23 Charles Sidney Sandford
1939-49
24 Charles Richard Stephen Sandford
1949-63
25 John Tharratt Riddle
1963-78
26 Dr Herbert Harkness Pilling
1978-1992
27 Stephen Albert Paul Hunter
1993-

ALLOTT James, of Attercliffe, gent. 10.14. O.c. of James of Wakefield and Margaret (Clay) of Bridgehouses. m. Esther, d. of William Burton of Royds Mill, s.p. From 1763 principal partner in S. Lead Works. Elected CB. 4.5.1768 and resigned 3.7.1776. GS(G). Original member of 'The Monthly Club'. One male servant in 1780. D. 30 August 1783, aged 50, and bur. A. Chapel; bulk of his estate passed to the Greaves of Page Hall.

ASHTON Alexander, of Whiteley Wood, gent. 11.7. 2nd s. of Robert of Stoney Middleton and High Sheriff of Derbys. and Joan (Sharpe). Uncle of Charles Ashton, D.D., Master of Jesus College, Cambridge. m. at Bd. 18.5.1659, Alice, d. and c.h. of Thomas Dale of Whiteley Wood. 1681 constable for H. and E. CB. until his death; bur. at S. 18.5.1682.

BAMFORTH George, of High House, Owlerton, lord of the manor. 11.8. Bap. S. 14.8.1625, (e).s. of George, GS(G)., yeo. and sh. of High House, and Winifred (Oxspring). App. to his father; F. 1653, having 3 smithies in 1670. CB. 6.8.1682 and continued until his death. GS(G). m. at E. Chapel 28.5.1683, Margaret, d. of Thomas Danid of Dronfield, and who, with their son, made bequests to the poor and to Wadsley school before her death in 1727. In 1677 he bought Wadsley Manor from the Duke of Norfolk. In 1688 he was collector for the V.'s money. George d. at S. 21.10.1701.

BAMFORTH George, of High House, gent., lord of the manor. 8.11. Bn. S. 17.5.1684, (e).s. of George above. Educated at S. GS. and St. John's College, Cambridge, pensioner 1701, fellow-commoner 1701/2, B.A. 1704/5. m. 1st, 8.8.1709, Anne, d. of Henry Hancock, and who was bur. 19.5.1717, Esther, d. of William Burton of Royds Mill, and who subsequently m. Robert Chappell, barrister, and Paul Meyer (q.v.). GS(G). Started the Bamforth Charity. Received 40 law books by the will of his uncle John Danid. In 1709 he paid 43s. towards the GS. Master's house. He was connected with St. Paul's Church. w.d. 23.4.1730. Bur. at S. 26.4.1730; inventory taken 13.7.1730 totalled £2,718 7s. 6d.

BAMFORTH Leonard, gent., Gray's Inn. 7.4. Connection with the Bamforths of High House is probable but not established. Witness to a Bd. marriage settlement in 1569; his own children bap. at Bd. from 1577 to 1585, his wife's name being Anne. Bought various properties in Bd., Ecclesfield and Silkstone districts. Steward for Cowley Manor in 1583. One of four judges in 1587 E. Manor case. Warden of S. Stock, 1587. An under-steward at S. 1589-90. An officer and friend of the Shrewsburys, being given a farm in Earl George's will and leasing Ardsley Manor and lands in Darfield and Earl Gilbert. Only CB. for a few months before his death; w.d. 6.8.1594, bur. within the Chancel of S. Church on 25.10.1594.

BANKS Joseph, Shirecliffe Hall, Attorney. 6.10. Bn. at Giggleswick 6.9.1665, s. of Robert of Beck Hall, an army officer at one time under Sir John Reresby at Bridlington and Margaret (Frankland). Served his articles under Thomas Chappell.

m. on 5.8.1689, Mary, d. of Rowland Hancock of Shirecliffe Hall, where he spent the early part of his married life. Under-Sheriff for Yorks. Agent for Dukes of Norfolk, Leeds and Newcastle, with 'his finger in every local pie'. Assessed for £4 4s. in 1692, with wife, child, two clerks and two servants. In 1697/8 bought Hoyle House, H., from John Unwin. Part owner of Handsworth Colliery. Elected CB. 23.4.1697 and TT. 3.11.1703, and resigned on removal to Scofton, near Worksop; also lived at Revesby Abbey. M.P. for Grimsby and Totnes. w.d. 27.7.1726. d. 27.8(?9).1727.

BARBER Bertram Harold, O.B.E. 1.22. Elected CB. 1957. b. 28.11.1901. s. of Harold Priestman, Chartered Accountant and Winifred Mary (Spratt). Ed. Shrewsbury. m. 3.3.1939, Nancy Lorraine (Belsham). Director of Marsh Brothers & Co. Ltd, and the Effingham Steelworks. J.P. Governor and Trustee S. Savings Bank. General Commissioner of Income Tax. Trustee Bluecoat Educational Foundation, S. GS. Exhibition Foundation, CB. Educational Foundation. Chairman S. Council of Boys' Clubs. Former Member Committee and Trustee Yorkshire County Cricket Club. d. 2.3. 1982.

BARLOW Edward, cutler. 8.4. Elected CB. 4.3.1672/3, vice Edward Saunders. who was probably his brother-in-law. Bap. at S. 13.12.1607, 4th s. of Francis (below) and his 2nd wife Ann (Hill), who remarried Christopher Capper, CB. 6.5. m. at S. 30.6.1630 Isabella, d. of Christopher Capper by his 1st w. Elizabeth (Hoole). CW. for the town in 1640 and 1649, constable in 1642, MC. in 1653 and TC. in 1655. 'Religiously disposed and well-affected' in 1645. m. 2nd 25.9.1655 Elizabeth (Newbowne), wid. of William Wadsworth, clerk to the Cutlers' Company. 1665, four hearths. It was presumably another Edward Barlow who was MC in 1670. W.d 4.9.1675 and bur. at S. 7.1.1675/6.

BARLOW Francis, The Cock Inn, chapman and ironmonger. 12.6. Younger s. of Henry of A. and Alice (Swift), bap. at S. 27.9.1563. m. 1st Isabella Frankish at S. on 24.6.1593 and 2 on 5.11.1599 Ann, d. of Edward Hill, coverlet weaver of B., and Margaret (Shemeld); Ann remarried Christopher Capper, CB. 6.5. CW. for the town in 1599. Paid 10s. in 1606 GS. Assessment. Only CB. for a short time before his death; w.d. 1.8.1616 and bur. at S. 16.8.1616.

BARLOW Francis. 10.8. Bap. S. 26.9.1626, (e).s. of Humphrey, vintner and grocer (2nd s. of Francis, CB. 12.6) and Dorothy (Sylvester). He succeeded his father both as vintner and ironmonger, having the Angel Inn and being a partner with William Simpson and Dennis Heyford in the iron works. His wealth is indicated by having 11 hearths taxed in 1665. He was actively connected with the TT., being TC. in 1661 and 1687, and was given honorary F. by the Cutlers' Company in 1681. GS(G)., but only CB. for a few years before his death (this despite his nonconformity). His children by his wife Catherine all d. young and he made his nephew Thomas, s. of his Quaker brother Samuel, his heir; w.d. 6.12.1688. He d. 18.3.1689/90 and was bur. in the chancel of S. church; MI.

BASSETT Albert Edward. 8.23. Elected CB. 8.12.1944. b. 12.2.1873 London, s. of Robert, soda merchant of London. Joined Mappin & Webb Ltd., silver plate manufacturers 1888, Director 1912, Director Associated Companies S. Silver Plate & Cutlery Co. Ltd. and Heeley Silver Rolling Mills Ltd. Member St. John's Ranmoor, PCC and Finance Committee. m. 1903 Beatrice (d. 1.11.1945) of Thomas George Sharp, London timber broker. d. 27.11.1945.

BATTIE John, Church Gates, attorney. 12.13. s. of Robert and Isabella. m. 1st Mary Handley, d. of Richard, apothecary and 2nd Margaret Ward, d. of William, attorney of London. Steward of the Manor Court, and also of the Bright Ecclesall and other estates, he trained many prominent local lawyers from his office in Paradise Square. He paid 10s. towards the GS. Master's house in 1709. He was connected with St. Paul's Church, trustee in 1739. Elected CB. 29.1.1729/30. Had 2 shares in Don Navigation Co. d. 22.3.1747/8, aged 64.

BATTIE William, Sharrow Head, attorney. 12.14. Bap. at S. 13.6.1711, s. of above John by his 2nd w. Clerk to the CBs., elected 27.5.1735, resigned 1766 and succeeded by James Wheat. Steward of Eckington and also for the Bright Ecclesall and other estates. His 'clients . . . come from many parts of England and vary considerably both in social standing and financial position'. Trustee for St Paul's in 1739. Elected CB. 16.4.1748 succeeding his father, and remained until his death. GS(G)., TT. d. unmarried 21.4.1774.

BAYLEY Richard, J.P., Castle Dyke, Ecclesall and Whirlow Grange. 1.16. Bn. 1801, (e).s. of Richard of Broomfield, a merchant and ironmonger, and Ellen (Hurst) of Wakefield. Elected CB. 13.6.1835 and resigned 4.11.1850. Also GS(G). and original Trustee of the Collegiate School. Poor Law Guardian for E. 'Munificent patron of art, and his collection of pictures is said to be one of the finest in the county'. Voted for Wortley in 1835, for Overend in 1852. Governor of Dronfield GS. from 1868. d. at S. 18.10.1884.

BELK Charles, J.P., Holmwood. 9.24. Bn. in S. and app. to Fr. Newton & Sons, Portobello Works. 1863, partner with Samuel Roberts at Furnival Works. 1877 F. by purchase, knife maker. 1885 MC.; also lectured on the history of the Company before the Lit. and Phil. Soc., of which he was President in 1886. Also President of the Chamber of Commerce 1887, and active in Conservative politics. Trustee of S. Savings Bank and Council Member of Firth and University Colleges, S. CB. from his election on 25.3.1897 until his death, aged 65, on 28.11.1904.

BLAKE Major William Greaves, D.L., J.P., Sharrow House and Mylnhurst, E. 6.22. Bn. 26.1.1833 at Norbury Hall, Pitsmoor, s. of Thomas (MC. in 1836, and subsequently of Upper Norwood, Surrey) and Elizabeth (Greaves). Educated at the Collegiate School and studied. in Germany. Served in Crimean War and Indian Mutiny (Captain 9th Lancers); Major in West Yorks. Militia. On 24.6.1863 m. at St. Mary's, S., Caroline Rebecca Watson. In 1869 m. 2nd Rebecca, d. of Thomas Jessop of Endcliffe Grange. Partner in Stephenson, Blake & Co., typefounders. 1880-82, Church of England member of the School Board. Chairman E. Board of Guardians. Conservative in politics. 1885, Director of S. and Rotherham Bank. A S. Savings Bank Governor, trustee of Jessop Hospital for Women and Chairman of S. Girls' Charity School. CB. from his election on 16.1.1896 until his death on 25.7.1904.

BLAKELOCK Ralph, Leavygreave. 9.17. (e).s. of Luke of Lastingham and Anne (Moore) of Leeds. Partner in bank of Parker, Shore & Blakelock. m. Mary, d. of John Ogle of Chesterfield. Subscribed to Youle's Arithmetic in 1813 and gave 10 gns. to the new S. GS. in 1823. CB. from his election on 11.7.1822 until his resignation on 22.2.1827; GS(G). for the same dates. d. on 2.11.1827, bur. at E., w.p. 25.4.1828.

BODDY Thomas Norman, T.D., J.P., D.L. 3.21. Elected CB. 1967. b. 6.9.1904, y.s. of John William, mining engineer and Mary Jane (Burdess). Ed. St.Peter's, York. m. 17.9.1932 Muriel (Firth). Chairman and Managing Director Boddy Industries Ltd. R.A. (T.A.) 1938. M.E. Italy 1940-1945 Major 1940 Lt. Col. 1943 T.D. 1946. J.P. 1959. Chairman City Magistrates 1970-74. High Sheriff of Hallamshire 1965/66. General Commissioner of Income Tax 1966. D.L. South Yorks. 1974. Resigned CB. 1984. d. 1986

BOVILL Percy James Clarke, J.P., BSc. 3.20. Elected CB. 1962. b. Cornwall 15.10.1898, s. of Percy Charles Edward Bovill, artist, and Ellen Stephens (Drew). Ed. Cheltenham College and S. University, B.Sc. Lt. RASC 1918/19. Director of many firms including Newton Chambers Ltd. (Managing 1956-63), Chairman S. No 1 Hospital Management Committee 1951; member Regional Hospital Board 1964. J.P. West Riding; Council Member Chamber of Commerce. Active boy scouts. MC. 1959/60. High Sheriff of Hallamshire 1966/67. m. 27.6.1936 Peggy Lever Brunhill (Pickering). d. 15.5.1967.

BRAYE Thomas, High Street. 1.2. Servant of Shrewsbury. Gave account books to CBs. and TTs. Actively concerned, with the Swifts, Smythes, Fentons and Parkers, in post-Reformation land sales. m., by 1558, Ann, d. of Richard Fenton, mercer, and Anne (Smythe) and sister of Richard, CB. 3.1. Thomas was CB. in succession to Robert Swift of Broom Hall and held lands in Little S. from the CB. In the 1569 assessment he was the second highest rated. Had Whiston mill and a farm at Treeton. W.d. 11.11.1569; bur. at S. on 11.9.1570. His wife and s. were concerned in a partition of lands in S., A. and Bridgehouses in 1579.

BRIDDEN Wharton, High Street, apothecary. 3.10. (e).s. of John of Bawtry, gent., and Ann (Wharton). 1739, failed to be elected TT. On 3.10.1734 m. Mary, d. of James Crawshaw Jun., silversmith, MC. 1721, and Joan, d. of William Hawley, CB. 4.6. Elected CB. 19.12.1741. GS(G). Trustee for St. Paul's. Voted for Turner in 1741. d. 11.5.1742.

BRIGHT Henry, Whirlow Hall. 7.8. Bap. at S. 17.1.1601/2, s. of John of Whirlow, yeo, and Grace (Bright). m. Gertrude, d. of John and Isabel Ramscar of B. Elected CB. 19.10/1652 and resigned in 1673. Dd. 14.6.1684 and bur. in parish church.

BRIGHT James, mercer. 9.5. Bap. at N. 24.8.1592, 3rd s. of Thomas of Bradway and later Carbrook, and Joan (Martyn als. Catley). Inherited property in the Market Place. Fined £10 for refusing knighthood. m. first by 1623, Jane Wordsworth, bur. 18.10.1627, and then, 27.8.1628, Anne, d. of William Spencer, lord of the manor of D., and Alice (Mitchell); Anne remarried John Dawson of Misterton. TC 1620. Succeeded Hugh Rawson (d. 1628) as CB. and continued until his death, s.p.; bur. in the Choir 18.8.1653. W. d. 1.4.1652 mentions estate at Nether Shatton, Derbs.; executor, nephew John Bright, CB. 4.4.

BRIGHT John, Whirlow, yeo. 10.3. s. of Richard, Whirlow, arrowheadsmith. Mentioned as son-in-law, also supervisor, in 1546 will of Thomas Creswick of Upperthorpe; possibly a 2nd wife, Agnes, who had administration of his goods in 1587, or that some of these entries refer to an older John. Bought 2 closes in Whiteley Woods in 1577. His wid. Agnes probably m. (as 2nd wife) Robert Staniforth the elder, shearsmith, on 5.2.1587/8 and was bur. S. on 30.9.1609. CW. for E. in 1559, 1571 and 1578. CB. in succession to Richard Jessop (d. 1580) until his death; bur. at S. 24.4.1587, inq. p.m. at Pontefract.

BRIGHT Rev John, M.A. 2.8. Bap. at N. 17.1.1594/5, 4th s. of Thomas Bradway and Carbrook, yeo., and Joan (Martyn). Admitted to St. John's College, Cambridge, in 1610; B.A. 1613/4, M.A. 1618. Ordained deacon 22.12.1616 and priest (London) 23.5.1624. C. of Highgate Chapel and M.S., before he succeeded Thomas Toller as V. on 20.8.1635; he was presented by Wm. Jessop (CB. 2.7) and maintained Toller's Puritan tradition. m. Joan Smales of Whalley, Derbs. Only example of V. being a CB., elected in 1641 but bur. at S. 23.4.1643.

BRIGHT Sir John, Bart, Carbrook and Badsworth, lord of the manor of E. 4.4. Bap. S. 14.10.1619, (e).s. of Stephen, bailiff, CB. 4.3, whom he succeeded as CB., GS(G). and bailiff. Protested against royal intention to raise armed forces. 'The most active in . . . Sheffield . . . for the Parliament'. 1643, W.R. Commissioner for sequestering the estates of delinquents. Made Colonel and Governor of S. Castle. Served under Cromwell in Scotland, but retired from the army in 1650. W.R., M.P. and Yorkshire High Sheriff, 1654-55. Visitor for Cromwell's College, Durham, 1657. Created baronet 1660. Commissioner for disbanding the army, 1660-61. Patronised ejected ministers, having William Bagshaw, the 'Apostle of the Peak', as domestic chaplain at Carbrook. Hunter gives details of his four marriages, which served to increase his considerable wealth, partly obtained from coalmines at Handsworth. Usually lived at Badsworth, but continued as CB. until his death on 13.9.1688. The Wentworth Woodhouse Muniments contain many family and official records.

BRIGHT John, Banner Cross. 5.6. Bap. S. 27.4.1634, (e).s. of Robert, CB. 5.5, whom he succeeded as CB. until his death, being bur. at S. on 11.11.1686. m. a d. and c.h. of Thomas Dale of Whiteley Wood. Left his Dobbin Hill messuage to his d. Elizabeth, £50 to his d. Anne, wife of Thomas Watson. of Stumperlow, and the rest of his property to his s. John; w.d. 21.12.1680, proved 4.2.1686/7.

BRIGHT John Sen., Banner Cross and Chesterfield. 5.7. Bap. at S. 7.3.1657/8, s. of John, CB. 5.6, whom he succeeded, until his resignation on 13.7.1703. Had moved to Chesterfield before his resignation in 1703. He had property at Hasland. He was clerk to Ald. Richard Youle of Chesterfield, whose d. Mary he married; they lived at Mary Gate, Chesterfield. Also GS(G). 1714, Mayor of Chesterfield and, 1722, High Sheriff of Derbs. w.d. 9.2.1721. d. at Chesterfield 19.6.1734.

BRIGHT John Jun., Banner Cross and Chesterfield. 5.8. (e).s. and h. of John, CB. 5.7, whom he succeeded as CB. until his resignation in 1722, probably on moving to Chesterfield. On 4.3.1701/2 married Barbara, youngest d. of Francis Jessop of Broom Hall, CB. 3.7, and had Banner Cross from his father; marriage settlement was dated 1.2.1701/2. In 1709 he paid 10s. towards the GS. Master's house. In 1717 he leased the red lead mill on Hunloke estate at Wingerworth. In 1736 he bought property at Bolsover and Palterton from Nicholas, Earl of Scarsdale, and in 1744, Scarcliffe corn tithes. Also had property at Hasland, Walton, Tapton and Matlock. Leased Rawmarsh estate from Southwell Chapter. Partner with Richard Milnes, Nicholas Twigg and Henry Thornhill in many lead mines. Connected with St. Paul's Church, trustee in 1739. Also GS(G). In 1738 established charity for master of a petty school. Voted for Turner in 1741 election. d. without male issue at Chesterfield on 3.4.1748, aged 68.

BRIGHT Joseph, Nether Edge and Greystones, J.P. 2.16. Bap. at S. 21.4.1687, s. of Thomas of Greystones and his 2nd wife Elizabeth (Bright). m. Elizabeth, d. of John Bright of Banner Cross, CB. 5.7. Voted for Cavendish in 1734 (freehold at Hathersage) and for Turner in 1741. Connected with St. Paul's Church. Succeeded as CB. by his s.-in-law John Nodder. Also had property at N. Elected CB. 9.10.1722 until his death on 25.3.1743; w.d. 19.1.1740/1.

BRIGHT Robert, Banner Cross, yeo. 5.5. Bap. S. 7.10.1593, (e).s. and h. of John of Banner Cross and grandson of John, CB. 10.3. On 10.7.1633 m. at S., Helen (or Emote), d. of William Shaw of Hall Broom, and wid. of John Parkin of Hunter House. 3 hearths in 1665. Held 2 messuages, 4 cottages and 60 acres of land at Banner Cross and Millhouses at his death. W.d. 1.8.1667 and d. at S. 7.8.1667, being succeeded by his son John, CB. 5.6.

BRIGHT Stephen, Carbrook, gent. 4.3. Bap. N. 27.12.1583, (e).s. of Thomas of Bradway and Carbrook, and bro. of James, CB. 9.5, and John, CB. 2.8, and V. of S. On 25.9.1610 m. at S., Jane, d. of George Westby and wid. of William Smales. 'Much employed by the Earl of Arundel', being bailiff -1623-37-. Fined £25 for not taking knighthood. GS(G). An arbitrator in Cutlers' dispute in 1625. On

4.11.1635 m., at Laughton, Barbara, d. of Ralph Hatfield. Bought E. Manor for £1,800 in 1636, and had a grant of arms as 'a person of £1,000 a year estate'. Gave £1 towards the new Cutlers' Hall in 1638. W.d. 20.5.1642 and d. 6.6.1642, being succeeded by his son John, CB. 4.4. Had lands in Dore, Totley and Edale, and was paying a pension of £12 p.a. to the former V., Thomas Toller.

BRIGHT Stephen, Raisin Hall. 8.7. 2nd s. of John of Brincliffe Edge and Raisin Hall, and Helen (Wilkinson). On 13.12.1684 m., at S., Ann, d. of Thomas Bright of Greystones who, in 1693, bought Brincliffe Edge from Stephen's cousin John of Lees Hall and Dronfield. Elected CB. 18.8.1696 but resigned shortly afterwards, being succeeded by Thomas Diston. Bur. at S. 9.11.1727.

BRIGHT Thomas, Hawley Croft, gent. 8.15. o.s. of James of Brincliffe Edge and Judith (Fenton). His wives, Elizabeth and Margaret, d. in 1755 and 1762. His large house was formerly the Ball Inn. Described as 'a goodly-looking personage, with powdered wig, cocked-hat, gold-headed cane and silver shoe-buckles'. Elected CB. 19.4.1764 and resigned, as also GS(G)., on 24.6.1778. d. 19.3.1796, aged 74.

BRITLAND (Bretland) Thomas, grocer, Market Place. 6.9. Probably connected with a family of Chesterfield where there was a contemporary namesake, lead merchant and ald. On 4.5.1642 m., at S., Sara Dodson (c.f. George Dodson, CB. 6.6); after her death in 1662 he m. by licence, on 26.10.1663, Mary, d. of William Cart, the puritan rector of Handsworth and wid. of Robert Hoole, CB. 6.8, whom Britland succeeded and through whom he had a close, Little Turning, in A. In 1645 'religiously disposed and well affected'. Had 4 hearths in 1665. Said to be a nonconformist and was certainly associated with several others on the TT., both before and after its reorganisation in 1681. GS(G). Issued a halfpenny token with William Cooke (q.v.) in 1670. His wife, Mary, bur. at S. 1683/4, and their d. Ruth m. Nevil Simmons, the stationer, in 1687. Assessed for 8s. (one servant) in 1692. d. 18.12.1696 aged 89 (?81) and bur. in chancel of the parish church, MI.

BROOMHEAD Christopher, Prior Row, High Street, gent. 9.8. s. of Henry, yeo of Fd, and Alice. F. 26.9.1674, having been app. to his bro.-in-law, William Creswick. On 6.2.1676/7 m. Sarah Archdale, wid., at S. TT. from 1690 and lent them £100 'to carry on the Navigation affairs'. MC. in 1696. GS(G)., giving 10s. towards the new Master's house in 1709. In 1692 assessed for 4s. personally, but also his wife, 4 children and 2 servants. His 3 ds., Elizabeth, Sarah and Margaret m. Robert Drake, s. of the V. and S. surgeon, John Balguy, s. of the GS. Master, himself Usher and later V. of Northallerton, and Christopher Robinson, also GS. Master. Broomhead bought his Prior Row house from Samuel Revell in 1705. Was connected with St. Paul's Church in 1719. W.d. 15.4.1729. d. 20.8.1729 and bur. N. aisle of parish church.

BROWN Sir John, Knight, Deputy Lieutenant, J.P., Endcliffe Hall. 12.20. Bn. 6.12.1816, Favell's Yard, Fargate, 2nd s. of Samuel, slater, and Ann (Roberts). 1830 app. to Earl, Horton & Co., small cutlery and file manufacturers and factors of Orchard Place. Factory in Furnival Street. In 1839 m. Mary, (o).d. of Benjamin Schofield; she d. 1881 s.p. Atlas Works (formerly Queen's Works) started in Savile Street, 1856. Councillor for St. Peter's 1856 and Ald. 1859, Mayor 1861-63. Conservative in politics. Guardian of the Poor for E. in 1857, chairman 1873-93. Chairman of limited company formed in 1864, which became particularly famous for its rolled armour plating. Elected CB. 5.1.1864, TT. 6.4.1864, and MC. 1865-66. Built Endcliffe Hall 1864. Knighted 1867. Elected GS(G). 27.1.1870. Church member and Chairman of the School Board 1870-79, and Trustee of Firth College. Director of various companies, including Sheffield Waterworks and Great Northern Railway. d. 27.12.1896 at Shortlands, Kent and bur. E.

BROWN Walter, solicitor, Endcliffe Crescent. 5.15. Bn. 25.2.1801, s. of John, attorney, and Sarah (Ward); his father came from Lincoln, was a partner with the Kenyon Parkers and founded the practice of Brown & Son of St. James' Street, which he joined. Elected CB. 27.12.1879 and GS(G). 9.12.1880. Conservative in politics. d. 16.1.1901, aged 79.

BROWNELL Charles, J.P., merchant and manufacturer. 9.18. Bn. 27.7.1802, 3rd s. of Peter (of Newfield, TT. and MC. 1807) and Marian (Wilkinson). Educated at S. GS. m. Susanna, d. of Laurence Peel of Ardwick, near Manchester, s.p. CB. and GS(G). 22.2.1827 to 6.8.1840 when he went to Liverpool as the representative of the family business, merchants, steel convertors and razor manufacturers of Carver Street. Active supporter of John Thornely, the Tory candidate in the 1837 election. d. 24.1.1863, bur. N.

BURROWES (Borrowes) William, yeo. 9.1. Probably cousin, witnessing the will of an earlier William Borrows who d. in 1537, making various bequests to the chantry priests and left 6s. 8d. to his godson, William Borows, 'towards his scholchyre'. His s. Robert was described as of Crookesmoorside, Tapton House, Endcliffe, and had land in Stannington. William was a CW. or CB. in 1549/50 before the CB. charter, and rented 'Black Lands' from the Burgesses. His wid. Margaret held a tenement called 'Ivelands' in 1564. W.d. 12.1.1557/8, w.p. 6.4.1558.

BURROS (etc.) William, yeo., Shirecliffe Hall. 1.3. 2nd s. of Richard (d. 1556) and Margery of Tinsley, and probably mentioned in the above 1537 will. Rented Shirecliffe Hall by 1564 from its various owners and apparently from his e.bro. Robert of Tinsley, to whose s. Richard it was later let. Two other bros., Richard and Nicholas, were of Rotherham, the former being a rich lead miner. In 1568 William bought Raisin Hall. He was CW. for B. in 1561 before election as a CB. His wid. Margaret was probably a d. of Ralph and Agnes Lee of Ecclesfield. W.d. 15.4.1587, bur. 20.4.1587.

BURTON William, Royds Mill, gent. 9.10. Bap. S. 25.6.1704, 2nd s. of William of Royds Mill and Anne (Fenton). On 23.12.1731 m., at Tinsley, Margaret, d. of

George Bamforth, CB. 8.11, who died 1749, and through whom he inherited the manors of Wadsley and Owlerton. William's sister, Esther, had already married his father-in-law. Freehold in Dronfield in 1734, voted for Cavendish. Elected CB. 15.1.1734/5 vice Thomas Heaton, also GS(G). Bur. in parish church 19.5.1764, w.p. 18.6.1764.

BURTON William, surgeon and apothecary. 12.15. Bap. S. 1.7.1743, 3rd s. of William, CB. 9.10. On his father's death he became co-lord of Wadsley with his bro. Michael, a S. attorney. On 13.4.1767 m. Elizabeth, d. of David Hussey of A. Forge. She d. s.p. in 1768 and William m. Maria, d. of Rev. John Bill. He moved from Bull Stake to Paradise Square. Elected CB. and GS(G). 9.5.1774, vice William Battie. Residuary legatee of Madam Bamforth, wid. of his uncle George, (e).s. of George, CB. 8.11. Of B., paid tax on one servant in 1780. d. 24.5.1798 and bur. in parish church.

BUTCHER Samuel, J.P., Banner Cross Hall. 9.21. His father, James, was a cutler of Charles Street, dead in 1801 when Samuel was app. to Richard Nayler, razor maker, for 7 years. Had 2 ds. by his 1st wife and several children by his 2nd, Maria Fosberry, from Liverpool. He and his bro. William (MC. 1845) headed the merchants and manufacturers of Philadelphia Works, Eyre Lane. Elected a Councillor for E. in 1843, he became Ald. and 3rd Mayor in 1845. S. Savings Bank Governor and Trustee, lived at Endcliffe and voted for Parker and Overend in 1852 and 1857. Elected CB. 17.12.1855 and, in 1860, GS(G). d. 1.12.1869, aged 73.

CAPPER (als. Hudson) Christopher, tanner. 6.5. Mentioned in 1602 will of John Saunderson, Tanner of Grimesthorpe and s. of Christopher; called 'my servant' and given large sum of £10. On 6.11.1605 at S., m. Elizabeth, d. of Robert Hoole, sh. of A., and Isabel (Mounteney), and bro. of John, CB. 12.7. In 1606 assessment paid 10s. 10d. CW. for the town in 1607-8 and searcher for leather in 1609. In 1617 was executor for, and occupied a house belonging to, Edward Saunderson, tanner of Grimesthorpe, and who had himself been executor for his uncle John above. With Saunderson and others he erected a loft in the parish church. Immediately after his wife's death he m., on 15.8.1618, Ann, wid. of Francis Barlow, CB. 12.6. TC. in 1623 and 1630; he borrowed £100 from Burgery. Paid £22 rent to the lord for Hall farm, Bullowes farm and part of Perrins farm; also had a house in Dixon's Lane and tanyard near Pond Mill. W.d. 10.9.1636 and bur. 25.10.1636.

CHALNOR (etc.) Hugh, Darnall, yeo. 8.1. His family had been prominent as CWs. and bailiff for 150 years. Hugh is called a godson in the 1537 will of William Borows. His father, William, was apparently living at Brampton when the CBs. obtained their charter and Hugh was appointed. His 1st wife (she or a d. named Jennet) was a d. of Thomas and Dionise Scargill, while his 2nd, Elizabeth, was a d. of Thomas and Elizabeth Parker of Whitley Hall. Records exist of several sales of property about 1590. He, or his 3rd s. Hugh, acted as CW. for AD. in 1592 and 1603. In 1601 paid rent for West Carr. W.d. 15.1.1602/3 ('sick' and desired to be bur. at S. but there is no record of this in the P. R.) W.p. 6.10.1603, Inq. p.m. at Rotherham 15.11.1604 showed that he had a house and 40 acres at Owlerton, Costenot Hall and cottages and other property in A. and D.

CHAPPELL Thomas, attorney. 2.14. Bap. at S. 6.7.1665, s. of Thomas, gent., attorney, GS(G)., TT., steward for Duke of Norfolk and Lydia (Stacye). In 1689 m. Hannah, (o).d. of Robert Sedgwick of Badsworth, gent., and the marriage settlement details property in D. which passed to the surviving children, Robert, barrister and GS(G)., and Ann, in 1703. In 1692, like his father, he was assessed for £4 4s. besides that for his wife, child and 2 maids. Elected CB. 6.2.1693/4 and succeeded his father as GS(G)., TT. and steward. Speaking of this family, Leader said that they had a 'finger in every local pie'. Bur. at S. 2.12.1703.

CHESTERMAN William, J.P., Belmayne, Clarkehouse Road and Eastwood Grange, Ashover, Derbs. 5.16. Bn. December 1837, s. of James, whom he succeeded in 1867 as head of James Chesterman & Co. Ltd., manufacturers of measuring instruments, Bow Works, Pomona Street. His wife, Emma (Bedell) d. on 21.6.1908, aged 62. Bought his F. in 1871, as a sh., and was MC. in 1880, being a member of the special committee appointed to secure greater independence for the Company. S. Savings Bank Governor and Trustee. Elected CB. 31.1.1901 and resigned 26.3.1920. TT. and President of S. Ratepayers' Association. d. 6.1.1930.

CLAY Joseph, Bridgehouses, gent. 5.10. s. of Robert, CB. 7.11. bn. 3.2.1712 and bap. 22.2.1712. m. on 29.12.1737, Elizabeth, d. of Arthur Speight, CB. 5.9, whom Joseph succeeded, being elected 7.4.1739; Elizabeth d. 25.1.1748 and was bur. at A. GS(G). On 25.2.1754 m. Sarah, d. of Ralph and Ann Elmsall of Thornhill, who was bur. at A. on 7.10.1799. In 1766 signatory to Rockingham address. In 1785 he was a subscriber to the Tontine Inn and shortly afterwards bought Wadsley manor from Michael Burton. In 1795 he guaranteed £300 to the Corn Committee. Partner with John Fell, CB. 8.13, in Colnebridge, Staveley and Carburton Forges. Shareholder of Stoke Sough and Eyam Consolidated Titles. Held Padley and Totley Lead Smelting Mills. Helped to promote Chesterfield to Hernstone Lane Head turnpike. Partner in various mines at Eyam. d. 22.6.1797, bur. A. Chapel.

CLAY Robert, Chesterfield, Walkey and Bridgehouses, lead merchant. 7.11. On 15.1.1687 m. at Chesterfield Hannah, d. of Jonathan Slater; their s. Robert removed to Philadelphia and founded an important American family. Shortly afterwards he m. Joan, posthumous d. of John and Sarah Rawson of Walkley, bap. 25.8.1670 and who d. 24.2.1747, having borne many children. In 1709 paid 10s. towards G.S. Master's house; GS(G). Had Dore Lead Smelting Mill in 1714 and was assessed for Hawksworth and Staniforth Farms and coal pits in 1716. Partner in mines at Eyam and Taddington. In 1742 actively connected with Don Navigation Scheme but only had one share in 1729. In 1734 voted for Cavendish, as a freeholder in Totley. Bur. S. Church 30.6.1737, his w.d. 13.9.1736 mentioning Upper House and Oxspring Wood, Walkley, smelting mill at Dore, mines, lands at Dronfield, houses at Tickhill and Bridgehouses.

COOKE William, mercer, gent. 1.8. (e).s. of William and Ann (Heton), aged 16 in 1647. His two younger brothers, Thomas and Robert, were of Shirecliffe Hall at the same time as Rowland Hancock. William was described as a woollen draper when he m. Elizabeth Lambert of Badsworth at S. on 8.11.1655. Another William was constable in 1646 and CW. for the town in 1648. In 1665 assessed for 5 hearths. Issued tokens in 1670. TC. 1675-6 and appointed TT. in 1681 when he obtained an honorary F. Only CB. for a short time but apparently acted as Collector for Col. John Bright in 1662 and 1686. In 1692 assessed for £2 4s., his wife, bro., s. and 2 servants being extra. Bur. 11.5.1694; his wid. probably moved to Leeds.

COOMBE John Newton, solicitor Brocco Bank and Abbeydale House. 4.15. Bn. Islington 8.11.1854, s. of Rev. Charles George, V. of Crookes and St. Paul's, Worthing. Educated at Broombank House and St. Peter's, York. Articled to Henry Rodgers, CB. 6.18, and admitted solicitor in 1876. 1877-87 partner with Charles Branson and then with Thomas Gould in Gould & Coombe, which later amalgamated with Messrs. Bramley & Son; President S. Law Society in 1908. Was vice-chairman of E. Conservative Association and Council Member of Firth and University Colleges and of the University 1890-7-1905-20. His wife, Francis Mary, d. of Ald. Joseph Burdekin Jackson, d. 1928. Active Conservative, vice-chairman of E. Church of England, member of the School Board 1882-8, vice-chairman 1885 and chairman 1894-7. Council member of University College and associated with University; 1900 President of the Literary and Philosophical Society, and of the Microscopical Society. Elected CB. 27.2.1902 and resigned in 1920. Retired to Worthing in 1926 and d. 11.12.1936.

CRESWICK James, the elder. 7.6. It is difficult to identify individual members of the widespread Creswick family, as there were often several contemporaries with the same name. For this reason several of the statements below are still doubtful. Not to be confused with James who succeeded his father Thomas (d. 1607) as parish clerk, and wrote and witnessed many of the contemporary legal documents. Possibly s. of Robert and Cecily (Philippe), bap. 28.7.1578. Is described as 'the elder . . . burgess' and also as 'the elder of Sheffield yeoman' when he acts as a trustee for Robert Rollinson, whom he succeeded as CB. In 1638-39 gave 10s. towards the new Cutlers' Hall, but is described as a non-cutler; consequently, probably not the MC. of 1632 who had a mark in 1614-15. More probably TC. in 1618. Probably bur. at S. on 15.3.1642/3, although a subsequent writer has added the word 'scribe' by confusion with 30.6.1642.

CRESWICK James, the younger, High Street and Church Gates. 7.7. Bap. 10.4.1583, s. of Thomas, Cutler, and Anne (Shemeld). On 10.8.1607 m. at S. Margaret, d. of Thomas Webster of Owlerton, and in 1616/7 was supervisor for her brother, Thomas Webster, receiving his bows and arrows and quivers. Described as 'the younger burgess' in 1621/2 and as 'James son. of Thomas' when he had a cutler's mark in 1624-5. Held part of S. Park, sharing it with his bro.-in-law,

Leonard Webster, in 1619. In 1631 he leased a High Street house from Edward Hill and bought it in 1651. In 1634/5 bought the Church Gates House from John Vesey of Brampton. Shared a wheel in Little S. Moor in 1626 and later Morton Wheel, Neepsend; MC. 1638; gave £1 to new Hall. Described as 'a most zealous Commonwealth man, and a sequestrator under the Parliament of England.' His d. Sarah m. Thomas, who was s. of the Puritan Rector of Staveley, Thomas Birbeck, M. and C. of A., ejected from Ackworth and licensed as a Presbyterian. His nephew, James, s. of Thomas of High Street, MC in 1635, was a Fellow of St. John's College, Cambridge, and ejected from Freshwater. On 2.11.1651 James m. Mary Dodson, probably related to George Dodson, CB. 6.6, and who later m. Martin Isles of Leeds. Bur. S. Church 15.10.1652, administration June 1653.

CRESWICK James, silver plater, Moorgate, Crookes Moor. 9.19. Bn. S. 28.6.1789, 2nd s. of James, file manufacturer and silver plater, and Mary (Smith); bro. of Thomas, CB. 12.19, and Nathaniel, CB. 9.20. m. Hannah, d. of John Jubb of Balliefield Hall, Handsworth. 1837 unsuccessful as TT. but elected CB. and GS(G). on 6.8.1840. Actively opposed S. Charter in 1838, was also a merchant and employed 50 men in 1851. d. 14.8.1854, bur. Crookes.

CRESWICK Nathaniel, silver plater, Easthill House. 9.20. Bn. 16.12.1793, younger bro. of James, above, whom he followed as CB., elected 2.9.1854. Partner in family business. Subscribed 5 gns. for new GS in 1823 and supported his bro. James in opposition to S. Charter in 1838. m. Elizabeth, d. of John Jubb of Balliefield Hall, Handsworth. d. 22.11.1855, bur. Heeley.

CRESWICK Thomas, lord of Owlerton Hall. 12.5. Bap. 12.5.1566(?), s. of John the elder of Owlerton Hall and Anne (Rawson). Held manorial courts in 1601 and 1607. Probably TC. 1597, occurs as 'burgess' in 1604-5. 1606 one of the assessors for the GS. Church collector in 1611 but resigned before his death. In 1613 he sold Owlerton Manor to Malin Stacie (CB. 5.4); in this and other sales he was associated with his s. Thomas and his wife Agnes (? née Barber, m. at S. 5.10.1584). Bur. 2.10.1617, administration 22.12.1617.

CRESWICK Thomas, silver plater, Ecclesall Grange. 12.19. Bn. 21.1.1788, (e).s. of James and Mary (Smith); bro. of James and Nathaniel above, and senior partner in family business. m. Phoebe Ann, d. of Peter Lomas of Cheshire and, after her death in 1819, secondly Mary Ann, d. of Nathan and Sarah Astley of Cheshire, and who d. in 1825. Subscribed 5 gns. to new GS. in 1823. Lived at East Hill House before E. Grange. Supported his bro. James in opposition to S. Charter in 1838. Was surveyor of E. highways in 1844. Elected CB. and GS(G). on 1.2.1844. d. Dec. 1863.

CRESWICK William, the elder, cutler. 2.4. Probably s. of Thomas of Little S., Cutler and bro. of Thomas who m. Anne Shemeld and had James, CB. 7.7. On 15.6.1578 m. at Ecclesfield, Margaret, d. of Richard Carr, yeo. of Butterthwaite and his wife Elizabeth. assessor for tax in 1593, TC. 1599 and Assessor for G.S. tax in 1606, himself paying 13s. 4d. Left his house at Morehills, Little S. to his wife and his 'interest in a grinding trough at Morton Wheel' to his sons, Edward and William. His d. Ann was mother of Charles Hoole, the famous schoolmaster of Rotherham and elsewhere, while Mary m. Edward Wood, TC. and GS(G). By his w.d. 1.8.1612 he left 6s. 8d. 'to the repair of the Causey leading to Little Sheffield Moor'. Bur. 5.7.1613.

CRESWICK William, cutler, Church Lane. 12.9. Possibly the s. of William, CB. 2.4, mentioned above and definitely cousin of Thomas of High Street, bro. of James, CB. 7.7. On 11.5.1631 m. Alice, d. of William Rawson of Walkley, CB. 1.6. In 1637 had land near Broomhall Lane and Church Lane, his house in the latter being occupied by Jonathan Eaton at his death. In 1639 gave 4s. to the Cutlers' Hall. TC. in 1653 and MC. in 1659. In 1665 had 4 hearths. Had land in Townfield Knowle from William Lee. W.d. 1.4.1666, bur. 23.5.1666.

CROOKE John, cutler. 1.7. Bap. 17.6.1599, s. of John, t.E. and Helen (Whitehead), and probably brought up by his great-uncle Thomas Housley. On 15.6.1625 m. Sarah, d. of William Unwin; their s. John educated at S. and Magdalene College, Cambridge, became C. of E. and C. and V. of Denby, from whence he was ejected in 1662 and retired to a family estate nr. Wakefield. Mentioned as a cutler in 1624-5 he had as app. his two nephews, ss of Thomas Rollinson, nephew of Robert Rollinson, CB. 7.5, who left John 'Mr Perkins booke upon the Creede and Mr Lathers booke upon the Gallatians'. MC. in 1637 and paid £1 6s. 8d. to the new hall. Made a bequest for a reading school in 1657. CW. and Constable, he lived in Church Lane. TC. 1637 and prominent in Burgery affairs. Parliamentary sequestrator. GS(G). d. 10.1.1668/9, bur. in church; MI.

DICKENSON. William, bailiff. 2.3. Bn.1540, s. of William. Apparently only paid 1s. 3d. in 1569. From 1574 Shrewsbury's bailiff, succeeding James Turner, CB. 2.2, on whose death he was elected CB. Probably started his note-book on taking office; among other items this shows a house built in High Street in 1575. Was an original GS(G). In 1587 he had a mortgage on Hazelbarrow Farm from William Selioke. He leased Black Land from the CB. in 1595. Actively interested in the Burgery. TC. 1588-90. His wife Margaret bur. in the church in 1594. Paid 40s. in the 1606 GS. assessment. Bur. 10.5.1606, an inventory showing above £40.

DISTON Thomas, ironmonger, Sheffield Park. 8.8. M. at Sheffield. on 19.9.1678 Jane, d. of Richard Boughton. 1685 Overseer of the High Ways. In 1682 an assessor for the Poll Tax and in 1692 paid £2 4s. GS(G). TT. from 1701. His daughters Jane, Mary and Elizabeth, m. Arthur Speight, CB. 5.9, John Ellis., CB. 3.9, and Benjamin Ferrand, M. and C. of A. Bur. 1.1.1702/3, w.d. 24.12.1702 and proved by his widow. Jane, to whom he left Parkgate and Riches Farms.

DIXON Henry Isaac, J.P., merchant, Cliffe House and Stumperlow Hall. 10.22. Bn.

30.6.1820, younger s. of James, of Broom Lodge and Page Hall, a descendant of William Dickenson, CB. 2.3, and his second wife Ann (Nowell). Educated at a Broomhall St. dame's school, a Doncaster ladies' school, Mr Wilkinson's Broomhall school and Hyam's Wesleyan School, Doncaster. Travelled on the continent for the family firm of James Dixon & Sons, silver and electro-plate manufacturers, Cornish Place works. 1852, Page Hall, voted Parker and Overend. 1857 voted Overend. On 8.8.1850 m. Anne, second d. of Frederick Woolhouse of Sheffield, grocer. 1854 bought Stumperlow Hall. 1856-59 councillor for Upper Hallam; conservative in politics. Elected CB. 28.1.1864 and resigned 14.3.1901. Director Sheffield Banking Co. and of Cleveland Bridge & Engineering Co. GS(G)., trustee for Birley and Hounsfield Charities and for the two Charity Schools. d. 24.11.1912, bur. Fd. and left £60,423 net.

DIXON James, J.P., silver-plater, Tylecote, Ranmoor, and Stumperlow Hall. 2.23. Born at Cliffe House, Ecclesfield 26.10.1851, (e).s. of Henry Isaac, CB. 10.22. Educated Whiteley Wood Hall (Rev. E. B. Chalmer), 1860-3 Stanley House Academy, Blackpool, Dr. Spiers' School, Weybridge, and 1867-8, Neuwied, Germany. Entered family firm and was senior director on his retirement in 1919. m. 2.9.1887 Edith Fawcett, d. of Benjamin and sister of Arthur Wightman, solicitors. 1887 MC. Council member of Firth College 1888-90, Fellow of the Royal Meteorological Society, Governor and Trustee of S. Savings Bank, President of the Deaf and Dumb Society. TT. 1888-1904 Poor Law Guardian for Ecclesall. 1890-4 Councillor for Fd.; conservative in politics. Elected CB. 14.3.1901, retiring to the south in 1925, but bur. Fd. 30.1.1947.

DODSON George, draper. 6.6. Little definite known about this family, but possibly connected with the Dodsons of Kirkby Overblows. George had m. by 1611 and came to S. a few years later, when the death of an infant child is registered. In 1620 the CB. paid him for the goodwill of his house. Sara and Mary, who m. Thomas Britland, CB. 6.9, and James Creswick, CB. 7.7, were possibly his daughters. Another relative was probably Nathaniel Dodson who was M. in 1619 at Emmanuel College, Cambridge, 1628-31, and then usher at the GS. until Michaelmas, 1634, C. of Bd., and bur. at S. in 1646. George bought part of Sicutt field, near Watery Lane, from William Lee. Bur. 1.4.1642.

DONCASTER James, Henry. 6.24. Elected CB. 9.6.1930, resigned 2.2.1940. b 15.2.1873, 2nd s. of Charles, steel manufacturer, Abbeydale, and Hannah Mary, e.d. of James Henry Barber of S. Banking Co. Ed Oliver's Mount School, Scarborough and Kings College, Cambridge; exhibitioner M.A. 1898. Joined family firm 1895, director 1902 when firm became Daniel Doncaster & Co. Ltd., also Secretary until 1929. 1931 succeeded his uncle, Samuel Doncaster as Chairman until 1944. J.P. Director S. Gas Company and S. District Public House Trust Co. Ltd. Council member, Chamber of Commerce, 1909, President 1924/5. Chairman High Speed Steel Assn. and Crucible Steel Assn. 1927/9. Member of S. Education Committee for many years, Treasurer 1932. Pro-Chancellor of University 1919-40. TT. m. 1919 Alice C. P. Lunn, Headmistress Girl's High School. d. 16.1.1948.

DRABBLE James, merchant, Highfield. 5.12. Born 1782, s. of Joseph and Ann (Whitham). m. Marianne, d. of Peter Brownell of Newfield and Marian (Wilkinson). First manager of S. Banking Co. Voted for Wilberforce and Lascelles in 1807, Parker in 1832 and Wentworth in 1835. CB. and GS(G). from 22.6.1819 to 28.4.1841. Subscribed Surrey Street Library. d. 1.9.1841, bur. St. Paul's.

ELLIS Sir William Henry, G.B.E., Commander of the Crown of Italy, J.P., Hon D.Eng (S). 5.17. Elected CB. 26.3.1920. Born 10.8.1860, s. of John Devonshire, Chairman John Brown & Co. Ed. Uppingham. Started career at Tannet Walker & Co., Leeds; joined John Brown & Co. 1887, Director 1906, Managing 1919-31. Knighted and G.B.E. 1918. Deputy Chairman Disposals Board; member Overseas Committee, Board of Trade 1920. President Iron and Steel Institute 1924/5; President Institution of Civil Engineers 1926; member governing body Imperial College of Science and Technology and of government Commission on Drainage in Doncaster area. J.P., MC. 1914-18. TT. Member University Council, Board of Royal Infirmary and Savings Bank. Mountaineer and organist. President S. Amateur Musical Society and Literary and Philosophical Society. m. 1889 Lucy, d. of F.E. Telby of Leeds. d. 4.7.1945. Bequests to CB.s for clergy stipends.

ELLISON John, apothecary. 3.9. s. of John, grocer and landlord of The Cock Inn, and Sarah (Shore). On 28.2.1719/20 m. Mary, d. of Thomas Diston CB. 8.8, and on 23.10.1734 Ellen, d. of John Fell, CB. 10.10; Ellen survived him and m. Ralph Elmsall of Thornhill. In 1723 lived in a High Street house belonging to William Swift. Elected CB. 10.10.1734; also GS(G). and TT. Original shareholder in Don Navigation Co. Subscribed to 'Dr Short's Mineral Waters'. Trustee for St. Paul's Church. d. 1.12.1741, aged 49, bur. in chancel of parish church. MI.

ESAM William Burnett, J.P., solicitor, Broom Hall. 7.18. Bn. 24.11.1847, s. of Charles, insurance company secretary. Educated at Milk Street Academy and articled to Sir H E Watson. Admitted solicitor 1871, later head of Watson, Esam & Barber, legal adviser to Cammel Laird's. President S. Law Society in 1896. His wife, née Bowling, d 1922. C.E. member of School Board from 1894 and then of Education Committee; Council member of University College; GS(G). Active in conservative politics. Director of Sheffield Banking Co. from 1900. Elected CB. 31.1.1901, remaining until he d. 5.5.1932, leaving £37,000.

EVERARD Charles Clifford, C.O.S. 10.25. Elected CB. 1948. b. 8.9.1899, s. of Rev. Ernest Vores and Louisa Alice (Spafford). Ed. K.E. VII, S., S. University, Royal Dental Hospital. m. 5.6.1937 Margaret (Meggitt). Dental Surgeon. d. 5.1975.

FELL John, gent, A. Forge. 10.10. Bn. 19.2.1665/6 at Hooton Roberts, s. of William Fell of Rotherham and Susanna (Kaye). Clerk to Hayford of Wortley and A. Forges, later leasing the latter. m. Ellen, d. of William Milner of Burton Grange and Ann (Elmsal); she d. 7.1.1724/5 aged 60. Trustee for Francis Barlow, CB. 10.8. GS(G)., paying £1 towards Master's house in 1701. Had a house at A. Hill Top. d. 30.4.1724, bur. in parish church.

FELL John, the younger, New Hall and A. Forge. 8.13. Bn. 6.3.1696, (e).s. of John, CB 10.10. m. Alice, d. of Richard Bagshaw of Castleton and The Oaks, Norton; she d. s.p. 8.8.1737. Built New Hall, A. Had three shares in Don Navigation Co. and was a Committee Member. Elected CB. 24.3.1732/3, also GS(G). and Bamforth Charity Trustee. m. 3.7.1740 at A. Elizabeth, d. of Henry Laughton of Scotter, Lincs., who was patronised by Madam Parkin of Ravenfield and was said to be 'well born, well conducted, pretty and of graceful manner', later being called Madam Fell, best known for her gift of £1,000 towards the Infirmary. 1741 voted for Turner. Chairman and Treasurer of Don Navigation Co. Had a share in Ladywash Mine, Eyam. Gave £10 to 1745 Defence Subscription. He was a partner with Joseph Clay, CB. 5.10, in Colnebridge, Staveley and Carburton Forges. d. s.p. 17.5.1762, bur. in the parish church.

FENTON Francis, merchant and police superintendent, Woodhill, Grimesthorpe Road. 1.15. Bn. 1755, nephew of John Fenton, CB. 9.11; he, or an earlier Francis, painter, and possibly father, was the latter's residuary legatee. m. Elizabeth, d. of Benjamin Roebuck, senior, in whose merchant business he was first a partner and then sole controller until his bankruptcy in 1808; she d. 6.3.1790. Elected CB. and GS(G). on 19.1.1785. Leading officer in the local militia, being promoted to Lt.-Col. Commandant vice the Earl of Effingham in 1807. In March 1793, m. Helen, d. of James Crosland of Deadmanstone, Halifax, attorney; she d. 5.3.1838. Elected TT. 22.6.1801, becoming an active member; the Trust presented him with a horse. 1807 voted for Wilberforce and Milton. Member of Lord Milton's election committee in 1810. Member of S. Pitt Club 1815. In 1818 first Surveyor to the Commissioners of Police in Sheffield. Subscribed 5 gns. to new GS. in 1823 and supported subscription for bells for St George's in 1824. Described by Barbara Wreaks as 'a good natured fellow'. Governor and Trustee S. Savings Bank. Subscribed Surrey Street Library. d. at S. 18.5.1835, MI.

FENTON John, Little Sheffield, gent. 11.12. Bap. 8.3.1687/8, s. of Alexander and Elizabeth Fenton of Gleadless, Handsworth. Guest of Duke of Norfolk in 1721. On 24.1.1721/2 m. Ann, d. of Jonathan Lee, CB. 9.7. Elected CB 22.4.1732; also GS(G). Was a trustee of St. Paul's Church. Freeholder at N. in 1734; voted for Lord Cavendish. His sister m. John Nodder, CB. 8.12. Bur. 5.2.1761.

FENTON John, MD, surgeon and apothecary, Portobello. 9.11. Bap. 16.2.1708/9 s. of Matthew and Mary (Hawksworth). 1734 and 1740 subscribed to 'Dr Short's History of Mineral Waters'. Occupied Horse Pastures, Little S. Elected CB. 13.6.1764; also GS(G). In 1766 signatory of Rockingham Address. w.d. 3.6.1775, w.p. 11.1.1777, his nephew Francis the painter being executor and residuary legatee; property at Bradfield Dale, Portobello, Woodthorpe, Moor Side, Red Croft S., Crookes and Hathersage.

FENTON Richard, mercer and gent, S. and Doncaster. 3.1. o.s. of Richard, mercer, who was concerned in many land deals, often in connection with the Swifts, in the period of Reformation; the father's first wife was Cecily, d. of Robert Swift of Silkstone and Rotherham and Agnes (Anne), and aunt to Robert Swift the younger of Broom Hall, CB. 1.1, and widow. of Nicholas Abson, alias Tomson. Richard's mother was Anne, d. of Lawrence Smythe of A., bailiff, and sister of Hugh Smythe, CB. 2.1. A step-sister, Emot, m. Nicholas Shirecliffe of Ecclesfield Hall, Nicholas Scott of Barnes Hall, and Edmond Dearnelly, while sisters m. Thomas Bray, CB. 1.2, and James Rawson, CB. 9.3. In 1548 he had the rest of the 'ferme of Sheffelde Church' from his grandfather Lawrence Smythe. He was under age when his parents wrote their wills in 1549/50 and 1552 and his uncle Hugh Smythe was named as his guardian. In 1558, with William Swyfte, he was godfather at the Rotherham bap. of Richard, s. of John Snell. In 1560 he was heir to his uncle, Hugh Smythe of A. and North Lees. In 1564 he was paying rent to the CB. but the next year he was described as a merchant of Doncaster, when selling S. 'Church Gates' property. He was Doncaster public collector in 1565 and Mayor in 1568-9. He bought D. Manor in 1565 and sold it to Thomas Bright in 1596. In 1566 he was still paying rent to the TT. for 'Swift's land' and in 1568 his wife Joan is mentioned in a S. sale. He sold a house in Market Street to Thomas Bray and was supervisor for the latter's 1569 will, probably then holding North Lees. In 1571, as gent. of Doncaster, he sold N. property; the next year he bought 1/3 of A. tithe; in 1573 he was consulted by the Burgery. In 1577, as Alderman of Doncaster, he was a recusant, worth more than £10 p.a. in lands, but he apparently acted as CB. collector in 1578. In 1580-1 his wife, Joan, was presented at Doncaster for not going to church. In 1582 he was of North Lees, supervisor of his sister, Anne Bray's, will. In 1585 his servant, Ralph Elves, conveyed a letter to the Queen of Scots, and he paid £25 instead of providing 'one light horse'. He appears several times, with his wife, Joan, in the 1592-3 recusant rolls, having property in Hathersage, A., Doncaster and Frickley, and was described as a 'dangerous recusant', released from prison in 1599. In 1604 his widow, Jenne, again appears on the recusant roll. Many of his later sales were in connection with his d. Margaret and her husband, and George Anne of Frickley.

FENTON William. 8.6. Bap. 4.6.1643, s. of William of Gleadless, Handsworth (descending from Richard above), and Ann (Nodder). m. Ruth, Born 1633, d. of Richard Rhodes and Elizabeth (Barnsley) and wid. of John Wright of A. Mill. He lived opposite Royds Mill. His d. Ann was mother of William Burton of Royds Mill, CB. 9.10; an elder sister, Hannah, m. Thomas Handley, CB. 4.7. In 1688 was collector for the Vicar's money. Bur. at S. 3.8.1696.

FIRTH Ambrose, J.P. Elected CB. 11.6.1952. b. 14.10.1896, (e).s. of Thomas Henry, engineer and Ethel Mary, d. of Stephen Johns. Ed. Rugby and then student engineer at Dusseldorf 1913-14. Joined family firm Brightside Foundry & Engineering Co. Ltd. in 1914. 1914-18 Lieut. in Army, later transferred to R.F.C. Director Brightside Foundry & Engineering Co. Ltd. 1932, Chairman 1940. Joint

Managing Director Brightside Engineering Holdings Ltd. until 1960. J.P. President S. Society of Engineers and Metallurgists. For many years associated with S. Scouts of which he was Hon. Treasurer. m. 1925 Muriel, d. of John William Boddy, mining engineer. d. 15.11.1962.

FIRTH Edward Willoughby, J.P., steel manufacturer. 11.20. Bn. 7.4.1867(?2), s. of Edward, a younger brother of Mark, of Oakbrook and the Norfolk Works. Partner in Thomas Firth & Sons, and Director of Thos. Firth & John Brown Ltd. Educated at Rugby 1882-5. Purchased F. in 1895. Secretary of S. Musical Festival. Active in conservative politics. Elected CB. 12.6.1902. Council member of S. University College 1903-5 and then of the University until he retired to Bournemouth. Governor of the Charity Schools, President of the Literary and Philosophical Society in 1907 and member of the Court of the University. In 1920 retired to Bournemouth (where he d. 18.6.1937), but continued to attend CB. meetings until his resignation in 1935.

FISHER Jasper, attorney, Hallam. 8.2. Occurs as witness to S. deeds from 1579. m. at N. on 5.6.1586 Bridget Parker. CW. for A.D. in 1593 and of A.D. in 1606 when he paid 7s. in the GS. assessment; paid legal charges by GS(G). 1619-24. Probably his s. Jasper who was a cutler in 1624-5 and lived next to John Smith of A. in 1620-1. Bur. 15.4.1634, w.d. 15.8.1633, mentioned his (?step-) brother Francis North and made James Darwen, with whom he lived, executor.

FLATHER David, J.P. 8.22. Elected CB. 27.10.1930, resigned 8.12.1944. b. 1.7.1864, (e).s. of William Thomas and Phebie, d. of Mr. Darwin of Queen's Foundry. Ed. S. Collegiate School and Firth College, 1879-80. Metallurgical chemist John Brown & Co. Ltd. 1880-86. Joined father's firm, W. T. Flather & Co. Ltd, becoming Director 1898, Chairman 1918-41, life Director 1946. Original member and Treasurer S. Committee on Munitions of War. MC. 1926. Member Council of Chamber of Commerce, District Council F.B.I. and numerous metallurgical and engineering societies. Guardian of Assay for S. Prominent Mason, Director of S. Masonic Hall Co. Ltd. and researched into Masonic history. President S. Literary and Philosophical Society, 1925. Member Yorkshire Archaeological Society and Egyptian Exploration Society. Society for Preservation and Old S. Tools founded under his chairmanship and the existence of Abbeydale Works and Shepherds Wheel as industrial monuments owes much to him. J.P. 1928. Diocesan Lay Preacher. m. 1896 Kate, elder d. of Edmund Mainprize of East Riding Gasworks. d. 21.4.1948.

FLETCHER Douglas Leslie. 11.25. Elected CB. 1980. b. 28.9.1918, s. of James Edwin Fletcher, silversmith, and Alice Renshaw. Ed. King Edward VII School, S. m. 24.1.1942 to Marjorie (Hodgson). Partner, Moore Fletcher & Co., Chartered Accountants, 1956-84. Chairman, House of Laity, S. Diocesan Synod, 1970-82. Chairman, S. Diocesan Board of Finance, 1981-1997. War service: Royal Engineers, 1939-46 with G.H.Q. 2nd Echelon North Africa and Italy, 1942-46.

FORDER Howard Poulsom. 5.19. Elected CB. 1968, resigned 1984. b. 14.2.1911 s. of William Howard, wooltrader and Ada Elizabeth (Mundy). Ed. Tonbridge. m. 13.8.1938 Cecily Mary (Rust). General Manager Samuel Fox & Co. Ltd 1956-64. Deputy Managing Director and Managing Director United Steel Companies Ltd 1964-67. Assistant Managing Director BSC (Midland Group) 1967-1969 – Managing Director BSC Special Steel Division 1970-72. Chairman, Arthur Lee & Sons plc 1976-79. Chairman Alloy Steel Rods Ltd 1980-81. Member of Council, S. University 1972-84 and Pro-Chancellor S. University 1972-79 MC. 1963/4. d. 23.7.1990.

FOX Ulysses, yeo., Fulwood. 11.5. s. of William, CB. 11.3. On 4.2.1612/3 m. at Bd. Elizabeth, d. of William Green, gent., of Smallfield in Bd. and Ann (Rhodes). CW. for H. in 1615. Concerned in dispute about milling rights. w.d. 14.10.1648, to be bur. on the south side of the church. bur. 26.4.1649, for which his s. John paid the usual 6s. 8d.

FOX William, yeo., Fulwood Hall. 11.3. (e).s. of William of Fd. Hall and head of a family long resident in Fd., and also having considerable property in Bd. In 1586 associated with Robert Mitchell about a Furnival grant to the people of Stannington. Succeeded Mitchell as CB., but appears to have resigned almost immediately. w.d. 21.9.1609 mentioned 6ds. and 2ss., (?2) wife Joan and his books. bur. 1.5.1612.

FOX William, Fulwood Hall, gent. 6.7. Bap. at S. 12.12.1613, (e).s. of Ulysses, CB. 11.5. m. at Bd. on 8.9.1636 Anne, d. of John Morewood of the Oaks, Bd. and who later m. Henry Balguy of the Hagg, Hope, gent. Ed. at Bd. for 7 years and then by Thomas Rawson at S. GS. for one year before entering Sidney Sussex College, Cambridge, as a pensioner in 1632. CW. for H. in 1641. w.d. 24.8.1648, he was bur. in S. church, probably on the 31st.

FURNISS Henry, J.P., Whirlow House, E. 5.13. Born 1803, s. of Matthew of Foolow and The Edge, S., silver plater. m. Ann, e.d. of Thomas Sanderson and became partner in Sanderson Bros. & Newbould, steel manufacturers, who had A. Forge and furnaces at D. Subscribed Surrey Street Library. Elected CB. and GS(G). on 28.4.1841. Voted for Overend in 1852 and 1857. Poor Law Guardian for E. d. 25.9.1872.

GRANT Sir Allan John. 6.25. Elected CB. 2.2.1940, resigned 15.6.1945. b. Surrey of Scots descent 8.9.1875, s. of Alexander Allan and Jane Maria (Tidd). Ed. Cheltenham College; pupil at Laird Bros., Birkenhead, marine engines and shipbuilders, and Walker Engineering Laboratories; Whitworth exhibitioner Liverpool University 1896. He came to S. as Assistant Managing Director John Brown & Co. Ltd, Director 1915. Managing Director Thos. Firth & John Brown Ltd. 1925-44. Chairman Firth-Vickers Stainless Steels Ltd. 1934-44. Director Craven's Railway Carriage & Wagon Co. Ltd., Park Gate Iron & Steel Co. Ltd. and

British Acheson Electrodes Ltd. President British Iron & Steel Federation 1932. Member Board of Trade Advisory Council 1933-36. Member Council Institute of Mechanical Engineers 1939-45. Chairman Ministry of Production East & West Riding Regional Board 1940-42. Vice-Chairman 1942-45. President Chamber of Commerce 1937-38. Member University Council 1935-45. Hon. Colonel 13th Light A.A. Regt. R.A. (T.A.) Chairman N. E. Derbyshire Conservative & Unionist Asstn. 1934-45. Knighted 1941, the first to be so inside a factory. m. 1909 Isa Florence, d. of William Hillyard of London. d. holidaying in Isle of Skye 19.7.1955.

GREAVES George, merchant, Sheffield and Attercliffe 10.15. b. 1733, s. of George Greaves, a button-maker of Lambert Street, and Mary (Marriot). m. Jane, e.d. of Richard Bustard of Lotherton and Bramham, and who d. in 1785, aged 59, their o.c., George Bustard, lord of Wadsley, being born in 1759. Leased 'Carlton House', Oakes Green, A., in 1777 and later bought Page Hall, built by Thomas Broadbent. There was a contemporary namesake MC. in 1762; one signed the Rockingham Address in 1766. Elected CB. and GS(G). on the 3rd and resigned on the 31st of July 1776. Registered his pedigree and arms at Herald's College in 7.1.1782. Two male servants in 1780, Tontine Inn subscriber in 1785, and (with his son) guaranteed £500 to buy corn in 1795. d. 20.12.1801.

GREAVES Henry Marwood, MA, J.P., Hesley Hall, Notts., Banner Cross and Ford Hall. 4.12. Bn. at Page Hall 6.2.1793, 3rd s. of George Bustard Greaves (see above) and Ellen (Clay), a grandson of Joseph Clay, CB. 5.10. Educated at Atherstone under Dr. Charteris before going to Clare College, Cambridge, 1810-14, M.A. 1817. Captain in the Tickhill troop of the 1st West Yorks. Yeomanry Cavalry, director of the Don Canal Co., and patron of the Church Educational Institute. Member S. Pitt Club 1815. Dep.-Lieut. for Derbs. On 24.9.1829 m. at Chapel-en-le-Frith Mary Catherine Anne, (o).d. and h. of Rev. Wm. Bagshawe of Banner Cross and Ford Hall; their (e).s. took the additional surname of Bagshawe. Elected CB. 28.2.1856. d. at Banner Cross 10.3.1859 and bur. at Chapel-en-le-Frith. His funeral sermon at E. by the Rev. Edward Newman, was printed.

GREAVES John, draper or merchant, Fargate. 10.19. Bn. 1743, s. of John, merchant of Fargate, and Ann (Shepherd). Probably one male servant in 1780. Elected TT. 16.8.1784. On Corn Committee in 1795. Elected CB. and GS(G). 14.3.1798. Bankrupt in 1821. d. 7.4.1828. MI.

GUNNING Thomas, merchant, High Street. 2.18. Bn. 1735, 2nd s. of John Gunning of Cold Ashton, Glos. Signatory to Rockingham Address in 1766. On 24.11.1766 m. Mary, d. of Thomas (CB. 4.8) and Mary Shirecliffe of Whiteley Hall. Elected CB. 24.3.1722; also GS(G). and TT. From 1774 partner in S. Lead Works. On 7.5.1781 m. at Royston Olive, d. of Robert and Frances Wood of Monk Bretton. w.d. 14.4.1784, d. 6.5.1784, MI.

HALDSWORTH (var.), James, vintner and mercer or draper. 6.2. In 1564/5 supervisor of the will of Gilbert Haldsworth, who was possibly his brother, was a servant to James Turner, CB. 2.2, and to whose son James he left a Bible as heirloom. In 1566 paid rent for Mr. Eyre's land to TT. In 1567 CW. for the town. TC. for several years, various references to his inn; signed for arms bought from Shrewsbury in 1576 and was chairman of the Sembly Jury in 1578. Paid 5s. 6d. at 1569 assessment. Joint guardian of the 4 ss. of Gilbert in 1580, after the death of their mother who had m. 2nd Robert Urton, who named James as one of the supervisors of his 1574 will. In 1587 first warden of S. stock. His widow, Agnes (or Anne) had a d. by an earlier marriage and was closely connected with the Hollands of Dovehouse. w.d. 8.3.1596/7 (described as yeo.), bur. 14.3.1596/7.

HAMILTON Stewart McKee. 5.20. b. 12.1.1937, o.s. of John Ian Hamilton, sales manager, and Marjorie Rintoul Young (McKee), teacher. Ed. at Oundle School and King's College, Cambridge. M.A. (Cantab). 1960-65 Rolls Royce Ltd. 1965-66 Tubewrights Ltd. Liverpool. 1966 joined T.G. Lilleyman & Son Ltd, (drop stampers of scissors, surgical instruments and orthopaedic implants), Production Director 1966-76, Managing Director 1977-1995, also Managing Director of Thornton Precision Forgings Ltd 1994-1995, then Chairman 1995 to date. J.P. City of Sheffield 1972. C.Eng. M.I. Mech.E. 1967, F.I.Mech.E. 1995, F.Inst.F.T. 1995, F.R.S.A. 1995. Chairman, Council of Cutlery and Allied Trades Research Association 1977-1987. J.G.Graves Charitable Trustee 1980-. Yorkshire Historic Churches Trustee 1991-1996. High Sheriff, South Yorkshire 1990-91. Special Trustee former United Sheffield Hospitals 1996 -, Chairman, Central Sheffield University Hospitals NHS Trust 1996 -. m. 21.7.1960 to Susan Marie Lilleyman, pharmacist.

HANDLEY Thomas, The Bridge-House and Hall-Carr gent. 4.7. Bap. S. 9.2.1670/1, o.s. of James and Hannah, d. of George Wild, CB. 7.9. On 4.9.1690 m. Hannah, d. of William Fenton, CB. 8.6. Some of their children were bap. at Upper Chapel. Bought property in A. from John Hoole. In 1709 paid £1 towards GS. Master's house. In 1731 he sold property in A. to Arthur Speight, CB. 5.9. Elected CB. 1.10.1713, despite opposition as not being a good Churchman, and resigned 18.10.1746. Lived to be 90.

HARLAND Albert, J.P. 9.27. Elected CB. 4.2.1921, b. 6.9.1869, 2nd s. of Rev. Albert A Harland, V. of Harefield and Louisa Ellen, d. of Henry Wilson of Westbrook House (CB. 2.21). Ed. Rugby and Corpus Christi College, Cambridge. Came to S. 1891. With elder bro. William became directors of Westbrook Snuff Mill (believed that they ran the Top Mill as a separate enterprise in competition with the successors of Henry Wilson (their grandfather – CB 2.21) who ran the Bottom Mill). Mill remained with Harland family until 1953 when sold to Imperial Tobacco Co. Ltd. President F. Graucob Ltd. and Nu-Swift Ltd. Member City Council 1902-11, 1929-36, Alderman 1932-36, J.P. 1912, TT. 1929-52. Conservative M.P. Ecclesall 1923-29. Patron S. Royal Institution for the Blind.

Strong supporter of Scout movement. Presented stained glass windows for CB. Room. d. 25.2.1957.

HARRISON James William, Tapton Park Road, Ranmoor. 9.23. Bn. at S. in 1816, s. of James and Mary. App. aged 14 to Stuart & Smith, stove-grate manufacturers. Joined Thomas Sanson & Sons, cutlers, Norfolk Street, which became Harrison Bros. & Howson in 1847, and from which he retired in 1875. Governor and Trustee S. Savings Bank, Director of S. Water Co., Gas Co., Ths. Jessop & Sons Ltd. Elected CB. 3.10.1878; also GS(G). Conservative in politics. Guardian for E. d. 1.3.1897, unmarried, bur. Fd.

HAWLEY William, sen., Grimesthorpe, gent. 4.6. Is the first entry in the pedigree of the Hawley Croft family and may have come from Shepley where he had property. His wife was named Dorothy but the marriage and baptism of the children are not recorded in the P.R. There was a John Hawley who had 5 hearths in 1665 and paid rent to the TT., and a William, whitesmith, living in the High Street in 1675. In his w.d. 27.8.1713 William is described as 'late of Grimesthorpe', so it is possible he was CW. for the town in 1709. Gave 5s. towards the Master's house in 1709. The younger s., Joseph, was a dyer and TT., and his elder brother William obtained his house in Campo Lane after his death. William, jun., also a dyer, was Overseer of the Poor in 1720 and a GS(G). William, sen., d. 31.8.1713.

(H)EATON Thomas, jun., ironmonger, Church Gates, High Street. 9.9. Bap. at S. 27.7.1686, s. of Thomas, who was probably an ironmonger and shopkeeper like his s. and supposed to have come from Manchester, and Ann (Wallhead). One of them paid 10s. in 1709 towards the Master's house. In 1710 he bought a house at the Church Gates from Joseph Banks; also had a country villa in the Pickle. Was assessed for 3-1/2d. in 1716 and connected with St. Paul's Church. On 23.12.1718 m. Sarah Hawke. The published letters from Phyllis Balguy of Hope show how strong were his Jacobite sympathies. He was also a TT. and GS(G).; closely connected with starting the Don Navigation Scheme, having two shares for himself and one for his e.d Anne. In 1731 trustee for Jonathan Hurt, the High Street mercer. w.d. 13.12.1734, d. 19.12.1734, MI. describing him as 'easy and agreeable . . . and died generally lamented.'

HOBSON Francis, jun., merchant and steel manufacturer, The Mount. 11.19. Bn. 1840 s. of Francis of Collegiate Crescent and Burnt Stones, Don Steel Works, Savile Street, and Bridget. Educated at the Collegiate School. Joined family firm. Lived at The Mount and Elmdale, Ranmoor. Elected CB. 30.1.1873 and resigned 12.6.1902, retiring to Trowbridge. Also GS(G). d. 1.1.1913, leaving £81,606; bur. E.

HOLLAND John, tanner, Dove House, Greystones. 10.1. The family was widespread, with various other spellings such as Holand, Howland, Hoyland and Hoiland making identification uncertain. The Christian name John was very popular, but Williams and Richards are also frequent. The family was closely connected with the pre-Reformation chantries. A priest, Sir Robert, another Robert, V. 1569-97, and his s. James were all at Christ's College, Cambridge. There were four main branches, the Vicar's and those residing at Dove Houses, Greystones, E. (Button Hill) and H., which are very difficult to disentangle and to relate. The original CB. was probably s. of another John, baker, who obtained a messuage in H. in 1496 and held Dove House in 1500. If so, it was probably his 2nd wife, Elizabeth who m. Richard Dale of High Storrs and perhaps his d. who m. 2nd James Holdsworth, CB 6.2. d. about end of 1571.

HOLLAND John, yeo., Button Hill. 10.4. Sometimes called Senior to distinguish from younger contemporary, s. of the last CB. and also a tanner of Dove House. May have been s. of John Holland (CB. 10.1) of Dove House and only a boy when his father d. He lived at Dove House until his 2nd marriage by licence at S. on 19.1.1619/20 to Emmot, wid. of Thomas Lee of Button Hill, when he moved there. His s. John lived at Dove House and d. on 1634, predeceasing his father. Possibly the 2nd s. of John of Ecclesall who was CW in 1567 and 1574 and Collector in 1568; he d. in 1580, to be followed shortly afterwards by his (e).s. Richard. The elder John was probably s. of a Richard whose wife Agnes (Stickbuck) had m. William Taylor, CB. 4.1. CW. for E. 1592, 1610 and 1631. Original GS(G)., and paid 13s. 4d. in 1606 assessment. bur. 3.12.1641.

HOLMSTROM Carl Eric, J.P. 5.18. Elected CB. 1945. bn. 28.7.1893, s. of Carl Albert, engineer, and Katherine Annette (Leresche). Ed. Haileybury College. Thos. Firth & Sons Ltd (export manager in 1926); Director Firth-Vickers Stainless Steel Ltd; Chairman John Bedford & Sons Ltd. Prominent in British Iron and Steel Federation; Chairman Stainless Steel Manufacturers Association. President S. Chamber of Commerce 1944-5. Active S. scouts; Chairman Sheffield Association 1953-9. JP for Sheffield from 1947. m Joan Leslie 30.4.1925 d. at North Anston 1.6.1968.

HOLT James Peter Rees, J.P. 10.26. Elected CB. 1975. b. 30.10.1929, (o).s. of Frederick Peter and Eleanor (Rees). Ed. Shrewsbury, Coll. Estate Management, University of London. m. 22.10.1955 to Cecilia Margery (Edwards). Chartered Surveyor, Senior Partner Eadon, Lockwood & Riddle and then Lambert Smith Hampton. J.P. 1975. General Commissioner of Income Tax 1973. Custodian Trustee TSB England & Wales, 1985. Chairman Yorks. Regional Board TSB, 1985. Central Board TSB Group, 1985. Board of UDT Holdings, 1985. Deputy Chairman of the Board of Trustees of the Lloyds/TSB Foundation for England and Wales. Retired as a Burgess 1997.

HOOLE John, shearsmith, B. 9.2. (e).s. of Robert and Margaret of 'Brikford' – the father d. in 1546 when John was still unmarried. Mark 10.2.1564/5. His wife was Catherine, d. of Nicholas Hatfield of Shiregreen, and she m. 2nd Edward Hiley, CB. 3.3. John was a juror for Southey in 1565 and benefited from the 1566 will of Jeffrey Cooke of Ecclesfield. bur. 9.2.1572/3.

HOOLE John, yeo., A. 12.7. Bap. S. 25.2.1581/2, (e).s. of Robert, a shearsmith of A. who d. in 1584. He was the (e).s. of John, CB. 9.2., and m. Isabel, d. of John Mountenay of Creswick, and who married 2nd Nicholas Staniforth of A., GS(G). The younger John helped with the GS. assessment in 1606, but was not GS(G). His sister was 1st wife of Christopher Capper, CB. 6.5. He was trustee for John Hill in 1605/6 and for Edward Sanderson, CB. 11.4, in 1617. m. at Laughton, Mary, d. of John Mirfield, who m. 2nd John Wilson, CB. 3.5. CW. A.D. 1613. w.d. 9.11.1621, bur. 3.12.1621.

HOOLE Robert, yeo., A. 6.8. Bap. S. 28.3.1616, (e).s. of John, CB. 12.7. His sister, Mary, was 1st wife of James Nicholson, CB. 2.12. Robert m. Mary, d. of William Cart, Rector of Handsworth; her bro. John was ejected from Handsworth and her brother-in-law, Matthew Bloom, was a leading S. Presbyterian and both were trustees for Robert's children. His freehold farm in Dean Field, A., contained the barn where Bloom preached. He had moved from A. when he wrote his will, 5.2.1658/9, and was bur. in the choir at S. on 11.2.1658/9.

HOOLE William, yeo., Crookes. 1.4. Younger s. of Robert and Margaret of 'Brikford', and brother of John, CB. 9.2. m. 1st, on 8.11.1562, Alice Wilson, bur. 19.4.1588, and then, 18.2.1589/90, Elizabeth Hobson. CW. for B. 1566 and 1581. Paid 13s. 4d. in 1606 Assessment. His (e).s., Charles, a corviser, m. Ann, d. of William Creswick, CB. 2.4, and had Charles, bap. S. 6.8.1609, the famous schoolmaster, before they moved to Wakefield. William was often supervisor for wills and was trustee for the V., Robert Holland. In 1611 he paid £21 rent to the lord for his farm near the Don. w.d. 21/6/1626; bur. 10.1.1627/8.

HORN William Ibberson, merchant, Carwood, Grimesthorpe Road. 11.18. s. of Joseph of London and Mary, d. of William, saw and fender maker, and Hannah (Brownhill). Set up as tilter and roller at Wisewood and merchant and steel, file, saw and edge tool manufacturer, Bridge Street. Voted for Bailey and Parker in 1832 and 1835, for Wortley in 1835, Wortley and Denison in 1841 and for Overend in 1852. Opposed S. charter in 1838. Overseer for the Poor 1848. Governor and Trustee S. Savings Bank 1868. Elected CB. 16.2.1854, also GS(G). from 1856 until he d. 3.1.1873, leaving £17,500 to charities.

HOUNSFIELD Bartholomew, merchant, Clough House. 8.18. bap. 13.10.1774, 6th s. of George, merchant and factor, Wadsley House, and Elizabeth (Twigg). Bought F. as a forkmaker in 1798. Partner with brother John, MC. 1819, in Pond Street. Wisewood allotment from 1821. Subscribed 10 gns. for new GS. in 1823, and opposed S. charter in 1838. Original partner S. Coal Company. m. Elizabeth, d. of Richard Gregory, and who d. 6.5.1817, aged 38. Elected CB. 3.11.1831; also GS(G)., J.P., (W.R.). Subscribed Surrey Street Library. Director S. and Rotherham Bank. Of Arundel Street, voted for Bailey and Parker in 1832 and 1835, and for Wortley in 1835. d. 12.4.1841, bur. Tinsley.

HOUNSFIELD George, merchant, Clough House and High Hazels, Darnall. 8.19. bn. 4.7.1806, o.s. of Bartholomew, CB. 8.18. Succeeded his father as director Coal Co., S. & Rotherham Bank (Chairman 1861), Wisewood allotment, CB. and GS(G)., elected 28.4.1841. m. at Edgbaston on 10.1.1838 Maria, (o).d. of Joshua Scholefield, M.P. for Birmingham, and who m. 2nd William Overend Q.C., M.P., in 1871. Subscribed Surrey Street Library. Treasurer S. Gas Co., chairman S. Water Co., director Midland Railway, Governor and Trustee S. Savings Bank. J.P. for W.R. and Derbs. Voted for Overend in 1857. w.d. 12.1866 and d. 11.2.1870, leaving bequests to Infirmary Hospital and Charity Schools, and started Pensions Fund connected with CB.

HOYLE James Rossiter, J.P. 9.26. Elected 24.10.1913, resigned 4.2.1921. b. Manchester 1856, s. of William Jennings (member of an old Yorkshire family). Ed. Owen's College, Manchester and in France. Entered engineering industry in Paris where he met Charles Henry Firth who brought him to S. 1881. Joined Thos. Firth & Co. Ltd. which he persuaded to manufacture heavy armaments, 1893 Director in charge of gun dept. Responsible for buying a Russian armaments firm and, with Armstrongs, for establishing projectile manufacture in Italy. Director Projectile Engineering Co. Ltd. Member Institution of Civil Engineers and Council Institution of Mechanical Engineers. President S. Society of Engineers and Metallurgists, 1909-11. J.P. 1912. MC. 1912-13. President S. Musical Union. m. 1883 Augusta, e.d. of Alexander Muir of Liverpool. 1919 retired to Hartfield, Sussex. d. 14.3.1926.

HUDSON Edward, East Cliffe, East Bank. 1.17. bn. 1806, 2nd s. of Henry, ironmonger, Leeds. m. Maria, sister-in-law of Henry Furniss, CB. 5.13, and 2nd d. of Thomas Sanderson. Partner in Sanderson Bros., merchants and steel manufacturers, West Street. Overseer for Poor 1847. Elected CB. 14.11.1850. Also GS(G). from 1854 and director S. Gas Co. from 1858. Voted for Wortley and Denison in 1841 and for Overend in 1852. d. 20.1.1887.

HUNT John Philip, T.D. 1.21 Elected C.B. 5.10.1951. B. Sheffield 27.4.1907. 2nd s. of John Edwin of Hope Derbs. Ed. Malvern College. Throughout life closely connected with Hallamshire Battalion, York and Lancaster Regiment, Hon. Col. 1965. Joined Hallamshire Steel and File Co. Ltd., succeeding father as managing director 1934. Master Cutler 1948-9. Managing director Staveley Coal and Iron Co. from 1954 and director several other companies. Town Trustee 1953. M. 1935 Jean Margaret, d. of C.A. Nicholson, Resigned 10.4.1957 d. at Holme Hall Bakewell 9.7.1970.

HUNTER Stephen Albert Paul J.P., M.A. 12.27 born Sheffield 11.9.52 and educated locally. Son of Horace Hunter and Rachel (Goudstikker). Married Anne (Ferguson) 1975. 2 Sons, Jonathan 1978 and Matthew 1979. Elected C.B. April 1993. Chairman of Unigraph (UK) Ltd. and Chairman and/or Director of several other companies. Director of the Sheffield Diocesan Board of Finance. Governor of

Birkdale School, Sheffield, Chairman 1995. Appointed Lay Inspector of Schools by OFSTED 1993. Appointed J.P. 1996. Appointed a non-executive director by Secretary of State for Health to Sheffield Childrens Hospital NHS Trust 1997 -. Appointed by Secretary of State for Health as a Special Trustee to the 'Former United Sheffield Hospital Special Trustees.' 1997 -.

HUNTSMAN Francis, steel manufacturer, Loversall Hall, near Doncaster, and A. 11.17. bn. 1785, s. of William, steel refiner, A., descendant of the inventor of crucible steel, and Mary. The 'Steel King of Attercliffe', he built himself a house in Worksop Road but later moved to Crook Hill, near Doncaster. m. 20.2.1812 Fanny, d. of John Hawksworth, knife manufacturer, A. Subscribed 5 gns. for new GS. in 1823, and opposed S. charter in 1838. Voted for Parker and Bailey in 1835, for Wortley and Denison in 1841, and Overend in 1852 and 1857. Elected CB. 28.4.1841 but resigned on 16.2.1854; also GS(G). Subscribed Surrey Street Library. d. 21.2.1879; bur. in family vault at Wadsworth.

HUSSEY John, surgeon apothecary. 11.13. bap. S. 1.4.1703, (e).s. of Peter, A. Forge, and Ellen (Goddard). Supplied medicines for Don Navigation Company in 1732. Subscribed for Dr. Short's 'Mineral Waters' in 1733, 1740. Messuage in Wadsley in 1739. Subscribed to S. Assemblies in 1747-8. Supported election of John Dickinson as M. in 1749. Elected CB. 24.2.1761, having already been GS(G). for nearly 20 years, and was succeeded after his death in both posts by Joseph Matthewman, who m. his niece. Trustee for Thomas Young, TT., in 1737 and for Elizabeth Parkin in 1766. Signatory to Rockingham Address in 1766. Guest at 1771 Cutlers' Feast, then a 'surgeon in considerable practice'. d. 6.3.1773 unmarried.

HUTTON Nicholas James Anthony, b. 7.8.1948. 8.25 C.B. 1988. Son of Colonel William Antony Robinson Hutton and Patricia Ann Georgina Cotterill. m. 12.4.1971 Elizabeth Anne Mundy. Ed. Wycliffe College and London College of Printing. Chairman of Greenup and Thompson Limited Manufacturers of Printed Packaging. Chairman British Carton Association 1988-90. President British Printing Industries Federation 1993-5. Fellow Institute of Packaging. Fellow Royal Society of Arts. Chairman Age Concern Sheffield 1987-1993 and 1996-7. Trustee of the Zachary Merton & George Woofindin Convalescent Trust. Member of the Finance Committee Sheffield Diocesan Trust and Board of Finance.

HYLEY John, yeo., A. 3.3. (?e.) s. of Edward, also a yeo., cutler of A., and his 1st wife Joan (?d. of John and Elizabeth Dale); Edward m. 2nd Catherine (Hatfield), wid. of John Hoole, CB. 9.2. Mark for knives 18.2.1565/6. CW. A.D. 1583, 1591; juror 1591. Presumably his wid. who paid 5s. 4d. in 1606 GS. Assessment. bur. S. 'municeps' 11.8.1604, w.p. 14.11.1604 by wid. Emott.

IBBERSON Joseph, Highfield. 12.16. bn. 1745, s. of Joseph, MC. in 1759 and TT., and Mary. Tontine subscriber 1785. Leased part of Wicker Tilts & Wheels in 1786, Spur-Gear Wheels in 1794. Guest at Cutlers' Feast in 1771 and 1790. Guaranteed

£200 to Corn Committee in 1795 and subscribed £40 for National Defence in 1798. Elected CB. and GS(G). 18.6.1798, and resigned 5.10.1798. d. 12.7.1800, leaving his wid. Truant a share in S. Theatre; she married Thomas Watson in 1801.

JACKSON Arthur, surgeon. 6.21. bn. 21.2.1844, 4th s. of Henry, surgeon, St. James' Row, and Frances (Swettenham). Educated and trained S. Collegiate School, Cheltenham College, S. Medical School and Infirmary, St. Bartholomew's Hospital, M.R.C.S. 1866, L.S.A. Then took over his father's practice, became surgeon to S. Public Hospital & Dispensary until 1877, also treasurer. From 1877 honorary surgeon to the Infirmary; secretary S. Medical Society 1871-6, of S. Medical School 1869-80, and Yorkshire B.M.A. from 1880. m. on 8.8.1878 Alice, 3rd d. of Bernard Wake, solicitor, and who d. 21.10.1918, having previously endowed the Arthur Jackson Chair of Anatomy at the University in her husband's memory. Town Councillor 1885-92; a convinced Tory. Elected CB. and GS(G). 23.12.1885. Keenly interested in local history, he built up the Collection now named after him and in the City Library. d. 29.12.1895, bur. Ecclesfield.

JESSOP Francis, Broom Hall. 3.7. bap. 25.4.1638 e. (surviving) s. of William, CB. 2.7, and 2nd wife Jane (South). Fellow-commoner at Trinity College, Cambridge, 1654. Admitted Gray's Inn 11.3.1655/6. Elected CB. 14.5.1661, and GS(G). Marriage settlement with his cousin Barbara, d. of Robert Eyre of High Low and Holme Hall, Derbs. dated 11.4.1664, details his inheritance, including mill, wheels, tithes, and S. advowson and property in Notts. Familiar with many prominent scientists, particularly the naturalist John Ray, he visited Montpellier and Lyons, attended meetings of the Royal Society and contributed to the Philosophical Transactions. Friendly to nonconformists, employed William Ronksley as clerk and was helped by V. Fisher's sons in his experiments. Strong opponent of Sir John Reresby of Thrybergh. Assisted Cutlers' Co. against the Hearth Tax and was rewarded with their Honorary Freedom in 1681. His book on Hydrostatics published in 1687. w.d. 10.4.1688, bur. S. 3.4.1691.

JESSOP George, Brancliffe, Anston, Esq. 2.6. bn. Broom Hall 29.5.1584, 2nd s. of William, CB. 3.2 and 2.5. Perhaps at St John's College, Cambridge, like his father. Admitted Middle Temple 9.2.1602/3, barrister 14.5.1613. 'Amongst the Catholics' when his brother wrote his will, 1615. m. Martha Goodrick from Lincs. and had children bap. at S. 1616-24. During this period succeeded his father as CB. and was followed by his nephew, probably when he moved to Worksop about 1626. Paid 13s. 4d. for Broomhall Tithe Hay in 1637. Nominated on Commission of Charitable Uses for S. in 1640. w.d. 9.1.1651, bur. 17.11.1651.

JESSOP Richard, Broom Hall, gent. 10.2. s. of William of Rotherham and Emote (Charlesworth). His marriage, about 1561 to Anne, e.d. and c.h. of Robert Swift and Helen (Wickersley) of Broom Hall, led to the foundation of the S. family. He presented the S. Vicars in 1567 and 1569. Succeeded John Holland as CB, acted as Collector in 1573. In 1572 associated with a recovery of over 500 acres of moor, heath and pasture near Worksop. Grant of Arms in 1575. Connected with repair of Heeley Bridge in 1580. w.d. 8.10.1580, d. 25.11.1580, bur. in church next day paying usual 6s. 8d. Inquisition at Pontefract 6.4.1581. He left bequests to the poor in the parishes where he had property and had £700 banked with a London goldsmith.

JESSOP William, Broom Hall, Worksop and North Lees (Hathersage, Derbs.), Esq. 3.2. and 2.5. bn. 4.1561 (e).s. and h. of Richard, CB. 10.2. Matriculated pensioner at St. John's College, Cambridge, Michaelmas, 1576, student of Middle Temple, 1579. Not of age when father d. but soon elected CB. m. at S. on 21.1.1581/2 Margaret, d. of Sir John Atherton of Lancashire. Their 1st s. bap. Worksop 1583, but next at S. 1584, and Margaret was bur. in S. Church 26.4.1585. He soon m. 2nd Anne, d. of Lyon Goodrick of Kirkby, Lincs., and wid. of Benjamin Bolles of Osberton, and moved to Worksop, having resigned as CB. He presented the puritan Toller as V. of S. in 1597/8, but during the period 1591-1611 was described as of North Lees, a seat connected with the families of Eyre, Smith, Fenton and Savage; assessed for land worth more than £10. Paid 13s. 1d. chief rent in S. in 1601. His return to S. possibly connected with his 3rd marriage to Jane, d. of Edward Disney, who survived him and m. 2nd at S. on 26.11.1635 Lionel Fanshawe of Dronfield. Again CB. in 1613, but had resigned in 1623 in favour of his s. George, 2.6. bur. 8.9.1630.

JESSOP William, Broom Hall, Esq. 2.7. bap. Worksop 8.4.1610, o.s. and h. of Wortley of Scofton, e.s of William, CB. 3.2 and 2.5, and Catherine (Doyley). Possibly matriculated pensioner Magdalene College, Cambridge, at Easter 1627. Admitted Middle Temple 30.6.1628. On 1.2.1630/1 m. at S. Mary, d. of Stephen Bright, CB. 4.3. Described as of Scofton when he presented John Bright as V. of S. in 1635, and had children bap. at Worksop 1632-4. Mary was bur. at S. 13.5.1635 and on 4.6.1637 he had a marriage settlement with Jane, d. of Sir Francis South, Knight, of Kelsterne, Lincs. and seems to have returned to S. where his younger children were bap. bur. S. 15.4.1641 by wid. Jane, who had tuition of young children, including Francis, CB. 3.7.

JESSOP William, Broom Hall, gent. 3.8. bap. S. 22.2.1664/5 (e).s. and h. of Francis, CB. 3.7. Admitted Gray's Inn 24.4.1683, bencher. Succeeded his father as CB. and GS(G); paid 23s 6d towards the new Master's house in 1609 and was trustee for Ronksley's English School at Crookes. Marriage settlement 19.10.1696 and licence at St. Paul's, London, 15.1.1696/7 for Hon. Mary, d. of James Darcy of Sedbury. Had William Ronksley as tutor and subscribed towards the new GS. Master's house in 1709. MP. for Aldborough 1702-13, 1715-34. Justice of Assize in North Wales 1707, called to the Bench 1715, Commissioner and Receiver-General of the Alienation Office 1717, Puisne Judge of Chester 1728/9, lived Lincoln's Inn Fields. Consulted and treated by TT. and connected with dispute about St. Paul's Church, S., 1719. d. at Broom Hall 15.11.1734 and bur. in parish church, MI.

KENYON John, file maker and merchant, Hollis Croft. 2.19. bn. 1738, s. of Joseph, MC. 1738 and founder of John Kenyon & Co., and Elizabeth. Educated at S. GS. and Paris 1754. Travelled in Russia and Germany, and was later 'one of the pioneers who opened up direct trade with the Continent, making protracted journeys to Germany and Portugal'. Became partner with his bros. in 1762. Signatory to Rockingham Address 1773. Guest at Cutlers' Feast 1771; F. 1771 and often Assistant between 1773 and 1797, when he retired owing to infirmity. Elected CB. and GS(G). 3.6.1784. Guaranteed £200 to Corn Committee in 1795. d. 28.1.1809, bur. parish church, MI.

LAMBERT Matthew, linen-draper, Market Place. 3.11 bap. at Handsworth 9.7.1710, his mother being Ann, d. of Alexander Fenton of Gleadless, s. of James, gent., of City of London. Inherited property in Hartshead and Crookesmoorside from bro. Edmund of Manchester and, 1743, bought house in Hartshead from Ann Hancock. m. Jane, d. of a rich dyer, Joseph Bever of New Miller Dam, and children included the writer Jane (Gosling). Elected CB. 29.4.1742; also GS(G). and TT. Owlerton juror 1744. Mercer's business at top of King Street, had Leavy Greave Closes and, in 1764, erected a new furnace at Lambert Croft. Signatory to Rockingham Address 1766. w.d. 1.5.1764. d. 1770.

LAVERICK John Henry Wales, J.P., LL.D.Eng. 11.21. Elected CB. 4.7.1935, resigned 7.2.1951. b. 20.7.1865 at Chesterton Hall, Staffordshire, (o).s. of George Wales, mining engineer, and Eleanor (?). Ed. Retford and Leeds University. Began mining career 1882. 1904 General Manager, Newdigate Colliery Co. Ltd., Warwickshire. 1907 Tinsley Park Colliery, later Managing Director until 1941. Chairman Renishaw Iron Co. Ltd, retired 1951. Associated with a number of other So. Yorks. coal, iron and chemical undertakings. Pioneer in So. Yorks. Gas Grid Co. and in use of coke oven gas in S. industry. President Midland Institute of Mining Engineers, 1919-21 and S. Furnacemen and Stokers' Technical Society. 1931 Chairman University Convocation; 1932 Hon. Doctor of Engineering conferred by University. m. Kate (Walker), d. of a civil engineer. d. 23.3.1955.

LEE George (?MD). 11.10. Born S. 12.8.1687, o.(surviving) s. of Jonathan, CB. 9.7. Educated at S. GS. under his cousin George Lee and admitted pensioner St. John's College, Cambridge, 6.5.1704, with Thomas Bosvile as tutor, matriculated 1704, M.B. 1709. m. 10.6.1714 Elizabeth, wid. of William Fenton of Gleadless, and later wife of John Cowley of Doncaster. Elected CB. 8.10.1717; also GS(G). Connected with St. Paul's dispute. w.d. 15.11.1719, bur. S. 27.6.1720.

LEE Jonathan, lead merchant, Little S. 9.7. s. of Roger, CB. 9.6. m. 5.5.1681 Anne, d. of Malin Sorsby, MC. 1649, and sister of Robert Sorsby, CB. 10.9; she was bur. 26.1.1697/8. Succeeded his father as GS(G). and CB., elected 2.7.1683. Collector of V's. money 1688, trustee for Crawshaw E. Charity 1690. Paid £1 towards new GS. Master's house in 1709. w.d. 29.9.1713, bur. 12.10.1713.

LEE Peter Wilton, CBE, D.L., M.A,. 4.20. Elected CB. 1977. Born 15.5.1935, (e).s. of Sir Wilton and Lady Lee (Master and Mistress Cutler in 1950-51), grandson of Mr/Mrs Percy W Lee (Master and Mistress Cutler in 1927). Ed. Uppingham School, Queens' College, Cambridge, M.A. in Engineering. 2nd Lieut. Royal Engineers 1953-55. Graduate Apprentice of Davy & United Engineering Co. Ltd. of S. 1958. Project Manager Alloy Steel Rods Ltd., 1962. Joined Arthur Lee & Sons in 1962. Joint Managing Director 1970, Group Managing Director 1973, Chairman and Managing Director of the Arthur Lee Group of Companies 1979. President of British Independent Steel Producers Assn. 1981-83. 1993-95 Deputy Chairman, Carclo Engineering Group plc. 1994 Chairman Edward Pryor & Sons Ltd. Director Sanderson Group plc. 1993. Chairman C.B.I Yorkshire and Humberside Regional Council 1993-95. 1994-96 President Engineering Employers Sheffield Association. High Sheriff of South Yorkshire 1995-96. Master Cutler 1985-86. Vice Lord-Lieut. for So. Yorks. Chairman of Council and Pro-Chancellor of S. University. Chairman of Governors of Monkton Combe School. Companion of the Institute of Management. Fellow of Royal Society of Arts. Vice President of So. Yorks. County Scout Council. Former Chairman of Council of S. Industrial Mission. Vice President and former Chairman of S. District Y.M.C.A. Trustee South Yorkshire Foundation. CW. for Fd. m. 3.1962 to Gillian Wendy (Oates).

LEE Roger, butcher, Prior Row. 6.4. Possibly s. of William, to whose lands he succeeded. There were other Roger Lees, at E. in late C15 and a physician to Shrewsbury late C16. Records of various purchases in S. and E. from 1576, including Townfield Knowle, from Richard Skinner. m. (?2nd) Margaret, d. of Thomas and Elizabeth Parkin, at S. 12.6.1580 – their (e).s. George was a yeo. butcher of Little S, GS(G)., while their 3rd s. Dennis was a surveyor and E. parish clerk, author of an early commercial Arithmeticke. Roger's wife's stepfather, William Sylvester, CB. 7.3, left him Moorhills in Little S. Roger was Church Collector in 1594 and 1605, TC. 1598 and 1612, an early GS(G)., assessed for 18s. in 1606, CW. for E. in 1593 and a juryman of the Sembly Quest in 1609. w.d. 26.4.1614, bur. S. 'municeps' 4.6.1614; inventory totalled £307, 15.6.1614.

LEE Roger, merchant, Little S. 9.6. bap. S. 19.12.1621, s. of George, (e).s. of Roger, CB. 6.4, and Ann (Stones). Possibly away from S. (? at London) in 1640s. m. Elizabeth and had Martha, who m. Thomas Marriott, CB. 12.11, and Jonathan CB 9.7. CW. for E. 1653. Elected CB. 21.9.1653, also GS(G). and TT., Honorary F. 1681. Bought Great Park Field, Little S. from Rev. James Creswick 1673. Traded in lead, ore and coal, having s. Jonathan as partner and £3,000 capital. w.d. 16.5.1683, bur S. 'municeps Eccles & Scholae' 12.6.1683, leaving £50 for 12 poor and aged in E.

LEE William, gent. 5.3. Difficult to distinguish from at least two others of the same name, one a bayliff (Leighe) and the other a scribe or attorney who founded a family of scribes closely connected with the CB's and d. in 1644. Bap. at S.

28.5.1570, s. of Robert and Alice (Morehouse). Original GS(G). and, as a 'lawyer', the CB. was assessed for 10s. in 1606. He left law books to James Creswick, Philip Gill and Thomas Bate – the latter had 'Fyningley Winde Mill' and his father William an estate and close called Brighouse Croft. He was bur. at S. 3.4.1609 and his w.p. 29.6.1609 also mentions property in Little S., suggesting a relationship with the other CB's.

LEVICK Henry Swift. 4.18. 20.8.1879, (o).s. of Thomas Swift and Emmie (Ensor), d. of a Leicestershire pottery manufacturer. Elected CB. 25.10.1939. Ed. Wesley College. Began with father's firm, Swift Levick & Co. 1895, worked in So. Wales, 1912 introduced magnet manufacture to S., Managing Director 1919, Chairman 1926. V.'s Warden St. Augustine's for 7 years, Deputy Warden Ranmoor. m. 1904 Julia, d. of Rev. John Chesman, C. of Hunslett, Leeds. 1947 retired to North Wales and later to Bournemouth where d. 4.11.1952.

LUDLAM George, Ox Close, cutler. 10.5. bap. 2.6.1590, s. of Roger of Ox Close and Agnes (Satterfett). m. on 5.7.1620 Margery, d. of John Hunter of Walshbridge, Rustlings Park, yeo.; his brother Thomas, MC. 1646, had m. Margery's sister, Ann. CW. for E. 1630; E. juror 1637; bur. S. 12.11.1651.

MARRIOTT Thomas, merchant, Ughill. 12.11. bap. Bd. 23.7.1643, s. of John, yeo., Ughill, a celebrated Parliamentarian, and Anne (Revell). His sister, Ann, m. John Hoole, M., who was ejected from Bd. but later conformed, ministering at Coley, Bd. and Midhope. m. by licence at S. on 13.7.1670 Martha, d. of Roger Lee, CB. 9.6. Lived in S., CW. 1675, Honorary F. 1681, GS(G)., TT. 1686 (TC. 1689), rated for £4 4s. in 1692 and described as 'merchant or gentleman'. Connected Derbs. lead mines. Elected CB. 28.11.1682 and resigned 8.6.1706. Inherited Ughill estate from his nephew Thomas in 1685. Erected or enlarged Ughill Hall in 1697. Took an active part in Bd. life, particularly in Stannington Chapel, encouraging nonconformist ministers, being, for example, executor for William Bagshaw in 1713. Conveyed Spout House to trustees for minister of chapel in 1714. w.d. 24.6.1715; d. 26.7.1715.

MARSH Harry Parker, merchant and manufacturer, Broomgrove House. 10.23. Born S. 24.2.1857, (e).s. of Theophilus, merchant and steel manufacturer, Ponds Works, and Jane (Parker). Educated at S. Collegiate School, Clifton College 1872-4, and then at Dresden, Germany. Became a partner in Marsh Bros., succeeding his father as Chairman in 1881. On 10.6.1879 m. Ann Jane, d. of John Lockwood. Conservative councillor for E. from 1888, Ald. 1905-26, Lord Mayor 1907; vice-chairman Education Committee. Officer E. and S. Conservative Associations. TT., GS(G)., J.P., Honorary Secretary S. Chamber of Commerce – President 1899 and 1900. Elected CB. 14.3.1901. Governor and Trustee S. Savings Bank. Chairman Effingham Steel Works. Guardian Assay Office. Council Member S. University, LL.D. (Hon.) 1926. d. 14.3.1933.

MATTHEWMAN Joseph, merchant, Townhead Cross. 11.14. Born 1731, s. of Joshua, of Townhead Cross and White House, Crookesmoor, and Dorothy (Brookes). His sister Margaret m. John Smith, M. and Head Master S. GS. Connected with early schemes for supplying water. Guest at 1771 Cutlers' Feast. m. at S. on 18.11.1773 Mary, d. of David Hussey of A. Forge, and niece of John Hussey, CB. 11.3. Mary had a £5,000 fortune and her sister Elizabeth m. William Burton, CB. 12.15. Elected CB. and GS(G). 18.3.1773, and TT. 19.11.1778. Paid tax for two servants in 1780. Property in Market Place 1784. Had two pews in church. d. 1.11.1791.

MATTHEWS Ronald Wilfred, Kt., D.L., J.P. 12.22. Elected CB. 5.1.1925, resigned 23.2.1939. b. 25.6.1885, s. of Wilfred Arthur of London and Julia Maud, d. of Henry Silvester of Beverley. Grandson of William, Mayor of S. and MC. Ed. Cheam and Eton. 1904 entered S. family steel firm of Turton Bros. and Matthews Ltd. Managing Director, Chairman. 1914-18 K.O.Y.L.I. Captain. 1922 MC. (youngest ever). President Chamber of Commerce 1929-31. President Association of British Chambers of Commerce 1940-42. Chairman L.N.E.R. 1938-48, General Refractories Ltd. and Philips' Furnishing Stores Ltd., deputy Chairman Independent Television Authority from 1955 and Legal & General Assurance Soc. Ltd.; Director Thomas Cook & Son Ltd., Gresham Life Assurance Society Ltd. and Gresham Fire & Accident Insurance Society Ltd. Chairman S. Royal Infirmary. Deputy Lieut., West Riding J.P. Vice-Consul S. for Czechoslovakia. Member Council of University. Knighted 1934. m. 1912 Vera, d. of W.B.E. Schufeldt of Wisconsin. d. 1.7.1959.

MERRYWEATHER James White, MC., T.D. 6.26. Elected CB. on 15.6.1945, resigned 31.3.1966. b. Carbrook Vicarage 8.10.1883, (o).s. of Rev. James White Merryweather, C. of S. Cathedral, and Constance Mary (Webster), d. of a solicitor. Ed. St. Lawrence College, Ramsgate. For many years senior partner of T.G. Shuttleworth & Son, Chartered Accountants. Territorial Commission, R.E. 1915-36. Major M.C. 1919. C.O. S. Auxiliary Fire Service Second World War. CW. St. Andrew's, Sharrow for 26 years. m. Coralie, e.d. of Robert Oates Wever, a S. stockbroker. d. 6.6.1966.

MEYER Paul, Baker's Hill, Esq. 1.12. 2nd s. of Sir Peter of London. His 1st wife was Mary, d. and c.h. of Francis Mason of Crofton, Wakefield. The length of his stay in S. and his local connections are not established – there was a contemporary, Henry Mayer, Usher at the GS. On 17.12.1740 m. at S. Esther, d. of William Burton of Royds Mill, a sister of William Burton, CB. 9.10, wid. of George Bamforth, CB. 8.11, and of Robert Chapell, a barrister and GS(G)., s. of Thomas, CB. 2.14. Freehold at Crofton; voted for Turner in 1741. bur. S. 27.12.1743.

MILNER Gamaliel, ironmaster, A. 7.12. bn. 1699 2nd s. of Gamaliel Milner of Burton Grange, gent., and Olive (Hall). m. 1st on 18.6.1735 his cousin Elizabeth, d. of John Fell of A. Forge, CB. 10.10, and Ellinor (Milner), Gamaliel's aunt.

Elizabeth's sister, Ellen, m. John Ellison, CB. 3.9. Elizabeth, d. in 1736/7 s.p. Gamaliel m. 2nd on 13.5.1742 Susan, d. of John Wilson of Broomhead. Elected CB. 16.8.1737 and also GS(G). Voted for Turner in 1741. Committee member of the Don Navigation Co., treasurer in 1747. d. 5.1.1784, bur A. Chapel.

MILNER Gamaliel, A. House, Esq. 3.13. bn. 15.6.1747, o. (surviving) c. of Gamaliel, CB 7.12, and 2nd wife Susan (Wilson). Overseer of the Poor 1773. Elected CB. and GS(G). 23.11.1774. m. Susan, d. and h. of John Walton of Thurlstone, near Penistone, and she d. 13.6.1816. Paid tax on one servant in 1780. J.P. 1784. Guaranteed £200 to Corn Committee 1795. Voted for Lascelles in 1807. Benefited from A. Enclosure 1810. d. 6.5.1825.

MITCHELL Robert, yeo., Stumperlow. 11.2. s. of Thomas, CB. 11.1, by his 1st wife. A 'man of business' under the Shrewsburys. In 1557 m. 1st Alice, wid. of George Shemeld, she was bur. 19.2.1568/9; and he m. 2nd Alice Parkin 16.10.1569 and after she was bur. 6.4.1599 he m. 3rd, 1602, Helen who survived him. Elected CB. after his father's death, Collector 1574 and 1598. E. juror in 1581. Obtained certificate of Furnival grant to Stannington in 1586 dispute. Paid 6s 10d rent for land in Hallam in 1601. Original GS(G)., paid 15s in 1606 Assessment. w.d 25.3.1610; bur. S. 27.3.1610.

MITCHELL Thomas, Stumperlow. 11.1. s. and h. of Robert of Stumperlow, from whom he obtained Odecroft in 1525. Supervisor of various wills. m. 2nd in 1549 Katherine, d. of Robert Machon, all his children being apparently by his 1st wife. Original CB. Collector in 1562. bur. S. 15.3.1563/4.

MOORE George, Sheffield and Greenhill, Norton, gent. 5.2. s. of Robert, CB. 5.1. Possibly at Christ's College, Cambridge, matriculating as a pensioner in November 1568, but was paid 4d. by TT. for writing in the next year. In 1572-4 active in suit against Shrewsbury for tenants' rights to waste land. TC. 1577-8. Before his father's death in 1583 he had from him a messuage and lands in Greenhill, Whirlow and Newbould. Details extant of many land transactions, mostly of sales of S. property when in 1595 he moved to N. From 1589 sales linked with his wife, Elizabeth, d. of Thomas Stringer of Whiston, a Shrewsbury agent. CW. for S. Town in 1591 and in 1591-2 John Bower was his deputy as TC. Capital messuage at Greenhill, besides property in Chesterfield. w.d. 3.1.1621/2, contained £1 annuity to Richard Edwards, V. of N.; bur. N. 21.8.1622; inventory totalled £253 13s. 10d.

MOORE Robert, merchant. 5.1. Also described as mercer, chapman, ironmonger and yeo. CW. or B in 1549/50 and then at incorporation; Collector 1568 and 1580. His wife, Margaret, was possibly d. of William and Elizabeth Rawson and sister of James, CB. 9.3, and John, CB. 12.2. In 1569 paid 8s., largest assessment, and helped to equip soldiers. TC. 1570. Connected with various land sales and wills. Property not specified in w.d. 11.1.1568/9, but in 1583 grant to his s. (q.v.); bur. in S. church 9.8.1583.

MOSELEY James, gent. 2.9 and 3.6. Apparently the same, bap. S. 30.7.1609, 2nd s. of William of Barker's Pool, gent., whose children were beneficiaries in the 1615 will of Ellis Young, yeo. and GS(G). William had part of Horner Farm, Sheldon House, Pond Meadow and Spittle Farm in 1637, was TC. and a s. of John, who had been Church Collector in 1573 and 1578. William or James went to London for the TT. in 1631. James was apparently away from S. until his father's death and returned in 1643-7, having a d. Jane bur. in the church. He was then away from S. for a further few years, but on his return was re-elected CB. (3.6) and also GS(G). He was consulted by the TT. in 1657. On 15.12.1658/9 he m. 2nd at S. Elizabeth, d. and h. of William Halton of Clerkenwell and Clee, wid. of William Palmer of Winthorpe and Lincoln – this suggests he may have been away in Lincs. or have gone there after his resignation as CB. on 14.5.1661 'for employment abroad' – on the other hand if he was of the Eyam family he may have resided there. The TT. was connected with £6 p.a. for the poor which may have been left by James.

MURRAY Charles Graham, M.B.E. 9.28. Elected CB. 1957. b. 28.1.1920, (o).s. of Dr Charles Graham, General Practitioner and Margaret Elizabeth, 4th d. of William Greaves Blake (CB. 6.22). Ed. Stowe. m. 26.2.1949 Susan Madeleine (Stephenson), grand-daughter of H. K. Stephenson of Hassop Hall, CB. 1.19. daughter W.R. Stephenson M.C 1949. 1940-48 R.A. (Major) Mentioned in Despatches. Director Tempered Spring Co. Ltd. 1951-55. Managing Director 1956-1981 MC.1974. Guardian of the Sheffield Assay Office. Hon. Treas. Diocesan Board of Finance 1953-82. J.P. 1962. D.L. 1975. TT 1977-.

NEILL Philip, C.Eng F.I. Prod. E. T.D. 4.19. Elected CB. 1952. b. 27.3.1907, s. of Robert Alexander, steel manufacturer and Cecilia May (Bocking). Ed. Westbourne Preparatory School, St. Bees School. m. 2.9.1932 Barbara (Hallam). 1925-1964 James Neill & Co. (S.) Ltd. 1939-45 R.E. Later R.E.M.E. H.Q. 49 Div. W.O., H.Q. 21 Army Group. Lt. Col. Resigned 1977. d. 1986.

NEVILE Dennis, Eastwood, Rotherham and Button Hill, gent. 11.11. bap. Chesterfield 31.7.1650, o.s. of John of Thorney, Notts., and Rebecca (Clarke). Witnessed a N. deed in 1672 and was of N. in 1696 when he bought Button Hill from Cornelius Clarke. His wid. was bur. Dronfield in 1757. Lived for some time at Dronfield. m. Anne, d. of John Poole of Killamarsh. w.d. 13.3.1729/30, leaving Button Hill to his wife and her relations, mentions friend Francis Sitwell, attorney and Cutlers' Clerk. d. 28.3.1732.

NEWBOULD Henry, merchant, Sharrow Bank, 3.14. bn. 1790, 3rd s. of Samuel of Bridgefield, merchant and manufacturer, MC. 1800, and Elizabeth (Taylor). On 4.6.1817 m. Mary, d. and c.h. of William Williamson of Buntingford, Herts.; their s. William Williamson Newbould F.L.S. was an original member of the Ray Society and well-known botanist. Elected CB. and GS(G). 26.5.1825. Subscribed Surrey Street Library. Bought Cherry Tree Hill and Button Hill property in 1834. 'A steady churchman of the staunch Tory school', voting for Parker in 1835 and Overend in 1852 and 1857. d. 15.1.1871, bur. E., w.p. 29.3.1871.

NEWBOULD Thomas, merchant, Highfield. 12.18. bn. 1772, (e).s. of William, merchant of Broomhill, and Sarah (Holy), and cousin of Henry, CB. 3.14. In 3.1799 m. Sarah, d. and c.h. of Jonathan Watkinson, MC. 1787, and wid. of William Watson. In 1807 a factor, with Freehold in Nether H., voted for Wilberforce and Lascelles. Elected CB. and GS(G). 30.1.1811. Captain in Volunteers in 1816. Connected with Gas Company. Subscribed Surrey Street Library. d. 25.5.1844.

NICHOLSON James, maltster, Attercliffe 2.12. s. of Thomas by his 1st wife. m. at S. on 20.7.1653 Mary, d. of John Hoole, CB. 12.7, and who was bur. 5.4.1656. m. 2nd at S. on 15.6.1657 Mary, d. of John Wilson, CB. 3.5, and wid. of John Bate of A., maltster. Trustee for 1659 will of Robert Hoole, CB. 6.8. w.d. 15.4.1671 mentions his 'loving friends Mr William Spencer, Mr Matthew Bloome and . . . loving brothers Joseph Wilson, Thomas Britland and James Wilson'; bur. S. 18.7.1671. His wid. Mary was an original member of the Shirecliffe Hall nonconformist congregation.

NICHOLSON Joseph, Attercliffe 2.13. bro. of James, whom he succeeded as CB., being elected 10.8.1671. m. on 16.11.1651 Mary, e.d. of Robert and Margaret Carr. Overseer for Poor 1676; Constable for 'ye house and land late Mr John Spencers' in 1679. Assisted Cutlers' Company against Hearth Tax 1680. Both he and his wife were members of Shirecliffe Hall nonconformist congregation and then, in 1681, at A. In 1688 collector for TT. payment to V. bur. S. 5.1.1693/4, w.p. 18.6.1694.

NODDER Isaac, scrivener and attorney. 1.13. bap. 26.11.1718, s. of John, CB. 8.12, and brother of John (q.v.), CB. 2.17. m. 15.5.1741 to Mary Stevenson. Voted for Fox in 1741. GS(G). Elected CB. 21.1.1743/4 and resigned 21.1.1768 when he moved to Tideswell. Bankrupt in 1767, assignment to Joseph Clay of Bridgehouses and John Stacye of Ballifield.

NODDER John, Handsworth, Woodhouse and S., gent. and lead merchant. 8.12. Bn. 1680. Marriage settlement 24.4.1711 with Deborah, d. of Alexander Fenton of Gleadless. Was interested in Hucklow lead mines in 1711 and had shares in Eyam mines in 1730. Elected TT. 16.2.1729/30; active in promoting and had a share in Don Navigation Scheme. Elected CB. 20.5.1730. w.d. 5.2.1732/3, left £1,500 to his d., property in Gleadless and Derbs. (lead mines at Eyam); d. 28.2.1732/3 and bur. in the chancel at S.

NODDER John, Cutthorpe and The Edge, attorney. 2.17. Bap. Handsworth 27.10.1715, (e).s. of John, CB. 8.12. Voted for Turner in 1741. Rented Dore smelting mill in 1743 and was a partner in mines at Eyam and Great Hucklow 1747-50. In 1763 subscribed to Richard Roose's . . . 'Compleat Accomptant'. m. Mary, d. of Joseph Bright, CB. 2.16, whom he succeeded, elected 16.4.1743, resigning 12.3.1772. Elected TT. 28.4.1739, TC. in 1745 and 1861; also GS(G). Partitioned property in Aston and Hope, Derbs., with bro. Isaac, CB. 1.13.

Promoter of Rockingham Address 1766. He was thrown from his horse and found dead between Dunston and Cutthorpe. w.d. 25.4.1753; d. 7.6.1772; bur. in the chancel at S.

OBORNE Walter, Ravenfield, merchant. 6.13. Bn. 1722, s. of a Bristol merchant, but adopted by his relative (?aunt) Madam (Elizabeth) Parkin. Educated S. GS. under John Cliff, being a class-fellow of Thomas Younge, CB. 1.14. m. Mary, d. of Henry Laughton and sister-in-law of John Fell, CB. 8.13. Lived at the Old Cock Inn, High Street, also assessed for '2 Steel Houses' and 'Sicker Meadow' in 1756. Closely connected with the Don Navigation Co., being chairman in 1758. Agent for Mrs. Fell, managing the Duke's Ironworks on her behalf in 1762. Managed Madam Parkin's affairs and inherited Ravensfield in 1766. Succeeded Samuel Staniforth as CB. and GS(G). Magistrate. Guest at 1771 Cutlers' Feast. d. 22.5.1778, MI.

OLIVIER William Herbert, T.D., DL., J.P., M.A., LL.D., F.C.A. 11.24. Elected CB. 1971. b. 29.4.1904, s. of Herbert Arnould, portrait painter and Margaret Barclay (Peat). (cousin of Lord Olivier, the actor). Ed. Eton and Trinity, Oxford. m. 1933 Katherine Mary, d. of Sir Frederick Jones, Bart. 1939-45 R.A. Lt. Col. 1943. Mentioned in Despatches. Partner in firm of Peat Marwick Mitchell & Co. Past President S. & Dist. Society of Chartered Accountants. Treasurer S. University, Pro-Chancellor. Resigned 1980. d. 1992.

OSBORN Samuel Eric. 1.20. Elected CB. 2.12.1947. b. 13.9.1891, o.s. of William Fawcett and Alice, d. of Richard Groves Holland. Ed. Rugby and Heidelberg. Joined Samuel Osborn & Co. Ltd. 1910, Managing Director 1919, Chairman 1950. MC. 1945, a position held by his father, paternal grandfather, Samuel (founder of the family firm) and maternal grandfather. President of S. Branch Commercial Travellers Association; member Chamber of Commerce Council. Treasurer Adult Deaf and Dumb Association. C.W. Ecclesall. Captain Lindrick Golf Club. m. 1922 Aileen Decima, youngest d. of Colonel Sir Arthur Holbrook, M.P., newspaper owner. d. 19.7.1951.

PALMER Arthur, gent. 2.15. Employed by Duke of Norfolk. m. at S. 1.8.1709 Bridget, d. of George Beaw (?Bewe), Rector of Sproatley, E.R., she m. 2nd Matthew Biggs of Rotherham. Paid £1 towards new GS. Master's house in 1709. Probably connected with William Palmer, a surveyor for the Don Navigation Scheme. w.d. 3.3.1711/12, left £10 to S. Charity School and £10 to 'the poore decayed Husekeepers, in the Parish of Stoxley County, York'.

PARKER Thomas, Attercliffe. 12.1. Difficult to place in the Parker of Norton pedigree. Only acted as CB. for a short time. Probably m. Elizabeth, d. of William and Elizabeth Rawson and sister of James Rawson, CB. 9.3, and of John Rawson, CB. 12.2, who succeeded his bro.-in-law. Elizabeth had CB. 5.1, Robert Moore, as another bro.-in-law. By her first husband, Thomas Parker, she had (at least) two sons, John and Thomas of Angley, Notts. She had married and was widowed again by 1562 when her s. sold property, including some at A. The second husband was probably a junior member of the Broomhead Wilson family.

PARKIN Thomas, gent. 12.12. Bn. 1644, baptism not found but probably of the Wadsley-Owlerton family. On 25.4.1678 m. Mary, d. of Jasper Bosville, and she d. 23.1.1714. Assessor for 1692 Poll Tax and rated at £2 4s., also for wife, three children and servant. TC. 1701. Bought the Cock Inn 1702 and bequeathed it to his granddaughter Elizabeth (Madam Parkin). Grocer and ironmonger. Also GS(G)., paying £1 for the Master's house in 1709. In 1716 assessed for 1s. 4d., besides Steele House, Sittar Meadow, Kits. Land and More Close. Connected with St. Paul's Church. w.d. 27.11.1722, leaving house to Charity School and mentioning property in South Kirkby and Bd. d. 6.1.1729/30.

PARSONS John, silver plater. 10.17. Bn. 1745 but parentage unknown. Partner in Winter, Parsons & Hall of S. Market Place (formerly Rose & Crown and later Todd's Post Office) with John Winter, CB. 10.16, whom he succeeded as CB. and GS(G)., elected 12.3.1792. Retired from the firm in 1793. Resigned from both offices 17.8.1795 on leaving the parish. Returned to S. and was living in Howard Street when he d. on 25.12.1814 aged 69; his sister and heir, Mary, endowed a charity to her brother's memory.

PEILE John Basil, M.A., B.Sc. 8.24. Elected CB. 1946. Born 6.1.1909, 2nd s. of Basil Wils., Brewery Managing Director, and Katherine Rosamond (Taylor). Ed. Charterhouse and Christ Church, Oxford. m. 11.5.1935 to Faith Octavia Winifred (Hoare). Member, Archbishop's Commission on Evangelism 1944-45. J.P. 1947. City Councillor 1948. Member, Home Office Advisory Committee on Commonwealth Immigrants 1962-65. MC. 1967. Lord Mayor 1970. High Sheriff of So. Yorks. 1974. Director of Turton, Brothers & Matthews, Ltd. 1941-59, Managing Director 1959-72. Director Neepsend Steel & Tool Co. Ltd.1968-72. D.L., W.R. of Yorks. (later So. Yorks.) Member Eastern Board, B. Rail, 1955-73, Deputy Chairman 1963-73. Retired as a Burgess 1987.

PETERS John Frank William. 6.28. Elected CB. 1981. b. 20.10.1935, s. of Albert William Peters, company director, and Doris Alice (Carter). M Evlyn Joy Gaze 1959. Ed. Maidenhead County Boys' School, King's College, London University. Ll.B. Partner in Taylor & Emmet (Solicitors) 1969-85. President of Mental Health Review Tribunals (Trent Region) 1978 -. Registrar of High Court Distict Registry in S. and of County Courts in S., Rotherham, 1985-90. District Judge 1991 -. Governor of Birkdale School, 1994.

PICKARD-CAMBRIDGE Arthur Wallace, K.T., O.B.E., M.A., D.Litt., LL.D., F.B.A. 4.17. Elected CB.23.2.1932, resigned 25.10.1939. b. 20.1.1873, s. of Rev. Octavius, M.A., F.R.S., of Wareham, Dorset and Rose, d. of Rev. James Lloyd Wallace of Sevenoaks, Kent. Ed. Weymouth College and Balliol, Oxford; graduated 1895, won Craven University Scholarship, fellow, lecturer in Latin and Greek literature; Professor of Greek, Edinburgh University, 1928-30; Vice-Chancellor S. University 1930-38. Chairman Northern Universities J.M.B. 1937-38. On governing bodies Rugby, Harrow, Stowe, Trent and Mill Hill Schools; Deputy Chairman Public Schools' Governing Bodies Association. Member Executive Committee British Council, Council British Academy and London Tribunal for Conscientious Objectors. Served on Councils of Lady Margaret's and St. Hilda's Colleges, Oxford. Chairman St. Hilda's. President S. Branch of League of Nations. Member Council, Chamber of Commerce, 1937-38. Prominent in diocesan affairs, 1934-45; member Church Asembly. O.B.E. 1946. Knighted 1950. m. 1901 Hilda Margaret (Hunt). Retired to Surrey 1938. d. 7.2.1952.

PILLING Herbert Harkness. 12.26. Bn. 23.10.1920, s. of Herbert William Pilling, insurance agent, and Jane Gertrude (Harkness), teacher. Ed. at Liverpool Collegiate School and Liverpool University. m. Joyce (Yeomans), teacher, on 18.8.1945. M.B. CH.B. 1944 Liverpool; Barrister 1958 Gray's Inn; LL.M. (Honoris Causa) 1976 S. H.M. Coroner, City of S., 1964-74; So. Yorks. (West District) 1974-85. R.A.M.C. 1945-1947. Elected CB. 1978. d. 1992.

PORTER John, wine merchant, Spring Head House. 4.11. Bn. 16.9.1785, (e).s. of John, grocer, King Street, and Mary (Bright). Inherited father's Howard Street house 1812. m. at Treeton on 14.10.1816 Hannah Willott, d. of James and Tabitha Taylor. Conducted wine business from 'Old Stone House', High Street. Also GS(G)., subscribed 10 gns. for New School in 1823, but sent sons to Collegiate School. Improvement Commissioner. Edited *The Churchman's Family Prayer Book*. Opposed S. charter in 1838. Elected CB. 4.4.1856. d. 10.2.1857, bur. E. and w.p. 2.4.1857.

POTTS Lawrence, merchant, Western Bank. 11.16. Nephew of Lawrence of Lowfield. m. at Worsborough on 2.5.1816, youngest d. of Richard Elmhirst of Wadingworth, Lincs. Closely connected with St. James's Church as Trustee and CW. Partner in Potts, Baxter and Brumby, manufacturers and merchants of Arundel Street. Lived in Norfolk Street and Broomspring. Voted for Wortley in 1835. Elected CB. and GS(G). 6.12.1838 and resigned in 1841. Opposed S. charter in 1838. Emigrated to Australia and lived at Annandale Cottage, Sydney.

PYE-SMITH Brian Charles, O.B.E., M.A., J.P. 6.27. Elected CB. 1966. b. 3.6.1903, y.s. of Edward Wilfred (CB. 10.24) and Mary (Westron). Ed. Cheltenham College and Trinity, Oxford. John Wylie Scholar. m. 8.10.1935 Evelyn Marjorie (Walker). Partner Pye-Smith and Son (Solicitors) later Broomhead, Pye-Smith and Reed. Law Clerk to CB's 1936-66. J.P. 1937. Chairman Juvenile Court Panel 1944-56. Chairman Probation Committee 1945-56. Deputy Chairman City Magistrates 1950-53. Chairman 1954-66. Chairman G.P.D.S.T. High School for Girls 1950-57. Chairman Osborn House Probation Hostel 1951-62. Chairman Assn. in Aid of Adult Deaf and Dumb 1961-67. Chairman Bluecoat and Mount Pleasant Ed. Fdn. 1962-67. Governor of Standard of Wrought Plate from 1938. Chairman Freshgate Trust Foundation from 1950. Freeman Company of Cutlers in Hallamshire 1951.

Law Clerk G.S. Exhibition Foundation from 1936. Deputy Chairman Arthur Davy & Sons Ltd. 1953-58. Deputy Chairman Samuel Osborn & Co. Limited 1966-69. President S. Dist. Inc. Law Society 1971-72. President S. Council of Boys Clubs from 1963. Vice President National Association of Boys Clubs. Golf Half Blue (Oxford) 1924 and 1925. Resigned 1981. d. 22.2.1984.

PYE-SMITH Edward Wilfred. 10.24. Elected CB. 1933. b. 18.9.1870, (e).s. of John William (Mayor of S. 1885) and Harriette (Rawlinson), grands. of John William (Mayor of S. 1856) and great grandson of John, F.R.S., DD. Ed. Wesley College and Bishop Stortford School. Articled to Reginald Bens. of S.; admitted solicitor 1.1893. Partner with Henry Shelley Barker (Pye-Smith & Barker) until 1924. Practised on his own until 1932 when joined as partner by his younger son Brian Charles (q.v.). Solicitor to Royal Infirmary and Hospital. Deputy Chairman Governors, High School for Girls, Trustee Bluecoat School and other charitable trusts. m. 1900 Mary, younger d. of Charles and Emma Westron of Exeter. Retired from practice 1945 and moved to Budleigh Salterton, East Devon, where d. 28.10.1948.

RAWSON Edward, tanner. 12.3. o.s. of John of Upperthorpe, yeoman. CB. 12.2. m. at S. on 13.6.1569 Helen Barber. Bought lands at Walkley. CW. for H. 1579 and 1592. Succeeded his father as CB. but d. within a few years. w.d. 12.10.1597, bur. at S. 15.10.1597.

RAWSON Edward, yeoman, Upperthorpe. 2.11. Bap. at S. 25.10.1607, (e).s. of John of Upperthorpe and grandson of Edward, CB. 12.3. m. Martha, d. of Percival Hobson of Dodworth, yeo., post-nuptial settlement 20.3.1635/6. CW. for H. 1652. Succeeded father as GS(G). He or his cousin of Walkey had 2 hearths in 1665. d. 10.9.1669, bur. at S., MI.

RAWSON Hugh, cutler, tanner and yeoman, Norwood. 9.4. o.s. of James, CB. 9.3. On 26.8.1587 m. at S. Isabella, d. of Alexander and Isobel Hatfield. Held Shirecliffe Park, at first with father, then alone. Had tanyards at Grimesthorpe and Pitsmoor, together with 36 acres at the latter place. Surrendered his messuage at Norwood to his 2nd s. John. Overseer for repair of A. bridge. CW. for B. 1592 and 1610. An active original GS(G)., he paid 20s. in 1606 assessment. Went to London about Cutlers' Company incorporation and was granted a Mark. Bur. S. 6.12.1628.

RAWSON James, yeoman, Norwood. 9.3. s. of William, tanner, and ELizabeth, and bro. of John, CB. 12.2. m. Katherine, d. of Richard and Anne Fenton and sister of the recusant CB. 3.1, Richard; his wife paid a fine for recusancy in 1592-93. CB. Collector in 1560, but succeeded John Howle as CB. Provided timber for Sheaf bridge in 1593. Held part of Shirecliffe Hall. d. at S. 1.6.1603, bur. next day, inquisition post-mortem 23.11.1604 detailed 76 acres.

RAWSON John, yeoman, Upperthorpe. 12.2. s. of William, tanner and Elizabeth, and brother of James, CB. 9.3. m. (?Elizabeth) d. of Henry Hatfield. Succeeded as CB. bro.-in-law Thomas Parker, and was followed by his o.s. Edward. CW. for H. in 1559. w.d. 12.6.1594 and bur. S. 28.6.1594.

RAWSON John, F.R.C.S., West Don House, Hallam. 9.15. Bn. 14.12.1749, 2nd s. of Thomas of Wardsend and Douglas (Carr) and descended from William, CB.1.6. Guaranteed £200 to Corn Committee in 1795. Also TT. and GS(G). On 17.12.1801 m. Mary, d. of Rev. Edward Mason of East Retford; his wid. m. William Rodgers. In 1807 voted for Fitzwilliam. Freehold at Creswick. d. 10.2.1819.

RAWSON William, yeoman and tanner, Walkley. 1.6. Bap. S. 29.10.1574, (e).s. of Edward, CB. 12.3. m. at S. on 9.7.1599 Alice, d. of Richard and Elizabeth Dale of High Storrs. Original GS(G). and paid 18s. in 1606 Assessment. CW. for H. in 1605. Possibly built Walkley Hall, was a principal landowner in that district, being assessed at 17s. 2d. in 1601. w.d. 1.9.1647, bur. S. 13.1.1648/49.

REVELL Samuel, sugar refiner, Norfolk Road. 6.16. Bn. 1775, probably s. of Samuel of S. Park, yeo., and Mary. m. 13.5.1800 Mary Ashworth, Born 1785. Also lived at Union Street and Cricket Inn Road, Park. Elected CB. 24.9.1829, also GS(G). His s. Samuel went from S. GS. to St John's College, Cambridge and became PC. Wingerworth. Opposed S. charter in 1838. d. 29.12.1859.

RICHARDSON Samuel Gray, cutlery manufacturer, Stone Grove. 8.21. Born 1851, 2nd s. of Samuel, manufacturer, Stone Grove, and his wife, Mary. Educated Broombank House and S. Collegiate School. In 1868 entered father's business, Messrs. Southern and Richardson, Don Cutlery Works, Doncaster Street, and later became head of it. F. by purchase in 1880, various offices until 1903, including MC. 1889. Governor and trustee S. Savings Bank from 1890. J.P. Elected CB. 21.12.1895 and resigned 27.10.1930. C. of E. member S. School Board. m. 1st Eleanor Mary, youngest d. of John Watson of Broomhall Park, Assay Master; she d. in 1916 and he m. 2nd in 1920 Sophia Margaret Vavasour Waddington of Gloucester. Retired to Lower Guiting near Cheltenham, and d. there on 16.5.1934.

RIDDLE John Tharratt, O.B.E., J.P. 12.25. Elected CB. 1963. b. 15.9.1905, s. of John Coulson and Sarah Elizabeth (Tharratt). Ed. Solihull School. m. 4.2.1931 Dorothy (Clarke). Chartered Surveyor, Partner, Eadon Lockwood & Riddle. 1939-45 Kings Own Royal Regt., Lieut. 1939, Colonel 1944-45. Governor and Trustee S. Savings Bank. General Commissioner for Income Tax 1960. J.P. 1952. Retired 1978.

ROBERTS Samuel, Queen's Tower. 4.13. Bn. 13.4.1800 at Park Grange, (e).s. of Samuel and Elizabeth (Wright). Educated Milk St. Academy, Whitley Hall, Ecclesfield and S. GS. Admitted fellow-commoner St. Catherine's College, Cambridge, 19.2.1830, matriculated Easter 1830, B.A. 1834, M.A. 1837. J.P. 1836. Married first on 7.6.1837, Elizabeth (daughter of Thomas Creswick of Easthill, Sheffield, (CB. 12.19), by his 1st wife; Elizabeth d. 1838) and m. 2nd on 5.1.1841 Sarah Anne ((o).d. of Robert Sorby). Town Councillor 1844-46, TT. from 1847 and GS(G). from 1864. Trustee, Council Member and Treasurer of Firth College from 1879. Elected CB. 24.3.1859 and remained until his death on 29.11.1887.

ROBERTS Samuel, Junior, Bart. 3.16. Bn. 30.4.1852 at Queen's Tower, o.s of Samuel, CB 4.13. Educated privately at Great Malvern and at Repton 1866-71. Admitted pensioner at Trinity College, Cambridge 23.2.1871, matriculated Michaelmas 1871, blues for athletics and football, B.A. 1875, M.A. 1878. Admitted Inner Temple 20.11.1877. Was a Trustee and Council Member of Firth College from 1879 and succeeded his father as Treasurer in 1885. m. on 21.12.1880 Martha Susan, (o).d. of Archdeacon Blakeney, V. of S. Went to live at Park Grange, S. in 1885. Elected CB. 3.10.1885. Also GS(G). from 1885. TT. from 1895. Director S. Banking Co. J.P. Conservative Councillor for E. 1887-1903. Lord Mayor 1899. Deputy Lieutenant for WR. 1900. Unsuccessful Conservative candidate for High Peak Division 1900, but M.P. for E. 1902-23. Knighted 1917. Baronet 1919. P.C. 1922. Hon. Freedom of S. 1924. d. 19.6.1926.

RODGERS Henry, solicitor, Broomfield. 6.18. Born 1.11.1824, 3rd s. of Robert, solicitor, Endcliffe House, and Maria (Eboral). Became a partner in father's firm, later called Rodgers and Thomas. m. on 12.11.1846 Mary, d. of Thomas Creswick, CB. 12.19; she d. 1851 s.p. Elected CB. 9.4.1874. Also GS(G). from 1878, Treasurer S. Church Educational Institute, member of committee of Boys' Charity School. d. 25.4.1882.

ROLLINSON Robert, mercer, Market Place. 7.5. Bn. 1541, probably (e).s. of Hugh, yeoman, Little N., and his wife Marjory. m. at S. on 13.5.1573 Helen, d. of Francis Houseley, CW. and CB. Collector in 1575. TC. in 1595. An original GS(G)., he paid the maximum rate in the 1606 School Assessment and left money and land to the School. Best known for his reconstruction of Barker's Pool, but he also helped the Cutlers' Company to build the new hall and gave two houses for the Ms. He d. 8.11.1631, was bur. in S. Church, MI., w.p. 18.4.1632.

SANDFORD Charles Richard Stephen, 12.24 C.B. 1949 b. 27.3.1914. 2nd son of Charles Sidney Sandford (12.23) (Surveyor) and Rachel Walkden. m. May 1946 Joan Barber. Ed. Shrewsbury School. Surveyor to the Trust from 1964-1982. Resigned as a Burgess 1963. Agent to the Duke of Norfolk's Sheffield Estates 1949-1982. Surveyor to the TT 1972-1982. Agent and Receiver for the Shrewsbury Hospital Trust 1949-1982 d. 8.1985

SANDFORD Charles Sidney. 12.23. Elected CB. 23.2.1939 (succeeded by son Charles RS). b. S. 7.10.1873, y.s. of Rev. George Sandford, V. of Ecclesall and Elizabeth Anne, d. of Rev. Henry Barlow of Pitsmoor; bro. of Henry Barlow Sandford (CB. 6.23). Ed. S. Collegiate and Felsted Schools. Articled 1891 to Frederick Fowler. Fellow of Surveyors' Institution before he set up in practice as chartered surveyor and land agent in 1899; senior partner in Fowler, Sandford & Co. Agent to Earl of Westmorland 1917, the Duke of Norfolk 1928, and to Trustees of Hospital of Gilbert, Earl of Shrewsbury 1929. m. 1908, Rachel, 2nd d. of Arthur Walkden, brewer of Derby. d. 2.11.1949.

SANDFORD Henry Barlow, J.P. 6.23. Elected CB. 18.5.1904. b. Ecclesall 21.5.1862, 2nd s. of Rev. George, V. of Ecclesall and Elizabeth Anne, d. of Rev. Henry Barlow of Pitsmoor; bro. of Charles Sidnes Sandford (CB. 12.23). Ed. S. Collegiate School. Articled to Arthur Thomas, Solicitor (CB 6.19), 1884 succeeded to practice of Rodgers, Thomas and Sandford, later Rodgers & Co. Notary Public. City Councillor 1906-12, Chairman Finance Committee 1909. TT. One of secretaries for scheme of making S. a diocese; Diocesan Registrar and Legal Secretary to Bishop in which post succeeded by son, Victor Henry (CB. 7.19). Member Recruiting Appeal Tribunal for West Riding 1914-18. Director Hadfields Ltd. Associated with numerous charities including Deakin Institution and Withers' Pensions. m. 1886 Eleanor, younger d. of Charles A Branson of Broomgrove. d. 15.6.1930.

SANDFORD Victor Henry, M.A. 7.19. Elected CB. 1932, Capital three times. b. 15.6.1897, (o)s. of Henry Barlow (CB. 6.23) and Eleana (Branson). Ed. Rugby and Magdalen, Oxford. m. 22.9.1926 Margaret (Mort). Solicitor. 1914-18 2nd Life Guards, Lieut.; 1922-37 Capt. Q.O. Yorks. Dragoons. TD. TT. 1964. Diocesan Registrar and Legal Secretary to the Bishop 1932-76. Treasurer and President S. District Law Soc. Expert on Stamps of Paraguay. Died 24.7.1977.

SAUNDERSON Edward, tanner, Grimesthorpe. 11.4. Bap. S. 15.1.1576/7, o.s. of Nicholas, tanner, and Margaret, d. of John Rawson, CB. 12.2. His father died in 1580 and willed that Edward should be brought up in learning and then apprenticed to William Hoole. m. at S. on 7.8.1599 Isabella, d. of Nicholas and Isabel Shiercliffe. Not a GS(G)., but active in connection with endowment; paid 20s. in 1606 Assessment. CB. Collector 1610, CW. for B. 1613, and connected with erection of loft in church. w.d. 21.4.1617, left bequests to V. and three other clergy. Bur. S. 24.4.1617.

SAUNDERSON Edward, tanner. 8.3. Bap. S. 17.8.1602, 2nd s. of Edward, CB. 11.4. m. at S. by licence on 23.1.1622/3 Anne, d. of Francis Barlow, CB. 12.6, and step-d. of Christopher Capper, CB. 6.5, of whose will Edward was executor. She d. in 1655 and he m. 2nd at S. on 10.10.1659 Immen, wid. of Richard Taylor, a tailor and father of the Congregational Minister. Had property in E. Assessor for Owlerton Bridge in 1638. Constable in 1641. Parliamentarian sequestrator in 1645. Prominent in Burgery. Assessed for 3 hearths in 1665. w.d. 28.3.1670. bur. S. 19.2.1672/3.

SAUNDERSON Nicholas, gent. 1.5. bap. S. 3.8.1600, (e).s. of Edward, CB 11.4. His wife came from the Norton family of Sandal-Magna. Supervisor of Christopher Capper's (CB. 6.5) will. Held Castle Meadows with George Hill. Borrowed money from GS(G)s. in 1642. Apparently living in 1655/6 when his d. Mary m. John Cart, the Rector of Handsworth, later ejected.

SCARGELL Thomas, yeoman. 7.2. His mother belonged to the Shemeld family.

The more influential mercer, William, descended from his brother, Robert, whose 1557-58 will Thomas supervised. m. Dionise, wid. of Thomas Hall (or Hale). CW. in 1558 and 1570. Paid 5s. in 1569 assessment. TC. 1570-2. w.d. 8.8.1575, bur. in S. Church 30.8.1575.

SCARGELL William. 6.3. (? e. surviving) s. of Thomas, CB. 7.2, and bro-in-law of Hugh Chalner, CB. 8.1. m. at S. on 9.2.1565/6 Elizabeth, probably d. of Thomas and Elizabeth Rose of Heeley. Paid 15s. rent to TT., several times TC. Paid 1s. in 1569 assessment. CW. 1573 and 1585. Bur. at S. 26.10.1602.

SHEMELD Humphrey, tanner, Grimesthorpe. 2.10. Bap. S. 13.7.1596, s. of William of The Cock Inn and Ann (Swift), who both d. when he was young. His guardian, and probably god-father, was his uncle, Humphrey Swinden, yeoman, Grimesthorpe. Bro. of Richard, CB. 12.8. m. at S. on 1.7.1629 Ann Sales from Laughton. CW. for B. 1636 and 1652 and connected with repair of the bridge 1638. w.d. 20.8.1657, bur. S. 26.8.1657.

SHEMELD John, yeoman, Fulwood. 12.4. (e).s. of Richard of Fd. m. in 1566 Rose, d. of Henry and Sibil Dale. CW. for H. in 1573 and 1582. Often occurs as supervisor of wills. Connected with Thomas Creswick of Owlerton Hall, probably through his mother. w.d. 3.6.1603, bur. S. 11.7.1603.

SHEMELD Richard, ironmonger. 12.8. Bap. S. 12.6.1586, s. of William of The Cock Inn and Ann (Swift); bro. of Humphrey, CB. 2.10. m. at S. on 20.10.1613 Isabella, d. of William Slack, blacksmith, Owlerton, an original GS(G); she d. in 1620 and he m. 2nd 1620/1 Elizabeth, d. of Malin Stacey, CB. 5.4. TC. in 1619. Connected with building the workhouse in 1632. Held part of the Spital Farm with James Bright, CB. 9.5. Accumulated considerable wealth (his inventory totalled £6,675), probably from trade in iron and lead, and had property in S., Crookes, Dore and Rotherham. He left £4 to S. poor, while his d. Ann founded a charity for apprentices and was commemorated in a window in the new GS. for her gift towards it. w.d. 29.9.1645, bur. S. 15.10.1645, inventory taken a week later.

SHIRECLIFFE John, gent, Whitley Hall. 4.8. Bap. Ecclesfield 22.6.1720, (e).s. of Thomas, Whitley Hall, and Elizabeth (Pearson). m. 6.4.1740 at Peak Forest, Mary, 2nd d. of Benjamin Steer, mercer and TT. Elected CB. 18.10.1746. Also GS(G). and TT., elected in 1746/7 to replace his father-in-law and resigned in 1756 on leaving town. 1750-5 kept the Blackmoor's Head, subsequently the Grey Horse in Whitley Hall in 1754. TT. trustee for Don Navigation shares. Succeeded his father at Whitley Hall in 1754. Partner in S. Lead Works from 1774. Taxed on one servant in 1780. His d., Mary, m. Thomas Gunning, CB. 2.18. d. 13.5.1789, bur. Ecclesfield.

SIMS Geoffrey Donald, O.B.E. B.Sc, M.Sc, Ph.D., FIEE, FCGI, F.Eng, Hon. D.Sc, Hon ScD, Hon D.Sc Eng, Hon Ll.D. 3.22. b. 13.12.1926, s. of Albert Edward Hope Sims and Jessie Elizabeth (Shortman). Ed. at Wembley County GS. and Imperial College of Science and Technology (London). m. 9.4.1949, Pamela Audrey

(Richings). Elected CB. 1984. Vice-Chancellor, University of S. 1974 -1990. Planning Committee for British Library 1971-73. Annan Committee on the Future of Broadcasting 1974-77 (Vice Chairman). Assn. of Commonwealth Universities (Symons Medallist 1991). Hon. Deputy Treas. 1984 -1990. Conference of European Rectors, Member of Bureau and Permanent Committee 1984-93. Committee for International Cooperation in Higher Education, Vice-Chairman 1985-1991. BBC Engineering Advisory Committee, Chairman 1981-89. Museums and Galleries Commission, Member 1983-1988. Committee of Vice-Chancellors and Principals of the UK, Member 1974-1990. Guardian of the Standard of Wrought Plate within the Town of S. 1984-. Worksop College Council, Custos 1984-93. Fellow Woodard Corporation and director of Woodard Schools (Midland Division) Ltd. 1977-1996 Hon Fellow 1997-. Charterhouse Japhet Venture Fund Management Ltd. 1984-93. Council for Education in the Commonwealth – Executive Chairman 1991-1996, Hon Life Fellow 1996 -.

SITWELL William, attorney. 8.9. Bap. 16.10.1662, 4th s. of Francis of Renishaw and Catherine (Sacheverel). Assessed for 4 gns. in 1692. m. at Ecclesfield 21.9.1693 Mary Reresby. Lived near Lady's Bridge. Also GS(G). d. 25.6.1703.

SMYTHE Hugh, bailiff, A. and North Lees, Hathersage. 2.1. o. (? surviving) s. of Lawrence of A., bailiff, and Agnes (Shirecliffe). This family had long been connected with the Church and was probably that of Thomas Smith who endowed the GS. Hugh's sister, Anne, m. Richard Fenton, mercer and father of CB. 3.1, for whom Hugh was named as guardian. Hugh's wife, Margaret, may have been the e.d. of Richard Fenton, mercer, by his first wife Cecily (Swift), but they do not seem to have had any children. Hugh had been charged by his father with a payment of 13s. 4d. for A. Chapel and left as his heirs Richard Fenton, CB. 3.1, and his sisters. He had leased Owlerton and S. mills. By his will, dated 8.9.1560, he left Ecclesfield parsonage to his Shirecliffe relatives. bur. S. (probably in the Church) 15.9.1560.

SMITH John Jobson, Portobello House, Grange Cliff, Ecclesall. 9.22. Bn. Alnwick, Northumberland 10.1800. Opposed S. charter in 1838, was a commissioner for the flood disaster in 1864-65 and was an active conservative. Entered his uncle's firm, Robert Jobson, stove-grate manufacturers, Roscoe Place. President S. Chamber of Commerce 1859-62. Chairman S. and Lincs. Railway Co. Director S. Banking Co. Governor and Trustee S. Savings Bank. Elected CB. 23.12.1869. Also TT. 1870-6 and GS(G). from 1871. J.P. d. 9.9.1878, bur. E. on 14th.

SMYTHE Robert, 7.1. Nothing known about his origins or death or relationship with Hugh, CB. 2.1. Occurs in S. wills from 1537 to 1555. Leased CB. property in 1555, but had been succeeded as CB. by 1559.

SMITH Thomas, ironmonger, High Street. 3.12. Bn. 1725, (e).s. of Thomas of Wakefield and Ann (Wordsworth). m. on 15.7.1753 Susan, d. of John Battie, CB. 12.13, and Margaret (Ward). Signatory to Rockingham Address 1766. Elected CB. 11.10.1770. Guest at Cutlers' Feast 1771. d. 1774.

SMITH Thomas, Broomfield and Dunston Hall, near Chesterfield. 4.9. Bn. 1763, s. of Thomas, CB. 3.12. Elected CB. 8.6.1789 and resigned 5.2.1798. Also GS(G). m. on 25.8.1791 Elizabeth Mary, d. of Robert and Elizabeth Mower of Barley Woodseats; she m. 2nd John Frederick Smith and d. 12.8.1829. Guest at Cutlers' Feast. d. 13.4.1811.

SMITH William, Westwood House, Brocco Bank, solicitor. 7.17. Bn. 17.4.1822, s. of William of Dam House and Elizabeth (Woollen). Educated at S. and apprenticed to Robert Rodgers, solicitor. Promoter Athenaeum Club. m. on 30.4.1852 Louisa, d. of Charles and Mary Picksley; she d. 28.2.1907. Councillor for E., later Ald. Clerk to Improvement Commissioners. Secretary Chamber of Commerce, President 1872. TT. and their representative on GS(G). Active in C. of E. Educational Institute. President S. Amateur Musical Society. Elected CB. 27.12.1895. d. 20.1.1901.

SORBY John. 10.20. Bn. 15.1.1786 e.(surviving) s. of John, edge tool maker of Spital Hill, and Elizabeth (Swallow), descended from a younger bro. of Robert, CB. 10.9. m. 1st on 29.10.1810 Rebecca, d. of John Bishop, merchant; she d. 1.8.1822 and he m. 2nd in 5.1825 her sister Anne. He was several times Assistant in the Cutlers' Co, but refused promotion; the family firm became Lockwood Bros. Elected CB. and GS(G). on 24.4.1828 and resigned 30.10.1844. On Water Works Committee. d. 12.8.1861.

SORBY Thomas Austin, J.P., Park Grange. 3.15. Bn. 1823, 2nd s. of Robert of Park Grange, founder of Carver St. firm, and cousin of John, CB. 10.20; his mother, Sarah, was (o).d. of Joseph Mycock, manufacturer. Original pupil of S. Collegiate School from 1836 to 1838. Joined father's firm and became senior partner. His sister m. Samuel Roberts, CB. 4.13. m. 1st on 7.3.1850 Dorothy Martha Heathcote of Blackwell, Derbs., and 2nd . . . Bishop. Conservative in politics. Elected CB. 26.1.1871, GS(G). 30.1.1873 and TT. 3.2.1881. Trustee Boys' Charity School. d. 12.8.1885.

SORSBY Robert, cutler and gent. 10.9. Bap. S. 25.12.1636, s. of Malin, MC. and GS(G)., and Elizabeth, d. of John Rawson, CB. 12.2. F. 1658, MC. 1669. m. at S. on 3.6.1674 Elizabeth, d. of John Revel of Whiston; she was bur. 17.11.1690. TT. from 1681, TC. in 1686 and borrowed money from the Trust. Succeeded father as GS(G). Assessed for 4 gns. in 1692 (3 children and 4 servants). His sister Ann m. Jonathan Lee, CB. 9.7, while his bro. Malin became a Fellow of St. John's College, Cambridge, D.D., and Rector of Ryton, Co. Durham. Held Hackings, near Crookesmoor. w.d. 21.6.1690, bur. S. 3.2.1700/1.

SORSBIE Robert, gent. 11.9. Bap. S. 12.1.1678/9, s. of Robert, CB. 10.9. Sold High St. house to Henry Waterhouse, attorney and GS(G). Also GS(G)., paying £1 towards new Master's house in 1709. Resigned CB. in 1717 and had faculty to erect a loft, seat or stall in parish church in 1724. TT. from 1703 until death, bur. 2.3.1754.

SPEIGHT Arthur, gent., Attercliffe. 5.9. Possibly from Doncaster, but first known in S. from marriage on 10.6.1708 to Jane, d. of Thomas Diston, CB. 8.8; their d. Elizabeth m. Joseph Clay, CB. 5.10. Was Overseer of the Poor for A. in 1710. About 1710 lived at A. Hill Top in house belonging to Leech family. In 1727 he bought an eighth share in the Duke of Norfolk's ironworks. In 1731 bought A. property from Thomas Handley, CB. 4.7. As ironmaster connected with John Fell, CB. 8.13, and others. Trustee of St. Paul's Church in 1719. Elected CB. 1.12.1722. w.d. 10.3.1737/8, mentions property in Earls Heaton, Dewsbury parish, and relatives at Hunslet Park, Leeds; d. 16.3.1738/9, bur. A. Chapel, MI.

SPENCER Thomas, gent., Attercliffe and Bramley Grange. 7.10. Bap. S. 3.4.1670, 2nd s. (bur. e. surviving) of William, CB. 10.7. Shortly after his father's death was 1st pupil admitted to Richard Franklin's famous nonconformist academy when it moved to A. Hall. Despite this and his youth, elected CB. m. Elizabeth, d. of William Fairfax of Steeton. Bur. S. 21.6.1703.

SPENCER William, Esq., Attercliffe and Bramley Grange. 10.6. Bap. S. 31.1.1612/3, (e).s. of William of A., Lord of D. Manor and GS(G)., and Alice (Mitchell). Admitted pensioner Emmanuel College, Cambridge, 1627/8, graduated B.A. 1631. Also entered Gray's Inn. m. 1st at N. on 30.10.1634 Elizabeth, d. of Leonard Gill, the founder of N. GS., and sister of Edward, Parliamentarian commander, Governor of S. Castle and W.R. M.P. Elizabeth d. in 1636 and he m. 2nd Sarah, d. of George Westby of Gilthwaite. Became a Parliamentarian lieutenant-colonel; was imprisoned by Earl of Newcastle, had his goods plundered and paid £350 for his release. Commonwealth J.P. Taxed for 17 hearths in 1665-6. Succeeded as GS(G). and CB. by his s. when he d., bur. S. 28.1.1667.

SPENCER William, gent., Attercliffe. 10.7. Bap. Braithwell 20.1.1641, (e).s. of William, CB. 10.6, and Sarah (Westby). Educated SGS. and Magdalene College, Cambridge, admitted a pensioner 24.4.1657, subsequently a fellow-commoner, and graduated B.A. 1659/60. Admitted Gray's Inn 1.5.1661. Succeeded his father as GS(G). and CB., but resigned both offices. Member of Shirecliffe nonconformist congregation, which migrated to A. in 1681; his s. Thomas, CB. 7.10, was educated at A. nonconformist academy. Bur. S. 19.8.1686, w.p. at York by his wid. Elizabeth.

SPOONER Hugh. 8.10. Probably of the Crookesmoor family. m. at S. on 10.4.1694 Elizabeth, d. of George Fox of Bd. and Fd. Hall, s. of William, CB. 6.7. Bought part of Bd. tithes from his bro.-in-law, Henry Fox. Held Market Place shop from George Bullas. In 1712 paid 10s. towards new GS. master's house. Bur. S. 8.10.1712.

STACEY Malin, Attercliffe and Darnall. 5.4. Parentage and activities uncertain owing to existence of more than one of these names, but presumably of the Ballifield, Handsworth, family. m. 1st at Handsworth on 10.8.1597 Margaret, d. of John and Alice Nodder of Handsworth; she was bur. 18.6.1603 and he m. 2nd on

24.9.1605 Anne, wid. of William Slacke, leading original GS(G), and d. of Alexander and Isabel Hatfield. Anne's d. m. Richard Shemeld, the rich ironmonger, CB. 12.8. Malin was also an original GS(G). and was succeeded by his s. Robert, who m. Margaret, d. of John Rawson of Upperthorpe. Lived in A. and D., when he paid 18s. in 1606 School Assessment. TC. in 1609. Concerned in various property sales on S. district and bought, in 1613, Owlerton Manor from Thomas Creswick, CB. 12.5. In 1624 was paying £4 rent for Slacke wheel on Loxley. In 1630 paid £10 fine for refusing a knighthood. In w.d. 10.11.1636 described as of S. parish, left money for poor of S. town and of H. and bequeathed some silver. Bur. S. 18.11.1636.

STANIFORTH John, gent., Darnall. 4.5. Bap. S. 18.9.1636, (e).s. of John of D., steward of Hallamshire, and Mary (Gower), and grandson of another John, both GS(G). m. at Ecclesfield on 2.2.1686 Elizabeth, d. of the V. there, Thomas Wright. Seems to have succeeded father as agent of Earl of Arundel, receiving £40 p.a. Taxed on 8 hearths in 1665-6. Member Shirecliffe Hall and A. Dissenting Congregations. Collected money for the V. in 1688. w.d. 11.3.1700, bur. S. 12.4.1704.

STANIFORTH Samuel, gent., Darnall. 6.12. Bap. S. 16.1.1688/9, (e).s. of Griffith, bro. of John, CB. 4.5, who made Samuel his principal heir. Gave 10s. for new GS. master's house in 1709 and later became GS(G). TT. 1720-4, resigning on account of distance from town, but later borrowed money from the trust. Connected with St. Paul's dispute, later becoming trustee. On 17.9.1722 m. at Bd. Alethea, 5th d. of Thomas and Susan Macro of Bury St. Edmunds. Had 5 shares in Don Navigation Co. Probably voted for Turner in 1741 election, described as clerk of D. w.d. 14.11.1748, executors were his friends John Fell, CB. 8.13, and William Hoole. d. 15.11.1748, bur A.

STANIFORTH Samuel, wine merchant, Darnall. 8.16. Bn. 1739, 2nd s. of Samuel, CB. 6.12; his sisters m. the bros. John Trevers and Dr. Thomas Younge, CBs. 7.13 and 1.14. Difficult to be certain of all references as several of these names, but probably failed election as TT. in 1761, but successful in 1801, holding office until his death, like the linen-draper of the same names. Signatory to Rockingham address in 1766. Guest at Cutlers' Feast, 1771. Elected CB. and GS(G). 24.6.1778 and resigned 31.7.1820, being succeeded by nephew, Charles Younge. One of the largest landowners in A.-D. district, benefiting from 1810 Inclosure Act. By his w.d. 11.9.1815 left £20 for poor of D. d. 26.9.1820, aged 81.

STANIFORTH William, yeoman, Brincliffe Edge. 4.2. Probably bn. 1527, s. of Richard of Brincliffe Edge, from whom he obtained smithy gear and scythes by his 1551/2 will, and his wife, Agnes. Juror and CW. for E. Witness, yeo. aged 60, in 1587 E. Manor case. Trustee and guardian for children of his bro.-in-law, Robert Holland, V. of S. One s., Richard, went to Cambridge and while V. of Owston was presented for not using the Book of Common Prayer; he had 3 ss. nonconformist ministers. Paid 6/8 in 1606 GS. Assessment. w.d. 28.2.1619/20. bur. S. ('municeps') 29.1.1620/1.

STANIFORTH William, Attercliffe. 10.13. Bn. 4.8.1717, (e).s. of John of A. and Elizabeth (Younge). Elected CB. 16.9.1760 and GS(G). 24.2.1761. His marriage on 14.5.1767 to Mary Macro of Norton, near Bury St. Edmunds, led to his removal there and he resigned as CB. on 4.5.1768. w.d. 2.3.1786, of Littlehaugh, near Bury St. Edmunds, by which he left to A. £50 for the upkeep of the family vault and alms for the poor. d. 11.11.1786.

STEEL Gerald, C.B.E., J.P. 11.22. Elected CB. 16.3.1951, resigned 12.10.1956. b. 15.2.1895, 2nd s. of Henry of United Steel Companies Ltd. and grandson of Henry, a founder of Steel Peech & Tozer Ltd. Ed. Charterhouse and Oriel, Oxford. Joined Steel Peech & Tozer Ltd. 1919; Managing Director United Steel Companies (India) Ltd. 1928. General Managing Director Samuel Fox & Co. Ltd. 1932; Director United Steel Companies Ltd. 1941, General Managing Director 1954. Greatly interested in works education and welfare; first Chairman Training Committee of Iron & Steel Federation; Chairman Central Council of Wages Association; Member Social and Industrial Council. West Riding J.P. 1941-51; for 5 years Chairman Upper Strafforth and Tickhill Division. Director National Provincial Bank Ltd. 1956-7. C.B.E. 1956. President elect British Iron & Steel Federation 1957. Chairman Church Extension Committee of Diocese & S. Bach Society. m. 1922 Ruth, (o)d. of Robert Crawshaw of Doncaster. d. at Wimbledon 14.9.1957.

STEER George, mercer, Market Place. 6.11. Bap. at S. 13.12.1683, 5th c., 2nd s. of William, cutler and chapman of D., and Sarah, d. of George Ludlam of D., yeo. His e.bro. William was the well-known V. of Ecclesfield. George was associated with, but must not be confused with, his father's younger bro. of the same name. In 11.1710 m. at Northowram Jane Clough from Stockport, who survived him. Connected with St. Paul's Church. First public post seems to have been GS(G)., but standing indicated by his choice to go to London in connection with the River Don Act, 1726. As CB. he succeeded the influential Joseph Banks whose niece was the wife of George's bro., William. Elected TT. 20.10.1729. Held share in Don Navigation Co. Given £150 by mother's will, but probably made part of his wealth from mines in Wales and Derbs. Probably author of *The Compleat Mineral Laws of Derbyshire*, published in 1734 with a dedication to the Duke of Devonshire. w.d. 15.8.1738, d. 22.10.1738.

STEER Joseph, mercer. 10.11. Bap. at S. 16.1.1688/9, 7th c., 3rd (surviving) s. of William and bro. of George, CB. 6.11. On 17.11.1715 m. at Bd. Mariah, d. of Samuel Morewood of The Oaks, gent.; she d. 4.4.1758. Like his bro., George, was connected with St. Paul's (Trustee in 1739), and a GS(G)., and succeeded him as TT. on 4.1.1738/9. Had 2 shares in and was a committee member of Don Navigation Co. Left £200 and land in Aston by his father's will; joint trustee for and guardian of children of bro. John of D. Overseer of the poor, 1735. Voted for Turner in 1741 election. Norfolk tenant. w.d. 8.6.1744, d. 16.6.1744 and bur. St. Paul's 2 days later.

STEPHENSON Sir Henry, Knight, J.P., Endcliffe Vale. 1.18. Bn. Allen St., S., o.s. of John, engraver and typefounder, partner with W. G. Blake, CB. 6.22. Became head of the family firm of Stephenson Blake & Co. in 1860. In 1862 m. Emma, d. of Thomas James Parker, solicitor, High St. Councillor for St. George's, 1883, Mayor 1886, Knighted 1887. Director of S. Gas Co. Elected GS(G) and CB. 4.2.1887 and succeeded by s. who was, however, educated at Collegiate School and Rugby. C. of E. member of School Board. Other educational interests included Girls' High School and University College; was a trustee for Firth College (a 'Second Founder') and also Vice-Principal. City Freeman 1900. d. 24.8.1904.

STEPHENSON Sir Henry Kenyon, Bart., D.L., Hassop Hall. 1.19. Bn. 16.8.1865, o.(surviving) s. of Sir Henry, CB. 1.18. Educated Collegiate School, S., and Rugby. In 1883 joined family firm, Stephenson Blake & Co. partner 1888 and later chairman. m. in Jan., 1894 Frances, e.d. of William Greaves Blake, CB. 6.22, and his 2nd wife. Also director S. Gas Co. 1896, chairman 1918; director and chairman Thomas Turton & Co., Sheepbridge Coal & Iron Co. Ltd.; director William Deacon's Bank. TT. Lieut. 4th W.Y. Vol. Artillery 1886, Lieut-Col. 1915-8, D.S.O. Like his father, actively interested in S. University, Council Member, first Treasurer, Pro-Chancellor and Chairman of Council, LL.D. Mayor 1908 and 1910, Alderman until 1935, member of Education Committee. MC. 1918-9. M.P. for Park Division until 1923. J.P., City Freedom 1929, High Sheriff for Derbs. 1932, Baronet 1936. d. 20.9.1947.

STEWART Thomas Ruddiman, M.D., physician, Paradise Square. 10.18. Bn., and probably trained at Edinburgh. Prominent supporter S. Library, President in 1780. Physician to the Infirmary 1797-8. m. at Doncaster on 19.11.1798 Dorothea Catherine, d. of Lowther and Dorothea Rutter; she d. 4.10.1858 at Burford, Oxon. Elected CB. and GS(G). 17.8.1795 and resigned 14.3.1798, retiring to Doncaster. In 1799 Stewart bought a residence in Hall Gate, Doncaster. He d. at Doncaster 7.9.1816, MI.

STURTEVANT Joseph, cutler, Attercliffe. 8.5. s. of John of Kneesall and app. to William Robinson of A. and John Bullus of D. in 1630 and 1635; F. 1639. m. at S. on 9.7.1649 Mary Staniforth, wid. Elected CB. 1.2.1675/6, but resigned before his death; bur. A. 16.2.1686/7.

SWALLOW Richard, steel refiner and merchant, Attercliffe Forge and New Hall. 9.13. Bn. 18.2.1729, (e).s. of Richard, Captain in the Horse Guards, and Frances (Beresford). Left orphan in 1743 and brought up by John Fell, CB. 8.13, for whose widow he was agent at A. Forge. In 1757 m. Anne, d. of John Smith, engineer, and his wife Mary; Anne d. 1792. Mined coal at A. Hill Top. Guaranteed £500 to Corn Committee in 1795. Trustee for General Infirmary, of which he laid the foundation stone. Elected CB. and GS(G). on 17.2.1796, and succeeded by s. Richard. His d. Elizabeth was mother of John Sorby, CB. 10.20. w.d. 7.2.1801, he d. 2.3.1801.

SWALLOW Richard, Attercliffe New Hall. 9.14. Bn. 1763, o.s. of Richard, CB. 9.13, whom he succeeded as CB. and GS(G)., but he resigned after only a few months. m. Maria, d. of John Parker of Woodthorpe; she d. 23.5.1844. On Lord Milton's committee for 1807 election. Voted for Parker in 1832. d. 26.9.1835.

SWIFT Robert, Esq., Broom Hall. 1.1. Bn. 1500, (e).s. of Robert, mercer of Rotherham, and Anne (Taylor). Obtained Broom Hall through his wife Ellen, d. of Nicholas Wickersley, and exercised great influence in S. district, partly through his relatives the Fentons and Smythes. Connected with many sales of property in an extensive district in South Yorkshire and Derbyshire and, in particular, with endowments of Rotherham College and Worksop Abbey. Principal agent of Earl of Shrewsbury. d. in Jan. 1558/9, predeceasing his father; left three daughters, the eldest, Anne, was the wife of Richard Jessop, CB. 10.2.

SYLVESTER William, yeoman. 7.3. Parentage unknown, but presumably related to pre-Reformation priest Thomas Sylvester. Wealth indicated by assessment for 4/6 in 1569. CW. for S. town. Helped to take 1593 assessment. Held Broadfield, E. His first wife possibly sister of his bro.-in-law Thomas Holland of H. m. 2nd at S. on 28.1.1565/6 Elizabeth, wid. of Thomas Parkin and Nicholas Dey. Left £10 for S. poor, £2 for Rotherham and Killamarsh, and £1 each for Bd., Ecclesfield, Handsworth, Eckington and N. w.d. 29.2.1593/4, bur. in S. church 1.3.1593/4.

TAYLOR William, yeoman, Holt House, Ecclesall. 4.1. Perhaps s. of John of S., mercer, and grandson of William, a CW. concerned with CB. endowments. John's sister, Anne, m. Robert Swyft of Rotherham and had Robert Swyft of Broom Hall, CB. 1.1, from whom he bought Archerfield and Whitfield in 1547. Held houses and shops from TT. m. Agnes, d. of William Stickbuck of Fd. and wid. of Richard Holland. By w.d. 22.4.1587 he left his property to John, s of his bro. John; bur. S. 25.4.1587.

THOMAS Arthur, solicitor, Endcliffe House. 6.19. Bn. S. 10.5.1830, (e).s. of Henry, Leavygreave, surgeon, and Ann Maria (Rodgers). Educated S. Collegiate School; showed his interest in old school by giving annual prizes. Articled to his uncles, Messrs T. W. & Henry Rodgers, solicitors, Bank St., admitted solicitor 1860 and later became a partner. On 28.4.1864 m. Mary, d. of James Culshaw of Trenchfield, Aughton, Lancs., s.p. Vice-chairman, S. Conservative Association. In 1878 published *Church Property in S.: Its Origin, Progress and Present Position*. Elected CB. 11.5.1882 to replace his uncle. Also Treasurer C. of E. Educational Institute. d. 25.11.1884.

TINDALL Frederic Markham, J.P. 4.16. Elected CB. 13.9.1920, resigned 28.1.1932. b. 26.4.1872 in A., 3rd s. of Francis Markham, brewer of Pitsmoor and Elizabeth (Heath). Ed. by Rev. Canon Godfrey of Redbourne. Entered father's brewery, took over firm in 1902 on death of father and later sold it to Whitworth, Son and Nephew, of which he became Director and later Chairman. Supported many church and social welfare organisations, including Girls' Charity School, Council of Social Service and Church Assembly Orphan Home Trust. m. 1895 Margaret Firth, d. of Marriott Hall, a S. doctor. Retired 1928 to Beaminster, Dorset, where he was active in voluntary work. d. 6.1.1962.

TOLL Henry Limbrey. 9.16. Bn. Kingsclere, Hants., 1776, o.s. of John Frederick, V. there and Jane (Limbrey). Matriculated, The Queen's College, Oxford, 13.2.1793. Major in S. Devon Militia. m. on 25.5.1813 Margaret Joan, d. of Rev. Alexander Mackenzie, C. of St. Paul's, and his wife Margaret. Obtained part of Kenwood estate through his wife and after her death, s.p. in 1821, he m. 2nd in 1823 Anne, e.d. of William Vavasour, Esq., of Heath, Yorks. Elected CB. 3.3.1819 and resigned 11.7.1822; also GS(G). J.P. and D.L for Devon, living at Perridge House, Exeter. d. 6.8.1844.

TOLLEY George, B.Sc., M.Sc., Ph.D., C.B. I.M. Hon. D.Sc., D.Univ. 1.23. b. 24.5.1925, s. of George Enoch Tolley, ironworker, and Elsie (Billingham). Ed. at Halesowen GS., Worcs. and Birmingham Central Technical College. m. 21.6.1947 to Joan Amelia (Grosvenor). Elected CB. 1980. Curate St. Andrew's, Sharrow 1967-90; Hon. Canon of S. Cathedral 1976-. Head, Dept. of Chemistry, College of Advanced Technology, Birmingham, 1954-58; Head of Research., Allied Ironfounders Ltd. 1958-61; Principal, Worcester Tech. College, 1961-65; Senior Director of Studies, Royal Air Force Coll., Cranwell, 1965-66; Principal, S. Coll. of Technology, 1966-69, S. City Polytechnic, 1969-82; Manpower Services Commission 1983-86. Institute of Training and Development. Chairman: Council, Plastics Inst., 1959-61; Further Education Unit, 1978-82; Council of the Selly Oak Colls, Birmingham, 1984-1992; Hon. Sec., Assoc. of Colleges of Further and Higher Educn, 1975-82; Member: CNAA (Chm., Cttee for Business and Management Studies) 1972-83; Yorks and Humberside Economic Planning Council, 1976-79; Royal Society of Arts, Council 1985-1991; Hon Fellow: S. City Polytechnic, 1982; Columbia-Pacific Univ., 1983; CGLI, College of Preceptors 1985. Hon. D.Sc. S. 1984; D.Univ. Open, 1984. D.Sc. (C.N.A.A.), 1986; D Bus. Admin (Int. Mgt. Coll; Buckingham 1987). Chairman, Central S. University Hospitals NHS Trust 1991-1996. Author, *We of our Bounty, A History of the Sheffield Church Burgesses*, 1999.

TURNER James, yeoman. 2.2. Probably s, of Richard, a S. husbandman, and e.bro. of Thomas who was apprenticed to a London stationer in 1564, subsequently published in London and was guardian of James's s. George. m. at S. on 1.2.1562/3 Elizabeth Marriott; she was bur. S. 11.2.1591/2. Succeeded Hugh Smythe as bailiff and CB. Paid 6/8 in 1569 assessment. Had property at Gleadless and Keiton (?Kiveton) tithes. Anthony Turner of Bampton one of supervisors of w.d. 24.4.1583; bur. S. 1.5.1583.

TURNER John, merchant, Hartshead. 9.12. Parentage, apprenticeship and marriage unknown. Held various offices in Cutlers' Co. 1761-74, including MC. 1767. Also TT., elected 29.12.1773. Elected GS(G). and CB. 8.1.1777 and left £100 each to Boys' and Girls' Charity Schools. Had property at Portmahon as well as at Hartshead, which he bought from Broadbents in 1782. This was left to friends Vincent Eyre, TT., John Kenyon, CB. 2.19, and James Wheat, CB. 6.14, in trust for children of his bro. James, and sister, Anne. w.d. 14.1.1796 also includes considerable bequests to members of Creswick family; his wife and son were both dead. d. 20.1.1796, aged 75.

TURNER Robert, silk mercer, Angel St. 4.10. Perhaps one of the 22 children of Samuel, of Market Place, mercer. m. 1st in 1774 Ann, d. of John Webster, jersey comber, and she died shortly afterwards. His 2nd wife, Jane, d. of William Jennings of York, d. 16.4.1786; he m. 3rd, on 28.1.1790, Sarah, d. of Joseph Mitchell, merchant, and she d. 4.7.1802. Often described as a leather seller, later in partnership with Elias Lowe. Leading Tory, voted for Milton in 1807. Elected CB. and GS(G). on 5.2.1798 and TT. on 22.6.1801, keeping these offices until his death. Subscribed for various local books, member of the Pitt Club and original promoter (Governor and Trustee) of S. Savings Bank. Benefactor to Parish Church, Infirmary and Charity School. w.d. 7.4.1808; he d. 19.3.1822, aged 67.

TURNER Thomas, J.P., East Bank. 7.16. Bn. S. 10.1.1829, (e).s. of Thomas. founder of the cutlery manufacturers, Suffolk Works. Educated by Rev. John Cockerton at Hillside Academy, Dronfield. Entered family firm and was head on his retirement in 1893, when the business was sold to A. & W. Hobson. Liberal in politics, Councillor for Park and St. Peter's Wards. Held various offices in Cutlers' Co., MC. 1871. Temperance supporter. Elected GS(G). 1879, also committee member for Charity Schools. Elected CB. 3.9.1874 and resigned 27.2.1895. Retired to Scofton House, Worksop, and took great interest in the gardens. w.d. 12.3.1915 (net £40,780); d. 18.3.1916, survived by his 2nd wife, Jessie A.

TURTON Nicholas, yeoman, Attercliffe. 3.4. s. of Richard of Whitley. He was m. three times at S.; 1st on 11.8.1583 to Elizabeth Rawson, who was bur. 3.5.1591; 2nd by licence on 8.12.1592 to Katherine Allen, who was bur. 10.5.1594; 3rd by licence on 16.2.1595/6 to Elizabeth Willey, who was bur. 27.12.1628. Children by all wives mentioned in his will, son William having Osgathorpe Hills property. Concerned with many local sales. Prominent in various directions: court juror, CW., overseer for repair of A. bridge in 1608, helped take School assessment in 1606, paying 10s. w.d. 19.1.1625/6; bur. S. 27.3.1626.

UNWIN Henry, J.P., steel merchant and coal owner, Broom Cross. 5.14. Bn. Cradley 18.8.1810, 2nd s. of Philip, penknife manufacturer. Poor Law Guardian for E. 1848. m. on 3.8.1835 Hannah, youngest d. of John Wilson of Oakholme, and sister of Thomas, CB. 8.20. Had Whiteley Woods Forge. Partner in Unwin & Shaw, coal owners. Also chairman Truswell Brewery Co. Ltd., chairman Nunnery Colliery

Co. Ltd., director Samuel Fox & Co. Ltd., Gas Co. and Water Co. Elected CB. 23.10.1871. Also GS(G)., elected 4.3.1875, and Trustee Girls' Charity School. d. 10.2.1879.

UNWIN William, yeoman, Greystones. 11.6. Bap. S. 12.10.1597, (e).s. of William of Greystones and Mary (Cutt); bro.-in-law of John Crooke, CB. 1.7. m. at S. on 4.2,1623/4 Joan, d. of (?William and Alice) Dungworth. CW. for E. 1640. Leased E. corn and hay tithe and left to s. William, of Little S., who was executor of w.d. 19.2.1662/3. Other children had Porter Fields, Hoyle House and Baisin. bur. 3.3.1662/3.

VICKERS Charles Edmund, Ecclesall. 12.21. Bn. Sharrow Head 10.5.1848, o.(surviving) s. of Henry of Holmwood, solicitor, and Sibilla (James). Educated at Worksop and Weybridge. Articled to his father, whom he succeeded in April, 1882, as clerk to the City Justices, resigning in June, 1908. Also, at first jointly with his father, Law Clerk to the TT. S. Director for Alliance Assurance Co. m. on 19.8.1875 Mary Bateman Sugden of Brighouse. Conservative in politics. Elected CB. 27.2.1896 and resigned 5.1.1925. d. 16.6.1933.

WAINWRIGHT Benjamin, M.D., Norfolk Street and Richmond Hill. 5.11. Formerly at Rotherham. Invited to 1790 Cutlers' Feast. Gave £300 to 1795 Corn Committee. Physician to the Infirmary 1797-1811. Held River Don shares. Elected CB. and GS(G). 14.7.1797. Member Town Library. d. 29.5.1819 after falling from a horse; bur. Handsworth.

WALKER George, coal owner, J.P., Osgathorpe. 6.17. Bn. Woodall, near Harthill, 1801. Began as a grocer, developed into sugar refiner and then into coal owner, closely connected with Wharncliffe Silkstone Co. Director Great Northern Rly. and S. & Rotherham Bank. Councillor for Park Ward. Elected CB. 26.1.1860 and GS(G). 28.1.1864. d. 24.3.1874.

WALTON William, innkeeper. 6.1. Presumably related to the Roger Walter who was CB. in 1499; William was also CB. at least four years before the Charter. Paid 2s. in 1569 assessment. Occupied Little Gill Carr. 1st wife Elizabeth bur. S.27.8.1571; he m. 2nd at S. on 28.7.1572 Alice, wid. of Ralph Holland. w.d. 29.4.1573 mentions bro.-in-law Gregory Revell, of Stannington Hall, and cousin Ralph Walton; bur. S. 12.5.1573.

WARD Paul Terence, solicitor. 7.20. b. 13.12.22, (o)s. of Edwin Ward, Provision Merchant and May Louisa (Bray). ed. Wellington School, Somerset. m. Audrey Winifred Mary Lock on 28.11.46. Elected C.B. 1977. Partner in Rodgers & Howe, Solicitors, 1954-1989. Clerk of the Peace, 1959-64. Diocesan Registrar, 1976-1990. Vice President, Sheffield Bach Society. Chairman of Royal School of Church Music, Sheffield and South Yorkshire Area 1986-1992 d.1.1998.

WATERHOUSE John, M.D., High St. 1.10. Bap. S. 30.8.1666, s. of Robert, apothecary and gent., GS(G)., and Eliza (Midgley). Matriculated Merton Coll., Oxford, in 1683/4. m. 1st at Silkstone on 16.11.1695 Rebecca, d. of . . . Shippen and wid. of Nathaniel Bower. m. 2nd at Dronfield on 26.10.1712 Mary, e.d. of John and Sarah Cart; Mary became the 2nd wife of James Walker of Manchester. Also GS(G)., gave £2 towards master's house in 1709. His will mentions s. John and property in Barnsley and Conisbrough. Left a farm to V. of Conisbrough and £15 to V. of S. for a sermon every Jan. 30 insisting on 'the Inconstancy of human Affaires without medling with party cause'. Also left £50 to new S. School. bur. S. 15.8.1714.

WATERHOUSE Rev. Robert. 8.14. Bap. S. 16.4.1707, 5th s. of Henry, attorney, and 1st wife Ann. Educated S. GS. under Christopher Robinson before entering St. John's College, Cambridge, as a pensioner, on 1.4.1725. B.A. 1728/9, Fellow 1729/30-39, M.A. 1732. Ordained deacon (Ely) 18.9.1730, priest (London) 19.9.1731, rector of Bowers Gifford, Essex, 29.3.1738. Later resided in S., 'unbeneficed and disengaged'. Elected GS(G). and CB. 12.6.1762, but resigned 10.4.1764. w.d. 12.12.1777, left £100 to S. Charity School; d. 16.1.1778, bur. in S. church.

WATERHOUSE Thomas, gent, High Street. 10.12. Bap. S. 31.8.1699, 4th s. of Henry, attorney, and elder bro. of previous Robert. Trustee for St. Paul's Church. Elected CB. 7.7.1744, GS(G). 6.6.1748. Voted for Fox in 1741 election. Leased property Chapel-en-le-Frith. w.d. 15.5.1749, d. 21.8.1760, unmarried.

WATSON Sir Henry Edmund, Shirecliffe Hall. 2.22. Bn. 1815, youngest s. of John of Shirecliffe Hall, attorney, and Anna Maria (Wright); nephew of next. Educated at Rev. Henry Hunt Piper's School, Norton and at Sandall, near Wakefield. Articled to his father, until 1872 partner with his father and bro. Thomas, and then with W. B. Esam, CB. 7.18. Governor and Trustee S. Savings Bank. Elected TT. 4.5.1876, CB. 9.12.1880, GS(G). 11.5.1882. Original trustee and Council Member of Firth College. Director Charles Cammell & Co. Ltd. Conservative in politics. Deputy Lieutenant for W. R. Knighted 1886. d. 16.2.1901.

WATSON Thomas, silver plater, Broomhill House. 2.20. Bn. 1773, 3rd s. of Thomas, landlord of 'The George', and Hannah (Newbould). Continued at 'The George', Hartshead, and then at 'The Rose and Crown'. On 4.12.1800 m. Mary Tennant. Bought Matthew Fenton's silver plating stock and established firm of Watson & Bradbury in Mulberry St. In 1807 voted for Wilberforce and Lascelles. Elected CB. and GS(G). 16.2.1809. Subscribed 20 guineas for new GS. building in 1823 and left bequests to Infirmary, Boys' and Girls' Charity Schools and National School. w.d. 9.6.1832; d. at Harrogate 30.7.1832.

WEBSTER John Dodsley, F.R.I.B.A. 9.25. Elected CB. 19.12.1904. b. 1840. Ed. Mansfield GS. Served articles with Samuel Worth, a well-known S. architect and soon after 1865 set up on his own. Elected F.R.I.B.A. 1873. A diocesan surveyor for

York and architect to Ecclesall Birlow Union Guardians. In practice with his son and partner, John Douglas, in name of S. D. Webster & Son, he was architect of numerous S. churches, hospitals, public buildings and monuments, including St. Bartholomew's, St. Cuthbert's and St. Augustine's churches. Former member and Chairman of Children's Hospital for which he was architect. Director of S. Gas Co., People's Warden St. Mark's. m. Emily, d. of T. B. Cockayne of S. d. 1.10.1913.

WHEAT James, solicitor, Norwood. 6.14. (e).s. of Thomas of Retford and Ann (Cockshutt). Articled to William Battie, attorney, CB. 12.14, to whose practice he succeeded in 1766; this included the clerkship of the CB. Moved office to Paradise Square in 1777. Elected CB. 24.6.1778. Solicitor to General Infirmary. Became unpopular with many people because of his active part in local enclosures. In 1770 m. Sarah, (o).d. of John Milnes of Newark. For last 30 years resided at Norwood Hall. Taxed for one servant in 1780. Gave £200 to Corn Committee in 1795. w.d. 17.12.1794; d. 24.1.1805, bur. in chancel of S. church.

WHITTAKER John Macnaghten, M.A., D.Sc. (Edin), M.A. (Cantab), LL.D. 11.23. Elected CB. 1956, resigned 1970. b. 7.3.1905, 2nd s. of Sir. Edmund Whittaker, F.R.S., Professor of Mathematics and Mary Ferguson Macnaghten (Boyd). Ed. Fettes, Edinburgh University and Trinity, Cambridge. Vice-Chancellor University 1952-65. Professor of Pure Mathematics, Liverpool Univ. 1933-52. F.R.S. 1949. 1940-45 R.A. (A.A. Comd. Western Desert, Tunisia, War Office) Lt. Col. 1944, Deputy Scientific Adviser Army Council 1944. Freedom of City of S. 1965. Married Iona Elliot 1933. d. 30.1.1984.

WILDE George, yeoman, Hall Carr. 7.9. The pedigree given by Hunter is clearly incorrect. Probably bap. S. 13.4.1616, 3rd s. of William of Crookes, cutler. App. to e.bro. John of Little S.; F. 1637. Of Little S. when younger bro. Samuel app. to him. Licence in 1637 to m. Ann, d. of Stephen Fox of Little S. She was only bap. in 1624; the marriage is not recorded at S. and the first known c. was only bn. in 1649; Ann was bur. S. 29.4.1663. Through his wife, George obtained Hall Carr. His e. sister m. Richard Slack, MC. 1642. His bro. John's d. m. William Stone(s), C. of E. Rayney Lecturer, Worsborough, from whom George bought property in Whiteley Woods. George's ss. d. young and he left his property to his grandchildren, Thomas Handley, CB. 4.7, and Mary, d. of John Webster, MC. 1687. His 3rd d. Martha m. Henry Hancock of S., mercer, and had Anne, the wife of George Bamforth, CB. 8.11. Elected CB. 28.8.1673, but apparently resigned before his death. In 1688 collected supplement to V.'s salary. w.d. 23.12.1689; d. 5.1.1689/90.

WILSON Charles Macro, solicitor, Waldershaigh, Bolsterstone. 4.14. Bn. 25.2.1835, 3rd (2nd surviving) s. of James of Brincliffe Tower, solicitor, and Elizabeth (Alderson); grandson of William, CB. 6.15. Educated S. Collegiate School 1843-50. Articled to his father, admitted solicitor 1856, became partner and ultimately head of Younge, Wilson & Co of East Parade; succeeded father as clerk to Cutlers' Co. in 1865. On 30.3.1865 m. Mary Elizabeth, 2nd d. of Richard Thorp of

Barnsley; she d. 18.4.1909. Elected CB. 22.12.1887 and GS(G). 17.5.1888; also supported Boys' Charity School. Governor and Trustee S. Savings Bank. 'Sound Conservative'. Member W.R.C.C. and chairman Stocksbridge U.D.C. Member Wortley Board of Guardians. D. 3.2.1902.

WILSON David Clement, B.A. 2.26. Elected CB. 1958. Bn. 1.3.1917, y.s. of Prebendary Clement Eustace Macro and Hon. Adele Emily Anna (Hamilton). Nephew of Reginald Thorp (CB. 2.24). Ed. Winchester and Trinity, Cambridge. m. 10.7.1948 Jocelyn Frances daughter W.R Stephenson Master Cutler 1949 and grand-daughter of H.K. Stephenson C.B. 1.19. Solicitor. 1940-42 Shropshire Yeomanry R.A. 1942-46 Army Air Photographic Intelligence, G.S.O. II India/Burma. Mentioned in Despatches twice. Law Clerk to Cutlers' Company 1958-73. Governor Trustee Savings Bank, 1959-75. Trustee 1970-75. Member Local Board Yorks & Lincs T.S.B. 1975. Chairman Dio. Dilapidations (later Parsonages) Committee 1956-1985. Played First Class Cricket 1938-39. Trustee Bluecoat Edu. Foundation. Council Member S. Chamber of Commerce.

WILSON George, J.P., Banner Cross Hall. 6.20. Bn. Broughton Ferry 1829, 2nd s. of George of Haugh Mill, Fifeshire, flax spinner, and Isobel (Ralph). A boarder at S. Collegiate School 1839-41, sent by Charles Cammell; then at Madras College, St. Andrews, and Edinburgh University. Entered Cammell's Furnival St. Works, became managing director in 1879. In 1856 m. Clara Maria, d. of Charles Prangley. MC. 1874. Active Conservative. Elected CB. 18.12.1884 and GS(G). 4.2.1885. d. of a stroke 1.12.1885, bur. E.

WILSON Henry, snuff manufacturer, Westbrook, Sharrow Moor. 2.21. Bn. Westbrook 27.10.1807, 2nd s. of Joseph, snuff manufacturer, and Elizabeth (Pearson). Educated by Rev. H. H. Piper at N. Entered father's firm and eventually became head of J. & H. Wilson, snuff manufacturers, having erected Westbrook (upper or top) mill. m. 10.1830 cousin Elizabeth, d. of Rev. Henry Pearson V. of N.; she d. 4.12.1895. Elected CB. and GS(G). 16.8.1832. Supported many churches and gave moiety of advowson of parish church to the Church Burgesses. Church member of School Board 1870-6. Guardian for E. Prominently connected with S. Collegiate School from its foundation until his death; at one period took full financial responsibility. w.d. 7.12.1871; d. 16.11.1880.

WILSON John, gent., Whaley and Alfreton, Derbs., and Attercliffe. 3.5. Possibly of a local family, but of Alfreton when he m. Elizabeth, d. of George Westby, and of Whaley in 1623 when licensed to m. at S. Mary, d. of John Mirfield of Laughton and wid. of John Hoole, CB. 12.7. Their d. Mary m. James Nicholson, CB. 2.12. Took a leading part in building A. chapel, held part of A. Forge meadow and co-lessor of corn tithe. Commissioner for dispute about Dronfield School in 1635. Perhaps dead by 1651, as not mentioned in w. of son-in-law, John Bate.

WILSON Ralph Macro, M.A. 2.25. Elected CB. 18.4.1953. b. 20.2.1903, elder s.

of Reginald Thorp (CB. 2.24) and Gladys, d. of James Willis Dixon, silverplate manufacturer. Ed. Winchester and Trinity, Cambridge. Entered family solicitors firm of Younge, Wilson & Co. Senior partner and Law Clerk to Cutler's Company 1953. Special Constabulary and Home Guard 1940-45. Hon. Secretary Chamber of Commerce. Chairman Wheatley & Bates Ltd.; local Director Eagle Star Insurance Co. Ltd.; member Management Committee S. Savings Bank; Director S. United Cricket and Football Club Ltd. Manager Bolsterstone School. President Penistone Divisional Conservative and Unionist Association. Chairman Stocksbridge Conservative Branch. People's warden Bolsterstone Church. Trustee Bluecoat School. Member Yorks. County Cricket Club Committee; Vice-President S. Cricket League. d. 6.7.1958.

WILSON Reginald Thorp, M.A., Solicitor, Waldershaigh, Bolstertone. 2.24. b. at Barnsley 1.2.1866, (e).s. of Canon William Reginald Wilson V. of Bolsterstone, and Martha, d. of Richard Thorp of Monk Bretton; nephew of Charles Macro Wilson, CB. 4.14. Ed. Shrewsbury School and Trinity College, Cambridge, M.A. 1892. Admitted Solicitor, 1891, and joined family firm of Younge Wilson & Co., senior partner 1917 and Law Clerk to the Cutlers' Company. m. 1900 Gladys, d. of James Willis Dixon, silver plate manufacturer, and great niece of Henry Isaac Dixon, CB. 10.22. An expert on trade mark law; full time secretary Chamber of Commerce, 1905-18 and thereafter honorary advisory secretary and council member; Member Merchandise Marks Committee, appointed by the Board of Trade 1919. Honorary Treasurer of S. District Incorporated Law Society 1928-1951, and President 1925. Chairman Management Committee of S. Savings Bank 1930-1953; Clerk to Assn. of Millowners of the Rivers Rivelin, Loxley and Don, and Secretary of High Speed Steel Association. People's Warden Bolsterstone Church for over 20 years. Elected CB. 5.1.1925 in place of James Dixon, a half cousin of his wife. d. 15.2.1953.

WILSON Thomas, cutlery manufacturer, Oakholme. 8.20. Bn. 1831, (? 4th) s. of John, cutlery manufacturer, Sycamore St., and his wife Mary; his sister m. Henry Unwin, CB. 5.14. Partner in family firm until 1897. Also prominent in S. Coal Co. Moved to Oakholme after death of his mother in 1870. Originally Congregational, worshipping at Queen St. Chapel, but joined C. of E. and attended S. Stephen's and St. Mark's. Elected CB. 3.3.1870 and GS(G). 23.10.1872. Treasurer Girls' Charity School. Staunch Liberal and Church benefactor. w.d. 27.1.1904; d. 22.5.1905, unmarried.

WILSON Thomas Kingsford, J.P. 3.17. Elected CB. 16.7.1926. b. 8.10.1861, youngest s. of George (2nd cousin of Henry CB.2.21) and Emily, d. of John Kingsford of Brothers Ltd., brewers, 1882, director and head brewer 1887, Managing Director 1895, Chairman 1921. Director Joseph Rodgers & Co. Ltd. Vice-President Royal Hospital, Trustee George Woofindin Convalescent Home. Member Church Extension Scheme 1911-15. Helped with formation of S. Diocese. First President S. Ratepayers' Assn. President Hallam Ward Branch Municipal

Progressive Party 1933. Celebrated game shot. m. 1894 Beatrice Helen, youngest d. of Henry Isaac Dixon, J.P. (CB. 10.22). d. 21.9.1937.

WILSON William, liquor merchant, Highfield. 6.15. Bn. 1754, 4th s. of John of Broomhead known as 'the Yorkshire Antiquary', and Susannah (Oates). The family firm of John Wilson & Sons was at Pond St. for over 50 years. Voted for Wilberforce and Lascelles in 1804. Elected CB. and GS(G). 4.2.1805; subscribed 20 gns. for new school in 1823. d. 30.8.1829; bur. Bd. church.

WILSON Zachariah, linen-draper, Broomhead. 1.9. Bap. Bd. 13.3.1638/9, 7th s. of Christopher, Broomhead, and Mary (Ibbotson). Perhaps app. to Robert Housley, linen-draper, whose d. Mary he m. by licence at S. on 28.4.1662. From this time, living in S., active in TT.; issued his own tokens. Elected CB. 28.8.1673. Bur. S. 25.7.1702.

WINSTON Alfred Henry. 3.18. Elected CB. 16.9.1937. b. 29.12.1876, eldest s. of Rev. Ripley, a Wesleyan minister. Ed. Kingswood School, Bath. 1892 joined Francis Newton and Hamer Chalmer Merchants and manufacturers of cutlery. 1902 joined Richard Groves Holland, importer of Swedish iron; managing director 1910. Director of several companies. Organist Fulwood Church and St. George's. m. 1904 Clara Beatrice, 2nd d. of Richard Groves Holland. d. 7.4.1952.

WINTER John, silver plater, Market Place. 10.16. Probably s. of John, cutler, app. to Thomas Law, F. 1755. A partner in Winter, Parsons & Hall, but had apparently retired by 1787 when described as gent., Churchyard. MC. in 1775, holding various offices 1767-81; presented largest known silver cup to Co. in 1779. Elected TT. 10.8.1772, CB. and GS(G). 31.7.1776; also trustee Boys' Charity School. Wife Mary probably survived him, was present at 1790 Cutlers' Feast and included, with child and 2 servants, in 1792 assessment. w.d. 3.8.1787; d. 12.2.1792.

WOODROVE Richard, gent., Woodthorpe. 12.10. Bap. S. 6.2.1620, s. of Richard of Crookesmoorside, husbandman and chapman, and Alice (Hunter). His 1st wife, Mary, bur. S. 11.8.1658; m. 2nd at S. on 3.7.1662 Anne Stone, wid., who was bur. 31.6.1681. Had property at Greystones, Lydgate and Crookes; bought High St. house from Rev. James Creswick for £200; obtained considerable property at Woodthorpe from John Nodder. Overseer for poor in 1664. Friend of John Crooke, CB. 1.7. Bur. S. 11.11.1682.

WRIGHT Thomas, attorney, Bridgehouses. 1.11. Parentage unknown, but came to S. as a clerk to William Simpson; his bro., Joseph, was a London goldsmith. m. Mary, d. of William Clayton of Whitwell, Derbs., and wid. of Richard Bacon, GS(G)., who d. in 1701. GS(G)., paying £1 in 1709 towards Master's house. Clerk to TT. from 1707. Steward Eckington Manor 1713-35. Closely connected with Francis Sitwell. Left manor of Birkin in 1715. Trustee for St. Paul's Church. Voted for Cavendish in 1734 Derbs. election, and for Turner in 1741 W.R. election. d. 17.11.1741; w.p. at York by his nephew Rev. Thomas Wright the next February.

YOUNGE Charles, silversmith, Brincliffe Edge. 8.17. Younger s. of John Trevers, CB. 7.13. Educated S. GS., steward at Old Boys' Feast in 1805. Constable in 1798, then of Union St. Voted for Wilberforce and Lascelles in 1807. Elected CB. and GS(G). 31.7.1820, vice his uncle, Samuel Staniforth. Subscribed 20 gns. for new school in 1823. d. 9.10.1831, unmarried.

YOUNGE Charles Frederic, silversmith and banker, High St. 10.21. Bn. 24.9.1792, s. of Simon Andrews, CB. 12.17 and Jane (Hall); bap. St Paul's 24.10.1792. Voted for Bailey and Parker in 1832. Director Manchester, Sheffield & Lincs. railway. Had already moved to Thurcroft Hall before election as CB. and GS(G). on 30.10.1844. On 16.4.1863 m. Emily, d. of William Barker of Huddersfield, solicitor. Resigned both offices in Jan., 1864, and moved to Forestside, Grasmere, where he d. 17.11.1866.

YOUNGE John Trevers, merchant, Union St. 7.13. Bap. S. 20.8.1719, (e).s. of Thomas, mercer, and Mary (Trevers); bro. of Dr. Thomas, CB. 1.14 m. on 25.12.1746 Elizabeth, d. of Samuel Staniforth and sister of Samuel, CB. 8.16; their sister, Mary, m. Dr. Thomas Younge. Elected CB. 6.6.1748, also GS(G). Signatory to Rockingham address in 1766. Elected TT. 23.7.1778. Benefited from E. Enclosure in 1778. Guaranteed £200 to Corn Committee in 1795. Member S. Town Library. d. 19.1.1807.

YOUNGE Robert, wine merchant, Greystones. 7.15. Bn. Charles St. 1801, s. of Samuel, CB. 7.14, and grandson of John Trevers, CB. 7.13. Succeeded his father as silver plater (Union St.) and wine merchant (Old Haymarket), and as CB. and GS(G)., elected 6.8.1840. Secretary S. Literary & Philosophical Society 1829, vice-president 1837. Took active part in Trevor controversy in 1850. Poor Law Guardian. Connected with Infirmary & Deakin Institution and supported School of Art. d. 20.8.1874.

YOUNGE Samuel, silversmith, Brincliffe Edge. 7.14. Bn. 1761, s. of John Trevers, CB. 7.13, and bro. of Charles, CB. 8.17. Of Howard St. and constable in 1798. On 16.10.1797 m. Lydia, d. of Robert Marsden. In 1807 voted for Wilberforce and Lascelles, and in 1832 and '35 for Bailey and Parker. Also lived in Union St., head of family wine and spirit business. Elected CB. and GS(G). 29.1.1807, vice his father and succeeded by his s. Robert. Governor and Trustee S. Savings Bank. Subscribed 20 gns. to new School in 1823. d. 20.7.1840.

YOUNGE Simon Andrew, merchant and steel refiner, High St. 12.17. Bn. 1734, s. of George and Elizabeth (Andrews). His 1st wife Elizabeth, d. of Christopher Stevenson, Rector of Rawmarsh, d. 1.11.1770, and he m. 2nd Jane, d. of William Hall of S., merchant. Elected CB. and GS(G). 5.10.1798, and resigned because of old age on 30.1.1811.

YOUNGE Dr. Thomas, physician, Church St. 1.14. Bn. 1721, s. of Thomas, mercer, and bro. of John Trevers, CB. 7.13. Educated S. GS. by John Cliff before admission to St. John's College, Cambridge, in 1739. B.A. 1743/4, M.A. 1747; M.D. (Edinburgh) 1752. Then returned to practise in S. On 11.1.1759 m. Mary Staniforth, sister of Samuel, CB. 8.16. Signatory to Rockingham address in 1766. Elected CB. 4.5.1768, also GS(G), d. at Tankersley 14.12.1784 on way to Wentworth Castle.

YOUNGE William, physician, Sharrow Grange. 11.15. Bn. 30.1.1762, 2nd s. of Dr. Thomas, CB. 1.14. Educated S. GS. by Charles Chadwick and then at Edinburgh; M.D. 1786. Went on a continental tour with Sir J. E. Smith, founder of the Linnaean Society. Settled in S. in 1787 and issued circular letter urging an infirmary in 1789; served as physician to it from 1797. Elected CB. and GS(G). 23.11.1791, subscribed 20 gns. to new School in 1823. Governor and Trustee S. Savings Bank. Voted for Bailey and Parker in 1832 and '35. Retired from Church St. d. of apoplexy, unmarried, 9.11.1838, his Library later being sold by auction (catalogue extant).

Sources, Bibliography and References

RECORDS OF THE Church Burgesses up to 1947 are deposited with the Sheffield City Archives. They are well classified and catalogued. The reference C.B. followed by a number refers to a document in that collection. Records subsequent to 1947 are in the possession of the Law Clerk to the Burgesses.

Accounts are complete from 1557. Minute books start in 1798 (but see Election Book, below).

The first Account Book, from 1557 to 1574, was given by Thomas Braye, who also gave the first account book, at the same time, to what later became known as The Town Trust. The opening inscription in the Church Burgesses' Accounts reads:

> 'A remembrance that I Thomas Braye did give this Boke to ye Churche there to remayne for a presydente for ye takings of ye Reconynges from Tyme to Tyme and to th' ntente that it maye be a Testimonye how ye Rents belonginge to ye Capitall Burgesses of ye Towne of Sheffeld bee spente as shall appeare within this Boke Anno Dmi 1557.'

The Election Book, in the possession of the Law Clerk to the Burgesses, has been in use from September 1653. It records the election of Burgesses, and is still in use for that purpose. It served as a Minute Book from 1653 until other, fuller, minutes began at the end of the 18th century. It also includes copies of the Queen Mary Charter, Henry Bayley's Information and the Swyft-Tailour Petition, together with some of the Opinions of Counsel on matters put to them. The appointment of Assistant Ministers and the conditions of those appointments are also recorded. References to entries in the Election Book are prefixed by the letters E.B. with a page number, or date.

Plans by William Fairbank of the Burgesses' property for 1768, revised in 1794, are in the Church Burgesses' collection in the City Archives, Other sketch plans relating to the Burgesses' estates are in the Fairbank Collection in the City Archives.

A report, 'The Architectural Records of Sheffield Parish Church and Cathedral', by Mark. T. Bateson, dated 18 November 1994, is deposited in the City Archives. Although the report of an uncompleted project, it contains much useful material.

Sheffield Local Studies Library has much relevant material. A reference L.S. followed by a number and/or letters, indicates that it is to be found in the Local Studies Library.

Papers appearing in the *Transactions of the Hunter Archaeological Society* are given the reference, T.H.A.S.

Bibliography

S.O. Addy, *Church and Manor: A Study in English Economic History* (George Allen, London) 1913.

Clyde Binfield, *A Short History of the Sheffield Town Trust 1297-1997* (Town Trust, Sheffield), 1997.

Clyde Binfield and David Hey (Ed.), *Mesters to Masters – A History of the Company of Cutlers in Hallamshire* (Oxford University Press) 1997.

David Bostwick, *Sheffield in Tudor and Stuart Times* (Sheffield City Museums), 1985.

Edward Bramley, *A Record of the Burgery of Sheffield (Commonly called the Town Trust) 1848-1955* (Northend, Sheffield) 1957.

H. Cecil and J.R. Wigfull, *The Cathedral Church of SS. Peter and Paul, Sheffield* (Pawson and Brailsford, Sheffield), 1916.

L.N. Coombe, *Memorandum as to the Origin, Objects and Administration of the Trust commonly known as 'The Sheffield Church Burgesses Trust'* (Waterlow, London) 1913.

Bryan Dale, *Yorkshire Puritanism and Early Nonconformity*, Bradford, 1909.

A.G. Dickens, *Lollards and Protestants in the Diocese of York* (Hambledon Reprint) 1982.

Eamon Duffy, *The Stripping of the Altars: Traditional Religion in England, 1400-1580* (Yale, London) 1992.

Endowed Charities (City of Sheffield), Report of Inquiry carried out by the Charity Commissioners in 1895. Published as a 'Blue Book', H.M.S.O., London, 1897.

Report of the Charity Commissioners, 1829.

A.E. Gatty, *Sheffield, Past and Present* (Thomas Rodgers, Sheffield), 1873.

T. Walter Hall, *A Catalogue of the Ancient Charters belonging to the Twelve Capital Burgesses and Commonalty of Sheffield* (Northend, Sheffield), 1913.

A Catalogue of the Charters, Deeds and Manuscripts in the Public Library at Sheffield (Northend, Sheffield), 1912.

Descriptive Catalogue of the Edmunds Collection (Northend, Sheffield), 1924.

The Fairbanks of Sheffield (Northend, Sheffield), 1932.

John Harrison, *An exact and perfect survey and view of the Manor of Sheffield with other lands (1637)*. Transcribed and edited by John George Ronksley. (Privately printed for Arthur Wightman), 1908.

H.K. Hawson, *The growth of a City, 1893-1926* (Northend, Sheffield), 1968.

David Hey, *The Fiery Blades of Hallamshire: Sheffield and its Neighbourhood, 1660-1740* (Leicester University Press), 1991.

The History of the City of Sheffield, 1843-1993 (Sheffield Academic Press), 1993. Edited Clyde Binfield, David Hey et. al.

Joseph Hunter, Hallamshire. *The History and Topography of the Parish of Sheffield* (Pawson and Brailsford, Sheffield). Published 1819. New and enlarged Edition by Alfred Gatty, 1869.

A.C.E. Jarvis, *The Cathedral Church of St. Peter and St. Paul, Sheffield* (British Publishing Co., (Gloucester)), 1947.

W.K. Jordan, *Philanthropy in England, 1480-1660* (Allen and Unwin, London), 1959.

J.D. Leader, *The Records of the Burgery of Sheffield* (Elliot and Stark, London), 1897.

Sheffield General Infirmary, 1797-1897 (Sheffield) 1897.

R.E. Leader, *Sheffield in the Eighteenth Century* (Leng, Sheffield), 1905.

Reminiscences of Old Sheffield (Leader, Sheffield), 1875.

D.R. Lunn, *Chapters Towards a History of the Cathedral and Parish Church of St. Peter and St. Paul, Sheffield* (Sheffield, Typescript), 1987.

James Wilkinson, Vicar of Sheffield 1753-1805 (Sheffield, Typescript) 1997.

M. Mercer, *Schooling the Poorer Child, Elementary Education in Sheffield 1560-1902* (Sheffield Academic Press), 1996.

W. Odom, *Memorials of Sheffield, its Cathedral and Parish Churches* (Northend, Sheffield) 1922.

Hallamshire Worthies (Northend, Sheffield), 1926.

David Owen, *English Philanthropy 1660-1960* (Harvard) 1964.

S. Pollard and C. Holmes, *Essays in the Economic and Social History of South Yorkshire* (South Yorkshire County Council, Barnsley), 1976.

Samuel Roberts, *Autobiography and Select Remains* (Longmans, London), 1849.

Dennis Smith, *Conflict and Compromise: Class Formation in English Society, 1830-1914* (Routledge, Kegan, Paul, London), 1982.

E.P. Thompson, *The Making of the English Working Class* (Penguin, London), 1968.

Mary Walton, *Sheffield, Its Story and its Achievements* (S.R. Publishers, Sheffield), 1968.

A History of the Diocese of Sheffield, 1914-1979 (Diocesan Board of Finance, Sheffield), 1981.

W.R. Ward, *Religion and Society in England, 1790-1850* (Batsford), 1972.

John B. Wheat, *A History of the Trust* (Sheffield, Typescript), 1912.

Gilbert J. Wheat, *A Professional Family: (The Wheats of Sheffield)* (Hathaway Press, Nailsworth, Gloucs.), 1996.

E.R. Wickham, *Church and People in an Industrial City* (Lutterworth Press, London), 1957.

David Wilson, *A History of the Wilson Family of Broomhead and Various Connections* (Typescript), 1991.

References

Chapter I: Origins

1. Joseph Hunter, *Hallamshire. The History and Topography of the Parish of Sheffield*, Pawson and Brailsford, Sheffield. Published 1819. New and enlarged Edition by Alfred Gatty, 1869, 243. (Hereafter referred to as Hunter.)
2. R.L. Craig, 'The Origin and Development of the Sheffield Town Trust', *THAS*, 6, 1949, 245.
3. *Endowed Charities (City of Sheffield), Report of Inquiry carried out by the Charity Commissioners in 1895.* Published as a 'Blue Book', London, 1897, 79. LS 361 SQ
4. J.B. Wheat, 'Sheffield's Ancient Public Trusts, 1304-1566, THAS, 2, 1924, 338-340.
5. T. Walter Hall, *A Catalogue of the Ancient Charters belonging to the Twelve Capital Burgesses and Commonalty of Sheffield* (Northend, Sheffield, 1913), 41 (Doc. 67); 42 (Doc. 68); 109-113. (Hereafter referred to as Hall, Charters). LS 016.94274.S
6. Hall, Charters, 106-110.
7. Response of Robert Swyft and William Tailour to Information of Henry Bayley, ibid. 101
8. ibid. 102.
9. ibid. 84.
10. Reproduced in *Endowed Charities*, 1897, 505.
11. Petition to Queen Mary, Hunter, 239.
12. Information of Henry Bayley, Hall, Charters, 98. E.B. 91-93.
13. Hall, Charters, 44 (Doc. 71).
14. Hall, Charters, 101. E.B. 94
15. Hunter, 239.
16. Hunter, 75.
17. A.G. Dickens, *Lollards and Protestants in the Diocese of York* (Hambledon, Reprint, 1982), 209-210.
18. Eamon Duffy, *The Stripping of the Altars: Traditional Religion in England, 1400-1580* London, Yale, 1992, 468, et. seq.
19. A.G. Dickens, *Lollards and Protestants*, 211.

20. Hall, Charters, 107.
21. J.D. Leader, *The Records of the Burgery of Sheffield*, London, Elliot Stock, 1897, xxxi.
    J.B. Wheat, *Sheffield Church Burgesses Trust: A History of the Trust, Typescript, 1912, 8. (Hereafter referred to as Wheat, History).*
    R.E. Leader, *Sheffield Iris*, 24 November, 1906.
22. 'Endowed Charities', 1897, 104.
23. Sheffield Town Council Minutes, 6 January, 1851.
    J.B. Wheat, History, 87-95.
24. David Hey, *The Fiery Blades of Hallamshire, Sheffield and its Neighbourhood*, 1660-1740, Leicester, University Press, 1991, 206.
25. Hall, Charters, 43, (Doc. 69).
26. Hall, Charters, 92 (Doc. 75).
27. For early deeds bequeathing property to the Vicar of Sheffield, see Appendix I.
28. J.D. Leader, Burgesses Property, *Notes and Queries* 7 December 1874, 237. (LS 913.4274.SQ)
29. Samuel Mitchell, *An Essay on the History of the Burgery of Sheffield, commonly called The Town Trust*, Printed by H. & A. Bacon and sold by R. Leader, Sheffield, 1828. LS. Local Pamphlets, Vol.82, 042S
30. J.B. Wheat, *Sheffield's Ancient Public Trusts*, 338.
31. J.D. Leader, *Records of the Burgery of Sheffield*, xxxi.
32. ibid. xlviii. And, *Endowed Charities*, 1929, 578.
33. J.D. Leader, *Records of the Burgery of Sheffield*, xlix.
34. ibid. xlvii.
35. Mary Walton, *Sheffield: Its Story and its Achievements*, S.R. Publishers, Sheffield, 4th Edition, 1968, 71.
    See also: *Extracts from the Records of the Company of Cutlers in Hallamshire*, Cutlers Company, Sheffield, 1972, xii. (The Act of 1624 is reproduced in full on pp. 12-19).
36. J.N. Coombe, *Memorandum as to the origin, objects and administration of the Trust commonly known as The Sheffield Church Burgesses Trust*, Waterlow, London, 1913, 5. LS 942.74 SQ
37. ibid. 4-12.
38. Hall, Charters,
    Hunter, 244-245.
39. J.N. Coombe, Memorandum, 11.
40. S. O. Addy, Newspaper Cuttings, 1913, (LS, Vol. I, 9).
    R.E. Leader, ibid. March 1913.
41. J.B. Wheat, *History*, 8.

42. T. W. Hall, *Descriptive Catalogue of the Edmunds Collection*, Northend, Sheffield, 1914, 248-260. (LS 016.94274.SST).
43. S.O. Addy, *Church and Manor: A Study in English Economic History*, George Allen, London, 1913, 224, 249.
See also: James Tait, *The Medieval English Borough*, Manchester University Press, 1936, 245.
44. *Sheffield and Rotherham Independent*, 11 January, 1851.
45. *An Address to the Town's Trustees, with a letter to the Twelve Capital Burgesses by A Townsman*, James Montgomery, Sheffield, 1811. (LS. Local Pamphlets, Vol. 133, No. 7).
46. Hall Charters, 92, (Doc.75).
47. P.J. Wallis, Sheffield Church Burgesses: A Biographical History, THAS, 7, 1952, 51-62; 1953-54, 144-157; 1955, 194-199; 1957, 344-360.
48. R.E. Leader, The Church Burgesses of 1554, *Sheffield and Rotherham Independent*, 24 November 1906. (LS Newpaper Cuttings, Vol. 19, 229. 942.74S).

Chapter II: The Charity Schemes

1. David Owen, *English Philanthropy 1660-1960*, Harvard, 1964, 14.
2. Hunter, 244.
3. T.W. Hall, *Descriptive Catalogue of the Edmunds Collection*, Northend, Sheffield, 1924, 229.
C.B. Account Book, 161. LS 016.94274 SST.
J.N. Coombe, *Memorandum*, 12.
4. R.E. Leader, *Sheffield in the Eighteenth Century*, Sir. W.C. Leng, Sheffield, 1905, 194.
5. J.B. Wheat, *History*, 34.
6. ibid. 38.
7. CB 150.
8. CB 151.
9. CB 150.
10. CB 151.
11. CB 151.
12. Dennis Smith, *Conflict and Compromise, Class Formation in English Society, 1830-1914*, Routledge, Kegan, Paul, London, 1982, 262.

Chapter III: From Parish Church to Cathedral

1. Hall, Charters, 44 (Doc. 71).
2. Eamon Duffy, *The Stripping of the Altars*, 565, et. seq.
3. Hall, Charters, 60.

4. J.N. Coombe: *Notes on Pew Allocations, 1617-1797*, C.B. 1632 (33).
5. Samuel Roberts, *Autobiography and Select Remains*, (Longman, London, 1849) 13. LS BR 544 SST.
6. Edward Goodwin, Sheffield in 1764: *Gentleman's Magazine*, Vol. 34, April 1764, 157. LS 052 ST.
7. T. Walter Hall, *The Fairbanks of Sheffield, 1688-1848* (Northend, Sheffield, 1932), 100-103.
8. Sheffield City Archives, Records of Sheffield Parish Church and Cathedral, B5/2.
9. A Report of a Public Meeting held on 3 November 1800 in the Parish Church – published as a Public Notice: City Archives, Parish Church and Cathedral Records, B5/3.
10. Hunter, 249.
11. R.E. Leader, *Sheffield in the Eighteenth Century*, 250.
12. A.E. Gatty, *Sheffield Past and Present*, 1873, 163.
13. See, for example, J. D. Leader, *Records of the Burgery of Sheffield*, 340 et. seq.
14. Hall, Charters, 60.
15. Hunter, 262.
16. E.D. Mackerness, *Music and Musicians at Sheffield Cathedral*, 1979 (Sheffield Cathedral).
17. Hunter, 77, 102.
18. E.R. Wickham: *Church and People*, 71.
19. D.R. Lunn, Lecture: *James Wilkinson, Vicar of Sheffield, 1753-1805*, given at Sheffield Cathedral, 22 January 1997. (Typescript).
    See also: D.R. Lunn, *Chapters Towards a History of the Cathedral and Parish Church*, 14.

Chapter IV: Clergy Matters: Conflict and Commitment

1. J. D. Leader, *Records of the Burgery of Sheffield*, lii.
2. David Hey: *The Fiery Blades of Sheffield*, 29.
3. Hunter, 244.
4. C.V. Collier, Letters and other papers relating to Church affairs in Sheffield in the Eighteenth Century, *T.H.A.S.*, 3, 1927, 193-211.
5. C.V. Collier, ibid., 205.
6. R. E. Leader, Talks of the Town, *T.H.A.S.*, 1, 1918, 375-82.
7. Hunter, 266.
8. J.B. Wheat, *History*, 47-74.
9. Correspondence between J.B. Wheat and J.N. Coombe, 1914. C.B. 1622, Folio 32.

10. See: Hunter, 237.
J.B. Wheat, *History*, 112.
W. Odom, *Memorials of Sheffield, its Cathedral and Parish Churches*, Northend, Sheffield, 1922, 57.
D.R. Lunn, *Chapters Towards a History*, 8.
11. D.R. Lunn, *Chapters Towards a History*, 8.

Chapter V: The Building of Churches

1. Hunter, 273.
W. Odom, *Memorials of Sheffield*, 63.
Wickham, *Church and People*, 20.
R.B. Wragg, St. Paul's Church, Sheffield, *T.H.A.S.*, 11, 1981, 52-58.
2. For a review of the early 19th century see:
Wickham, *Church and People*, 70-107.
Clyde Binfield, *The History of the City of Sheffield, 1843-1993* (Sheffield Academic Press), 1993, 364-428.
3. Mary Walton, *A History of the Diocese of Sheffield 1914-79*, Diocesan Board of Finance, 1981.
4. Wickham, *Church and People*, 148; 275-280.

Chapter VI: The Burgesses and Education

1. For accounts of the establishment and development of the Grammar School see;
J.R. Wigfull: An Early Sheffield School: *T.H.A.S.*, 3, 1928, 336-343.
Sheffield Grammar School: *T.H.A.S.*, 6, 1935, 283-300.
Hunter: 305-312.
Florence Ball: The development of the Grammar Schools in Sheffield (Typewritten Dissertation, Totley Hall College of Education, Sheffield, 1971) L.S. 373.4274 SQ.
2. For information on Thomas Smith see:
P.J. Wallis: Thomas Smith, Benefactor of Sheffield Grammar School: *T.H.A.S.* 7, 1955, 188-193.
3. Malcolm Mercer: *Schooling the Poorer Child (Elementary Education in Sheffield, 1560-1902)*, Academic Press, Sheffield, 1996, 22.
4. For information on William Lee, see:
J.R. Wigfull: The Early Books of the Parish Register of Sheffield: *T.H.A.S.*, 2, 1920, 86.
5. Edward Goodwin, *Sheffield in 1764*, 159.
6. Report of the Charity Commisssioners, 1829. LS 361S.

7. G.C. Moore Smith: Sheffield Grammar School, *T.H.A.S.* 4, 1931/31, 145-160.
8. *The History of the City of Sheffield, 1843-1993*, Vol. II; Society, Academic Press, Sheffield, 1993.
9. G.C. Holland; *The Vital Statistics of Sheffield*, Robert Tyas, Sheffield, 1843, 221-223. LS J 314.274 S.
10. R.E. Leader: *Reminiscences of Old Sheffield*, Leader & Son, Sheffield, 1875, 31.
11. Information drawn from:
    Hunter: 320-322.
    Notes and Queries, Vol.I, No.2, Sept. 1899, Sir. W.C. Leng, Sheffield, 83.
    Endowed Charities, 1897.
    Report of Charity Commissioners, 1829.
12. W.G. Matthews: The Free Writing School, Sheffield, and its Masters, *T.H.A.S.* 10, 1977, 280-285.
13. Edward Goodwin, *Sheffield in 1764*, 159
14. John Salt: Early Sheffield Sunday Schools and their Educational Importance, *T.H.A.S.* 9, 1967, 179-184.
15. W.R. Ward: *Religion and Society in England, 1790-1850*, Batsford, 1972, 147.
16. E.P. Thompson: *The Making of the English Working Class*, Pelican 1968, 389.
17. E.R. Wickham: *Church and People*, 83.
18. W.R. Ward: *Religion and Society in England*, 13.
19. R.E. Leader: *Sheffield in the Eighteenth Century*, 334.
20. E.P. Thompson: *The Making of the English Working Class*, 415.
21. *The History of the City of Sheffield, 1843-1993*, 298.

Chapter VII: A Charity for all Seasons

1. David Owen: *English Philanthropy 1660-1960*, 36.
2. W.K. Jordan: *Philanthropy in England, 1480-1660*, Allen and Unwin, 1959, 80.
3. Hunter, 329

Chapter VIII: The Burgesses' Estates

1. David Postles: An Early Modern Town: Sheffield in the 16th Century, *T.H.A.S.*, 12, 1983, 61.
2. C.B. 884.
3. C.B. 1633.

4. David Postles: The Residential Development of the Church Burgesses' Estates in Sheffield, *T.H.A.S.*, 10, 1979, 360-364.
5. C.B. 699.

Chapter IX: The Men of the Trust

1. Hunter, 418.
2. Wickham, *Church and People*, 35.
3. Wickham, *Church and People*, 35.
4. D.R. Lunn, *Chapters Towards a History of the Cathedral*, 51.
5. Bryan Dale, *Yorkshire Puritanism and Early Nonconformity* (Bradford, 1909), 59-60.
6. ibid. 20.
7. Hunter, 285.
8. Hunter, 394.
9. Malcolm Mercer, William Ronksley (1650-1724), Schoolmaster, Writer and Philanthropist, *T.H.A.S.* 14, 1987, 14.
10. Wickham, *Church and People*, 151.
11. David Hey, *The Fiery Blades of Sheffield*, 213-217.
12. David Postles, An Early Modern Town: Sheffield in the 16th Century, *T.H.A.S.* 12, 1983, 61-67.
13. Hunter, 296.
14. W. Odom, *Hallamshire Worthies* (Northend, Sheffield, 1926), 101.
15. Thomas Fuller, *A Sermon of Reformation*, 1634, 23-24 (Quoted in Paul A. Welsby, Lancelot Andrewes, 1555-1626 (SPCK, 1964), 3.
16. Wickham, *Church and People*, 99-102.

Appendix III: Miscellanea

1. R.E. Leader: Talks of the Town, *T.H.A.S.*, 4, 1918, 386.

Index